Mill and Town in South Carolina 1880–1920

DAVID L. CARLTON

Louisiana State University Press
Baton Rouge and London

To my parents,
Robert C. Carlton and Sara L. Carlton,
for their support (moral and financial)
throughout a most prolonged adolescence

Manufactured in the United States of America

Designer: Albert Crochet
Typeface: Linotron Sabon
Typesetter: G&S Typesetters, Inc.

LIBRARY OF CONGRESS CATALOGING IN PUBLICATION DATA
Carlton, David, 1948–
Mill and town in South Carolina, 1880–1920.

Bibliography: p.
Includes index.
1. Textile industry—Social aspects—South
Carolina—History. I. Title.
HD9857.S6C37 307.7'66'09757 82-7753
ISBN 0-8071-1042-6 AACR2
ISBN 0-8071-1059-0 (pbk.)

Louisiana Paperback Edition, 1982
10 9 8 7 6 5 4 3

Contents

Acknowledgments ix

Introduction 1

I Origins of the "Town People" 13

II Mill Building as Town Building: The Industrial Impulse 40

III The Early Response to Industrialism 82

IV The Discovery of the "Mill Problem," 1895–1905 129

V Solving the "Mill Problem": The Reformers and the Operatives 171

VI The Bleaseite Challenge 215

Appendix: A Note on Table 9 273

Essay on Sources 277

Index 303

List of Tables

Table 1 Specialization in Cotton, 1850–1900 19

Table 2 Residences of Mill Directors 48

Table 3 Mill Directors Residing in the South Carolina Piedmont, 1880–1907, by Occupation 50

Table 4 Mill Presidents Residing in the South Carolina Piedmont, 1880–1907, by Occupation 51

Table 5 Enrollment, Number of Teachers, and Pupil-Teacher Ratios, Large Mill Districts, 1900 99

Table 6 Population Growth and Teaching Loads in Town Schools and Selected Mill Schools 100

Table 7 Factionalism in Spartanburg County, 1910–1916 218

Table 8 Mill, Town, and Bleaseism in Greenville County 219

Table 9 Ecological Regression Estimates, Mill Operative Support for Blease, 1914 and 1916 220

Map

South Carolina Spindleage, 1907 47

Acknowledgments

This volume had its genesis nearly nine years ago as a doctoral dissertation in history at Yale University. Its initial conceptualization owed much of its rigor to C. Vann Woodward, who insisted to a graduate student interested chiefly in indulging an old enthusiasm about southern cotton mills that the writing of history required thought as well as the collection of data. While Professor Woodward was a model of forbearance during the actual writing of the dissertation, his insistence that I make my intentions clear at the outset of my work gave it a shape and direction which it otherwise would have sorely lacked. The lengthy process of revision has benefited enormously from the comments of the other members of my dissertation committee, Professors David Brion Davis and William N. Parker.

Like all historical researchers, I have been dependent on libraries and archives, a dependence which, in my case at least, was not limited to the need for access to materials. The archival staff at the Baker Library of the Harvard University Graduate School of Business Administration allowed me to consult the R. G. Dun and Company credit ledgers, and, with the concurrence of Dun and Bradstreet, gave me permission to use that material in Chapters I and II. The aid of Mattie U. Russell and her staff at the Manuscripts Division of the Perkins Library of Duke University, and of Carolyn A. Wallace and her staff at the Southern Historical Collection of the University of North Carolina at Chapel Hill, were indispensable to me as they are to anyone dealing with a topic in southern history. Closer to my native ground, I am indebted to Charles E. Lee and his staff at the South Carolina Department of Archives and History in Columbia not only for their research assistance but for their financial assistance as well, as they provided me with part-time employment when my fortunes were at an ebb. Herbert Hucks of the South Carolina Methodist Archives at Wofford College in Spartanburg was an ever gracious host on my periodic forays upstate; Horace F. Rudisill of the Darlington County Historical Society passed on some remarkably revealing documents. My greatest single library debt is to E. L. Inabinett and his staff at the South Caroliniana Library of the University of South Carolina at Columbia, where I have virtually lived for most of the past decade. Like the Archives, the Caroliniana came through with a strategically timed part-time job, but it has also provided other services and personal favors too numerous to catalog. More important, both its staff and its corps of regular and occasional researchers have made the Caroliniana not simply a work place but also a scholarly community of distinction; what there is of virtue in the following pages has come in good part from the experience of having worked there.

Successive versions of this monograph have been passed out to numerous people over the years. Among those who read the dissertation manuscript in whole or in part were Carol Wasserloos, Rachel Klein, Robert Byrd, Tom E. Terrill, James L. Lancaster, Joseph Wilkins, and Marlene T. Sipes. The anonymous readers at the University of North Carolina Press and Louisiana State University Press made comments which were especially helpful in enabling me to outline my revisions. The revised manuscript has been read in its entirety by John Scott Strickland, Peter A. Coclanis, George D. Terry, Lacy K. Ford, and Allen H. Stokes, all of whom made valuable suggestions. Gavin Wright and Stanley Engerman read the early chapters and saved me from some serious economic errors; other partial readings, with equally valuable comments, were made by Hugh H. Hawkins, Don H. Doyle, and Drew Gilpin Faust. While he has not commented on any versions of this manuscript, Jonathan M. Wiener has, through his strong criticisms of several conference papers, helped me clarify my argument and consider its implications.

The work of revising the dissertation was undertaken during the academic year 1980–1981 under the auspices of a fellowship grant (Number FB-20004-80-0586) from the National Endowment for the Humanities, an act of faith on its part for which I am deeply grateful. My recent employer, the University of South Carolina–Coastal Carolina College, has aided in the completion of the manuscript; Jane Hansen of the Coastal Carolina staff typed a portion of the final version. Jerald S. Ulrey of the University of South Carolina Department of Geography produced the maps. Permission to make use of material from my essay "'Builders of a New State': The Town Classes and Early Industrialization of South Carolina, 1880–1907," in *From the Old South to the New: Essays on the Transitional South*, edited by Walter J. Fraser and Winfred B. Moore, including an earlier version of the map on p. 47, has been granted by the editors and by the publisher, Greenwood Press, a division of Congressional Information Service, Inc., Westport, Connecticut. Beverly Jarrett, Martha Hall, and Marie Blanchard of Louisiana State University Press have been capable and tolerant in guiding me through the unfamiliar process of book publication.

Special thanks are due to two close friends whose contributions cannot adequately be recognized. Lacy K. Ford and I have played intellectual ping-pong for so many years that he may deserve credit as coauthor of the first two chapters, at least. The ultimate responsibility for all that follows must, of course, rest on my head, but much of what the reader will find worthwhile in this work can be ascribed to his influence. His forthcoming dissertation on the social history of the South Carolina up-country from 1850 to 1900, currently being written for the University of South Carolina, should add significantly to our understanding of southern history. Allen H. Stokes, the Curator of Manuscripts at the South Caroliniana Library, has been involved in the enterprise virtually from its inception. His knowledge of the records and his helpfulness have long been legendary among those engaged in research on South

Carolina topics; I have especially benefited from his scholarly interest in the southern textile industry. That this volume, like many others, exists at all is in significant part due to his ability and his devotion to the advancement of scholarship.

Mill and Town in South Carolina
1880–1920

Introduction

August 9, 1912, was greeted by the citizens of Spartanburg, South Carolina, with varying emotions. It was the day of the biennial "stump meeting," when candidates for the Democratic party's gubernatorial nomination presented themselves before the voters. The air was charged, for this year the star attraction was the incumbent governor, Cole L. Blease, a man as loathed by the "professional and trading classes" of the up-country city as he was adored by the mill workers of the industrial suburbs surrounding it. Disorder and violence had been constant threats throughout the campaign; less than a week earlier another political meeting had degenerated into pandemonium, and elaborate measures were being taken to ensure that the stump meeting crowd remained orderly. It being a Friday, the mills were running full time, but many of their operatives skipped work to come to town and cheer for their favorite; on the other hand, many town folk, concerned either for their business duties or for their sensibilities, kept away.[1]

One townsman who did attend was D. E. Camak, a young Methodist minister nine years out of Wofford College. As an undergraduate Camak had been fascinated by Spartanburg's transformation from Piedmont country town to industrial city, and especially by the influx of rural and mountain folk into the villages sprawling

1. Ronald D. Burnside, "The Governorship of Coleman Livingston Blease of South Carolina, 1911–1915" (Ph.D. dissertation, Indiana University, 1963), 144–60; Spartanburg *Herald*, August 9, 10, 1912; Columbia *State*, August 4, 1912.

over the bare red hills on the outskirts of town. Fearful of the moral effects of factory life on the new white proletariat, he had determined to devote his ministerial career to "uplifting" the mill people; most recently, he had organized, under Methodist auspices, a part-time school for the benefit of young operatives denied a normal education by poverty and child labor. Thoroughly middle class by background and sympathies, Camak was a supporter of Blease's opponent for governor, Ira B. Jones; however, he attended the stump meeting not as a partisan but as an observer. "I not only meant to get a good view of the arch juggler of human passions [Blease]," he explained later, "but the people also—the people to whose intellectual, social and spiritual well-being I was giving my life."[2]

Camak got what he came for, and more than he cared for. The occasion, as he recalled it, was nothing less than a vision of hell. "Coley," of course, played the Prince of Darkness, in the manner of one of Dante's vulgar demons. Coming "with dash and tawdry show . . . he sprang to the fray. With glib tongue spouting billingsgate he launched a broadside of invective against his opponent," playing "with consummate art" upon "the passions of the mob." If the genteel Camak was disgusted with Blease, however, he was unnerved by the governor's supporting cast. The crowd was composed of South Carolinians of the purest "Anglo-Saxon" blood, but the "tornado of shrieks, yells and whistles" which arose from it suggested the clamor of the abyss. Nor were individuals any better. Mingling with a group of Bleaseites, Camak overheard conversations about "liquor, prisons, pardons, and automatic pistols," all drenched in "a shower bath of profanity and obscenity." He watched disdainfully as six Blease men parlayed two meal tickets into six barbecue plates in cavalier disregard for property rights. Most disturbing of all was the seeming lack of respect for law, civilization, even human life:

2. Watson B. Duncan, *Twentieth Century Sketches of the South Carolina Conference M.E. Church South* (Columbia: The State Company, 1914), 76–78; D. E. Camak, *Human Gold from Southern Hills* (Greer, S.C.: By the Author, 1960), Chaps. 2, 7; the quote is from p. 137.

"Wonder whut this automatic 'ud do," said one, "if I turn't it loose on that crowd." He patted his coat pocket proudly.

"Hit'd get yer in the pen," replied another, "but 'Coley' 'ud git yer out." They all laughed.

The experience left Camak shaken: "The human society, for whose well-being I lived and worked, seemed slipping into the sea, and I was sick with the slush of it."[3]

Camak's distress was by no means unique among educated, "respectable" South Carolinians of his time; indeed, the desire to understand what seemed to be the imminent dissolution of the state's social order created a major intellectual cottage industry. Most commentators were inclined to blame the Palmetto State's disgrace on "democracy," especially on the rise of the common man in state politics. The journalist William Watts Ball, an avowed reactionary, argued that the fondly remembered antebellum unity of white South Carolinians had flowed from their relatively undemocratic form of government, with the special protection it gave to property. Modern-style democracy, on the other hand, with its elevation of "King Numbers" over property rights, had been introduced into the state by its Reconstruction masters; its provenance notwithstanding, it had so corrupted the whites that they had not only retained it (for themselves) upon regaining power, but in succeeding years had carried it to absurd heights. The ultimate product of the democratic urge, the white primary, granted "the illiterate and propertyless" the privilege of choosing their leaders; such men could hardly be expected to favor representatives of the literate and propertied at the polls. Unlike Ball, the historian David Duncan Wallace, a "progressive," viewed the democratic revolution as an indigenous product, dating from the rise of Benjamin R. Tillman's Farmers' Movement in the middle 1880s. Furthermore, Wallace viewed the advent of democracy as a positive development; properly regulated, the rule of the people would ensure that the government would be run in the interest of all, not of a privileged few as was the case in slavery days. The difficulty lay, not in

3. Camak, *Human Gold*, 137–39.

democracy per se, but in "the lack of a true and enlightened democracy," and the presence of a large body of voters whose material, mental, and moral welfare had thitherto been neglected by South Carolina's political leadership. The positions of Ball and Wallace effectively defined the debate over the consequences of political democracy carried on in South Carolina during the Blease era, the "reactionary" camp favoring a retreat to some form of suffrage restriction while the "progressives" urged social programs and education.[4]

For present purposes, however, the most striking characteristic of the debate was the general agreement of all parties on a single proposition: that democracy, good or bad, native or foreign, was in fact a recent development in the history of the "aristocratic" Palmetto State. That proposition, however, glosses over a fundamental problem, namely that South Carolina had not, since the early nineteenth century, been especially *un*democratic. "King Numbers" was, to be sure, carefully hedged about with restrictions in the antebellum period; there were property requirements for office holding, indirect elections for most officials, including the governor and presidential electors, and a legislative apportionment scheme skewed toward the low country. The fact remains, though, that virtual universal white manhood suffrage existed in the state from 1810. Nor is there any reason to believe that the political culture of South Carolina was any less "democratic" than were those of other southern states in the Jacksonian era; there, as elsewhere, the slave regime rested on the support of the white voters, and politicians ignored them at their peril. If South Carolina was not uniquely undemocratic before the Civil War, neither was its behavior particularly unusual afterward. The turmoil it experienced in the late nineteenth and early twentieth centuries had its analogues elsewhere in the region, in the Populist revolt, in various local insurrections, and in the periodic political shooting stars la-

4. William Watts Ball, "Back to Calhoun," and "Back to Aristocracy," in Anthony Harrigan (ed.), *The Editor and the Republic: Papers and Addresses of William Watts Ball* (Chapel Hill: University of North Carolina Press, 1954), 37–78; D. D. Wallace, "The Democratizing of an Old Commonwealth" (MS address, probably 1913, in David Duncan Wallace Papers, South Carolina Historical Society, Charleston; microfiche copy in South Caroliniana Library, University of South Carolina, Columbia—hereafter cited as SCL).

beled "demagogues" by their detractors. While the rhetoric generated by these political electrical storms crackled with attacks on the "aristocracy," it did not reflect an assault on a quasi-feudal social order; like "democracy" itself, it was in fact a survival of the Jacksonian political culture, in which "aristocrat" was the ultimate term of opprobrium.[5]

Something other than the "rise of the common man," then, accounts for the turbulence Camak witnessed at Spartanburg. What was new in South Carolina politics was not widespread popular participation; that had long been present. What was new was the collapse of white unity. The white men of South Carolina, who had stood shoulder to shoulder in defense of their prerogatives against the Yankee army, the carpetbaggers, and, above all, the Negro, were now given over to violent factional division. Furthermore, in the case of Blease, the political cleavage had a disturbing social dimension, for "Coley's" ascendancy was intimately related to "the sudden coming into being of a segregated and class conscious industrial vote." The creation in the Palmetto State of a class of propertyless white wage earners, and the "stubbornly vexing problem" they posed in politics, was a particularly dramatic special case of a larger social trend pervading the post–Civil War South.[6] In these years the region was undergoing a transformation; whereas it earlier had a comparatively simple agrarian social structure in which whites had been mainly independent producers and blacks had been mainly slaves, the postwar years brought increasing complexity and hierarchy, as a small group of economically powerful whites came to dominate a mass of black and white sharecroppers, tenants, indebted farmers, and "wage slaves." The biggest losers in the process were the poorer whites (the blacks

5. Harrigan (ed.), *Editor and the Republic*, 45–46; Fletcher M. Green, "Democracy in the Old South," in J. Isaac Copeland (ed.), *Democracy in the Old South and Other Essays by Fletcher M. Green* (Nashville: Vanderbilt University Press, 1969), 65–86; for the antebellum political culture of another southern state, see J. Mills Thornton III, *Politics and Power in a Slave Society: Alabama, 1800–1860* (Baton Rouge: Louisiana State University Press, 1978); an argument along similar lines for South Carolina will appear in the forthcoming work of Lacy K. Ford. On the postbellum South, see C. Vann Woodward, *Origins of the New South, 1877–1913*, A History of the South, IX (Baton Rouge: Louisiana State University Press, 1951).

6. Harrigan (ed.), *Editor and the Republic*, 43.

having little to lose), and, not being docile, they fought back. As a result, the period between the end of Reconstruction and World War I was one of intermittent, sometimes violent contention among whites over the emerging shape of their society.

The outline of the story was first sketched a generation ago by C. Vann Woodward in his monumental work *Origins of the New South*; only recently, however, have historians betaken themselves to reconstructing the historical process by which the transformation was accomplished.[7] The present study is intended to contribute to that reconstruction by inquiring into the causes and consequences of one of the more striking developments in postbellum southern social history, the rise of the textile industry in the South Carolina Piedmont. By relating the industrialization of a single southern state to the larger socioeconomic changes it has experienced, I hope to shed some light on the origins and nature of the modern South. At the same time, I hope to successfully address the problem that so vexed Ball, Wallace, and their fellows: how the white men of South Carolina, who had marched united to war in 1861 and to "Redemption" in 1876, could by 1912 have become so rancorously divided, and how a state which had prided itself on the superior quality of its civilization could have produced the infernal scene witnessed by D. E. Camak.

Most of the writing on social and economic change in the post–Civil War South has concentrated on events in the countryside.[8] The reason for the agrarian emphasis is unobjectionable; agricul-

7. Examples of recent work include, in economic history, Roger Ransom and Richard Sutch, *One Kind of Freedom: The Economic Consequences of Emancipation* (Cambridge: Cambridge University Press, 1977); Gavin Wright, *The Political Economy of the Cotton South: Households, Markets, and Wealth in the Nineteenth Century* (New York: W. W. Norton, 1978); in political history, J. Morgan Kousser, *The Shaping of Southern Politics: Suffrage Restriction and the Establishment of the One-Party South, 1880–1910* (New Haven: Yale University Press, 1974); in social history, Lawrence Goodwyn, *Democratic Promise: The Populist Moment in America* (New York: Oxford University Press, 1976); and Steven Howard Hahn, "The Roots of Southern Populism: Yeomen Farmers and the Transformation of Georgia's Upper Piedmont, 1850–1900" (Ph.D. dissertation, Yale University, 1979).

8. Ransom and Sutch, *One Kind of Freedom*; Hahn, "Roots"; Jonathan M. Wiener, *Social Origins of the New South: Alabama, 1860–1885* (Baton Rouge: Louisiana State University Press, 1978).

ture dominated the southern economy and society until well into the twentieth century. A majority of workers in the old Confederate states tilled the soil or raised livestock as late as 1920, when only a quarter of the entire nation's work force was engaged in agriculture. Only after the economic disasters of the 1920s and the Depression did a majority of southern workers come to pursue callings off the farm. Understandably, then, southern historians have generally worked from the premise that the region's history has been fundamentally shaped by its thralldom to the soil.

However large agriculture has loomed in southern life, though, its relative importance has been in chronic decline since 1880. Conversely, while manufacturing has until recently played but a minor role in the southern economy, its development has been steady and strong throughout the past century. In no decade since 1880 has the growth in value added by manufacturing in the old Confederacy failed to outpace that of the nation as a whole; in only one have southern manufacturers failed to expand their payrolls faster than United States manufacturers generally. The full emergence of the industrial South may have had to await the aftermath of World War II, but it had been in preparation since the aftermath of Appomattox. Most men of the "New South" may have spent their lives on the farm, but the future of their society lay with the factory.[9]

The rise of the textile industry in South Carolina in the years after Reconstruction was thus a significant development, not only in itself, but also in its implications for the state's future. Between the beginning of the cotton manufacturing boom in the 1880s and the approximate end of the Progressive era in 1920 the Palmetto State became the third largest textile producing state in the Union. The number of wage earners employed by the industry increased over twenty-two times, from 2,053 in 1880 to 48,079 in 1920; in the latter year an estimated one sixth of the state's white population resided in its mill villages. To be sure, over 60 percent of South

9. E. S. Lee, A. R. Miller, C. P. Brainard, and R. A. Easterlin, *Population Redistribution and Economic Growth: United States, 1870–1950*, Memoirs of the American Philosophical Society, XLV (Philadelphia: American Philosophical Society, 1957), 609–20, 684–85, 694–95.

Carolina's work force persisted in agriculture in 1920. However, the great twentieth-century exodus from the farm had already begun, while the number of manufacturing wage earners continued to rise, even in the 1930s; within a generation only a quarter of the state's workers would be agricultural. Furthermore, the circumstance that the mill population was virtually all white added to the importance of its numbers, for white men governed this black-majority state, and all white men had the right to help choose its leaders.[10]

Of even greater impact than the quantitative impact of the industrial expansion was its relationship to the basic structural changes going on within South Carolina and propelling it toward modernity. Of these far and away the most significant were the development of two new social classes, each of whose members developed a strong group consciousness and tended to live together in more or less homogeneous communities. In fact, their places of residence determined the names by which they were known in South Carolina: the "town people" and the "mill people."

To contemporary South Carolinians the term "town people" referred to approximately the same social group as does the French term *bourgeoisie*, namely the business and professional classes of the state's commercial centers; the appearance of this incipient urban middle class was one of the most distinctive developments of the "New South." Merchants and professional men, of course, had been present in South Carolina in antebellum days, congregated in the coastal and river towns, clustered about courthouses, or scattered through the interior as local storekeepers. Prior to Secession, though, they were but minor adjuncts to an economic structure dominated by the slave plantation and the factorage system. Only after the demolition of that structure in the Civil War did they come into their own. While the Union victory produced no material changes in the distribution of land, the emancipation of the slaves and the disruption of the South's financial and marketing

10. *Ibid.*, 618; Edward Atkinson, *Report on the Cotton Manufactures of the United States* in *U.S. Census, 1880: Manufactures*, 15: *U.S. Census, 1920*, II, 31; X, 159; South Carolina Department of Agriculture, Commerce, and Industries, Labor Division, *Report, 1920*, 43.

system left many landowners without the resources needed to continue production. The need for agricultural credit, along with changes in the transportation system, provided expanded opportunities in local trade and led to an influx of fortune seekers into merchandising in the postwar years.

The tribe of tradesmen did more than increase; as it grew it began to develop a sense of identity, of cohesion, even of purpose. During the years following the Civil War several score small towns and cities grew up about the interior of the state, serving as local centers of trade. While the merchants and professional men who ran the towns were aggressive seekers of private profit, they also took great pride in their communities and in their embryonic "urban" civilization. They looked upon the town as their corporate property, and identified its advancement with their own self-interest. They began to organize for the sake of local development, and thus became appreciative of the power of social organization as an instrument for improving their welfare and expanding their wealth and influence.

The rise of the town, then, provided an opening wedge with which modern forms of social organization, including corporate enterprises, elaborate and hierarchically ordered divisions of labor, and bureaucracy could penetrate a South whose economic and social life had long revolved around autonomous white planters and small farmers. The most striking manifestations of the "new society" were the cotton mills. The townspeople became infatuated with mills, viewing them as human beehives capable of producing fabulous wealth. Using their acquired expertise in trade and organization, they began in the 1880s to band together in corporations to build factories; by the turn of the century the industrial fervor, fanned by fierce town rivalries, reached a fever pitch. While the manufacturing boom did not produce a "great leap forward" into instant industrial maturity, by World War I the townsmen had succeeded in installing the factory as a major feature of the Carolina landscape.[11]

The industrial growth so dear to the "town people," however,

11. For discussions of the nature of the "town people," see Liston Pope, *Millhands and Preachers: A Study of Gastonia* (New Haven: Yale University Press, 1941), 55 and *passim.*:

involved far more than stock subscriptions and factory construction; it also required creating a class of dependent, propertyless white mill operatives, a class then unprecedented in South Carolina. Although there were early misgivings about the prospect of a white proletariat in the midst of rural South Carolina, the industrialists and their supporters were able at first to assure a naïve public that "Anglo-Saxon" southerners would make perfect industrial workers and would pose no threat to the social order. By 1900, though, townsmen were beginning to suspect otherwise. The "cracker proletariat" streaming into the mill villages were rural folk from an essentially premodern world. Like the English workers described by E. P. Thompson, or the (northern) American workers described by Herbert G. Gutman, the "mill people" came to the factories bearing cultural traditions often ill-suited to the demands of industrial life.[12] Especially disturbing was their touchy resentment of all authority, all "bosses"; immigrants as they were from a society in which all white men considered "independence" to be their birthright, they disliked the increasingly elaborate regulations being imposed upon them in the interest of public order, safety, and economic development.

The response of the "town people" to what they termed the "mill problem" was to seek even greater control over the operatives. Like their Progressive-era contemporaries elsewhere in the country, they believed that the disorderliness of their society could best be controlled by placing it under the guidance of educated and disinterested "experts."[13] It was, of course, precisely the sort of "paternalism" to which the operatives were already objecting. The conflict between mill and town sharpened as progressives sought to use the state apparatus, especially the public schools, to break

---

Ralph C. Patrick, Jr., "A Cultural Approach to Social Stratification" (Ph.D. dissertation, Anthropology, Harvard University, 1953).

12. E. P. Thompson, *The Making of the English Working Class* (New York: Pantheon, 1963); Herbert G. Gutman, "Work, Culture, and Society in Industrializing America," *American Historical Review*, LXXVIII (1973), 531–88.

13. Robert H. Wiebe, *The Search for Order, 1877–1920* (New York: Hill and Wang, 1967); Samuel P. Hays, *The Response to Industrialism, 1885–1914* (Chicago: University of Chicago Press, 1957); James Weinstein, *The Corporate Ideal in the Liberal State, 1900–1918* (Boston: Beacon Press, 1968).

the allegedly pernicious influence of mill parents over their children, as movements arose to restrict the political rights of the "ignorant," and as the notion gained ground among the "better sort" that white supremacy need not entail white equality. Sensing themselves increasingly circumscribed and persecuted by arbitrary mill officials and meddlesome reformers alike, the mill hands finally struck back through their chosen scourge, Cole L. Blease. Because of its fundamental negativism and disorderliness, "Bleaseism" was but a brief, bizarre interruption in the flow of modern South Carolina history. In Blease, though, the operatives' outrage over their loss of control over their lives, and over their subordinate position under the rule of the "town people," found a voice so raucous and daring in its contempt for the new order that it briefly shook the confidence of the rising middle class in its ability to command its society.

In a fundamental sense, then, the scene that D. E. Camak so deplored in August 1912 was an expression, not of an ascendant democracy, but of its decline, a twisted, bewildered outburst against the impending death of a world in which every white man was a master of his own house and an equal beside his fellows, in which blacks, and only blacks, formed the mudsill of society, and in which personal honor was the supreme law. As we have already noted, this sense of constriction, of "enslavement" in the old, broad use of the word, was hardly unique to mill workers, or indeed to southerners. It has, in one form or another, been a theme of much American social history, appearing with the earliest large-scale New England cotton mills and reasserting itself with each extension of the market, each wave of business consolidation, each expansion of industrial scale, each major social reform. The passions aroused in South Carolina by the social process begun in the wake of Sherman's march and manifested in part by the smokestacks of the Piedmont mill districts appear in many other places and in many variant forms. Nonetheless, it is not unnecessary duplication of effort to retell the tale with a cast of characters from the Carolina up-country. If, as both Arnold Toynbee and C. Vann Woodward suggest, it is morally desirable to recognize that "history [has] happened to my people in my part of the world," it is often necessary to recount the same story with many different accents, in hopes that the reader will recognize his own.[14] It is my hope that the readers of this essay, whatever their antecedents, will hear, somewhere along the way, a familiar voice.

14. Toynbee, quoted in Woodward, *Origins*, xiii.

Chapter I

Origins of the "Town People"

The story of South Carolina's industrialization must begin with the men who, above all, were responsible for initiating it: the town-dwelling middle class. The burgeoning towns of late-nineteenth-century South Carolina, and the business and professional men directing their destinies, were themselves the products of larger developments transforming the society and economy of the Palmetto State, especially its upland regions, in the years following the Civil War. Wartime disorganization, Emancipation, changes in transportation and communication, and the decline of the cotton economy forced a drastic reorganization of the state's economic structure, making the small-town merchant, rather than the planter or factor, its pivotal figure. The appearance of the "town people," in turn, introduced a new, dynamic element into the life of the state. Like their counterparts on the western frontier, the townspeople were driven not simply by lust for private gain but also by a sense of common destiny; the "booster ethos" flourished in the Spartanburgs and Greenwoods of South Carolina much as it did in the Zeniths and Gopher Prairies of the Midwest. It was this "town spirit," this ceaseless drive for civic wealth, power, and glory, which led the burghers of the up-country to organize corporations to build cotton mills. More importantly, it was the booster's emphasis on organized effort to promote the general welfare which suggested to some townsmen that the ramshackle society in which they lived might well benefit from new, systematic methods of social control. As their power increased, the "town builders" of the late nineteenth century progressively widened their ambitions; by the twentieth century they would aspire to be the "builders of a new State."[1]

The interior town was an almost negligible feature in the countryside of antebellum South Carolina. Setting aside the forty thousand residents of Charleston, fifteen thousand people at most lived in towns of over one thousand in 1850, 40 percent of them in Columbia, the state capital; the remainder were divided among seven scattered communities averaging just over a thousand souls apiece. Together they contained no more than 2½ percent of the population of the state outside of Charleston, and less than 3 percent of the white population. Interior towns made some modest population gains as the prosperity of the 1850s quickened the commercial pulse of the cotton belt. The state's treelike railroad system, hitherto self-contained and extending no further than the fall line, sent shoots into the up-country to within sight of the Blue Ridge and reached across political boundaries to touch the rail networks of neighboring North Carolina and Georgia; total track mileage increased by two and a half times in the course of the decade. The new transportation system created new communities and expanded old ones. The town of Anderson, for example, was in 1850 a courthouse hamlet whose commerce could be handled by sixteen individuals; the coming of the railroad stimulated local business, however, and by 1860 forty-four men kept stores and shops there. Meanwhile, the larger towns of the lower Piedmont, Winnsboro, Chester, and Newberry, gained in commercial importance and by 1860 were supporting the first banks in the up-country. The economic expansion of the 1850s, while portending significant future developments, was, however, quite modest in its immediate impact on town growth. The free populations of the eight towns outside of Charleston grew by 45 percent during the decade, but only 4 percent of the non-Charlestonian free population lived in them on the eve of Secession, and the census of that year reported only

1. Marjorie A. Potwin, *Cotton Mill People of the Piedmont: A Study in Social Change* (New York: Columbia University Press, 1927), 33.

nineteen towns of any size in existence in the entire state.[2] Townspeople were marginal figures in the antebellum social landscape; it would take the events of the 1860s and 1870s to move them to the center.

The first of these events, of course, was the Civil War, which effectively shattered the old commercial system of the South. Before the war southern trade was dominated by factors operating in the coastal towns, who, by handling the movement of staple crops, effectively controlled commercial access to outside markets and financing. The wartime strangulation of the cotton trade, however, forced the factorage firms to suspend operations for the duration of hostilities; most merchants in interior towns likewise closed their doors, for want of things to buy or sell. What remained of commerce faced increasing difficulties as the Confederate military and economic position steadily deteriorated. The internal transportation system largely disintegrated through a combination of physical destruction and wartime neglect. The collapse of Confederate bonds and currency, along with widespread insolvency, brought about the virtual collapse of the state's financial structure.[3]

The impact of war and defeat did not, however, result in long-term commercial prostration; rather, by sweeping away the old economic organization, it cleared the ground upon which a new structure could be erected, with materials sifted from the debris of the old order.[4] The fall of the Confederacy, after all, did not suck

2. *U.S. Census, 1850*, 339, Table 2; *U.S. Census, 1860: Population*, 452, Table 3; *U.S. Census, 1870: Population*, 258–60, Table 3; Alfred Glaze Smith, Jr., *Economic Readjustment of an Old Cotton State: South Carolina, 1820–1860*(Columbia: University of South Carolina Press, 1958), 190, 194; R. G. Dun and Company Collection, Baker Library, Harvard University Graduate School of Business Administration: South Carolina, II, *passim*. See also J. Mills Thornton, *Politics and Power in a Slave Society: Alabama, 1800–1860* (Baton Rouge: Louisiana State University Press, 1978), 268–94, for parallel developments in Alabama; and Harold D. Woodman, *King Cotton and His Retainers: Financing and Marketing the Cotton Crop of the South, 1800–1925* (Lexington: University of Kentucky Press, 1968), esp. Chap. 23, for the larger southern context.

3. Woodman, *King Cotton*, Pts. 1–3, p. 214; Francis Butler Simkins and Robert H. Woody, *South Carolina During Reconstruction* (Chapel Hill: University of North Carolina Press, 1932), 9, 11–12; John F. Stover, *The Railroads of the South, 1865–1900: A Study in Finance and Control* (Chapel Hill: University of North Carolina Press, 1955), 42–43. Of the twenty-eight firms operating in Anderson on the eve of the war, only six continued to operate throughout the conflict. R. G. Dun Collection, South Carolina, II, *passim*.

4. Roger Ransom and Richard Sutch, *One Kind of Freedom: The Economic Conse-*

all the wealth of the South after it into the abyss. Many had preserved their assets by judiciously investing in specie, sterling bills of exchange, or commodities. Especially lucky were those who managed to preserve quantities of cotton through the war. Cotton prices, which in the prosperous 1850s only reached the middle teens, briefly exceeded fifty cents a pound in the aftermath of Appomattox, and merchants were frequently able to finance the resumption of their prewar businesses by selling their holdings. John Kyle, a Laurensville hardware merchant, bet on cotton during the war and won handsomely, being worth reportedly forty to fifty thousand dollars in 1870. O. H. P. Fant in Anderson emerged from the war with sixty bales, the proceeds of which made him a wealthy man and helped finance the reconstitution of the Anderson mercantile community.[5]

Furthermore, the privations of war and the economic difficulties of its immediate aftermath created an enormous demand for goods. In June, 1865, the Reverend A. Toomer Porter, an Episcopal priest from Charleston, obtained two thousand dollars' credit and carried two wagon loads of groceries and dry goods to Anderson, where no store had yet opened. From the very beginning his counter was thronged with eager customers, "for things they had not seen for four years were before them in quantities, and each seemed afraid lest what they wanted would be gone before they could get their share"; in two weeks the rector earned enough to pay his debts and resume his ministry. A similar venture in Spartanburg by an unemployed school teacher, W. K. Blake, had a more lasting result. Blake and his partners rode the speculative roller coaster of the late 1860s with consummate skill, and established themselves among the leading merchants of their town.[6] The short crops of the immediate postwar years kept demand for

---

quences of Emancipation (Cambridge: Cambridge University Press, 1977), 40–44, comments on the rapid recovery of transportation and manufacturing after the war.

5. Woodman, *King Cotton*, 214, 235–36, 248–50; Simkins and Woody, *South Carolina*, 21; R. G. Dun Collection, South Carolina, II, 72M, 73B; X, 132T; XI, 102A.

6. A. Toomer Porter, *Led On! Step by Step* (New York: G. P. Putnam's Sons, 1898), 201–205; W. K. Blake, "Recollections" (Typescript in Southern Historical Collection, University of North Carolina, Chapel Hill), 88–90. Blake was subsequently secretary-treasurer of a railroad, and sat on the original board of directors of the Clifton Manufacturing Company. Charleston *News and Courier*, January 22, 1880.

foodstuffs high and merchants busy. In 1867 the Greenville and Columbia Railroad shipped over 200,000 bushels of corn and over 1,000 hogsheads of bacon over its tracks to ease up-country food shortages, and as late as 1870 large-scale food imports were necessary to avert famine in the countryside.[7]

The fabric of South Carolina's commerce, then, came to be rewoven fairly quickly. However, the pattern that emerged was completely new, the product of the vastly altered circumstances of the postwar South. The most immediate and drastic change was the transformation of black slaves into free workers, which necessitated a radical reorganization of southern agriculture. Out of the chaos of the postwar southern countryside emerged a new labor system, in which work in gangs on large-scale productive units was largely abandoned in favor of sharecropping or tenant farming. While landholding remained as concentrated as it had been before the war, the productive units in the old plantation regions came to be split up into family sized farms. As a result, a new class of local merchants arose in the old staple-producing regions to supply goods to freedmen and white farmers and help market the local cotton production. Their power was based on the desperate need of most rural southerners for agricultural credit; since any merchant, to operate, either had to have capital of his own or access to capital in the North, the new storekeepers became the principal financiers of the countryside. The development of the crop-lien system, given legal sanction in 1866, formalized the new merchant dominion; the continuing postbellum stagnation of southern agriculture, due both to changes in the labor system and to a slackening in the growth of world demand for cotton, helped maintain it.[8] Even after 1880, when other sources of credit, such as banks, be-

7. Greenville and Columbia Railroad, *Minutes of Proceedings of the Stockholders at Their Annual Meeting, Held at Columbia, April 30, 1868* (Columbia: Julian A. Selby, 1868), 8; Anderson *Intelligencer*, July 20, 1871.

8. The historical literature dealing with the transition from the "Old" South to the "New," especially in the countryside, is burgeoning. For a useful interim survey, see Harold D. Woodman, "Sequel to Slavery: The New History Views the Post-Bellum South," *Journal of Southern History*, XLIII (1977), 523–54. The foregoing passage draws largely on Woodman, *King Cotton*, Chaps. 23 and 24; Ransom and Sutch, *One Kind of Freedom*; Jonathan M. Wiener, *Social Origins of the New South: Alabama, 1860–1885* (Baton Rouge: Louisiana State University Press, 1978), 3–34; Gavin Wright, *The Political Economy of the Cot-*

gan to reappear, Harry Hammond could report that in South Carolina "the system of credits and advances prevails to a large extent, consuming from one third to three fifths of the crop before it is harvested."[9]

Another major development shaping postwar commerce was the intensified involvement of small white farmers in the cotton economy. South Carolina produced 45 percent more cotton in 1880 than in 1860. Moreover, spectacular growth occurred in the western corner of the state, which before the war had been peripheral to the plantation economy. The five counties of Oconee, Pickens, Anderson, Greenville, and Spartanburg quintupled their cotton production during the period; Spartanburg and Anderson, each of which had raised only a few thousand bales a year in the 1850s, vaulted into the ranks of the state's leading cotton producing counties. In a period in which cultivated acreage in South Carolina was generally on the decline, these counties (except Spartanburg) and Lancaster, in the north central part of the state, were the only counties to expand cultivation.

The increase in cotton output involved a precipitous shift from a diversified small farming economy in which foodstuffs played a major role to one specializing heavily in production of an inedible crop for the international market. Table 1 illustrates the shift in terms of the relative proportion of cotton output to that of the major food crop, corn. While cotton production soared in the area between 1860 and 1880, corn production grew by less than 7 percent, and the number of swine, the principal source of meat, dropped by over 50 percent.[10] While the evidence is not conclusive,

---

ton South: Households, Markets, and Wealth in the Nineteenth Century (New York: W. W. Norton, 1978), Chap. 6; and Simkins and Woody, *South Carolina*, 273–77. The original crop-lien law appears in South Carolina, *Statutes at Large*, XIII (1866), 366[12]–66[13].

9. Harry Hammond, *South Carolina: Resources and Population, Institutions and Industries* (Charleston: Walker, Evans, and Cogswell, 1883), 153.

10. *U.S. Census, 1860: Agriculture*, 128–29; *U.S. Census, 1880: Report on Cotton Production*, II, 459; *U.S. Census, 1880*, III, 203–204. For antebellum production figures see Smith, *Economic Readjustment*, 61–62. This region was 31.2 percent black in 1860. The growth in corn output may have been illusory; the 1859 crop, from which the 1860 figures were derived, was reported to be one-third short in several upper Piedmont counties. See *U.S. Census, 1860, Social Statistics*.

Table 1. SPECIALIZATION IN COTTON, 1850–1900
Ratios of cotton (lb.) to corn (bu.)

	1850	*1860*	*1870*	*1880*	*1890*	*1900*
County:						
Anderson	3.25	3.46	5.79	20.13	36.20	34.96
Greenville	1.54	1.72	2.36	13.28	20.33	19.63
Pickens (incl. Oconee)	.86	.56	1.65	7.44	11.68	12.62
Spartanburg	3.05	3.13	2.44	18.46	22.95	24.47
Five county average	2.31	2.23	3.09	14.63	22.00	22.06
South Carolina	7.40	9.38	13.27	20.12	25.88	24.20

SOURCE: *U.S. Census, 1850*, p. 346; *U.S. Census, 1860*, p. 129; *U.S. Census, 1870: Industry and Wealth*, 239–40; *U.S. Census, 1880*, III, 203–204, 240; *U.S. Census, 1890: Statistics of Agriculture*, 382–83, 396; and *U.S. Census, 1900*, VI, Pt. 2, pp. 181–82, 433. The bale weights used are 400 pounds (1850 and 1860), 450 pounds (1870), 453 pounds (1880), 477 pounds (1890), and 500 pounds (1900), as estimated in Stanley L. Engerman, "Economic Aspects of the Adjustments to Emancipation in the United States and the British West Indies" (unpublished paper), Table 8 (used by permission).

it suggests that the largely white western counties were abandoning a diversified agriculture and a large degree of self-sufficiency and becoming reliant on cash income from cotton to meet their needs, a development which scholars have found to be characteristic of this period both for the South as a whole and for other predominantly white upland areas within the region.[11]

Exactly what brought this state of affairs about remains unclear. Some economic historians view it as a simple response to comparative advantage; specialization in cotton, they argue, was more profitable than diversified farming. Others see a darker significance to the shift; noting the increasing pressures of population upon the land, the devastation of the war, and the hardships of its aftermath, they argue that white farmers were "locked in" to pro-

11. Cf. Ransom and Sutch, *One Kind of Freedom*, 151–59; Wright, *Political Economy*, 164–76; Steven H. Hahn, "The Roots of Southern Populism: Yeomen Farmers and the Transformation of Georgia's Upper Piedmont, 1850–1900" (Ph.D. dissertation, Yale University, 1979), 189–211.

duction of the cash crop in a futile effort to repay the debts they began to incur in the disastrous 1860s.[12] Whatever the truth may be, the result was a striking enhancement of the role of the merchant, especially in those up-country counties destined to become the heartland of South Carolina's textile industry. It was the merchant who advanced the supplies that the farmer needed to live and work; it was the merchant who purchased and marketed his cotton. It was also the merchant who supplied him with guano, which made it possible to raise the fleecy staple in areas where previously the soil had been too thin or the growing season too short, and which first became a major item of commerce in the 1870s.[13] By concentrating control of agricultural produce and essential supplies in mercantile hands, the rise of cotton monoculture made possible the accumulation of capital by a new class of potential entrepreneurs, in a portion of the state which was well endowed with water power and had a heritage of small-scale manufacturing.[14]

Both Emancipation and the shift of white farmers into cotton cultivation, then, handed new power to South Carolina's merchants. New opportunities, of course, attracted new people, and the result was a "remarkable increase in the number of establishments engaged in trade."[15] A comparison of available lists of establishments in 1854 and 1880 indicates, in fact, that the number of trading establishments in the state outside of Charleston rose by 128.6 percent during the period.[16] Many of these new firms, espe-

12. For examples of the first argument, see Stephen J. DeCanio, *Agriculture in the Post-Bellum South: The Economics of Production and Supply* (Cambridge: M.I.T. Press, 1974); and Robert McGuire and Robert Higgs, "Cotton, Corn, and Risk: Another View," *Explorations in Economic History*, XIV (1977), 167–82. For examples of the second, see Ransom and Sutch, *One Kind of Freedom*, Chap. 8; Wright, *Political Economy*, Chap. 6; Gavin Wright and Howard Kunreuther, "Cotton, Corn, and Risk in the Nineteenth Century," *Journal of Economic History*, XXXV (1975), 526–51; Wright and Kunreuther, "Cotton, Corn, and Risk in the Nineteenth Century: A Reply," *Explorations in Economic History*, XIV (1977), 183–95; and Hahn, "Roots," 189–211.

13. Ransom and Sutch, *One Kind of Freedom*, 102–103, 187–89; Simkins and Woody, *South Carolina*, 258; Hahn, "Roots," 201–202.

14. Ernest McPherson Lander, *The Textile Industry in Ante-Bellum South Carolina* (Baton Rouge: Louisiana State University Press, 1969).

15. Hammond, *South Carolina*, 659.

16. The lists used are in *Southern Business Directory and General Commercial Advertiser* (Charleston: Walker and James, 1854), and R. G. Dun and Company, *The Mercantile*

cially in the heavily black areas, were crossroads merchants, who had, according to Hammond and many subsequent observers, "become an important factor in the organization of labor and in the distribution of wealth"; statewide, the number of trading communities with between one and three firms had risen by 71.6 percent.[17] However, the most striking commercial expansion occurred not in the countryside but in the towns. The number of trading centers containing ten stores or more rose from thirty-one to seventy-six, and accounted for 71.8 percent of the total increase in the number of establishments; a majority of the increase accrued to some thirty-eight settlements with twenty or more stores apiece. In the Piedmont, where country merchants had been comparatively numerous before the war, 81.8 percent of the growth in mercantile establishments occurred in settlements with at least ten stores, and 64.1 percent occurred in towns of twenty or more stores.[18] The changing economic patterns of the postwar period were shifting the focus of trade away from the coastal ports and their factors, but not to the country storekeeper. Rather, commerce was being reconcentrated at several score small centers, where merchants gathered to take advantage of transportation and communication facilities, and where farmers came to sell their cotton, obtain their provisions, and arrange their financing.

The tendency of merchants to cluster in towns was in large degree the product of the postwar expansion and reorientation of the state's railway system. The period between the Civil War and 1880

Agency Reference Book, 1880. My counts include stores, artisans' shops, and small manufacturers, but exclude professionals, such as doctors and dentists, not engaging in mercantile activity, such as operating drug stores. The 1854 listing has some inadequacies, but can be used with some profit. Charleston District is not included, because the data is incomplete and because I wished to exclude the City of Charleston from the estimates.

17. Hammond, *South Carolina*, 659. Ransom and Sutch, *One Kind of Freedom*, Chaps. 6 and 7, note the emergence of interior towns after the Civil War but stress the importance of the country merchant and his "territorial monopoly" in order to explain the high "credit prices" charged to southern farmers.

18. Aiken County was created between 1854 and 1880 from territory straddling the line between "Piedmont" and "non-Piedmont" counties. For purposes of comparison I apportioned Aiken's trading points in 1880 to their respective antebellum districts. "Piedmont" includes the area north and west of Edgefield, Newberry, Fairfield, Chester, and Lancaster districts as district lines were drawn in 1854. A similar pattern of merchant concentration in towns is reported by Hahn, "Roots," 257.

saw little change in South Carolina's total track mileage; during those fifteen years only 420 miles of track were added to the 1,007 miles already in existence. The track that was laid, however, filled crucial gaps in the network, providing the interior with direct links to northeastern ports and markets and diverting trade from its traditional course down to Charleston. The Columbia and Augusta Railroad, built in the late 1860s, completed a rail route running from Augusta to Charlotte, bisecting the old rail lines. Of even greater importance was the construction of the Atlanta and Charlotte Air Line, a road which had been dreamed of from antebellum times but whose construction across the western corner of the state was delayed until the early 1870s; the Air Line became a crucial link in a southeastern trunk line from Atlanta to Washington, which a succession of systembuilders managed to piece together by 1881.[19] Rail transportation was improved as much by managerial innovation as by physical construction; corporate consolidation removed many of the bottlenecks inhibiting free movement of goods, as did the development of connections between lines, car interchange agreements, and through bills of lading. Railroads also provided the rights of way along which the telegraph penetrated the interior in the postwar years, bringing with it opportunities for "futures" speculation by the reckless and "hedging" by the more cautious. By providing interior merchants with direct connections to northern suppliers and customers, and thus permitting them to dispense with the services of Charleston factors and wholesalers, the railroads both stimulated commerce and opened the interior to increased northern influence.[20]

The transformation of rural social and economic relationships

19. Stover, *Railroads*, 61, 99–121, 193, 233–38; Helen Kohn Hennig, *Columbia: Capital City of South Carolina, 1786–1936* (Columbia: R. L. Bryan, 1936), 356; Hahn, "Roots," 198–201; Anderson *Intelligencer*, June 8, 1871.

20. Stover, *Railroads*, 275–78; Woodman, *King Cotton*, 269–86, 289–94, 328; Lewis J. Bellardo, "A Social and Economic History of Fairfield County, South Carolina, 1865–1871" (Ph.D. dissertation, University of Kentucky, 1979), 138–43. Even in the antebellum period interior merchants preferred dealing with northern suppliers, chiefly because they offered better terms and prices than southern factors and wholesalers. Lewis Atherton, *The Southern Country Store, 1800–1860* (Baton Rouge: Louisiana State University Press, 1949), Chap. 6.

proceeding beneath the political tumult of Reconstruction, with the penetration of the railroads, then, resulted in the spawning of numerous small towns in the interior of South Carolina. Only nineteen such towns had existed in the state in 1860; by 1880 there were a hundred and six. The vast majority of them were mere hamlets, to be sure; only thirty-nine had more than five hundred inhabitants, and only eighteen had more than one thousand. Their importance, however, lay not in their size but in their appearance on the scene and their potential for future growth. By 1880 ten towns existed along the route of the Atlanta and Charlotte Air Line which less than a decade before had been mere gleams in a promoter's eye. Seneca, with 382 residents and 23 stores, Gaffney City, with 400 residents and 24 stores, and most of the others had been laid out in 1873.[21]

While new towns were coming into existence, older ones burgeoned. Greenville and Spartanburg, for instance, had been small, sleepy courthouse and railroad terminal towns on the eve of the Civil War, dealing in supplies and serving as summer resorts for low-country planters; according to Harry Hammond, no cotton was shipped from Greenville prior to the war. The completion of the Air Line, however, transformed the two rail terminals into major junction towns; a portion of the traffic which had formerly drained away from them toward Charleston reversed its flow and began to move through Greenville and Spartanburg on its way north. By 1880 Greenville's 23 stores had become 161, her population had quadrupled to over six thousand, and local boosters were boasting of having shipped as many as forty thousand bales of cotton in a year. Spartanburg's growth was less impressive, but only by comparison; the city's population grew by one and a half times between 1860 and 1880, and in the latter year was officially counted an "urban place," along with Greenville, Columbia, and

21. *U.S. Census, 1860*, 452, Table 3; *U.S. Census, 1880*, I, 327–30, Table 3; *R.G. Dun Reference Book, 1880*; Frances Holleman, *Seneca, South Carolina, Centennial, 1873–1973* (Greenville, S.C.: Creative Printers, 1973), 1, 7; Mattie May Morgan, *Central: Yesterday and Today* (Taylors, S.C.: Faith Printing Company, 1973), 26; Bobby Gilmer Moss, *The Old Iron District: A Study of the Development of Cherokee County, 1750–1897* (Clinton, S.C.: Jacobs Press, 1972), 208–209.

Charleston. In 1880 the city had 111 stores, versus 34 in 1854, and shipped twenty-five to thirty thousand bales of cotton each year.[22]

Other older towns benefited less conspicuously from the postwar economic transformation, but did handsomely all the same. Anderson, Greenville's rival thirty miles to the southwest, lost out in the complex contentions over the route of the Air Line in the early 1870s, but its position as entrepot for a broad area of the upper Savannah River valley was enhanced by the new northern connection, which drew cotton to its market that had formerly gone downriver to Augusta. The volume of local trade was further enlarged by the postwar surge into cotton. Anderson County, which grew barely five thousand bales a year in 1860, raised over twenty thousand bales in 1880 and over forty thousand in 1890, and the trade of the town kept pace; its annual shipments totaled twelve thousand bales in the early 1870s, twenty thousand by the 1880s, and nearly thirty-five thousand by the end of the century. Forty-four men were doing business in the town at the time of the last-prewar credit report; by early 1880 eighty-one shopkeepers were vying for local patronage.[23]

In contrast to the fairly steady growth of Anderson was that of Rock Hill, on the Charlotte and South Carolina Railroad just south of the North Carolina line. Unlike the other large upcountry towns, which had originated as clusters about local courthouses, Rock Hill had scarcely any prewar existence. A tiny depot before the war, its major expansion came afterward; thirty stores were in operation by 1880. Cotton prices were higher there, reports the city's historian, and "as a result cotton was hauled here from Lancaster and Chester Counties and from all over York County. Cotton, which for half a century had found its way to

22. *U.S. Census, 1860*, 452, Table 3; *U.S. Census, 1880*, I, 327–30; *R.G. Dun Reference Book, 1880*; Hammond, *South Carolina*, 709, 712–13; James M. Richardson, *History of Greenville County, South Carolina* (Atlanta: A. H. Cawston, 1930), 76.

23. Anderson *Intelligencer*, June 8, September 14, 1871; September 25, 1873; June 21, 1888; August 31, 1898; August 31, 1899; *U.S. Census, 1860*, 129; *U.S. Census, 1880*, III, 240; *U.S. Census, 1890: Agriculture*, 226; Hammond, *South Carolina*, 705. The number of men in business in Anderson is compiled from R. G. Dun Collection, South Carolina, II.

Camden, Columbia, and even Charleston, turned toward the Up-Country town where the best prices could be obtained. Rock Hill almost became a boom town, growing to the tune of turning wagon wheels carrying the cotton crop to its warehouses." In 1869 the Rock Hill cotton market handled two thousand bales a year; by 1883 fifteen thousand bales passed through the hands of its merchants. As the town was new, so were its citizens. Of the fifteen notables comprising the boards of directors of its first three cotton mills, only three had resided on the spot before the Civil War: a landholder, a physician, and a merchant who arrived in 1859.[24]

These towns, and numerous smaller ones in the interior of South Carolina, continued their rise through the remainder of the century. Between 1880 and 1900 their number rose from 106 to 193, and the proportion of the state's population outside of Charleston living in towns of one thousand or more inhabitants increased from 5 to nearly 12 percent. The commercial population of the state, hitherto concentrated in Charleston, thus increasingly shifted away from the old port. The census of 1890 showed that for the first time a majority of South Carolina's town population lived outside of Charleston; by 1900 the former metropolis of the state was the home of only one quarter of the state's townsmen. In that year twenty towns, half of them in the Piedmont, were classified as "urban" by the census, having populations of twenty-five hundred or more; Greenville and Spartanburg each had passed ten thousand.[25]

Not that the state was becoming "urban"; far from it. Even with Charleston included, the proportion of the state's inhabitants living in towns of one thousand or more rose only modestly, from 9.8 percent in 1880 to 15.6 percent in 1900, and the great bulk of

24. Douglas Summers Brown, *A City Without Cobwebs: A History of Rock Hill, South Carolina* (Columbia: University of South Carolina Press, 1953), 137 and *passim*; Hammond, *South Carolina*, 715; *R.G. Dun Reference Book, 1880*.

25. *U.S. Census, 1880*, I, 327–30, Table 3; *U.S. Census, 1900: Population*, 350–55, Table 5. The 1900 census probably understates the extent of urbanization to a considerable degree. Industrialization was well under way by then; most mill operatives lived in unincorporated mill villages whose populations were not returned separately in 1900. The 1890 census listed eight mill villages, four with populations of over one thousand and one with over twenty-five hundred. *U.S. Census, 1890: Population*, Pt. I, 306–10, Table 5.

South Carolinians continued to work the soil.[26] The importance of town development, however, far outweighed the number of people living in them. It represented a fundamental shift in economic and social power to a new class of merchants, a class whose influence had hitherto been heavily circumscribed by an economic structure based on the plantation and the factorage system. Of even greater significance was the role of the town in making these new businessmen *into* a class. By enmeshing them in a web of relationships and institutions and inspiring them with a common interest in the welfare of their communities, it converted their desire for individual aggrandizement into a powerful force for economic and social development, a force which began to transform the landscape and the people of South Carolina.

The explosive growth of the inland towns inevitably introduced an element of crudity into their appearance. Some of the older courthouse settlements, such as Anderson and Spartanburg, had central business districts built largely of brick, and the latter city had a mile of macadamized street in 1884. In newer towns, or in faster growing older ones such as Greenville, however, wooden structures proliferated; for the most part, streets were unpaved, and heavy rains turned the Piedmont clay into a crimson morass.[27] Both the courthouse towns and the newer creations of land speculators were commonly laid out according to rational plans, but growth was nonetheless frequently anarchic; Rock Hill, for instance, "had grown up like Jonah's gourd, almost overnight, and now sprawled here and there beginning at the depot, and working out along lines of least resistance, via cow paths, old trails, and the like."[28] The rawness extended to social as well as physical qualities.

26. *U.S. Census, 1880*, I, 327–30, Table 3; *U.S. Census, 1900: Population*, 350–55, Table 5.

27. *Historical and Descriptive Review of the State of South Carolina* (3 vols.; Charleston: Empire Publishing Company, 1884), III, 52, 54, 125, 149, 150, 202; "A Trip to Anderson," *Erskine Collegiate Recorder*, December, 1857, reprinted in Anderson *Daily Mail*, February 16, 1912; Richardson, *History of Greenville*, 93–94; Bellardo, "Fairfield County," 150.

28. Louise Ayer Vandiver, *Traditions and History of Anderson County* (Atlanta: Rural-

Greenville had as many as eighteen barrooms before liquor sales became a state monopoly in 1893; an attempt at prohibition failed decisively in the early 1880s. Rock Hill, with just over eight hundred inhabitants in 1880, had eight saloons, ranging from "dirty little grog shops to 'gilded palaces,'" virtually all of which had been built since the war. The Reverend W. P. Jacobs, Clinton Presbyterian minister and civic booster, characterized pre-prohibition weekends in his town as times of "unruly riot, yelling, swearing, drunkenness that made it impossible for ladies to go out on the streets or even sit on the front piazzas." The struggle for wealth pitted groups of businessmen against each other, as in the case of Gaffney, where the "East End" and the "West End" contended for preferment.[29]

The rough edges were knocked off or worn smooth after a while, thanks in large part to the concerted efforts of the "town people" themselves. Even so, there remained in the air of the new towns an aggressive spirit to be expected in communities composed of rising businessmen. They were populated with self-styled "practical men," whose view of the world around them was colored by their thirst for material gain. In the presence of an up-country waterfall, observed a Spartanburg editor, the typical townsman would see "something more than limpid streams, precipitous descents, trailing arbutis, and the like. Every pint of water from the Middle Tyger at this point means so much money." Aggressiveness in business was celebrated as a cardinal virtue by the proliferating promotional literature of the day. Rock Hill was celebrated for its drive. "We have struck no other town with as much push and energy as progressive little Rock Hill," claimed one puff sheet. "Here she is a mere infant by the side of some of her sister towns, with a population of less than five thousand, and has more industries than any [other] town in the State, except Charleston and Colum-

---

ist Press, 1928), 11; Holleman, *Seneca*, 7, 10–15; Moss, *Old Iron District*, 208–209; *Historical and Descriptive Review*, III, 50; Brown, *City Without Cobwebs*, 168–69.

29. Brown, *City Without Cobwebs*, 169–71; Richardson, *History of Greenville*, 96; *Our Monthly* (Thornwell Orphanage, Clinton, S.C.), XIX (1882), 258; Bellardo, "Fairfield County," 152; Moss, *Old Iron District*, 210, 211, 274–75.

bia." The town of Gaffney in the 1890s was remembered by a man who had moved there to make his fortune as a merchant and mill president as "an up-and-coming, businesslike place, reminding me of the hustle I had seen in some of the western towns."[30]

Occasionally the quest for money was described in less flattering terms, particularly by ministers and other guardians of tradition. A view of Rock Hill less rosy than the one cited above was offered at the turn of the century by a Methodist circuit rider:

> Rock Hill has no pleasure grounds, few gardens for flowers, no pretty public park with gushing fountain and shaded walks. There seems to be a dearth in the social atmosphere of sentiment and song, and lack of poetic shadings in the constituted nature of things. The town seems to have been built, not in a day, but hurriedly, and for business. And so, not having parks to walk and muse in, if you keep the streets, you will be continually jostling or meeting a banker or a butcher, a tradesman or a trafficer, a bucketshop man, or a broker shop man—all very busy men, and all insured or insuring.[31]

General Ellison Capers, son of the Methodist bishop and rector of Christ Church (Episcopal) in Greenville, was disturbed that "the one thing needful to man" in the eyes of his fellow townsmen seemed to be "the possession of this world's good," complaining that "our people must make money, let it cost what it will. Business is first and last, and everything must bend to business." A visitor to the Southern Baptist Convention, held in Greenville in the spring of 1882, reported sadly that the Mountain City, "once noted for its morality and religion, now impresses the visitor as a pushing, growing, worldly-minded city."[32]

Despite the preoccupation with moneymaking, however, the new communities were by no means simply agglomerations of clawing competitors. The rhetoric of individualism and worship of the "self-made man" which pervades American self-description must not be allowed to obscure the social dimension of American

30. Spartanburg *Herald*, November 3, 1886 (Industrial ed.); Sumter *Home Seeker and Business Guide* (April, 1895), 172; W. C. Hamrick, *Life Values in the New South* (Gaffney, S.C.: By the author, 1931), 107.

31. E. Alston Wilkes in *Southern Christian Advocate*, April 21, 1904.

32. Greenville *Daily News*, March 15, 1881; *Central Baptist*, cited in *Baptist Courier* (Greenville, S.C.), June 15, 1882.

business. South Carolina's townsmen, like their compatriots elsewhere, depended upon the community for aid in attaining their goals. Success in business for the individual was contingent on his obtaining, and maintaining, the confidence of colleagues and customers; furthermore, the continued viability and future growth of each individual enterprise was allied to that of the town as a whole. Townsmen were tied to their homes by affective bonds as well, by friendships and by familial and conjugal love. Economic and noneconomic motives alike thus impelled the "town people" to develop a community life of some vigor.

A look at a single case, that of the town of Anderson, will show how personal relationships contributed to the corporate consciousness of the business community. Any investigator studying the credit records of the period will be struck not only by the number and extent of family relationships among Anderson merchants, but also with the importance ascribed to family connections in determining credit risks. Young men starting out depended on relatives to provide capital and security, and derived their own reputations for reliability from those of their families. Thus, when P. K. McCulley opened his general store in 1870 the local credit reporter based his favorable assessment of the new firm on the fact that McCulley's father was one of the town's wealthiest men; John E. Peoples owed much of his success as a tinner to his status as son-in-law to Sylvester Bleckley, Anderson's most prominent merchant. Kinship networks in Anderson were complex, reaching out into the countryside and far into the past; at least half a dozen of the town's business and professional men could claim a blood or marriage relationship through one colonial settler, Edward Vandiver. Knowledge of a merchant's kin and antecedents reassured rural customers otherwise suspicious of the black arts of commerce and inspired the confidence necessary to attract trade.[33]

Those not blessed with the right family ties could succeed by attaching themselves to a successful and reputable patron, especially

33. R. G. Dun Collection, South Carolina, II, 76, 124, and *passim*; Joseph N. Brown, "The Vandiver Family," Anderson *Intelligencer*, June 6, 1900. Cf. Paul E. Johnson, *A Shopkeeper's Millennium: Society and Revivals in Rochester, New York, 1815–1837* (New York: Hill and Wang, 1978), 16–32.

by taking a clerkship. Clerking was still to some degree a master-apprenticeship relationship in the late nineteenth century, with the employer playing the role of surrogate parent. Clerks thus might succeed their patrons much as sons succeeded fathers. W. S. Ligon, son of the local schoolmaster and clerk to W. S. Sharpe, took over Sharpe's business in 1875, along with another clerk whose father was a local druggist. J. J. Fretwell, whose father was a farmer living near town, became a clerk for Sylvester Bleckley in 1867; in 1874 he was elevated to a partnership in Bleckley, Brown and Fretwell, which in the 1880s became one of the leading mercantile firms of the Piedmont. Personal relationships mattered not only to young men on their way up, but to established merchants as well; businessmen made use of their friendships to cushion themselves in times of trouble, which came frequently enough in the years after Appomattox. Bleckley, for example, received capital backing after the war from Alex Evins, a physician, and O. H. P. Fant; he himself later took in as a clerk, and later as a partner, E. W. Brown, a colleague having hard times. The web of affective relationships developed by the Anderson business elite contributed powerfully to its cohesion and continuity; of the twenty leading firms of the town in 1880, fifteen had some link to the antebellum business community through survivors, sons, sons-in-law, or former clerks.[34]

Personal relationships were supplemented by noneconomic institutions such as fraternal orders and churches, which served to tie each developing town elite to its fellows elsewhere. Lodges and churches were expected to uphold the values of personal and public morality essential to the smooth and reliable workings of commerce; a fraternal or church affiliation thus served as testimony of a man's reliability even when he was doing business among strangers. The regional and national networks formed by the various orders and denominations made it possible for mobile businessmen

34. R. G. Dun Collection, South Carolina, II, 72G, 72L, 72Z6, 73B, 114; J. C. Hemphill (ed.), *Men of Mark in South Carolina* (4 vols.; Washington: Men of Mark Publishing Company, 1908), I, 123–25; Anderson *Intelligencer*, Souvenir ed. (1896). The list of firms in 1880 includes those with an estimated worth of at least five thousand dollars, as reported in *R. G. Dun Reference Book, 1880*; the other information is compiled from R. G. Dun Collection, South Carolina, II.

to move from one community to another without having to give up their credentials as "respectable" men. In addition, they provided meeting grounds for men from different towns, thus developing among the "town people" an awareness of a common interest transcending their localities. Concerted effort in religious or fraternal endeavors suggested it in others as well; it was, accordingly, oddly appropriate that the Savannah Valley Railroad project to link Augusta and Anderson was first conceived by Anderson and Abbeville County businessmen at a meeting of a Baptist association.[35]

Noneconomic institutions and relationships gave the town elites much of their cohesion, but the most important and dynamic town institutions were economic. The central commercial institutions were the banks, and accordingly a significant measure of the rising economic influence of the interior towns is the proliferation of banking institutions after the Civil War. On the eve of the war nine of the state's eighteen banks, and the bulk of its banking capital, were located in Charleston; the remaining banks had their offices chiefly in Georgetown and in the fall line towns of Hamburg, Columbia, Camden, and Cheraw. The three Piedmont banks established in the 1850s were comparatively small. Serving chiefly to finance the movement of the cotton crop, antebellum banks were generally run quite conservatively, and, according to one economic historian, were "inadequate as far as the credit needs of the economy were concerned, particularly in meeting the needs of economic expansion and development."[36]

By 1880 the nature of banking in the state had fundamentally altered. At that time, according to R. G. Dun and Company, there were banks at twenty-one locations instead of eleven; thirteen towns had established banking facilities since the war, eight of them located in the Piedmont. A contemporary directory listed national banks in operation at Anderson, Greenville, Spartanburg, and Union as well as at Chester, Winnsboro, and Newberry; private bankers lent money in Greenville, Union, Rock Hill, York-

35. Anderson *Intelligencer*, August 19, 1886. Cf. Don H. Doyle, *The Social Order of a Frontier Community* (Urbana: University of Illinois Press, 1978), 156–69, 178–93.

36. Smith, *Economic Readjustment*, 194, 217.

ville, Walhalla, and even the hamlet of Fork Shoals.[37] The next two decades saw a proliferation of small-town banks; by the end of 1906 the State Bank Examiner reported 204 state and private banks, and 25 national banks, doing business at virtually every crossroads in the state. These banks were generally quite small, being operated chiefly for the accommodation of farmers and small businessmen; the financing of large-scale manufacturing enterprise, among other things, was beyond their capacities.[38] However, their existence in such numbers, in contrast to the antebellum period, suggests the degree of vitality to be found in the small cities and towns of South Carolina in this period. Banks also helped provide organization and leadership to local business communities. The banker, dealing with money as a commodity, occupied a central position in the economic life of a town, and was expected to be the man best qualified to direct its development.

If the bankers were the leading business organizers of the towns, the newspaper editors were their principal spokesmen and cheerleaders. The numerous local weeklies in existence in the late nineteenth century were commonly referred to corporately as the "country press," but the typical "country paper" was run chiefly in the interest of the town in which it was published. The local newspaper served as a disseminator of town gossip, a medium of advertising for local merchants, a bulletin board for town meetings, legal notices, and personal announcements, and a forum for local issues. Several of the larger "country" papers graduated to daily status during the period and by the 1880s were meeting their enlarged capital needs through incorporation. The backers of the new enterprises were generally leading town citizens; four current or future mill presidents were listed among the incorporators of the Greenville News Company in 1888, and most of the 1890 board of directors of the Spartanburg Herald Company were important mill officials, bankers, and merchants.[39]

37. *R. G. Dun Reference Book, 1880*; *South Carolina State Gazetteer and Business Directory for 1880–1881* (Charleston: R. A. Smith, 1880), 612.

38. South Carolina State Bank Examiner, *First Annual Report, 1906*, 3–4, 8–9. The average capitalization of a state or private bank was around $38,000; the average for national banks was $129,000.

39. South Carolina Secretary of State, Private Corporations, Charter Book A, 147 (in

None of this is to deny the importance of a farm readership to the "country" press. South Carolina, as we have seen, was still overwhelmingly rural, and the interior towns were generally too small to support newspapers on their own. Farmers were major customers of town merchants, and their patronage built up the town, adding potential subscribers and advertisers to its population; for that reason, for instance, newspapers typically devoted a fair amount of space each fall to touting the local cotton market. More immediately, the farmers were major consumers of the goods advertised in the newspapers, and advertising rates thus depended on attracting a rural readership. Accordingly, small-town editors generally showed great solicitude for local agriculture and agriculturists. Charles Petty of Spartanburg's *Carolina Spartan*, for example, was a former farmer well known for his copious commentaries on farm matters. However, much of his advice consisted of homilies extolling hard work and intelligent management. These were virtues, to be sure, and were sorely needed on Carolina farms, but against the backdrop of postwar rural poverty, the constant drain of the credit system, and the worldwide stagnation of cotton demand, the gospel of work was both inadequate and patronizing. As with most of its colleagues of the state press, "metropolitan" and "country" alike, the 1890s found the *Spartan* bitterly opposed to the Tillman movement and complaining loudly about the "communistic" enmity of the countryside toward the towns.[40]

Given their positions as chief spokesmen for and to the towns, the vast majority of the "country" newspapers, like their daily cousins, took up roles as civic promoters and agitators for all manner of improvements and community enterprises. The "booster ethos" flowered in South Carolina in the late nineteenth century much as it had done less than two generations before in the Midwest, and the editor was its prophet. In particular, editors in the

---

South Carolina Department of Archives and History, Columbia); *S.C. Stats. at Large*, XVIII (1884), 859; Spartanburg *Carolina Spartan*, August 13, 1890. Cf. Atherton, *Southern Country Store*, 199–203.

40. Spartanburg *Carolina Spartan*, January 19, 1887; May 17, 1893. Cf. Thomas D. Clark, *The Southern Country Editor* (Indianapolis: Bobbs-Merrill, 1948), 264–82, 292–93, 297–301.

Piedmont pressed for cotton mills, and at least three served on boards of directors of cotton manufacturing corporations.[41] The contribution of the press to the economic development of towns should not be exaggerated, however. A press campaign without backing from the local business elite was apt to be little more than gas. One envious daily ascribed Spartanburg's industrial success to the existence of a public spirit that "does not need arousing, where newspapers enjoy the pleasure of announcing large public improvements without first having to endure the pains of protracted pleading and mathematical demonstration to prove that benefits will benefit and paying investments will pay." And a cynical weekly proclaimed that "the country editors haven't built a single factory." The town of Anderson saw several press campaigns come and go before the community was prepared to risk its meager capital in cotton manufacturing.[42] Alone, the press could not motivate; its power derived from its ability to express the will of the local elites, transmit their attitudes to the populace, and mobilize the townspeople to act.

The "booster" spirit of the newspapers was an articulation of the tendency of the business and professional men of the towns to treat their communities as common enterprises, a tendency also manifested in the development of government services and the creation of private organizations for civic betterment. The leading merchants were also the leading municipal politicians. The mayor of Greenville in the early 1880s, who was responsible for such public improvements as the construction of a city hall and the establishment of a board of health, was a dry goods merchant. His contemporary in Spartanburg was Joseph Walker, a partner in the city's leading mercantile firm, whose administration was marked

41. Directors of cotton mills are gathered from South Carolina Secretary of State, Private Corporations, Charter Books G, 5; S, 575; and Charter Number 2696. They are identified in Hemphill (ed.), *Men of Mark*, II, 11–12, 33–34, 442–43.

42. Columbia *State*, May 8, 1899; Abbeville *Press and Banner*, November 2, 1887; Anderson *Intelligencer*, September 28, October 26, November 2, 1871; May 1, September 4, 18, 24, 1873; April 26, May 17–June 7, 1883; May 10–June 7, 1888; Broadus Mitchell, *The Rise of Cotton Mills in the South*, Johns Hopkins University Studies in Historical and Political Science, series 39, no. 2 (Baltimore: Johns Hopkins University Press, 1921), 58*n*. Cf. *ibid*., 112; "The cotton mill development sprang in large part from the activity of the press."

by major street improvements, the expansion of police and fire protection, and the completion of the opera house. Between its incorporation as a city in 1882 and the end of the century Anderson had five mayors; two were lawyers, two merchants, and one a physician. Further, of the forty-six aldermen serving during the period, all but a handful were merchants, bankers, and professional men. Business dominance carried over into quasi-public institutions as well. Membership in Rock Hill's volunteer fire company, organized in 1869 to protect the town from the fires which "rushed through its frail wooden buildings like sparks in prairie grassland," was considered prestigious, and the names of many of the local merchants appeared on its rolls.[43]

The interest of townsmen in public improvement extended to areas only indirectly beneficial to business, as can be seen in the immense pride they took in the local "graded schools." Prior to the Civil War there had been little genuine public education in the state; there was a system of "free schools" for the children of "paupers," but the principal means of education was the private academy. The only major exception was the public school system of Charleston, organized under the leadership of Christopher G. Memminger in the late 1850s. The first genuine state public school system in South Carolina was a gift of the Reconstruction constitution writers of 1868.[44] It suffered grievously from corruption before 1877, however, and then only slightly less grievously from the "narrow and reactionary" policies of the Conservative-dominated General Assembly in the years following "Redemption." In a general atmosphere of "indifference to education, if not hostility," state appropriations were cut, and the right of local school districts to tax themselves was abolished. That right could be restored, however, for individual localities with sufficient determina-

43. *Historical and Descriptive Review*, III, 63–64, 156; the Anderson officials are listed in Vandiver, *Traditions and History*, 29–30, and identified from a variety of sources. Cf. Samuel M. Kipp III, "Old Notables and Newcomers: The Economic and Political Elite of Greensboro, North Carolina, 1880–1920," *Journal of Southern History*, XLIII (1977), 373–94. Brown, *City Without Cobwebs*, 171–76.

44. John Furman Thomason, *Foundation of the Public Schools of South Carolina* (Columbia: The State Company, 1925), 161–66, 173; Simkins and Woody, *South Carolina*, 434–36.

tion; beginning with an enactment for Winnsboro in 1878, the General Assembly established a succession of special school tax districts to supplement the meager state allotments. Some ninety-six had been established by the time their further formation was prohibited by the Constitution of 1895. While a large minority of special districts were strictly rural, the majority were located in and about incorporated towns and villages. In the case of the larger towns they seem to have become status symbols; of those with more than fifteen hundred people in 1890, only Gaffney and Beaufort never established special districts. For smaller towns and villages, and for the countryside, special districts were far less common.[45]

The principal motives behind the public education drive of the towns in the 1880s were economic. Public education was seen as one of the major factors in the economic success of the northeast, which, despite the conventional hatred of all things Yankee, the new town classes admired and envied. The Orangeburg *Times and Democrat* cited the experience of New York, Pennsylvania, and even devilish Massachusetts in support of education by the state; the people of those commonwealths had "found, by practical experience, that the elevation and perfection of the public school system has been the greatest blessing to the people. Why should South Carolina be behind in this respect?" The public schools were expected to produce the skilled, intelligent labor force required for diversified economic expansion, and to supply the swelling ranks of store clerks and stenographers on which the business and professional classes relied. The schools were also used as symbols of civic pride and culture, and as tools of civic expansion. At the close of the century *The State* of Columbia reckoned "the creation of fine educational systems" to be equal to the extension of railways and the erection of factories as a "chief factor" in "the

45. Thomason, *Public Schools of South Carolina*, 223; David Duncan Wallace, *The History of South Carolina* (4 vols.; New York: American Historical Society, 1934), III, 482; Thomas E. Dukes, "Special Legislation Pertaining to Special School Districts Established in South Carolina Between 1868 and 1895" (M.A. thesis, University of South Carolina, 1927), compared to *U.S. Census, 1890: Population*, Pt. I, 306–310. Gaffney was the smallest of these towns, with an 1890 population of 1,631; Beaufort was much larger (3,587) but was also heavily black, and for that reason probably suffered from legislative hostility.

very rapid growth of our towns." The schools served as advertisements and drawing cards, attracting "from the country or from less progressive places a very considerable number of excellent people seeking education for their children." In advocacy of a new building for the Anderson Graded School, a local editor pointed out its role in "drawing into our citizenship people who buy and improve property and contribute to the permanent advancement of the city."[46]

On the other hand, the use of the public schools for broader social purposes, such as the transmission of values, was little bruited in this period. Prior to the industrial surge at the end of the century there was no major "proletarian" white population in the towns, and thus no movement to use the schools to inculcate new values and behavior.[47] The principal social concern of the townsmen, as of white South Carolinians generally, was with the black population; but blacks, defined as they were outside the body politic, could be dealt with in blunter fashion, and it was feared that schooling would make them dangerous. Aside from the race question, the townsmen felt their social order to be fairly secure. Although an occasional school advocate, responding to attacks on public education as "communistic," might equate schooling with law enforcement as a legitimate application of public funds, most viewed it principally as an attraction to be cited in advertising, an aid to community prosperity.[48]

The institutional development of the towns was the product of a rising "town spirit" among their citizens, a sense that all who lived in or near a town had a common interest in its progress. This "booster" mentality obtained its vitality from the application of the precepts of American individualism to community life. Towns, argued the boosters, like individuals, held their fate in their own hands, and success for towns, as for individuals, lay in their ability

46. Orangeburg *Times and Democrat*, November 19, 1880; Columbia *State*, April 26, 1899; Winnsboro *News and Herald*, November 27, 1878; Anderson *Intelligencer*, June 11, 1902.

47. Cf. Michael B. Katz, *The Irony of Early School Reform: Educational Innovation in Mid-Nineteenth Century Massachusetts* (Cambridge: Harvard University Press, 1968).

48. See the exchange of "B" and "Citizen," in Anderson *Intelligencer*, May 9–23, June 6, 1889.

to organize their energies in pursuit of a cherished goal.[49] Thus it was widely understood that the "pooling of interests and combination of resources" were "more than anything else conducive to the upbuilding of a city," and that the success of cooperation depended heavily upon "a solid population of determined business men." A young merchant who moved to Gaffney in 1895 listed among the town's attractions "the spirit of unity manifest in most of its leading citizens." "If we want our town to grow," argued a Newberry editor, "we must go to work all together to inaugurate such enterprises as will make it grow. . . . We must all work together for the common good." Cooperation in economic development was institutionalized in the ubiquitous boards of trade and chambers of commerce, each "pushing the claims of the town to the front and making it boom." Organization was to the townspeople the great lever of Progress, the tool with which men could shape their own lives rather than have them shaped by implacable external forces. Before its discovery, argued *The State*, the towns "were dependent upon agriculture and they gained no more in population than agricultural growth permitted." By the end of Reconstruction, however, "the towns realized that they had the power by a wise expenditure of money to increase greatly their populations and make themselves to a considerable degree independent of the vicissitudes of an unprogressive agriculture. They found that through their own exertions they could compel success, and one by one they created mills and railroads and grew by leaps and bounds."[50]

This budding sense of class power through organization was at least partially illusory. The strength of boosterism was everywhere sapped by personal factionalism and constrained by the larger world; in South Carolina, limited economic skills, the competition of the industrial North, and the mutual suspicion of town and country all played some part in stifling civic dreams of grandeur. Nonetheless, the principles of cooperation and organization had potentially enormous ramifications. Organized effort was solving

49. Doyle, *Social Order*, 62–64.

50. Columbia *State*, January 3, 1894; April 26, 1899; Hamrick, *Life Values*, 107; Newberry *Herald and News*, February 6, 1890; Anderson *Intelligencer*, January 31, 1900.

small problems; could it not solve larger ones? The towns remained fundamentally dependent on the trade in cotton, a fluctuating and chronically depressed commodity; could they not stabilize their economies and increase their wealth by manufacturing it?

The townsmen of South Carolina in the years after the Confederate surrender were beginning to create a new world. From little knots of country storekeepers only marginally distinguishable from the surrounding countryside they were developing an embryonic urban civilization. Corporately and individually, they were at the cutting edge of social change in the state, and their values and drives were becoming increasingly influential in shaping the social order. However, their full potential could not begin to be realized until they stepped decisively away from the countryside and began to industrialize. The rise of the mills about the southern towns, while increasing their wealth and power, would in time produce social changes for which the townsmen were unprepared. That story, however, came later. For the moment, the fascination of the "town people" was not with the "cotton mill problem" but with the factory as a generator of wealth.

Chapter II

Mill Building as Town Building
The Industrial Impulse

Although South Carolina's cotton textile industry did not become a significant economic and social force until just before the close of the nineteenth century, it was no creation *ex nihilo*. Yarn had been spun by power-driven machinery in the Palmetto State since the beginning of the century. Several establishments, notably William Gregg's famous mill at Graniteville in the Horse Creek Valley, were large, integrated operations producing for broad markets; more characteristic, however, were small, water-powered factories scattered about the foothills of the Blue Ridge, taking advantage of the numerous shoals and benefiting from markets naturally protected by up-country isolation. Some of these enterprises, such as D. E. Converse's mill at Glendale, survived the slave regime and prospered in the years after the Civil War. More significantly, the fund of experience acquired by these petty manufacturers was readily transferred to newer firms, and their demonstration of the feasibility of manufacturing in the South attracted men and money to the industry. In these senses the later developments in cotton textiles can be said to stem from a continuous historical tradition.[1]

That said, the fact remains that the cotton mill development of the Gilded Age was, so to speak, cut from an entirely different cloth. In 1880 South Carolina's textile industry consisted of fourteen firms employing two thousand operatives; by 1910 147 cor-

1. Ernest McPherson Lander, Jr., *The Textile Industry in Ante-Bellum South Carolina* (Baton Rouge: Louisiana State University Press, 1969).

porations were producing yarn and cloth with a work force of forty-five thousand. In those thirty years the state's spindleage increased by nearly forty-five times. Even more significant was the dramatic increase in factory size. The typical 1880 mill had fewer than six thousand spindles; by 1910 it had more than twenty-five thousand. The enlarged scale of operations reflected a fundamental shift away from small factories producing primarily yarn for local sale, to integrated cloth mills competing in national and international markets. Antebellum manufacturers had carried on their business, for the most part, little differently from the local grist miller; their postbellum successors were modern industrial capitalists.[2]

The dramatic emergence of the southern Piedmont, including its South Carolina portion, as one of the world's great cotton manufacturing regions has generally been attributed a historical importance overshadowing its limited direct impact on the South as a whole. "Burdened with emotional significance," writes C. Vann Woodward, "the mill has been made a symbol of the New South, its origins, and its promise of salvation."[3] That very identification of the textile industry with southern progress, however, has led to some difficulty in understanding the nature of industrial development in the region. The old Beardian dichotomy of "industrial North" and "agrarian South," coupled with the historians' preoccupation with plantation slavery, has made the working of factory smokestacks into the southern historical landscape a tricky matter. Thus some historians have suggested that the rise of mills in such a

2. *U.S. Census, 1880, Manufactures: Report on Cotton Manufactures of the United States*, 15; *U.S. Census, 1890*, XII, 188–89; *U.S. Census, 1900*, IX, 56–57; *U.S. Census, 1910*, X, 56, 58, 63; Gustavus G. Williamson, Jr., "Cotton Manufacturing in South Carolina, 1865–1892" (Ph.D. dissertation, Johns Hopkins University, 1954), 49–51, 113–15. The trend toward increased scale of operations dates from the Civil War; in 1860 the average mill had fewer than two thousand spindles. *U.S. Census, 1860, Manufactures*, xxi. Richard W. Griffin, in "Ante-Bellum Industrial Foundations of the (Alleged) New South," *Textile History Review*, V (1962), 33–43, argues that antebellum census figures for manufacturing are virtually worthless, and that the prewar southern textile industry was vastly larger than they indicate. His estimates seem wide of the mark; in the case of South Carolina, Lander's careful research suggests that the 1860 census figures are substantially correct. Lander, *Textile Industry*, 79.

3. C. Vann Woodward, *Origins of the New South, 1877–1913* (Baton Rouge: Louisiana State University Press, 1951), 131.

backward region could have come only through the intervention of Divine Providence; in one of the great mass conversions of all time, a whole region put away the Old Adam of sinful sloth and dedicated itself to the service of the god of Progress. Others, to the contrary, see not regeneration but restoration. A reactionary, antimodern planter class, it is argued, seized upon industrialization as a means of bolstering an authoritarian, even fascistic, social order modeled on "the social relations of the plantation." This "revolution from above" created a South superficially modern but informed by social values fundamentally different from the classical liberal beliefs supposedly held by most Americans.[4] As this line of reasoning makes clear, a proper understanding of southern industrial leadership and its motivation is essential to anyone seeking to comprehend the nature and evolution of the postbellum South.

In order to understand the men leading the cotton mill development in South Carolina, it is first necessary to determine who they were and how they related to their social milieu. Since cotton manufacturing firms in the state were almost universally organized in corporations, the individuals collectively most representative of the industry's entrepreneurial wellsprings were those who sat on the boards of directors of the various mills. Charged as they were with the general oversight of corporate affairs, mill directors were not only to have financial expertise, but were also to be representative of the various interests investing in the enterprise. One hundred and forty of these corporations were chartered between the beginnings of the industrial surge in the 1880s and the first comprehensive listing of mills in 1907; of these, one hundred, controlling 80 percent of the state's spindleage, were located in the Piedmont. It is on these mills and their founding officers, the names of whom are reported in the charter records, that the following analysis is based. Four hundred and seventy-six individuals served on the boards of the ninety-eight firms for which information is avail-

4. Broadus Mitchell, *The Rise of Cotton Mills in the South* (Baltimore: Johns Hopkins University Press, 1921), Chap. 2; Dwight B. Billings, Jr., *Planters and the Making of a "New South": Class, Politics, and Development in North Carolina, 1865–1900* (Chapel Hill: University of North Carolina Press, 1979).

able. Of these, three hundred and eighty-four, or over 80 percent, have been identified; they account for over 85 percent of the seats held.[5]

Who were these men? To begin with, the overwhelming majority were South Carolinians. Only twenty lived outside the state, and five of them made their homes just across the state line in North Carolina. Although, as we shall see, northern aid was essential to the development of the industry, only fourteen directors, holding twenty-four seats, dwelt north of the Potomac. The local cast of leadership was even more pronounced among the most important mill officials, the presidents. Only three of the seventy-two mill presidents identified lived outside the state at the time their corporations were organized, and those three lived in Charlotte and Gastonia, North Carolina, two manufacturing and commercial centers of the southern Piedmont, of which the South Carolina up-country was but a part. Obviously, in terms of personnel at least, the industrialization of South Carolina's Piedmont was largely the product of southern brains and hands.

The indigenous roots of the industrialists having been established, the more important question remains: from what *segment* of local society did the drive to industrialize arise? One important source of both capital and entrepreneurial leadership was the state's "metropolis," Charleston. In colonial times one of the major cities of British America, Charleston had lost much of its importance during the antebellum period as newer ports had arisen to tap the expanding cotton export trade. Despite its relative decline, however, it had remained a major center of cotton factorage in South Carolina, and its energetic merchant community had fought to

5. The names of mill directors are available chiefly through South Carolina Secretary of State Charter Records, Private Corporations, 1887–1907 (in South Carolina Department of Archives and History, Columbia). The basic listing of mills appears in August Kohn, *The Cotton Mills of South Carolina* (Columbia: South Carolina Department of Agriculture, Commerce, and Immigration, 1907), 214–17. The scope of the analysis is limited to the Piedmont because data in other portions of the state are often unavailable, and because much of the development in the Horse Creek Valley, one of the two major non-Piedmont industrial concentrations, predated 1880. The definition of "Piedmont" is that used above (Ch. I, n. 19). For more detail on the mode of analysis, see David Carlton, "'Builders of a New State': The Town Classes and Early Industrialization of South Carolina, 1880–1907," in Walter J. Fraser and Winfred B. Moore (eds.), *From the Old South to the New: Essays on the Transitional South* (Westport, Conn.: Greenwood Press, 1981), 58–64.

maintain its position by sponsoring the development of a system of railroads and waterways to tap interior commerce. Then came the war; the resulting disintegration of the slave economy, coupled with the reorientation of the rail network in the 1870s, left Charleston in a commercial backwater, producing an economic stagnation which a brief boom in phosphate mining was unable to counterbalance.[6] By 1880 the most perspicacious members of the Charleston business community were considering investment opportunities elsewhere, especially in up-country cotton manufacturing. Their interest had a history dating from the 1840s, when Charleston merchants and bankers supplied their fellow townsman William Gregg with nearly half the capital he needed for his project at Graniteville.[7] The success of Graniteville and other pioneer enterprises sharpened their appetite for textile profits, and the later years of the nineteenth century saw a considerable flow of Charleston capital to the Piedmont.

The leaders of the financial exodus were Ellison A. Smyth and Francis J. Pelzer. Smyth's background was impeccable; his father had been a famous Presbyterian minister and theologian, and his maternal grandfather had been James Adger, one of Charleston's preeminent merchants. Born in 1847, Smyth formed the ambition in childhood "to be a rich man"; after service in the Civil War, he pursued his goal in the Adger family business, in which he was soon a partner. In 1880, however, the firm's banking branch collapsed, and Smyth was handed the duty of closing the books. While the family fortune was not badly hurt, it was obvious that the road to riches no longer passed through Charleston. Smyth, familiar with the great financial success of the Graniteville, Lang-

6. Gregory Allen Greb, "Charleston, South Carolina Merchants, 1815–1860: Urban Leadership in the Ante-Bellum South" (Ph.D. dissertation, University of California at San Diego, 1978); Mitchell, *Rise of Cotton Mills*, 267; Francis B. Simkins and Robert H. Woody, *South Carolina During Reconstruction* (Chapel Hill: University of North Carolina Press, 1932), 279–87, 305–311.

7. Compiled from Graniteville Manufacturing Company Ledger, Stockholders' Accounts, 1846–1850 (in South Caroliniana Library, University of South Carolina, Columbia, hereafter cited as SCL). See also David Duncan Wallace, "A Hundred Years of William Gregg and Graniteville" (Typescript, 1946, in David Duncan Wallace Papers, South Carolina Historical Society, Charleston; microfiche copy in SCL), 28–29, 33–34.

ley, and Piedmont cotton mills, decided to remove to the up-country and try his hand with the new industry. His principal ally in the new venture was Pelzer, a member of Charleston's leading factorage firm and a phosphate manufacturer, who like Smyth felt increasingly cramped by Charleston's contracting commercial boundaries. Together they organized the Pelzer Manufacturing Company, chiefly with Pelzer, Smyth, and Adger capital, and built at a site on the Saluda River in Anderson County; while Pelzer remained in Charleston, Smyth moved to the new village of Pelzer to serve as president of the company. The Pelzer Company was a rousing success; by 1907 it was the second largest mill corporation in the state, controlling 130,000 spindles. Smyth, in control of several companies besides Pelzer, ranked as one of the great mill magnates of the South.[8]

In the years following the establishment of Pelzer numerous Charlestonians added up-country mill stocks to their portfolios. At least seventeen held directorates in Piedmont area mills, for a total of twenty-two seats. However, thirteen of those seats were clustered on the boards of three firms: Pelzer, Enoree in Spartanburg County, and Courtenay in Oconee County. All were large-scale, heavily capitalized water power developments almost completely under Charleston control. The remaining nine seats were scattered among nine different corporations. The few surviving lists of mill stockholders suggest that Charleston holdings were of little significance outside Pelzer, Enoree, and Courtenay; the Charlestonian on the board of the Pacolet Manufacturing Company in 1895 represented only a dozen investors and less than 10 percent of equity.[9] The influence of Smyth, Pelzer, and the other

8. W. P. Jacobs II, *The Pioneer* (Clinton, S.C.: Jacobs Press, 1934), 21, 30, 88–89, 108; Kohn, *Cotton Mills*, 94.

9. Pacolet Manufacturing Company, Stock List, December 31, 1895 (MS in Frank E. Taylor Papers, SCL); Allen Heath Stokes, Jr., "John H. Montgomery: A Pioneer Southern Industrialist" (M.A. thesis, University of South Carolina, 1967), 138–43, reprinting Spartan Mills Stock List, September 30, 1890; Lawrence B. Graves, Jr., "The Beginning of the Cotton Textile Industry in Newberry County" (M.A. thesis, University of South Carolina, 1947), 78–79, reprinting Newberry Cotton Mill Stockholders' List, May 7, 1883. Cf. Mitchell, *Rise of Cotton Mills*, 267: "Charleston money was a resource to South Carolina local communities pretty generally."

Charlestonians on the development of cotton manufacturing in the state was significant; the major sources of capital and talent, however, lay elsewhere.

Despite aid from outside the region, either from other southern cities or from the North, the entrepreneurial energy building the cotton mills was chiefly generated in the neighborhoods in which they were built. As Table 2 demonstrates, a large majority of Piedmont mill directors lived in the county in which their mill was located; three fifths of them used the same post office as the mill. At first glance this suggests the sort of "grass roots" movement described by Broadus Mitchell, or the sort of rural "industrial plantation" posited by Dwight Billings. However, the traditional imagery of "cotton mills in cotton fields" is not borne out by the actual geographical pattern of industrial development. Mills were not scattered over the countryside but tended to cluster about towns. Of the one hundred firms under consideration, seventy-six were located either in or adjacent to incorporated towns with 1910 populations of at least one thousand; nine others were located either in or near smaller towns whose existence had antedated that of the mill. Only fifteen firms built away from towns, usually in order to take advantage of a remote water power site. Over three quarters of spindleage and mill employment were accounted for by "town" mills, over one quarter by those in and about the three leading mill centers, Anderson, Greenville, and Spartanburg.[10]

There were sound economic reasons for locating mills in towns, having to do chiefly with access to transportation and communications facilities. The increasing efficiency of steam power relative to water power, along with the beginnings of hydroelectric generation and long-range electric power transmission in the 1890s, freed factories from the need to locate along rivers and cope with floods and droughts, although steam power did require reliable rail shipments of coal.[11] In addition, as industrialization proceeded,

10. Compiled from Kohn, *Cotton Mills*, 86–98.

11. Williamson, "Cotton Manufacturing," 148–49; Douglas Summers Brown, *A City Without Cobwebs: A History of Rock Hill, South Carolina* (Columbia: University of South Carolina Press, 1953), 236–44. The Columbia Mills factory in Columbia was the first textile plant to be operated by electric motors; see Sidney B. Paine, "The Story of the First Electrically Operated Textile Mill" (Schenectady, N.Y.: General Electric Company, 1930).

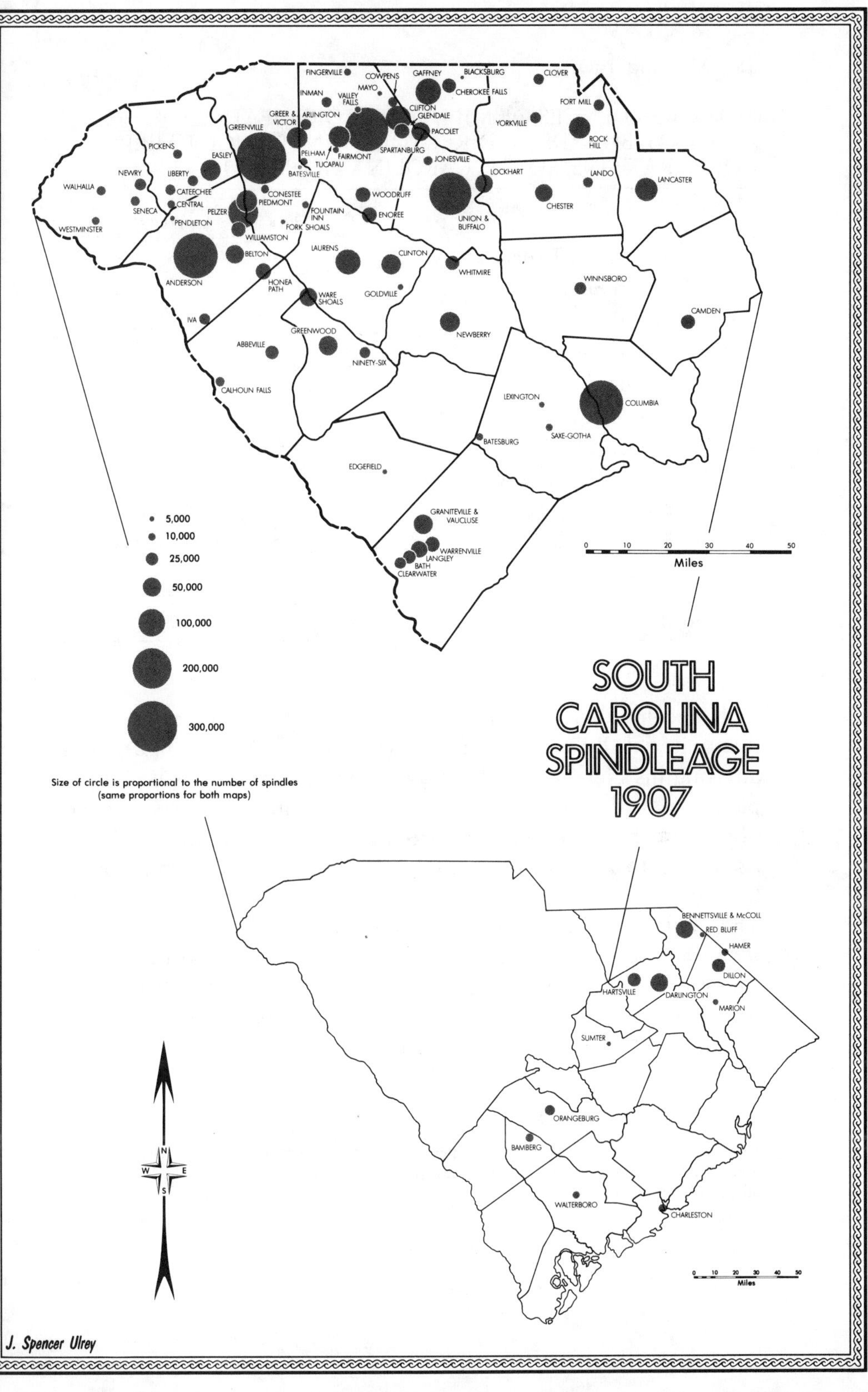

SOUTH CAROLINA SPINDLEAGE 1907
FINGERVILLE
COWPENS
GAFFNEY
BLACKSBURG
CLOVER
MAYO
CHEROKEE FALLS
INMAN
VALLEY FALLS
CLIFTON
FORT MILL
GREER & VICTOR
ARLINGTON
GLENDALE
YORKVILLE
GREENVILLE
PACOLET
ROCK HILL
PICKENS
SPARTANBURG
EASLEY
PELHAM
FAIRMONT
JONESVILLE
TUCAPAU
NEWRY
LIBERTY
BATESVILLE
LOCKHART
LANDO
LANCASTER
WALHALLA
CATEECHEE
CONESTEE
WOODRUFF
SENECA
CENTRAL
PIEDMONT
PELZER
FOUNTAIN INN
CHESTER
ENOREE
PENDLETON
FORK SHOALS
UNION & BUFFALO
WESTMINSTER
WILLIAMSTON
LAURENS
CLINTON
BELTON
WHITMIRE
HONEA PATH
WINNSBORO
ANDERSON
GOLDVILLE
WARE SHOALS
CAMDEN
IVA
NEWBERRY
GREENWOOD
ABBEVILLE
NINETY-SIX
CALHOUN FALLS
LEXINGTON
COLUMBIA
SAXE-GOTHA
BATESBURG
EDGEFIELD
GRANITEVILLE & VAUCLUSE
WARRENVILLE
LANGLEY
BATH
CLEARWATER
0 10 20 30 40 50
Miles
5,000
10,000
25,000
50,000
100,000
200,000
300,000
Size of circle is proportional to the number of spindles
(same proportions for both maps)
BENNETTSVILLE & McCOLL
RED BLUFF
HAMER
DILLON
HARTSVILLE
DARLINGTON
MARION
SUMTER
ORANGEBURG
BAMBERG
WALTERBORO
CHARLESTON
0 10 20 30 40 50
Miles
N
W
E
S
J. Spencer Ulrey

Table 2. RESIDENCES OF MILL DIRECTORS (SEATS ON ORIGINAL BOARDS OF DIRECTORS, NINETY-EIGHT MILL CORPORATIONS, SOUTH CAROLINA PIEDMONT, 1880–1907)

	No. Seats		*Percent*	
Persons outside Piedmont	68		11.8	
Northeast		24		4.2
Charleston		22		3.8
Charlotte		8		1.4
Columbia		9		1.6
Other		5		0.9
Piedmont residents	508		88.2	
Same locality as mill		356		61.8
Same county as mill		96		16.7
Adjacent county		43		7.5
Other		13		2.3
Total	576		100.0	

mills became increasingly dependent on distant sources for their raw material. By 1900 John H. Montgomery of Spartanburg was advising his New York selling agent that existing mills had completely soaked up the local cotton production, forcing his firms to obtain much of their supplies from areas further south. By 1907, according to August Kohn, mill consumption of cotton in seven leading textile counties exceeded local production by 138 percent. The quality of cotton also created a constraint on local supplies; manufacturers frequently found the neighborhood product unsuitable due to insufficient length or uniformity of staple, and so ended up buying from the richer areas of the Black Belt or the Delta.[12] The same rail lines used to ship materials in could, of

12. Williamson, "Cotton Manufacturing," 152–53; John H. Montgomery to Seth M. Milliken, January 17, 1900, in John H. Montgomery Letterbook (on microfilm), SCL; Kohn, *Cotton Mills*, 178; David R. Coker, "Papers Read Before the Manufacturers' Association of South Carolina at Their Annual Meetings, June, 1908 and 1911" (Hartsville, S.C.: Hartsville Publishing Company, n.d.).

course, be used to ship products out. Furthermore, the use of railroad routes as rights of way for telegraph lines helped assure that transportation points would also become centers of communication with the far-flung marketing networks for cotton and textiles.[13] It was no accident that one third of the firms organized during the period from 1880 to 1907 located along what is now the main line of the Southern Railway, with its connections to the Alabama and Mississippi cotton regions, the Birmingham coal fields, and the northeastern marketing centers.

The erection of mills in and near towns was dictated by more than the economics of location, however. Table 3 classifies by principal occupation the cotton mill directors reported in Table 2 to have been residing in the Piedmont. As it indicates, a solid majority of mill directors were drawn from commerce; furthermore, nearly one in five were professional men, chiefly lawyers. The predominantly commercial cast of industrial leadership is even more striking when mill presidents are considered. Table 4 shows that over two thirds of the identified mill presidents residing in the region came to manufacturing from commerce, especially from merchandising.

Men whose principal occupations were "farming" or "planting," on the other hand, played distinctly minor roles in mill development. In only a handful of firms was the agrarian role significant, and only two, the Norris Manufacturing Company in Pickens County and the Goldville Manufacturing Company in Laurens County, could be said to be dominated by "planter" interests. To be sure, in the heavily rural up-country the lines between "planters" and "merchants" or "lawyers" were not easy to draw. Commercial and professional men of means usually either acquired or inherited extensive landholdings, and agriculturists invested in merchandising and manufacturing. Whether landholders or not, however, it is apparent that most mill directors were extensively involved in commerce or in commercially oriented profes-

13. Alfred D. Chandler, Jr., *The Visible Hand: The Managerial Revolution in American Business* (Cambridge: Harvard University Press, 1977), 89, 188, 195; Harold D. Woodman, *King Cotton and His Retainers: Financing and Marketing the Cotton Crop of the South, 1800–1925* (Lexington: University of Kentucky Press, 1968), 273.

Table 3. MILL DIRECTORS RESIDING IN THE SOUTH CAROLINA PIEDMONT, 1880–1907, BY OCCUPATION

	No. Seats		Percent		No. Indivs.		Percent	
Commerce	315		62.2		204		60.0	
Merchants		250		49.2		158		46.5
Bankers		49		9.6		30		8.8
Other commercial		8		1.6		8		2.3
White collar		8		1.6		8		2.3
Manufacturing	38		7.5		24		7.1	
Cotton		29		5.7		17		5.0
Other		9		1.8		7		2.1
Professionals	91		17.9		63		18.5	
Lawyers		61		12.0		39		11.5
Other		30		5.9		24		7.1
Agriculture	59		11.6		44		12.9	
Other	5		1.0		5		1.5	
Total	508		100.0		340		100.0	

sions such as the law. Insofar as "planters" or "farmers" were involved, their interests ranged far beyond the agrarian sphere.

The geographical orientation of mills toward the towns, and the predominantly local and commercial cast of their officers, strongly suggests an intimate relationship between postbellum industrialization in South Carolina and that larger phenomenon, the rise of the interior towns and their "town people." The importance of the emerging town elites to manufacturing development can be further illustrated by briefly considering the mill directorate in one of the more important cotton textile centers, Anderson. Six major corporations were organized between 1899 and 1904 to build cotton factories in or about Anderson; the forty-three seats on their boards were held by twenty-nine individuals, all of whom have been identified. Twenty-one of the directors lived in or near Ander-

Table 4. MILL PRESIDENTS RESIDING IN THE SOUTH CAROLINA PIEDMONT, 1880–1907, BY OCCUPATION

	No Seats		*Percent*		*No. Indivs.*	*Percent*	
Commerce	58		68.2		49	68.1	
Merchants		50		58.8	42		58.3
Bankers		5		5.9	4		5.6
Other		3		3.5	3		4.2
Manufacturers	10		11.8		7	9.7	
Cotton		5		5.9	4		5.6
Other		5		5.9	3		4.2
Lawyers	6		7.1		6	8.3	
Other professional	1		1.2		1	1.4	
Agricultural	9		10.6		8	11.1	
Other	1		1.2		1	1.4	
Total	85		100.0		72	100.0	

son; of these, eleven were merchants, three bankers, three lawyers, one a physician and druggist, one a cottonseed products manufacturer, and one a career textile executive. Only two were farmers. If only the inner circle of men involved in the direction of more than one firm is considered, commercial and town dominance is even more pronounced; ten men, including seven merchants, two bankers, and the textile executive, held over half the available seats. Similar knots of enterprising men appeared in the other budding manufacturing centers of the Piedmont; their success in industrializing varied considerably according to local conditions, but they were all basically alike both in their commercial interests and in their commitment to economic development.

The paths taken by these men to manufacturing can best be illustrated with several individual examples. One of the more important early entrepreneurs was Leroy Springs of Lancaster, scion of a wealthy old planting family with extensive commercial, railroad, and manufacturing interests. After attending the University of North Carolina for two years, he began business life in 1881 as a drummer for his brothers' Charlotte wholesale grocery firm. In 1882 he set up an agency in Lancaster, and in 1886 became a partner in Heath, Springs and Company. In the meantime he had founded Leroy Springs and Company, which he built into one of the largest cotton exporters in the southeast; in the process he became knowledgeable about cotton and well-connected among cotton manufacturers. By the middle 1890s he had amassed a fortune, but much of it was invested in mortgages and uncollectable debts. Casting about for ways to break his dependence on agriculture, he decided to build a cotton factory, and laid the cornerstone of what became the Springs Mills empire in 1895.[14]

Not far from Lancaster was the booming little town of Rock Hill, the home of a small group of industrialists centered on W. L. and W. J. Roddey. William L. Roddey was the son of John Roddey, a local planter and surveyor who had laid out the town of Rock Hill in 1852, purchased one of the original lots, and owned the major store there before the war. William had been a clerk in Chester before going off to fight; in 1866 he moved to Rock Hill, bought up much of the town, and opened a branch of the powerful Chester firm of Wylie and Agurs, taking over full ownership of the branch in 1873. By 1890 W. L. Roddey and Company was, according to a contemporary promotional account, doing "a larger wholesale and retail business than any other firm outside Charleston," as well as managing a sizable cotton trade. In wealth the firm ranked with Heath, Springs and Company as the strongest in the up-country, its worth being estimated at between a quarter and a half million dollars. W. L. Roddey and his son, W. J. Roddey, were at that time serving as, respectively, president and vice-president of the local National Bank. Furthermore, one or both were on the boards of directors of virtually every industrial enterprise in the

14. Elliott White Springs, *Clothes Make the Man* (n.p., 1948), 12–14; J. C. Hemphill (ed.), *Men of Mark in South Carolina* (4 vols.; Washington: Men of Mark Publishing Company, 1908), I, 378–83; Katherine Wooten Springs, *The Squires of Springfield* (Charlotte, N.C.: William Loftin, 1965). John Springs, Leroy's grandfather, was an original subscriber to the stock of the Graniteville Manufacturing Company. *Ibid.*, 85–86; Graniteville Stockholders' Accounts, SCL.

city, including three cotton mills, and were ranked among the principal "upbuilders" of the town.[15]

In the considerably less important Laurens County town of Clinton lived Mercer Silas ("Mess") Bailey. Bailey, who had begun his career before the war as a "copperas-breeched young clerk" in a general store, went into business on his own after Appomattox with four bales of cotton for capital. Within twenty years he became the town's leading merchant; then he retired, handing his business over to his sons. Despite his retirement, though, he was constantly under pressure to lend his support to new enterprises. Some came from his son Will, who was cashier of the bank and became secretary-treasurer of the cotton mill; both bank and mill were headed by the elder Bailey but organized and managed by the younger. "Mess" was also exhorted to help develop Clinton by his minister and friend (and his son's father-in-law) W. P. Jacobs, the town's leading civic booster. Above all, his leadership was demanded by members of Clinton's business and professional community, whose desires were later described by one of Jacobs' sons: "They were poor. They had a job to do. Their country must be rebuilt. . . . They were about to build a city."[16]

While towns larger than Clinton were less dominated by individuals, they could frequently boast more powerful firms. A case in point was the Spartanburg establishment of Walker, Fleming and Company. The firm began in 1866 as a partnership between John B. Cleveland, an old, wealthy merchant, and Joseph Walker, one of his former clerks. By 1869 Walker was on his own, and, while possessed of little capital, had acquired a reputation as an energetic businessman and "a bold trader in cotton." "Be cautious," potential creditors were warned, "just the kind of man to

15. Brown, *City Without Cobwebs*, 74–79, 135; *Cyclopedia of Eminent and Representative Men of the Carolinas of the Nineteenth Century* (2 vols.; Madison, Wis.: Brant and Fuller, 1892), I, 381–82; R. G. Dun and Company Collection, Baker Library, Harvard University Graduate School of Business Administration, South Carolina, XIV, 138, 174; R. G. Dun and Company, *The Mercantile Agency Reference Book*, 1889; Charleston *News and Courier*, June 7, 1890.

16. R. G. Dun Collection, South Carolina, XI, 102F; J. C. Garlington, *Men of the Time* (Spartanburg, S.C.: Garlington Publishing Company, 1902), 14; Thornwell Jacobs, "My People" (Clinton, S.C.: n.p., 1954), 6, 10; Thornwell Jacobs, *Step Down, Dr. Jacobs: The Autobiography of an Autocrat* (Atlanta: The Westminster Publishers, 1945), 63.

make or break." Those who risked their money on Walker had no occasion for complaint, however; the firm grew stronger, and in 1872 Walker took in as a partner C. E. Fleming, a local physician and druggist just returned from a few months' sojourn in the West. At about the same time a young farmer and sometime merchant in the rural community of Hobbysville, John H. Montgomery, anticipating the burgeoning demand for fertilizers, came to town and set up shop as the southern agent of a Baltimore manufacturer. In 1876 he joined forces with Walker and Fleming, the new firm being styled Walker, Fleming and Company. Later, after Montgomery departed to pursue his career as an industrialist, the remaining partners took in another local merchant, J. H. Sloan. By 1890 Walker, Fleming and Sloan was handling annually over fifty thousand bales of cotton through twenty-three agents in South Carolina and others in Alabama and Mississippi; in addition, the firm dealt in securities, and was the largest fertilizer dealer in the state outside of Charleston.[17]

As striking as the mercantile success of Walker, Fleming was the degree to which the firm and its members were involved in cotton manufacturing, and indeed in the whole commercial life of Spartanburg. Joseph Walker was one of the original directors of the Clifton Manufacturing Company, Spartanburg County's first major postwar industrial enterprise; its success undoubtedly attracted the interest of the other partners. In early 1881 Walker, Fleming bought the Trough Shoals property on the Pacolet River downstream from Clifton. Consisting of three waterfalls contained in a mile-long natural trough, the shoals were capable, according to estimates, of driving one hundred thousand spindles. The next year saw the organization of the Pacolet Manufacturing Company with an initial capital stock of $103,000, much of it supplied by the parent firm. Montgomery began his career as a mill magnate with Pacolet, later becoming president of Spartan Mills. Fleming ultimately became president of the Whitney Mill, and J. H. Sloan organized the Beaumont Mill, both in or near Spartanburg. The

17. R. G. Dun Collection, South Carolina, XIII, 9, 14D, 16, 20, 28B6, 28D, 28G, 38, 91; Stokes, "Montgomery," 15–20; *Cyclopedia*, I, 344–45, 462–65, 482–83; Charleston *News and Courier*, July 28, 1890.

Walker, Fleming partners served on each others' boards of directors as well. Only Walker never became a mill president, being content to head one of the town's two banks, dabble in railroads, and help direct the newspaper.[18] It was a rare enterprise in Spartanburg that lacked Walker, Fleming money and influence.

There were, of course, sound technical reasons for the ascendancy of these and other rising merchants in the cotton mill movement. The few experienced mill men from antebellum times, such as H. P. Hammett and D. E. Converse, were enormously influential as examples and advisors to their fellows, but neither they nor the developing corps of career mill managers were sufficiently numerous to fill more than a small fraction either of directorates or presidencies. Merchants, on the other hand, were a proliferating species in the postbellum up-country, and furthermore owed their business success to many of the same qualities useful in cotton manufacturing. The principal duties of the directors and, especially, the presidents were mercantile in nature; for that reason nearly 60 percent of the presidents identified in Table 4 also performed the duties of the chief financial officer, the treasurer. Converse himself assured the promoters of Pacolet that they need not hold back because they lacked technical expertise; "any good business man that could control men and money," he reportedly said, "could manage a cotton mill." Hammett, endorsing a mill project headed by R. L. McCaughrin, a Newberry banker, declared that "your experience and reputation as a financier in this country, and your knowledge of and familiarity with the commercial part of the operations, is a guarantee to me that those departments will be well and wisely managed." As for technical expertise, "your judgement of the fitness of men will always enable you to keep a good manufacturer in the mill." The identification of successful businessmen with an enterprise helped assure local investors of its safety. The directorate of the Anderson Cotton Mill was thus touted as consisting of "men of both financial and executive ability . . . careful, prudent, and yet men of progress." Similarly, in New-

18. Spartanburg *Carolina Spartan*, March 23, 30, April 6, 1881; April 19, 1882; May 21, 1884; Charleston *News and Courier*, July 28, 1890; Garlington, *Men of the Time*, 429–30.

berry the local editor characterized the directors of the local mill as "without exception, men who, from a financial point of view, have avouched their merit by the best of all tests, the successful management of their own affairs. . . . By experience they know the importance of labor and the value of a dollar."[19] Success as a merchant, to be sure, was a less than perfect preparation for the more complicated duties of a manufacturer, as some painfully discovered.[20] Even so, commercial ability provided a solid foundation for engagement in manufacturing.

The confidence of local people was essential not only in and of itself, but also as a means of attracting northern investment. It was commonly understood by mill promoters that their chronically poor state could not successfully industrialize without considerable outside aid; it was likewise well known that northerners, their memories of the Civil War still fresh, were fearful that an absentee-owned and identifiably "Yankee" enterprise might confront local hostility. "Capitalists want the people at home largely identified with any enterprise they put their money into," Hammett advised two Laurens merchants in 1887; "they want this to protect it against local prejudices, adverse legislation, and that it shall have the moral support of the people living around it." Montgomery attempted to dissuade a merchant friend in Union from undertaking a mill project for which less than half the capital had been locally subscribed, warning him that he could not expect to make up the difference in New York or New England. Prudence led northern capitalists to delay any financial involvement in a new enterprise until its local organization and finances were on a firm basis; for that reason, Table 2, consisting as it does of data on the original directors of mill corporations, understates the extent of northern involvement in the southern industry. The original board of the Gluck Mills of Anderson consisted entirely of Andersonians, but within three months four outsiders, including two Bostonians,

19. Spartanburg *Carolina Spartan*, May 17, 1883; H. P. Hammett to R. L. McCaughrin, February 17, 1886, in H. P. Hammett Letterbooks, SCL; Anderson *Intelligencer*, June 7, 1888; Newberry *Herald and News*, May 10, 1883.

20. See, for example, John H. Montgomery to John A. Fant, November 15, 1899, in Montgomery letterbook, SCL, citing a merchant friend of Montgomery who gave up his store to acquire a small, unprofitable cotton mill, and who was now "terribly embarrassed."

were named directors as representatives of nonlocal investors. At the time of its organization in 1882 the Pacolet Manufacturing Company's directors were all South Carolinians; the following year, though, a Baltimorean and a Bostonian were placed on the board. By 1895 one third of all Pacolet stock was held north of the Potomac. A survey of eighty-five firms made in 1916 indicated that 28 percent of South Carolina mill stock was northern owned, with a median holding per firm of 20 percent.[21]

Northern investors were drawn into manufacturing in South Carolina not simply by evidence of local support but also by personal and business contacts with prospective local industrialists. While twelve of the fourteen northeastern mill directors from Table 2 were affiliated with the textile industry, only one was primarily a manufacturer, the rest being involved chiefly with commission sales, machinery, or engineering. As a result, they were concerned comparatively little with the possible effects of southern competition with northern factories. On the other hand, as suppliers of capital goods and services to the textile industry, they were anxious to expand their southern trade. Two groups of northern investors were particularly important to South Carolina. Woodward, Baldwin and Company of Baltimore and New York, a leading commission house, first entered the state as a selling agent for the Piedmont Manufacturing Company in the 1870s; the firm later became involved with the Pelzer Company, thanks in part to a marriage tie betweeen Ellison Smyth and the Baldwins. By the early twentieth century twenty-one South Carolina mills were Woodward, Baldwin clients; sixteen of them were located in counties lying along the Saluda River, the area where Piedmont and Pelzer influence was greatest. The other major northern group was headed by Seth M. Milliken of the New York selling house of Deering, Milliken and Company, and by Amos Lockwood and Stephen Greene, two New England mill engineers. Milliken's entry

21. *Ibid.*; South Carolina Secretary of State, Charter Books, Private Corporations, Charter No. 2785 (in South Carolina Department of Archives and History, Columbia); Anderson *Intelligencer*, May 5, 1887; January 14, March 11, 1903; Spartanburg *Carolina Spartan*, May 2, 1883; Mary Baldwin Baer and John Wilbur Baer, *A History of Woodward, Baldwin and Company* (Annapolis, Md.: private, 1977), 21; Pacolet Stock List (MS in Frank E. Taylor Papers, SCL); Greenville *Daily News*, August 18, 1916.

into South Carolina came through John H. Montgomery, who had been referred to the merchant by his fertilizer supplier; at about the same time, Montgomery's partner C. E. Fleming was meeting Lockwood and Greene. The alliance between the Milliken-Lockwood-Greene interests and the Montgomery-Walker, Fleming group began with the Pacolet mill and continued with operations at Spartanburg and elsewhere; in one case, that of the Spartan Mills, the northern group physically moved a Massachusetts factory to the up-country town. By 1905 Deering, Milliken sold cloth for thirteen mills, most of which had some connection with Spartanburg interests.[22]

The importance of northern connections transcended mere direct investment. The commission merchants in particular played crucial roles in organizing the industry. They brought prospective manufacturers together with engineers and machinery men; their knowledge of the ever-changing cloth market made them indispensable sources of advice on such major production decisions as determining the style of cloth to be made and the quantity in which to make it. The financial connections of the more important houses enabled them to place stock and bond issues in the money markets for their clients and, especially, supply short-term operating credit, which in the capital-starved South was chronically scarce.[23] To be sure, this latter role gave the selling houses enormous power over the southern industry, power sometimes wielded roughly. While Woodward, Baldwin generally made a policy of staying aloof from the management of its clients, Seth Milliken took advantage of his position to obtain control of a number of mills. The most spectacular takeover came in 1905 and 1906, when the Milliken interests, aided by their Spartanburg allies, ousted an opponent from the presidencies of the Darlington and Laurens mills following a widely publicized proxy and court battle; the embittered victim later anathematized the entire Milliken

22. Baer and Baer, *Woodward, Baldwin*, 20–28, 71; Stokes, "Montgomery," *passim*; Columbia *State*, May 16, 1905. At least seven other commission houses held South Carolina accounts in 1905.

23. Baer and Baer, *Woodward, Baldwin*; Williamson, "Cotton Manufacturing," 66–67, 220–22; Mitchell, *Rise of Cotton Mills*, 241–55.

clan as "the coldest-blooded lot that ever lived."[24] Milliken's behavior lends substance to the old charge that the selling houses were instruments of "colonial oppression" of the South by the North. Even so, it is difficult to see how the southern textile industry could have developed without them. Summerfield Baldwin of Woodward, Baldwin, admittedly an interested party, claimed that without the aid of commission merchants southern industrial development would have been retarded by twenty years.[25] Certainly, their alliance with the local town merchants provided the rising commercial elite of South Carolina with much of the backing it needed to commence industrialization.

The leading role of the town merchants in industrialization, then, reflected their entrepreneurial expertise, their preeminence in local affairs, and their function as conduits for northern financial and technical aid. It also reflected the postwar concentration of local wealth in their hands. While all these conditions helped make their industrial leadership possible, one crucial factor remains to be explored, namely that of motive. Although the rationale for entering any profitable business seems straightforward enough, there are nonetheless some complexities here worth examining. Town merchants hoped that the mills would make them rich, not only individually but corporately. It was, indeed, that corporate, communitarian aspect of cotton manufacturing which provided it with the resonant social meaning it held for South Carolinians and southerners generally. To understand the response to industrialization in South Carolina, we must learn what was expected of it.

What were the intentions of the mill builders? The most obvious answer is, "the pursuit of profit," and no one examining the public

24. Baer and Baer, *Woodward, Baldwin*, 21, 24; the Milliken-Lucas conflict is covered in Columbia *State*, May 15, 16, 19, 20, 22; June 7, 8, 9, 25; July 27, 28; October 8, 12, 31; November 2, 1905; April 8, 11, 13, 1906. The quote is from W. E. Lucas to William Watts Ball, September 16, 1907, in William Watts Ball Papers, Duke University, Durham, N.C. For other complaints against Milliken see E. R. Lucas to Ball, April 26, July 20, December 1, 1906, in Ball Papers, Duke.

25. Woodward, *Origins*, 308; Baer and Baer, *Woodward, Baldwin*, 21.

pronouncements of the period can avoid the conclusion that men built mills basically to make money. H. P. Hammett of the Piedmont mill could almost have been answering those who have claimed humanitarian motives for the pioneer industrialists when he stated that "the main object in building a mill by those who put their money into it, is the prospective profits upon the investments; there may be the laudable desire to give employment to the people and benefit the community—the latter is always incidental and secondary, if at all." Even among those members of the press giving the "philanthropic" argument the most play, there was a basic realization that "nobody is going to invest money, as he pays taxes, for the public benefit." The profitability of cotton manufacturing was well known and well publicized, both by newspapers and by promotional pamphlets such as J. K. Blackman's *The Cotton Mills of South Carolina*, which reported returns of 18 to 40 percent on capital stock among the state's mills.[26]

These publicized figures explain much of the enthusiasm of the so-called "cotton mill campaign" of the early 1880s, an enthusiasm which worried cooler heads. Too often the figures were blown far out of proportion by tricky accounting or by a misunderstanding of the nature of profits. Frequently all earnings were paid out in dividends, in disregard of the need to build a surplus or accumulate commercial capital; little attention was paid to depreciation, a cost which Hammett estimated was equivalent to 5 percent of the capital stock annually. Profit figures could be misleading even where prudent accounting procedures were followed, for the high reported earnings of many an older enterprise reflected long-term accumulation of financial strength; Graniteville's 20 percent net earnings would have shrunk by half were internally generated funds included in its capital stock, and other well-run mills would have appeared far less profitable had their equity been valued at the market price rather than at par. Newspaper reports, of course, glossed over the differing prospects of established firms with their

26. H. P. Hammett, "Southern Cotton Mills," address to South Carolina Agricultural and Mechanical Society and South Carolina Grange, reprinted in Charleston *News and Courier*, July 29, 1881; *ibid.*, March 22, 1880; [J. K. Blackman], *The Cotton Mills of South Carolina* (Charleston, S.C.: News and Courier Job Presses, 1880), 20.

retained earnings and brand new enterprises possessed only of their equity; thus, charged an "Observer," "the general public only reads the fact stated . . . and concludes that it is only necessary to get up a company and erect a mill and they, too, will earn twenty per cent." Despite their frequent unreliability, though, the fat numbers batted about in the press had their effect, providing a significant boost to the brief cotton mill boom of the early 1880s.[27]

The very credulity displayed by South Carolinians regarding the profitability of cotton manufacturing, however, suggests reasons other than the desire for high dividends for the various mill booms of the late nineteenth century. Indeed, an examination of the press and other literature of the period indicates that there is much substance in Broadus Mitchell's argument that "cotton manufactories were frequently motivated by the desire to help a community to its feet." The chief difficulty with the "community enterprise" argument is less its factual basis than its conceptual confusion. Especially troublesome is the meaning of the term "local community" as applied to the towns of the postbellum South.[28] As we have seen, the dominant elements in the rising inland towns of South Carolina were the business and professional classes. Their interest in the welfare of the town was, in a sense, proprietary; each town was seen as a sort of corporate enterprise belonging to the business and professional community, and its government was conducted with a view to "high returns" for the town's "stockholders." The welfare of the "community" was defined as that of the middle class, and "community" cotton mills were promoted accordingly. Certainly there was little desire in the "communities" to work in a cotton mill; as one cynic observed of his fellow townsmen, "all the advo-

27. Greenville *Daily News*, July 29, 1881; "Observer" in Charleston *News and Courier*, May 16, 1883; Williamson, "Cotton Manufacturing," 93–103.

28. Mitchell, *Rise of Cotton Mills*, 127. The same confusion appears in works other than Mitchell's. William J. Cooper, in *The Conservative Regime: South Carolina, 1877–1890* (Baltimore: Johns Hopkins University Press, 1968), argues that the theme of "class conflict in which farmers battled against a clique of planters, merchants, and industrialists" developed by C. Vann Woodward does not apply to South Carolina in this period. A key feature of Cooper's argument is his assertion that the "clique"-dominated General Assembly in fact "courted industry less ardently than did local communities," which he assumes to have been agrarian bailiwicks (pp. 17–18). The implied identification of "local communities" with farmers is, however, misleading; however small, the typical "local community" was dominated by "merchants and industrialists," not farmers.

cates of factories want to be stockholders, while they seem to think that somebody else may fill the place of operative."[29]

On the crassest level, there were profits to be made from the increased property values attendant on the establishment of a mill. The importance of land speculation as a motive for "boosterism" has been well understood by historians of the Midwest, and southern townsmen had much in common with the frontier promoters of Illinois and Kansas. One manufacturer recalled that "many mills were built with the primary object in view of adding to the population and property values of a town or section"; profitability, even solvency, "were, apparently, secondary considerations." Manufacturers sought support from farmers for tax exemptions for their mills by pointing to the appreciation in value of farm lands in the vicinity of an industrial development; the construction of Pacolet, for example, allegedly raised local land prices from ten to thirty dollars an acre. The Lancaster Cotton Mill increased its capitalization from $150,000 to $1,000,000 in 1900 because, according to Leroy Springs' son, "the pay roll was not large enough to bring on the real estate boom the stockholders had anticipated."[30]

A more important, albeit related, consideration, was the prospect of increased population and trade from the operatives. The *Carolina Spartan* urged the local citizenry to take stock in a proposed suburban mill; with $200,000 capital "a factory can be built that will require two hundred hands or more, and that will add one thousand to our population." The promoters being merchants, they planned no company store; thus, "all the trade . . . will come to this place." Another up-country paper hailed the expansion of the mills at Pacolet, citing "an increase of population and an increase of trade" as the principal "indirect benefits accruing to the town." When the Newberry mill commenced operation, predicted a local editor, "there will be a considerable influx of population, and we hope that trade and business of all kinds

29. Abbeville *Press and Banner*, September 26, 1883.

30. Leslie E. Decker, "The Great Speculation: An Interpretation of Mid-Continent Pioneering," in David M. Ellis (ed.), *The Frontier in American Development* (Ithaca, N.Y.: Cornell University Press, 1969), 357–80; W. C. Hamrick, *Life Values in the New South* (Gaffney, S.C.: private, 1931), 122; Spartanburg *Carolina Spartan*, April 11, 1883, May 21, 1884; Springs, *Clothes Make the Man*, 19.

will be livelier, and that there will be a new era of prosperity for Newberry."[31]

The cotton mill enthusiasts have been accused of being monomaniacal, stunting the development of the region by shifting their allegiance from "King Cotton" to "King Cotton Mill"; however, a major reason for launching into cotton manufacturing was the belief that it would stimulate a variety of other industries. A successful cotton mill in Spartanburg would attract "a foundry and machine shop, a shoe factory, and other similar enterprises," predicted the *Spartan*. Greenville prided itself not only on its cotton mills but also on its diversity of other factories, manufacturing machinery, paper, furniture, mattresses, whiskey, and wine, not to mention the more conventional fertilizer factories and cotton, lumber, and grain based enterprises. Rock Hill's pride and joy was less its cotton mills than its buggy factory. The *Spartan* promoted small industries, arguing that "it is not best for a community to carry all its eggs in one basket."[32]

To be sure, local industrial boosters were to be disappointed in their hopes for diversified economies, as local money, attracted by profits, poured into cotton manufacturing. Rather than launching into diversified economic growth, the towns developed single-industry economies heavily dependent upon the North for machinery, finance, textile finishing, and other auxiliary services. Unfortunately for the southern economy, it had to coexist, within national boundaries, with a well-developed industrial region which could provide strong competition to any southern "infant industry" requiring a skilled labor force and experienced entrepreneurs. For example, whereas New England, thanks in part to a British embargo on the export of textile machinery, had to create its own industry in order properly to equip its mills, southern mills found it easier to buy their machinery from an established, experienced industry whose existing investments were concentrated outside the region. Since the New England textile machinery industry created

31. Spartanburg *Carolina Spartan*, February 15, March 21, 1888; Rock Hill *Herald*, February 2, 1888; Newberry *Herald and News*, October 23, 1884.

32. Newberry *Herald*, May 3, 1883; Charleston *News and Courier*, June 7, 1890; Spartanburg *Carolina Spartan*, March 21, May 9, 1888.

a pool of skills and experience of crucial importance to the development of the larger American machinery industry, the southern failure had broadly deleterious effects on the development of the regional economy. Similar patterns appeared with other auxiliary industries, so that despite its sometimes spectacular growth the southern textile industry long remained a mere adjunct of a New England–dominated American textile industry. Not until the virtual collapse of the New England industry in the 1920s and the rise of the synthetic fiber industry, which developed within the region, did the Piedmont cotton mill belt begin to broaden its industrial base.[33] The disappointments lay in the future, however; the 1880s and 1890s were years of economic hope for the southern mill promoters.

Given the importance of cotton to the economies of the towns, and to that of the state in general, it is natural to find that the emphasis on cotton manufacturing derived in large part from its presence. Gerald W. Johnson wrote of those days that "the mainstay of the Southern economies was cotton, and he who was not involved with cotton, in one way or another, was running a side show."[34] The striking image of the cotton mill in the cotton field, popularized by the Charleston *News and Courier*, played a justly famous role in cotton mill promotion, as did the more down-to-earth argument that the South had an advantage in cotton manufacturing because of its plentiful supply of raw material.[35] The importance of cotton to cotton mills made the industry attractive to merchants in other ways as well. As long-time dealers in the staple they had developed connections with the textile industry that would prove helpful, especially for finance and technical advice; they also had

33. See Caroline Ware, *The Early New England Cotton Manufacture* (New York: Russell and Russell, 1931). Cf. Mary Josephine Oates, *The Role of the Cotton Textile Industry in the Economic Development of the American Southeast, 1900–1940* (New York: Arno Press, 1975).

34. Gerald W. Johnson, *The Making of a Southern Industrialist: A Biographical Study of Simpson Bobo Tanner* (Chapel Hill: University of North Carolina Press, 1952), 36.

35. The "cheap cotton" argument, however, has generally gotten short shrift from economic historians, who have found little comparative advantage to be gained from being near the cotton fields which was not offset by the greater distance from the finishing plants and the major markets and ports. See the discussion and review of the literature in Williamson, "Cotton Manufacturing," 129–54.

intimate knowledge of the cotton market, which was useful in procuring supplies of raw material for the mills. Most alluring of all, though, was the prospective impact of the erection of mills on the local cotton trade. Cotton money generally provided the commercial base for the towns, and any attraction that could bring in more was not to be overlooked. A Laurens County farmer predicted that as a result of the projected mill at Clinton "thousands of bales of cotton will go [there] that otherwise would have found market elsewhere, for it is a conceded fact that Cotton Manufacturers can afford to pay better prices for the staple when it is at their Mills. A cotton Mill at Clinton will assure the town of largely increased sales in merchandise and other articles, as farmers from every side, even across the Enoree, will take their cotton there." The prospect of an expanded cotton market was the principal attributed cause of the "cotton mill fever" that periodically stirred Abbeville in the late 1880s, and a Rock Hill editor gave credit for that town's "fancy prices" for the staple to the local factory; "give us more factories," he declared, "and better prices will be obtained."[36]

Higher cotton prices benefited farmers as well as merchants, and one occasionally finds farmers, such as the one quoted above, urging cotton mills for that reason. Farmers also appreciated the potential produce market provided by the new population. The projected Newberry Mill would "give us a market for milk, butter, eggs, poultry, wood and in fact everything, for these Factory people, as a general thing, spend all they make and spend it at home," argued one rural letter writer. The value of such benefits was not lost on the men who answered Benjamin R. Tillman's call for a Farmers' Convention in 1886. The assembled farmers passed a resolution urging "the speedy development of our manufacturing interests, thereby creating home markets for all our productions, and for the crude materials which nature has bestowed upon us with such lavish hands." Tillman, otherwise the virtual dictator of

36. Springs, *Clothes Make the Man*, 14; Mitchell, *Rise of Cotton Mills*, 256–57; "Upper Laurens" in Laurensville *Herald*, January 25, 1895; Abbeville *Press and Banner*, January 16, 1889; Rock Hill *Herald*, January 19, 1888.

the convention, was forced quietly to drop a resolution hostile to the mills.[37]

Occasionally farmers gave more concrete support to factories. The Westminster Cotton Mill in Oconee County was owned by several local farmers; it made use of the famous Clement Attachment, a device which combined ginning and carding into a continuous process and which was advertised as the surest means of bringing the cotton mills to the cotton fields.[38] In the fall of 1887 a movement was started among the farmers of Abbeville County to build a mill at the county seat; enthusiastic mass meetings were held, and subscriptions were solicited through the local Farmers' Clubs. However, by December the scheme had quietly died, a denouement anticipated by a local editor. "One enthusiastic farmer," he snorted, "said that he would be one of a thousand men to give *ten dollars*. Another farmer said he would give *twenty dollars*, and, if necessary to secure the success of the enterprise, he would double the amount."[39] An effort to build a mill at Anderson in 1883 foundered because of pessimistic crop prospects; when the Anderson Cotton Mill was finally organized it was nearly doomed by its inability to sell stock to local farmers.[40] No amount of enthusiasm could compensate for the farmers' chronic lack of capital. Nor could it hide their ambivalence toward cotton mills and the concentrations of economic power they represented.[41] The benefits of mills to farmers were comparatively minor considerations to the townspeople who led the more successful local "cotton mill cam-

37. "True Friendly Home" in Newberry *Herald and News*, March 1, 1883; Spartanburg *Carolina Spartan*, May 26, 1886, May 1, 1889; Francis Butler Simkins, *Pitchfork Ben Tillman: South Carolinian* (Baton Rouge: Louisiana State University Press, 1944), 101–105.

38. [Blackman], *Cotton Mills*, 18–19.

39. Abbeville *Press and Banner*, October 19, 26, November 9, December 14, 1887; *The Cotton Plant* (Greenville), December 1887. Similar stirs occurred in Abbeville in 1889 and 1890. They seem to have been an annual phenomenon, coinciding with the harvest, when farmers temporarily held a surfeit of cash. Abbeville *Press and Banner*, November 19, 1890. Abbeville finally built a mill near the turn of the century, but it was controlled by townspeople.

40. Anderson *Intelligencer*, April 19, May 17, 31, 1883; May 10, 24, June 7, 21, July 12, August 30, September 6, 1888; February 14, April 11, 1889; May 29, 1890.

41. See, for instance, E. M. Pendleton, "The Clement Attachment," *Land and Home* (Atlanta), January 22, 1880 (Typescript copy in John V. Stribling Papers, Southern Historical Collection, University of North Carolina at Chapel Hill).

paigns," and expositions of those benefits in the town press often had the air of patronizing lectures.

If farmers were ambivalent about factories, the "town people" were ambivalent about agriculture. They paid due tribute to King Cotton as the source of their wealth, even at times boasting of their vassalage, but beneath the hymns of praise could be heard constant low mutterings of discontent. Merchants as well as farmers were entrapped in the credit system; they depended on their northern suppliers to finance their stock, and on their customers to settle at harvest time. Commerce was thus sustained largely by long-term debt, secured by an unpredictable commodity. In the best of times business under these conditions would be risky and costly; in the late-nineteenth-century South, plagued with falling cotton prices, it was often precarious. While dependence on agriculture fostered chronic uncertainty and high credit costs, however, the cotton mill with its constant turnover seemed to offer a measure of stability. Anderson was a great cotton market, noted the *Intelligencer*, but it was less prosperous than Greenville with its mills, for "when there are big crops, we have a big trade, and when there are small crops we have a small trade." A farmer near Piedmont saw manufacturing as a means of escape from "the old slipshod, credit business"; steady wages for operatives would create a constant money flow and permit merchants to establish "a good cash, money-making business." Among the major attractions of manufacturing to Leroy Springs and his associates in Lancaster was the hope that a regular payroll would ease the growing credit stringency faced by the area in the waning years of the nineteenth century. Significantly, the pace of manufacturing development quickened during the economically disastrous 1890s, peaking just after cotton prices hit their postwar low in 1899.[42]

Townspeople, then, embarked on industrialization at least partially for defensive reasons. The need for a defensive strategy was

42. Woodman, *King Cotton*, 353–59; Anderson *Intelligencer*, May 26, 1887; March 14, 1889; Springs, *Clothes Make the Man*, 12–14. On the turn of the century mill boom, see pages 133–35 herein. The cotton price series is from Latham, Alexander and Company, *Cotton Movement and Fluctuation, 1904–1905* (New York: Latham, Alexander and Company, 1905), 127. The connection between the agricultural depression and industrialization was suggested by Stanley L. Engerman in letters to the author, January 2 and 26, 1981.

reinforced on the level of the individual town by the fierce commercial struggles accompanying the late-nineteenth-century proliferation of trading points. The sometimes violent competition among western towns for preeminence on the advancing frontier reappeared with only somewhat less vehemence on the "commercial frontier" of the postbellum Piedmont. Town contended against town for railroads, for rural customers, for public works, and for capital. Rivalries were rife, the one between Greenville and Spartanburg being especially virulent. Naturally the cotton mill became a prime weapon in such struggles for local supremacy. Mill promoters in every locality played upon the fear of civic decline. W. P. Jacobs pointed Clintonians to the county seat: "Laurensville is to have two big railroads. She already has the court-house, the jail, and a good many other things." Spartanburg worried not only about Greenville, but also about the small local centers growing up along the railroads and constricting its trading area. Abbeville was concerned with its decreasing importance, while in a neighboring town it was noted that "other towns are growing into prominence which attracts [*sic*] more or less trade from Greenwood, and their effects will be to eclipse our town and by a combination of other places, unless a factory is built, Greenwood may sink to the level of 'a dead cock in the pit.'"[43] Such fears of local failure were at least as effective as prophecies of local greatness in gaining support for mills. In the social darwinian vision of the boosters, the necessity of economic development decisively outweighed any risks. The more daring invested in mills for profit and prosperity; the more cautious built factories for security.

Almost as important as the pecuniary benefits of mills to towns were their symbolic attributes. The large size of the mills compared to virtually all other manufacturing enterprises in the state,

43. *Our Monthly* (Thornwell Orphanage, Clinton, S.C.), XVIII (1881), 101; Spartanburg *Carolina Spartan*, November 25, 1885; Abbeville *Press and Banner*, February 20, March 27, 1889; also Charleston *News and Courier*, September 16, 1887, on Camden. Cf. Don H. Doyle, *The Social Order of a Frontier Community* (Urbana: University of Illinois Press, 1978), 18–38, 62–91, 242–55; Robert R. Dykstra, *The Cattle Towns* (New York: Alfred A. Knopf, 1968), *passim*. Albert Fishlow, in *American Railroads and the Transformation of the Ante-bellum Economy*, Harvard Economic Studies, CXXVII (Cambridge: Harvard University Press, 1965), 184–86, 191–95, comments on the relationship of town rivalries to the expansion of the midwestern railroad network.

the great mechanical power amassed therein, and the powerful organizations welding men, machines, and materials into engines of production, stirred local promoters to flights of lyricism. A discussion of the machinery in the future Newberry mill, "the hugest work ever before begun" there, moved a local editor to both childish enthusiasm and a striking association. "We want to hear the jingle jangle, the bang, the rattle, the whir and whiz of its thousands of spindles. In plain words we want to see the 'veels go round,'" he said. "To see and hear all this will transport us in memory to the great industrial show in Philadelphia in '76; machinery Hall, its miles of belting and shafting, its grand Corliss engine, the size, the like and the make of which never seen before, will then be called to mind, and in fancy we will be there again." As the buildings for the Spartan Mills rose near the Spartanburg depot, they were compared to "a city on a hill, or rather several of them." The statistics of the smokestack (40 feet in diameter at the bottom, 12 feet, 8 inches at the top, 182 feet high) were recited lovingly, and the symbolism of that stack, overshadowing as it did the towers of nearby Wofford College, formerly the town's principal institution, was not lost on at least some observers. The mill was indeed "something about which the business men of the city can talk—boast of—'the best in the South' &c, something to please the ladies and something for the children to wonder at." The "lofty monument[s] to intelligent industry," made even more visible by the great plumes of smoke they emitted, served to advertise the town's achievements and energy both to rural folk and to travelers. Smoke from the factories at Anderson could be seen across the Savannah River; the blast of the Spartan Mill whistle could reportedly be heard fifteen miles away, and it became the time standard not only for the work force but also for the city and much of the surrounding countryside, where a farmer opined that "if the factory has served no other purpose it has established uniformity in time and the hours of labor."[44]

44. Newberry *Herald and News*, February 21, 1884; Spartanburg *Carolina Spartan*, May 30, 1883; June 19, 1889; April 9, July 9, 1890; June 17, 1891; Columbia *State*, July 8, 1901; Anderson *Intelligencer*, June 11, 1902; D. E. Camak, *Human Gold from Southern Hills* (Greer: private, 1960), 19.

Not only were the mills monuments, but the wealth they produced in turn built other monuments. Elliott White Springs recalled that the first dividend from the factory at Fort Mill organized by his grandfather was used in part "to erect marble monuments to the Soldiers of the Confederacy, the Women of the Confederacy, and the Faithful Slaves, and to build a new pavilion on the hill, which has since been known as the Bandstand." More important monuments, however, were also being erected with mill money. In the late 1880s the Methodists of Spartanburg constructed a new church building, one more "in keeping with the wealth of the congregation" and "the expectations of the Methodist people of the State." At the same time the city's leading businessmen were organizing a women's college, subsequently named for the most prominent local manufacturer, and the graded school was erecting a large building, reportedly the first building in the state outside of Charleston erected specifically to serve as a graded school.[45] Thus the new industrial wealth being created by the corporate effort of the townspeople was used not simply for private enjoyment but also for developing the amenities of town life.

In one striking case, cotton mills and the growth of a town became means to a theocratic end. The Reverend Dr. William Plumer Jacobs had taken a pastorate in the struggling little town of Clinton near the close of the Civil War. By 1871 he had found his calling, which was to prove "that a little village church could be made a lighthouse in Zion." To that end he dedicated his labors until his death in 1917, founding an orphanage and a college as well as building up one of the leading Presbyterian congregations in the state. His vision extended to more than his religious institutions, however, and he was as fervently devoted to Clinton as to any other part of his benevolent empire. Clinton was to be his "city on a hill," and to further its destiny he not only led the fight against demon rum in the 1870s but became the community's most vociferous promoter. Having cast his lot with the town, Jacobs' ambitions as a man of God became in his mind indistinguishable from the material ambitions of Clinton. The pages of his personal organ, the

45. Springs, *Clothes Make the Man*, 4; Federal Writers' Project, *A History of Spartanburg County* (Spartanburg, S.C.: Band and White, 1940), 214, 221–22; *Southern Christian Advocate*, January 21, 1885.

Thornwell Orphanage publication *Our Monthly*, teemed with exhortations to build up the town, though not, as one historian has argued, for reasons of moral uplift. While the rhetoric was as fervid as any in the secular press, the arguments employed were the familiar ones of town-building: enhancing the local market, expanding the local population and trade, etc. He urged the creation of railroads, banks, and factories, however, neither for his own profit nor even completely for the benefits the new wealth brought to his philanthropic enterprises.[46] The power and influence of Clinton became the means by which he expanded the power and influence of his ministry, which, with the arrogance of the true believer, he identified completely with the glory of God.

Too much can be made of Jacobs; indeed, too much has. Nothing else in the state compared with Jacobs' unique Calvinistic commingling of the things of the world and the things of God; far from being typical, Jacobs' mentality was an oddity in the increasingly secular culture of late-nineteenth-century South Carolina.[47] The case of Jacobs is nonetheless instructive, for it expressed in a religious idiom the ways in which the ambitions of an individual townsman could become inextricably intermingled with those of his community. If the sense of calling held by most "town people" was less explicitly Christian than was Jacobs', the desire to be known as an "upbuilder" of the community was no less powerful. The highest esteem went, not to the merely rich, but to those who contributed their wealth and talents to the larger ends of the community. It was in this general sense that investment in cotton mills became "a public philanthropy."[48]

The word *philanthropy* has a more specific meaning as well, a

46. *Our Monthly*, XVIII (1881), 101; XXIV (1887), 80; XXVI (1889), 90; XXXII (1895), 383. Jacobs invested $2,500 of orphanage endowment funds in Clinton Cotton Mill stock and served on its board of directors. *Ibid.*, XXXIV, 185, 594. The "village church" quotation is from Thornwell Jacobs, *Step Down*, 113. Cf. Mitchell, *Rise of Cotton Mills*, 136.

47. Thornwell Jacobs, *The Life of William Plumer Jacobs* (New York: Fleming H. Revell Company, 1918), is filiopietistic but captures the flavor not only of the elder Jacobs' mentality but also that of his progeny. A grandson, W. P. Jacobs II, became head of the publishing house founded by his father. He also became secretary-treasurer of the Cotton Manufacturers' Association of South Carolina and used his access to the press, and later the presidency of Presbyterian College, to propagandize for the industry.

48. Columbia *State*, January 20, 1895; J. W. Norwood (a Greenville banker) to Wilson

fact which has caused considerable mischief. Ever since Broadus Mitchell first suggested that southerners built cotton mills for basically humanitarian purposes, his interpretation has haunted the historiography of the postbellum South. According to Mitchell, "to give employment to the necessitous masses of poor whites, for the sake of the people themselves, was an object animating the minds of many mill builders." While he admitted that many people, including manufacturers, would disagree, he insisted that "a study of the facts shows how frequent and normal was the philanthropic motive."[49]

It cannot be denied that the potential work force figured in many of the public pronouncements on industry made in South Carolina during the period. The "philanthropic" aspect of mill development, however, was blown out of all proportion in Mitchell's work by misunderstandings and, especially, over-reliance on a single source. Aside from his extensive use of interviews with prominent industrialists and generally sympathetic observers, Mitchell relied chiefly on newspapers, especially the files of the Charleston *News and Courier* for 1881 and early 1882. That reliance led him to several of his major conclusions: that there was a unified, coordinated "cotton mill campaign" in the 1880s, that it was led by the *News and Courier* and its British-born editor Francis W. Dawson, that it had heavily "philanthropic" overtones, and that "the Charleston Manufacturing Company was the type enterprise of the Cotton Mill Campaign."[50] All of these statements were based on the assumption that Charleston was paradigmatic of South

---

G. Harvey, August 6, 1920, enclosed in Norwood to David R. Coker, August 19, 1920, in David R. Coker Papers, SCL, speaking contemptuously of a local man who, though wealthy, "I have never heard of . . . giving financial aid to objects for the public good." Cf. Anthony F. C. Wallace, *Rockdale: The Growth of an American Village in the Early Industrial Revolution* (New York: Alfred A. Knopf, 1978), 406–408, on the relationship of notions of "stewardship" to the impulse of local development.

49. Mitchell, *Rise of Cotton Mills*, 132 and *n*.: "The genuineness of altruism as a motive in the Cotton Mill Campaign is supported by observation of Southern character in other particulars and especially as operative in this period."

50. *Ibid*., 112–14, 127, 133–34, 157–58. Mitchell's other contemporary sources are the Atlanta *Constitution*, the Raleigh *Observer* (later the Raleigh *News and Observer*), and the Baltimore *Journal of Commerce and Manufacturers Record* (later Baltimore *Manufacturers Record*). Judging from the dates given in the notes, all were examined for periods of several years in the early 1880s.

Carolina, indeed of the whole southeast. In fact, though, there were critical differences. The concern for "furnishing employment to many in our midst" which flourished in Dawson's columns found only faint echoes in the "country press" of the interior, and seems indeed to have varied inversely with distance from the coast. For that matter, considering the record, it varied inversely with industrial success.[51]

What set Charleston off from the rest of the state in this regard was its size and vigor, or rather its lack of vigor. With nearly fifty thousand inhabitants in 1880 it was five times the size of the largest interior town, Columbia, and eight times the size of the leading up-country town, Greenville. It was, though, a city in the midst of a slow economic decline, the railroads passing it by, its market areas shrinking, its most astute businessmen moving their capital elsewhere. The city therefore had a sizable unemployment problem, bearing "most heavily upon the female population of the city. Among this class there is great destitution, and this is no matter of surprise when we know the miserable pittance they receive for their work." Humanitarian concern was mixed with economic and social concern, since "where a large proportion of the population of a city is made up of consumers who add nothing to its wealth, crime, lawlessness, and destitution will always exist."[52]

Complicating the situation was an appalling lack of business confidence; the ebullient rhetoric of Dawson's newspaper was less an expression of the Charleston spirit than a goad to it. The city had a reputation as a "thriftless and retrograde place," losing capital and managerial skill to the up-country and points west. The *News and Courier* readily admitted that "the right men to establish the factory are hard to find," and that "people are not going to put their money into a cotton factory . . . unless they have confidence not only in the integrity of the promoters, but also in their capacity to make the enterprise pay." The rhetorical altruism sur-

51. This was recognized by Mitchell. *Rise of Cotton Mills*, 193–94. For an example of rhetoric from a low-country newspaper showing the Charleston influence, see Orangeburg *Democrat*, March 3, 1881.

52. Editorial, "The Unemployed Problem," Charleston *News and Courier*, January 2, 1879.

rounding the Charleston mill may have deepened the gloom, for the *News and Courier* had to assure potential shareholders that the charitable objects of the enterprise did not include the management; the corporators, it insisted, were successful men who were involved out of desire for profit, "not because they have failed in other things or have nothing else to do."[53]

It was against this general despondency that Dawson and the *News and Courier* set themselves, and their strategy was the "cotton mill campaign." As Gustavus G. Williamson has noted, the "campaign" was not Southwide, or even statewide, but was essentially local, fading out after the accomplishment of its object, the establishment of the Charleston mill. The arguments, particularly those concerning the "poor women and children," were addressed specifically to Charleston. Even there, though, the major emphasis of Dawson's massive publicity campaign was on the commercial benefit to the city. According to the *News and Courier*, the mill would give the city "the life and vigor which nothing short of manufactures will assure us." "Two or three million dollars additional poured annually into the pockets of the shopkeepers and tradespeople would make them think that the commercial millennium had come."[54] While the *News and Courier* was statewide in its influence, and was certainly not shy about claiming a position of leadership, its role was essentially similar to that of its "country" cousins. Although its tactics were shaped by peculiar conditions, it, too, served its home town as a civic booster.

Not only did Charleston differ from the rest of the state in its economic conditions, but it also was conspicuous in the failure of its attempts to become a textile center. Ironically, the major problem was the labor supply. Allegations of unemployment notwithstanding, the people of Charleston steadfastly refused to work in the Charleston mill. Their disinclination to enter the factory was due to prejudice against mill work on the part of urban Charlestonians and the comparatively high wages paid workmen, which enabled working class women to remain at home. Turnover, too,

53. *Ibid.*, March 22, 1880; January 28, 1881. "Justice," *ibid.*, December 18, 1887, blamed the ultimate failure of the mill on the timorousness of local businessmen.

54. *Ibid.*, January 28, 1881; Williamson, "Cotton Manufacturing," 78, 80, 82–83.

was enormous. By 1887, when the original company collapsed, over one thousand Charlestonians had been trained as operatives, but only 98 out of a work force of 388 were natives of the city.[55] As the value of Charleston mill stock steadily sank, the mill management and the *News and Courier* became peevish, the latter remarking with some irritation that "hundreds of young girls in this city who earn a living by sewing and more menial work will not take advantage of the opportunity of learning a trade which will support them comfortably."[56]

At any rate, philanthropy as a motive for continuing the enterprise vanished within a year of its commencement. By the end of 1883 the company was recruiting its labor supply from other areas, especially from Orangeburg and the Augusta-Horse Creek Valley district, justifying the move by pointing out that "it was cheaper to bring skilled operatives here than to teach new hands to spin, weave, &c." However, the company had as much trouble with the imported help as with the natives. The cost of living was comparatively high in Charleston, forcing wages up; the *News and Courier* reported in 1883 that local spinners made four dollars a week, nearly twice the pay of spinners at the Piedmont mill in Greenville County. However, the mill was disinclined to provide the fringe benefits, such as free housing, then common among the mills; in 1884 it did build four tenements in an effort to depress rents, but charged fifty cents per room per week for their use. Even as regards "welfare work," the "idealistic" managers of the mill developed an unenviable reputation for callousness, a reputation hardly enhanced when in 1887 the managers blamed the impending bankruptcy of the firm on its labor force, and proposed a shift to black workers.[57] In the end another try was made with whites,

55. Mitchell, *Rise of Cotton Mills*, 194–96; Charleston *News and Courier*, May 11, September 22, October 7, 1883.

56. Charleston *News and Courier*, September 22, 1883, quoted gleefully in the anti-cotton-mill Abbeville *Press and Banner*, September 26, 1883; Charleston *News and Courier*, November 12, 1883. Charleston Manufacturing Company stock hardly ever sold above its par value of one hundred dollars per share, a record unique among the larger mills of the period. On the eve of its bankruptcy the firm's shares were quoted at $22.50 bid, $25.00 asked. *Ibid.*, September 14, 1883; May 10, 1884; November 25, 1887.

57. Charleston *News and Courier*, January 28, 1881; May 11, 1883; May 2, 3, 1884; November 30, December 15–18, 1887; Piedmont Manufacturing Company, Time Book, 1884–1886 (on microfilm, SCL).

followed by two with blacks; all were failures, and attempts to operate the factory were finally abandoned in 1901.[58]

While Charleston's economic health depended on providing employment to its own labor force, that of virtually every other town in the state depended on attracting labor from elsewhere. As we have seen, a major selling point of the cotton mill promoters was the increase of population resulting from the establishment of manufacturing in a town. The cotton mills served that function well; in Columbia, for example, the evidence suggests that only a handful of the one thousand operatives living in the city in 1899 had lived there before coming to work in the mills.[59] Although one finds an occasional moralist urging the town loafers to take mill jobs, it was almost universally assumed that the labor force would come from outside the towns.[60]

There were two different, and inconsistent, expectations about the new class of population. One was that it would be chiefly composed of women and girls drawn in from the countryside. Occasionally remarks on this segment of the labor force expressed concern for its well-being, but more often the promoters viewed it as a heretofore wasted resource which could be used more efficiently in the mill than on the farm. Although testimony is conflicting, there seems to have been a disinclination to use white women and girls in the fields except when "driven by necessity," and the cotton mill was frequently proposed as a means of soaking up the "excess" labor.[61] The South Carolina agent for the Clement Attachment,

58. *Ibid.*, January 26, 1888; May 26, 1897; Allen Heath Stokes, Jr., "Black and White Labor and the Development of the Southern Textile Industry, 1800–1920" (Ph.D. dissertation, University of South Carolina, 1977), 181–85, 231–36, 243–61.

59. *Columbia City Directory and Business Guide for 1885* (Columbia, S.C.: W. B. McDaniel, 1885); *Columbia City Directory, 1891* (Charleston, S.C.: Lucas and Richardson, 1891); *The Columbia City Directory, 1895* (Columbia, S.C.: The State Company, 1895); *Walsh's Directory of the City of Columbia for 1899* (Charleston, S.C.: Lucas and Richardson, 1899). A search of the 1899 directory uncovered 994 operatives (exclusive of foremen and skilled machinists) living in Columbia and its environs, 947 white and 47 black. Of these, only 38 were listed in earlier directories in occupations other than cotton mill operative. Even allowing for inadequate coverage and the omission of unemployed children in the earlier directories, the above figures seem to confirm the abundant impressionistic evidence that most mill operatives came from outside the town.

60. *E.g.*, Newberry *Herald and News*, August 28, 1884.

61. Charleston *News and Courier*, February 4, 1884, supplement, "South Carolina in 1884," including results of a questionnaire sent to county correspondents, including the

noting that his mill at Westminster required only eight hands, argued that "every neighborhood has at least that many idle girls, who are only burdens to the producers. We would make more producers without increasing the consumers." Likewise, the *Carolina Spartan* urged a cotton mill for Spartanburg, as "it employs labor, which otherwise might be idle; it decreases the number of non-producers." The *News and Courier* saw great untapped wealth, as well as an opportunity for charity, in the use of such labor: "Employment is given to white women and children who could find no other work equally well-adapted to their strength, and producing as large a return for their labor."[62]

On the other hand, promoters claimed that the new labor force would be not only an economic asset to the towns but a social one as well. According to the *Spartan*, the operative "would be a valuable addition to our population. There is, as a whole, no more orderly and law-abiding people in the country. There may be now and then a few bad and worthless characters among them, but it is the exception, not the rule. Such people are always punctual in their hours and industrious, it cannot be denied."[63] This argument was probably designed in part to reassure the anxious about the character of the industrial classes, but it was also an indication of the expectations being aroused by the promoters. That a population of unschooled and unskilled immigrants from the countryside might present as many problems as benefits, and would certainly not be the sort of community asset being promised, is obvious in retrospect but was assiduously obscured by the early industrial publicists. The industrialists and their commercial backers valued the potential labor force for its cheapness and availability, and for the money that it spent. The potential social ramifications of its creation, on the other hand, were hidden by clouds of roseate rhetoric.

To be sure, there was some thought being given to the shape

---

question, "Do women and children, white or colored, work in the fields, and to what extent?"

62. John V. Stribling to John W. Harper, March 19, 1879, in John V. Stribling Papers, Southern Historical Collection, UNC; Spartanburg *Carolina Spartan*, September 24, 1889; Charleston *News and Courier*, February 10, 1880.

63. Spartanburg *Carolina Spartan*, May 30, 1883.

of the future social order and the role of the factory in ushering it in, enough at any rate to give some substance to Mitchell's assertion that the southern industrial revolution was "deliberately planned."[64] The president of the South Carolina College, William Porcher Miles, foresaw a day "when manufactures shall thickly dot the banks of our streams and rivers; when little villages will have sprung up around them, and when the mass of our people are there gathered into communities." At that time, he thought, "we may hope to see a church and school-house within reach of every inhabitant of the State." Naturally the "social improvement" theme was taken up by the promoters. According to the *News and Courier*, the mills, "by bringing [the operatives] together in groups, where they are subject to elevating social influences, encourages them to seek education, and improves them in every conceivable respect, as future husbands and wives, sons and daughters, parents and children, in South Carolina." John V. Stribling, the chief local promoter of the Clement Attachment, included among his selling points "the assembling of [the South's] indigent, unemployed labor in villages, where through the influence of churches, schools, and factories, they could be improved mentally, morally, and physically, [and] many saved from vicious lives." In these pronouncements one can see a certain whiggish vision of the social benefits arising from economic development. Sentiments of this sort are not encountered often, however, and can hardly be considered central to the industrial impulse. The social dimensions of industrialization interested a few of the more intellectual; to the promoter they simply provided more grist for the advertising mill.[65]

If broadly social concerns were peripheral to mill building, so were religious concerns. The legend of the Salisbury, North Carolina, cotton mill, founded as the result of a revival, has no South Carolina equivalent. There were occasional religious dedications of cotton mills; several cases in North Carolina were reported in

64. Mitchell, *Rise of Cotton Mills*, 78.

65. William Porcher Miles, "Education as a Science," address to State Normal Institute in Greenville, reprinted as a supplement to Charleston *News and Courier*, September 17, 1881; Editorial, *ibid.*; John V. Stribling to James O'Brien, September 12, 1889, in John V. Stribling Papers, Southern Historical Collection, UNC. O'Brien was a prospective purchaser of the attachment.

the South Carolina press, and each new installation of machinery in the mills at Clinton was blessed with prayer. Even so, contemporary comments indicate that such practices were not only unusual but even provoked some skepticism. "If [such a dedication] had been done at the North," snorted a Spartanburg man, "and some distinguished anti-Southern preacher, such as Beecher or Bishop Simpson, had been called upon to dedicate a factory at Lowell, or a paper mill at Holyoke, then our papers would have cried out, 'A sharp Yankee trick,' 'a big advertising dodge,' 'Pharasaism in the extreme'; and the whole thing would have been denounced as sacrilegious." The editor of the *Spartan* agreed, arguing that "religion was degraded by being hitched to the starting of a factory." The religious press took a more benign view of the matter, but its attitude was due less to an uncritical endorsement of business enterprise than to evangelical Protestant beliefs concerning Christian calling and stewardship. The *Southern Christian Advocate*, for example, thought "the formal and solemn dedication of a secular interest and enterprise to the Lord" to be a splendid idea: "Ought not a man to realize amid the scenes and opportunities of his daily business, just as he realizes at his church on Sunday, the duty and the privilege of worship? Ought not his business to be to him a means of grace just as the service at church is a means of grace?" No endorsement of any enterprise was intended here, however: "This Randalman Company [the North Carolina mill being dedicated], if its owners are not hypocrites and Pharisees, will do a clean business. . . . From this factory we expect a good fabric, made of good material, measured off to buyers by a yardstick 36 inches long, and made by operatives who are worked a reasonable number of hours in the day, and who receive a fair equivalent for their service. Besides this we expect them as the Lord prospers them to devote a part of their dividend to the service and glory of GOD."[66]

Only in Clinton did the mill approach the status of a religious institution, and there it was due chiefly to the influence of W. P.

66. Spartanburg *Carolina Spartan*, March 24, 1880; June 28, 1882; *Southern Christian Advocate*, March 13, 1880.

Jacobs and his vision of the Laurens County town as the New Jerusalem. The blessing of God was placed explicitly on money making at Clinton, as "it is the Lord that gives us power to get wealth. . . . Clinton people do hardly anything without prayer. Is that the reason Clinton enterprises so generally prosper?" While Jacobs was only too happy to lend the prestige of the church to the financial schemes of his congregation, he was nonetheless capable of threatening its withdrawal when his flock displeased him: "If they fail to do their duty" for mission work in the mill village, he warned at a later time, "how can they expect the Lord to bless their property interest?"[67]

Whatever public blessings Jacobs placed on the Clinton Cotton Mill, he was privately perturbed. Beneath the optimism of the town classes and the mill promoters ran an undercurrent of anxiety over the impact of the new industrial departure on the stable traditional world of South Carolina, a world in which even those men doing their utmost to destroy it still fondly imagined themselves to live. The prospect of industrialization produced at first only a vague unease, a distress without a clear focus. It was easily soothed by the assurances of promoters and manufacturers that Coketown could not possibly be reincarnated in South Carolina, and was overwhelmed by the intense desire of the new middle classes to amass wealth and challenge their New England compatriots for supremacy in textiles. Even so, forebodings were present from the inception of the industry and were destined to increase in importance over the years. The tension between economic hopes and social fears was perhaps best expressed by Jacobs, whose God-drenched outlook made him the most curiously perceptive of South Carolina's industrial prophets. In December, 1895, he penned the following laconic entry in his diary:

> We have organized our Cotton Mills. I am elected a director.
> My purpose to accept it for three purposes:

67. *Our Monthly*, XXXIV (1897), 117; XXXIX (1902), 240, 730. On a visit to Clinton in 1900 the Georgia humorist "Bill Arp" was told by the townspeople that "Dr. Jacobs is in partnership with the Lord and that Mr. Bailey is the Lord's financial agent." Columbia *State*, February 24, 1900.

First—To have an influence in locating the same.

Second—To have a word as to religious and school privileges for operatives.

Third—To have my say as to regulations in regard to the moral character of the operatives.

These were not the things in the minds of those who elected me. God speed the work.[68]

68. Thornwell Jacobs (ed.), *Diary of William Plumer Jacobs* (Oglethorpe University, Ga.: Oglethorpe University Press, 1937), 317–18.

Chapter III

The Early Response to Industrialism

The unity and singleness of purpose fashioned by mill promoters in South Carolina was real and significant, but it was not the whole story. The boosters' stress on civic consensus inherently obscured a broad range of occasionally incompatible attitudes toward industrialization. Even the material possibilities of manufacturing were open to question. The triumphalism of the New South evangelists notwithstanding, the momentum of manufacturing development accelerated slowly and haltingly up to the great boom of the late 1890s. Only twenty-six of the one hundred mills in operation in the Piedmont in 1907 were organized before 1895; local promoters frequently suffered one or more miscarriages before bearing a major enterprise to full term, and such subsequently robust offspring as the Anderson and Spartan Mills had extraordinarily difficult births.[1] If the public voices of the towns were daring and entrepreneurial, the majority of potential investors were not. Small savers desired safety and steady returns; demonstrating that cotton mills satisfied their needs as well as those of the more adventurous required time and a steady accumulation of success stories.

The caution of many townsfolk reflected, as well, a concern over

1. David Carlton, "'Builders of a New State': The Town Classes and Early Industrialization of South Carolina, 1880–1907," in Walter J. Fraser and Winfred B. Moore (eds.), *From the Old South to the New: Essays on the Transitional South* (Westport, Conn.: Greenwood Press, 1981), 44–45; Allen Heath Stokes, Jr., "John H. Montgomery: A Pioneer Southern Industrialist" (M.A. thesis, University of South Carolina, 1967), 54–61. See also page 66 herein.

the social consequences of manufacturing. Their desire for prosperity by no means entailed a taste for the commotion of great cities, but neither did it completely preclude the sense that a major economic departure would likely have unsettling effects on their familiar social order. Thus, like many present-day Chamber of Commerce officials, townsfolk desired "clean industry" which would harmonize with the local "quality of life." Harmonizing factories and country towns proved anything but easy, though. However much farmers and townsmen might laud manufacturing as an aid to agricultural and commercial prosperity, they were also aware that concentrated corporate power posed problems to a society still dominated by petty producers and traders. Mills were periodically accused of manipulating cotton prices to the injury of local growers and merchants; shopkeepers complained of company stores monopolizing the mill trade, while small investors fretted over managerial incompetence and high-handedness. While rural resentment of industrialists found brief and ambiguous expression in the Tillman movement, the economic complaints of the townsmen were generally absorbed as an easily borne cost of Progress.[2] More pervasive, if even less visible, were concerns for the social health and stability of the future industrial South Carolina with its congested communities of landless white wage earners. The advocates of industrialization confronted a long-standing fear of industrial society which South Carolinians had inherited from their rural, conservative past and which had been strengthened by their observations of older manufacturing regions. One of the promoters' major tasks, then, was to convince their fellow citizens that they had nothing to fear from the formation of a proletariat in the Palmetto State, that a combination of the social controls of "cotton mill paternalism" and the operatives' "Anglo-Saxon" virtue would spare South Carolina the turmoil and class enmities of

2. Spartanburg *Carolina Spartan*, June 18, 1884; Laurensville *Herald*, October 18, 1895; Union *Times*, July 14, 1905; Columbia *State*, September 27, 29, October 11, 1899, May 8, 1900; for the complaints of a particularly querulous investor, see William Watts Ball Papers, Duke University Library, Durham, N.C., *passim*. See also Gustavus G. Williamson, Jr., "South Carolina Cotton Mills and the Tillman Movement," *Proceedings of the South Carolina Historical Association*, 1949, 36–49.

northern and British cities. Temporarily, at least, they succeeded.

Anti-industrial propaganda had played an important role in the antebellum debate over slavery. Although the most thoroughgoing southern critic of free labor society, George Fitzhugh, advocated limited industrialization as a means of freeing the South from its dependence on the world market, rejection of the factory system was at least implicit in southern attacks on the social order that spawned it.[3] More commonly, the conditions of industrial life provided raw material for *tu quoque* arguments, in which the bourgeois abolitionists of Old and New England were condemned for meddling in southern affairs while neglecting their own. In a letter to the British antislavery leader Thomas Clarkson, James Henry Hammond asserted that English working people were "more miserable and degraded, morally and physically, than our slaves; to be elevated to the actual condition of whom would be to these, *your fellow citizens*, a most glorious act of *emancipation*." Citing as evidence Parliamentary investigations revealing long hours, pitiful wages, and child labor in the mines and mills, squalid and destitute living conditions in the cities, and immorality, ignorance, and irreligion among the people, he challenged Clarkson "to deny that these specimens exhibit the real condition of your operatives in every branch of your industry."[4]

The object of William J. Grayson's poem "The Hireling and the Slave" was to convict abolitionists of hypocrisy, specifically to accuse "England's saintly coteries" of deciding "the proper nostrum for each evil known/ In every land on earth, except their own," while remaining unconcerned with "the sufferings, wants or sins,/ At home, where all true charity begins." He drew a lurid picture of conditions in the mining country, particularly condemning those

3. George Fitzhugh, *Sociology for the South: or the Failure of Free Society* (Richmond, Va.: A. Morris, 1854), 136–43; see also Eugene Genovese's discussion of Fitzhugh, industrialization, and slave society in *The World the Slaveholders Made* (New York: Random House, 1971), 202–11.

4. James H. Hammond, "Slavery in the Light of Political Science," reprinted in E. N. Elliott (ed.), *Cotton Is King and Pro-Slavery Arguments* (Augusta, Ga.: Pritchard, Abbott and Loomis, 1860), 657–60. See also Chancellor William Harper, *Memoir on Slavery*, reprinted *ibid.*, 549–626.

"ruthless hearts" who took the child away from "the breezy hill, the sunny glade," and made him "the drudge of labour." As for the colliers, they were

> Crammed in huts, in reeking masses thrown,
> All moral sense and decency unknown.
> With no restraint, but what the felon knows,
> With the sole joy that beer or gin bestows.
> To gross excess and brutalizing strife,
> The drunken Hireling dedicates his life.[5]

The proslavery argument became irrelevant at the end of the Civil War, but the siege mentality of the South was accentuated by Reconstruction and the reinforcement that victory in a "holy war" gave to Yankee self-righteousness. The need for polemical weapons against the continuing northern assaults on southern virtue, along with the persistence of the tariff as a sectional issue, made aspersions on northern industrial society an attractive pastime for South Carolina's spokesmen. Francis W. Dawson's *News and Courier* had little difficulty shifting from encomiums to progress in southern cotton manufacturing to gleeful recitations of the poor material and moral conditions of mill girls in New England.[6] On occasion the finger pointing could become ludicrous. In 1880 the *News and Courier* attacked protected manufacturers for piling up profits while paying their employees, on average, $1.16 a day; in the same year it reported South Carolina cotton mills paying an average of no more than $.78 a day while claiming profits of from 18 to 40 percent. In 1886 the newspaper applauded the quest of organized labor "to reduce the hours of work to reasonable limits, eight to ten hours a day" in New York and Boston; in 1887 it ridiculed an early effort to pass a ten hour law for factory workers in South Carolina.[7] While the *News and Courier* and others saw

5. William J. Grayson, *The Hireling and the Slave* (Charleston: John Russell, 1854), 23–24.

6. "Life in New England Mills," Charleston *News and Courier*, February 17, 1883, reprinting the testimony of Frank K. Foster before the Committee on Education and Labor of the U.S. Senate.

7. *Ibid.*, May 7, 1884, March 19, April 30, 1886, December 11, 1887; [J. K. Blackman], *The Cotton Mills of South Carolina* (Charleston: News and Courier Job Presses, 1880), 20. In April 1883 the average day wage at the Piedmont Manufacturing Company

no contradiction in attacking evils elsewhere that they condoned at home, an occasional critic of industrialization could use the existence of those evils to warn of the socially deleterious tendencies of factory life.[8] While such critics were rarely seen in print, the self-contradiction of the "New South" press could hardly have gone unnoticed by those unconvinced of the immunity of the South to northern evil.

By and large the weapons of the southern polemicists were forged by northerners or Englishmen, a reflection of the South's position as an outlying province of the English-speaking world. Even during the antebellum period southerners obtained most of their books from New York, Boston, and London, and kept in touch with the latest trends by reading northern and British journals. They traveled in the North and abroad, and often sent their sons outside the South to college despite the entreaties of cultural nationalists. Even the allegedly distinctive trappings of upper-class southern "romantic" culture, such as its "chivalric" self-image and its woman worship, were in large part adaptations of Victorian culture to the peculiar social conditions of the South.[9] The accelerating nationalization of American cultural and economic life in the period following the abortive southern attempt to leave the Union made southerners all the more aware of affairs in the developing industrial metropolises of Great Britain and the American northeast; along with that awareness came exposure to the accumulated experience of the oldest industrialized regions of the world.

South Carolinians were cognizant of the writings of the new

---

was fifty cents a day, while the median was forty-eight cents. Daily wage data is unavailable for the one-quarter of the work force on piece work; however, assuming a full work month of twenty-six days, the most productive weaver made ninety-eight cents a day. Data for two small departments (the cloth room and the repair shop) are missing. Piedmont Manufacturing Company, Time Book, April 1883–July 1886 (Microfilm copy in South Caroliniana Library, University of South Carolina, Columbia; hereafter cited as SCL).

8. "Early Marriages in Lancashire," Abbeville *Press and Banner*, August 22, 1883. The article appeared during an editorial campaign against cotton mills; see pages 122–24 herein.

9. Avery O. Craven, *The Growth of Southern Nationalism, 1848–1861*, A History of the South, VI (Baton Rouge: Louisiana State University Press, 1953), 253–56, 271–76; Rollin G. Osterweis, *Romanticism and Nationalism in the Old South* (New Haven: Yale University Press, 1949). For contemporary Victorian England, see Walter E. Houghton, *The Victorian Frame of Mind* (New Haven: Yale University Press, 1957).

breed of social investigators. They were well-read in Victorian literature, and were familiar with such "industrial" novels as Dickens' *Hard Times*; the images of Coketown and Josiah Bounderby appeared in their discourse and helped shape their view of the world. On a lower level popular fiction found in factory life the materials for tear-jerking romance seasoned with social significance.[10] Even patent medicine advertisements made their contributions to the southern stock of ideas about factories, including supposed occupational ills of operatives among the myriad diseases they claimed to cure.[11]

The citizens of the state were well briefed on the national news, which in the 1880s included the development of giant corporations, labor unrest, and the Haymarket riot. The antebellum southern perception of the North and West as dark hotbeds of radicalism survived the slave regime; there was the difference, though, that the generation surviving the Civil War had had personal experience of the destructive power of a militant ideology. South Carolinians also knew that the discontent stirring the great northern cities was associated with the development of a working class and the increasing dominance of large organizations in economic life.[12] The prospect of such conditions being reproduced at home was potentially disquieting; a speaker at a Greenville church meeting in 1888 warned his listeners to

> Look at the great northwest with millions of gold and its brilliant cities. There stands dimly outlined in the gathering mists that enshroud

10. *E.g.*, "Nan, the Factory Girl," Orangeburg *Times and Democrat*, December 28, 1882. *Baptist Courier*, April 10, 1884, congratulated the directors of the Piedmont Manufacturing Company for not behaving "in the spirit of 'Jos. Bounderby, Esq.,' but [showing] a wise and kind concern for the interest of the employees." See also page 124 herein.

11. An example encountered in the Charleston *News and Courier*, March 20, 1880; Greenville *Daily News*, November 5, 1881; and *Southern Christian Advocate*, November 5, 1881, read as follows: "Close confinement, careful attention to all factory work, gives the operatives pallid faces, poor appetite, languid, miserable feelings, poor blood, inactive liver, kidney and urinary troubles, and all the physicians and medicine in the world cannot help them unless they get out of doors or use HOP BITTERS, made of the purest and best remedies, and especially for such cases, having an abundance of health, sunshine, and rosy cheeks in them. None need suffer if they will use them freely. They cost but a trifle." "Hop Bitters" was made in Rochester, N.Y.

12. Charleston *News and Courier*, May 5, 1886; Spartanburg *Carolina Spartan*, June 13, 1883; Newberry *Herald and News*, April 7, 1886.

> the future the blood-dyed form of Anarchy, ready at any moment to swoop down and destroy all that this nation holds dear. Look eastward, and there find in the very "cradle of liberty" another destroyer of nations. Under the very statue of Liberty, thriving, growing, increasing, is found a spirit of communism that unless checked will destroy this government. . . .
>
> Turn your eyes Southward. To the sunny Palmetto groves of Carolina. No anarchy; no communism. Scan the horizon east and west. Surely you will not find any grim threatner of the nation. What is that black storm cloud that hovers just over the horizon? Once it dashed upon us with all of its fury and deluged our once smiling land with blood; swept off our wealth; made wives widows and prattling babes orphans; broke mothers' and sisters' hearts, and brought low the heads of the gray-haired patriots of our Southland. Will it ever happen again? *Never in the same form* [emphasis mine].[13]

As is suggested by the speaker's identification of the northern radicalism of the 1880s with the ideas that helped bring on the Civil War, the fear of disorder from concentrations of wage laborers was a heritage from antebellum times, if not from the early Republic. The mobs of dependent poor populating industrial cities were traditionally viewed as potential instruments for the destruction of liberty and property. The slaveholding elite, in particular, feared that a large body of propertyless whites might come to threaten the institution of property in man. Christopher G. Memminger warned James H. Hammond in 1849 that such a class would consist of "the same men who make the cry in the Northern cities against the tyranny of capital . . . and every one of these men would have a vote."[14] His concerns were shared so widely that it was necessary for industrial advocates to devote special attention to their refutation. The social structure of South Carolina had changed radically by 1880, but the state's intense conservatism remained; indeed, it was reinforced by the experience of the war and

13. W. J. Thackston in *Baptist Courier*, September 6, 1888.

14. The classic statement of southern agrarian fears of manufacturing and the "mobs of great cities" appears in Thomas Jefferson, *Notes on the State of Virginia*, ed. William Peden (Chapel Hill: University of North Carolina Press, 1955), 164–65; see also Christopher G. Memminger to James H. Hammond, April 28, 1849, reprinted in Thomas P. Martin (ed.), "The Advent of William Gregg and the Graniteville Company," *Journal of Southern History*, XI (1945), 414; Eugene Genovese, *The Political Economy of Slavery* (New York: Pantheon, 1965), 228–33.

Reconstruction, which had left the dominant element with its own special vision of the horrors of social upheaval. While the new middle class was avid for economic development, it was equally anxious that the social patterns it had inherited, which provided it with spiritual solace as well as economic protection, remain unshattered by the forces of change.

"Cotton mill paternalism," or more accurately the celebration of cotton mill paternalism, was the principal means by which the new industrialists and their apologists sought to reassure their fellow citizens that they had nothing to fear from the creation of a wage-earning white industrial class. The term *paternalism* must be handled with care. First, the practice was by no means uniquely southern. American manufacturers had concerned themselves with the control and education of their employees from the days when apprentices lived under their masters' roofs; the involvement of antebellum northern industrialists with the personal lives of their employees, and its later elaboration into "welfare capitalism," were to some degree an extension of the colonial ideal of "family government."[15] Furthermore, it is misleading to call southern mill villages "industrial plantations," insofar as that implies a correlation between southern white mill workers and black slaves.[16] As the remainder of this volume will argue, a white supremacist society could not even admit the suggestion that free-born white men could be "enslaved" without potentially explosive consequences. Finally, it must be borne in mind that "paternalistic" controls had a variety of uses, both broadly social and narrowly self-interested. Mill controls over villages were used to regulate the labor supply,

15. For a description of "paternalism" in northern cotton mills, see Anthony F. C. Wallace, *Rockdale: The Growth of an American Village in the Early Industrial Revolution* (New York: Alfred A. Knopf, 1978), 298–337; see also Caroline F. Ware, *The Early New England Cotton Manufacture: A Study in Industrial Beginnings* (New York: Russell and Russell, 1931), 200–203, 256–60, 284–85; and Stuart D. Brandes, *American Welfare Capitalism, 1880–1940* (Chicago: University of Chicago Press, 1976).

16. As do Melton A. McLaurin in *Paternalism and Protest: Southern Cotton Mill Workers and Organized Labor, 1875–1905* (Westport, Conn.: Greenwood Press, 1971), 16–40; and Dwight B. Billings, Jr., *Planters and the Making of a "New South": Class, Politics and Development in North Carolina, 1865–1900* (Chapel Hill: University of North Carolina Press, 1979), 96–113; both essentially follow W. J. Cash, *The Mind of the South* (New York: Alfred A. Knopf, 1941), 200–201. See also C. Vann Woodward, *Origins of the New South, 1877–1913* (Baton Rouge: Louisiana State University Press, 1951), 223–24.

and to suppress strikes and unions; later, more enlightened "welfare capitalists" sought to use mill village institutions as means of improving their "human capital."

The principal significance of "paternalism" for present purposes, however, lies in its social justification; it was to protect the operatives, and thus society, from the demoralization that many South Carolinians saw implicit in industrial life. The "paternalistic" regime as it was presented to the public in the state, and occasionally the national, press, was epitomized by a group of six "model factory towns": Pelzer, on the Saluda River in Anderson County; Piedmont, five miles upstream in Greenville County; Clifton, on the Pacolet River east of Spartanburg; Pacolet, six miles downstream from Clifton; and Graniteville and Langley on Horse Creek, a small tributary of the Savannah River in Aiken County. All six were built around large mills with strong capital backing, and were located in sparsely populated areas where water power was available, thus necessitating the construction of complete new communities. Their presidents were considered the industrial leaders of the state; Ellison Smyth of Pelzer, H. P. Hammett of Piedmont, D. E. Converse of Clifton, and John H. Montgomery of Pacolet were collectively known as the "big four."[17]

The best publicized of these showplaces was Pelzer, an unincorporated town under the complete control of the Pelzer Manufacturing Company, which by 1900 boasted a population of around forty-five hundred. In a sense Pelzer was the successor to William Gregg's famous regime at Graniteville, for Ellison Smyth had read Gregg's pamphlets in his youth and later termed Gregg the decisive influence in his career. Smyth became one of the greatest masters of philanthropic rhetoric among South Carolina's mill magnates, sitting on the United States Industrial Commission and generally serving as liaison between the manufacturers and the public.[18] The town he founded and ruled was perhaps the most elaborate exam-

17. W. P. Jacobs, *The Pioneer* (Clinton, S. C.; Jacobs Press, 1935), 30. All four were six footers. After Hammett's death in 1891, his place was filled (in both senses) by James L. Orr, Jr. H. H. Hickman of Graniteville and W. C. Sibley of Langley lived in Augusta.

18. *Ibid.*, 30, 32; D. A. Tompkins, *Cotton Mill: Commercial Features* (Charlotte, N.C.: Private, 1899), 205, reported a copy of Gregg's *Essays in Domestic Industry* in Smyth's library.

ple of benevolent despotism to be found in South Carolina in the early stages of its industrialization.

The village of Pelzer was located on the western slope of the Saluda River valley, to the north of the factory. A single street, entering the town from the south past the mill buildings and the officials' houses, connected the inhabitants to the outside world; it ended in a central square on which the school was built and from which radiated the residential streets. There were one hundred and fifty "comfortable houses" of from four to six rooms each, supplied to the operatives at no charge.[19] There was no sewerage system, and the water supply came from wells, but the generators that supplied electric light to the mill provided it to the village as well.[20] Pelzer had no company store—Smyth disapproved of them and preferred to pay his employees in cash—but the company owned the four store buildings.[21] The government, of course, was completely in the hands of the company, which enforced its own regulations and employed a town marshall, appointed by the governor but paid by the mill. The kinds of regulations imposed ranged from prohibition of saloons ("no drunkenness; no midnight broils to disturb the peace and quiet of its sober and orderly people") to prohibition of dogs ("the fact that dogs are in ninety-nine cases out of a hundred worthless and troublesome property has been fully established").[22]

At the heart of mill philanthropy were the church and the school; according to the publicists, the company did well by both.

19. Charleston *News and Courier*, July 9, 1885. By 1901 a rental charge of fifty cents per room per month was levied at Pelzer; Spartanburg *Carolina Spartan*, March 22, 1893; Leonora Beck Ellis, "A Model Factory Town," *Forum*, XXXII (September, 1901), 63. The limited access to and from the village was evidently deliberate. In 1900 Smyth single-handedly derailed a proposal for an interurban rail line between Anderson and Greenville via Pelzer, largely because "easy and cheap communication with a larger and livelier town would tend to demoralize the operatives." Columbia *State*, April 6, 1900. Nonetheless, a line was subsequently constructed in the 1910s.

20. Jacobs, *The Pioneer*, 92. The overwhelming majority of mill houses in the state were equipped with privies at the time of the federal child labor investigation. U.S. Bureau of Labor, *Report on Condition of Woman and Child Wage Earners in the United States*, Senate Document No. 645, 61st Congress, 2nd Session (19 vols.; Washington: Government Printing Office, 1910), I, 526.

21. Charleston *News and Courier*, July 9, 1885; Jacobs, *The Pioneer*, 92. Cf. *Woman and Child Wage Earners*, I, 599.

22. Charleston *News and Courier*, July 9, 1885; Ellis, "Model Factory Town," 62.

The church building was donated by Mr. and Mrs. Francis J. Pelzer; a five-thousand-dollar edifice in Queen Anne style, it seated six hundred worshippers, boasted a twelve-stop organ, and was touted as "a gem in church architecture." It was intended for use as a union church, its facilities rotating among the Baptist, Methodist, and Presbyterian congregations. In addition to its provision of a building, from the early 1880s on the company made small semiannual donations to the principal congregations.[23] The first school at Pelzer was established for the benefit of the children of construction workers. In its early years it used a vacant building, but in the middle 1880s the company constructed a schoolhouse, which an observer in 1886 found well-equipped and presenting "the air of a city school." It was completely financed and operated by the mill, which kept it open to all the children of the village and the surrounding countryside at no charge, probably for a ten-month term. The school had one teacher, a young Wofford College graduate, in 1885; by 1890 there were three.[24]

As important as equipment and personnel to the success of the school was its efficiency in reaching the children, and there Smyth's links to Gregg were most evident. After his first two years at Pelzer, Smyth placed a record book in the superintendent's office listing the ages of all residents of the town; also, at that time or later he inserted two clauses into the family work contract, one requiring attendance at school for all children between the ages of five and twelve, the other requiring all children over twelve to take jobs in the mill unless excused by the superintendent. Families failing to meet the stipulations of the contract were liable to dismissal and eviction from the village. Toward the end of the century Smyth supplemented this stick with a carrot by offering ten cents a month to each school child with a perfect attendance record for the previous month.[25]

23. *Baptist Courier*, January 15, 1885; Pelzer Manufacturing Company Receipt Book, 1881–1896 (Microfilm copy in SCL).

24. Charleston *News and Courier*, July 9, 1885, November 6, 1886; Jacobs, *The Pioneer*, 101; *Palmetto School Journal*, I (1890), 108. The statewide average length of term in 1885 was three and one-half months. South Carolina State Superintendent of Education, *Report, 1885*, in South Carolina General Assembly, *Reports and Resolutions, 1885*, 708.

25. Jacobs, *The Pioneer*, 101; S.C. State Supt. of Educ. *Report, 1900*, 138–40. Cf.

The Pelzer Manufacturing Company stood to reap great benefits from its educational philanthropy. Smyth credited his interest in education to his regrets at having had to leave school in order to join the Confederate army, and to a fervent belief in providing opportunity for advancement to the children under his charge. However, he was also concerned with "making improvements in their ideals of life and in their appreciation of the responsibilities of citizenship." What those ideals and responsibilities were can be inferred from his own "ideal" of the "perfect workman": "a high-toned moral life, loyalty to his friends and to his employer, honesty in fulfilling his contracts and in giving full return for value received." Outside observers shared his views, as witness the correspondent applauding "the good sense of the company in thus providing for the mental and moral culture of the children that are to become one day the operatives in the factory and the citizens of the town." While "education for citizenship" was an important long-range goal, the mill received more immediate benefits in public relations. The presence of the school, "appreciated by the thoughtful employees," assured the outside world that Pelzer was not a festering sore on the body of civil society, and the policy of admitting rural pupils at no charge provided a public service and helped counter suspicions of the mill in the countryside.[26]

Public relations played a role in other mill philanthropies as well, a far more important role than has commonly been noted. In fact, the realities of mill "welfare work" generally fell far short of the shining ideal depicted in the contemporary accounts of Pelzer, but those realities were usually obscured by promotional verbiage. The most common distortion was to applaud the mills for "benefactions" that were simply community necessities. The authors of the federal government's 1910 *Report on Woman and Child Wage Earners* refused to consider mill-owned housing and mill construction of schools and churches as "welfare work," reasoning that in

---

Graniteville Manufacturing Company, Rule Books, 1861–1867 (in SCL); Broadus Mitchell, *William Gregg: A Factory Master of the Old South* (Chapel Hill: University of North Carolina Press, 1928), 76–85.

26. Jacobs, *The Pioneer*, 93, 94, 101; Charleston *News and Courier*, November 6, 1886.

most cases the mills could not attract workers without building complete communities for them, and further noting that the mills themselves usually treated the expenditures as costs of doing business. In South Carolina in the late nineteenth century it was assumed that any cotton mill building in an isolated area was obliged at least to supply its employees with a school and a church. In fact, on occasion a mill promoter would use the putative saving of expense on community facilities as an argument for building a mill in town. In many cases, then, the mills were doing little more than what was generally expected of them. Nonetheless, when a mill donated a church or built a school its deed was usually hailed as philanthropic.[27]

A closer look at the mill schools suggests both the degree to which mill "welfare work" was exaggerated by publicity and the severe limits placed on mill philanthropy by its ultimate subjection to the interest of the firm. To begin with, the expenses of even the best mill schools weighed hardly at all on the pocketbooks of their corporate sponsors. As late as 1910, according to a prominent mill president, the total mill investment in school houses amounted to about one third of one percent of the total capital invested in cotton manufacturing; no mill spent as much as 1 percent of its capital a year on welfare work. As a former student recalled, in the 1880s the Graniteville Academy was well endowed, with a comfortable building, comparatively highly paid teachers, a dedicated principal, and free textbooks, all supplied at no charge for nine months a year. Even so, during the thirty-one-year administration of President Hickman the Graniteville Company spent an average of one thousand dollars a year on the school; the total amounted to less than 2 percent of the total amount of dividends paid during the period, around 3 percent of the total expenditures made on plant and equipment, and less than 5 percent of the cash reserve held by the company at the time of Hickman's retirement in

27. *Woman and Child Wage Earners*, I, 596; Charleston *News and Courier*, January 28, 1881, May 1, 1883. The most flagrant example of the practice is August Kohn, *The Cotton Mills of South Carolina* (Columbia: South Carolina Department of Agriculture, Commerce, and Immigration, 1907), which cited even the most niggardly expenditures of the mills as if they were major benefactions.

1899.[28] Graniteville charged no tuition; some other mills, however, supplemented the meager state funds with student fees, which frequently hampered the access of mill children to the schools.[29]

While much was made of the encouragement of education by mill officials, no corporation besides Pelzer and Smyth's mill at Belton took particularly elaborate measures to compel attendance. Only two other mills are known to have insisted upon schooling for young children in the postbellum period. William C. Sibley, president of the Langley Manufacturing Company, informed a committee of the United States Senate that at the time he took control "we had about a hundred and fifty urchins running around loose"; he promptly ordered all children in the village over the age of five into school. Sibley was pleased with the results: "Our people are fully 150 per cent more civilized than they were when the village was commenced."[30] In Graniteville, on the other hand, William Gregg's compulsory attendance rule was abrogated by the directors in 1869, shortly after the accession of Hickman to the presidency of the firm. There was at the time, Hickman later testified, "a great deal of dissatisfaction" with Gregg's school policies, and a petition of "citizens" had protested compulsory attendance. Neither the cause nor the source of the discontent is certain. Hickman himself viewed education beyond literacy as demoralizing to the work force, and the petitioners may well have been high-ranking employees wishing to place their children in a better school than the Graniteville Academy; on the other hand there is evidence for this period of operative resistance to schooling.[31] For whatever rea-

28. Thomas Fleming Parker, "The South Carolina Cotton Mill Village—A Manufacturer's View," *South Atlantic Quarterly*, IX (1910) (offprint), 4–5; W. E. Woodward, *The Way Our People Lived* (New York: Liveright, 1944), 354; Columbia *State*, April 22, 1899.

29. Spartanburg *Carolina Spartan*, June 28, 1882, September 12, 1883, December 21, 1887, January 18, 1888; Howard B. Clay, "Daniel Augustus Tompkins: An American Bourbon" (Ph.D. dissertation, University of North Carolina at Chapel Hill, 1950), 118; Marjorie Potwin, *Cotton Mill People of the Piedmont: A Study in Social Change* (New York: Columbia Univerity Press, 1927), 43.

30. U.S. Congress, Senate Committee on Education and Labor, *Report . . . Upon the Relations Between Labor and Capital, and Testimony Taken by the Committee* (4 vols.; Washington: Government Printing Office, 1885), IV, 796.

31. *Ibid.*, IV, 738, 745–47, 796; D. D. Wallace, "A Hundred Years of William Gregg and Graniteville" (Typescript, 1946, in David Duncan Wallace Papers, South Carolina His-

son, compulsion was rare, and the quality of enforcement in the few places where it existed was debatable. Although Smyth reported in 1900 that the Pelzer Company paid out $450 in perfect attendance awards over the school term, a federal investigation a few years later found that the compulsory attendance regulation was being widely ignored both at Pelzer and at Belton.[32]

Compulsory attendance, at any rate, was probably a meaningless luxury, given the quality of the schools. Few aspects of mill paternalism were as clouded by promotional rhetoric as the quality of mill education, but a rough profile can be drawn from scattered sources. It cannot be denied that in some cases the mill schools were good. The larger firms set the pace, running their schools for as long as forty weeks in the year and paying their teachers salaries comparable to those in the towns.[33] Even where mill schools failed to meet the town standard they could defend themselves with the argument that they provided more educational opportunity than did the rural schools which were the alternative for the bulk of the operatives. The rural schools, however, provided an abysmal yardstick for measuring mill schools, which had in their sponsoring corporations a source of financial support far greater than anything the countryside could offer. While most mill schools were a step upward for the operatives, their benefits can only be rationally measured by comparing them with the town schools, which then provided the best available public instruction in the state.[34]

Some of the smaller mills maintained schools with standards little different from those in the country. The length of the school term was often brief; in 1900 the one-teacher school at Reedy River Factory in Greenville County ran for eighteen weeks, and the school at Lolo (Valley Falls), near Spartanburg, was open for eight. In 1902, the year of its organization, the school at Saxon, also near

---

torical Society, Charleston; Microfiche copy in SCL), 205–206; Jacobs, *The Pioneer*, 93; W. E. Woodward, *Way Our People Lived*, 354.

32. S.C. State Supt. of Educ. *Report, 1900*, 140; *Woman and Child Wage Earners*, I, 597.

33. S.C. State Supt. of Educ. *Report, 1900*, Tables 1, 2, and 8.

34. The rural comparison was made by, among others, A. B. Stallworth in Spartanburg *Carolina Spartan*, December 31, 1890; Potwin, *Cotton Mill People*, 43, 117.

Spartanburg, operated for four months.[35] As for quarters, the building used at Fingerville, in upper Spartanburg County, was described as an "old shack"; a spare house served as both church and school at Cherokee Falls in 1883. The school at D. A. Tompkins' Edgefield mill, run for some years by Tompkins' sister Grace, was held in a room over the local bank, and later in a church; as late as 1920 the state supervisor of mill schools felt obliged to comment that "if the mill insists on running a school it should build a decent schoolhouse."[36]

If the smaller mill schools lacked facilities, however, they were able to compensate by providing some degree of personal contact between teacher and pupil. Evidently intimacy was less common in the larger mill schools, especially after the middle 1880s. The school at Piedmont employed two teachers for one hundred pupils in 1883, and Clifton's 1886 enrollment of 140 was taught by three teachers. The number of pupils to each teacher, 50 and 47 respectively, seems high by our standards, but was not out of line with the 45.5 pupils assigned to each teacher in contemporary town and city schools. Other reports, however, indicate a shocking imbalance between teachers and pupils at the mills. In 1890 three teachers were in charge of 175 pupils at Pelzer. In 1885 a Miss Greenleaf taught 80 to 100 children at Pacolet. By 1889–1890 another teacher had been added at the Pacolet school, but the average attendance had risen to 130. In the fall of 1890 there were 179 students at Pacolet, and the principal was forced to admit that there was some crowding, although he assured the public that the mill was coming to the aid of the school with enlarged facilities and more teachers. Nonetheless, by 1900 President Montgomery himself was reporting that his school employed four teachers to handle an enrollment of four hundred! Such was the condition of the school kept by one of the state's largest and wealthiest mill cor-

35. S.C. State Supt. of Educ. *Report, 1900*, Table 1; Potwin, *Cotton Mill People*, 43. By comparison, in 1902 the statewide average length of term in white rural schools was 20.3 weeks. S.C. State Supt. of Educ. *Report, 1902*, 13.

36. Report of the state supervisor of mill schools, in S.C. State Supt. of Educ. *Report, 1920*, 172, 185; Charleston *News and Courier*, May 1, 1883; *Southern Christian Advocate*, April 3, 1902; Clay, "Tompkins," 117–19; Kohn, *Cotton Mills*, 158.

porations, whose head allegedly gave the school his personal attention and boasted of it that "there is not a better one in the Up-country."[37]

Even granting the gross inaccuracy of the 1900 school statistics, they tell a striking story. The six large mill districts then in existence in Spartanburg County enrolled 75 to 125 pupils for each teacher, or an average of 111.5. Langley reportedly had four teachers for 299 pupils, and Newry, the village of the Courtenay Manufacturing Company, had two teachers for 164. Even Pelzer, with an enrollment of 700, had a pupil-teacher ratio of between 67.3 and 88.2.[38]

To be sure, the inadequacies suggested by these figures were not wholly attributable to niggardliness or negligence. Some of the larger "mill villages" were becoming sizable industrial complexes comprising several mills; had they been incorporated, Piedmont's three thousand inhabitants would have qualified it as an "urban place," and Pelzer's forty-five hundred would have made it the second largest town in Anderson County and the eleventh largest in the state. The swelling numbers of operatives, many with large families, put pressure on mill school facilities. The problems arising from an influx of industrial workers were shared by the incorporated towns as well. Spartanburg, whose population doubled in the 1890s, had around sixty enrolled pupils to every school teacher in 1900, and in Gaffney, where population growth was even more rapid, each teacher dealt with an average of fifty-seven

37. Abbeville *Press and Banner*, August 1, 1883; Spartanburg *Herald*, November 3, 1886 (Industrial Issue); *Palmetto School Journal*, I (1890), 108; Charleston *News and Courier*, May 16, 1885, July 28, 1890; Spartanburg *Carolina Spartan*, December 31, 1890; S.C. State Supt. of Educ. *Report, 1900*, 142–43.

38. S.C. State Supt. of Educ. *Report, 1900*. The school figures reported for Pelzer illustrate the statistical confusion of the period. The enrollment was given as 673 by the Anderson County superintendent of education (p. 175), and as 706 by Smyth (p. 143); the Pelzer school superintendent reported 700 (p. 263). The county superintendent reported eight teachers, but the local superintendent reported himself and nine others. There appears to have been considerable uncertainty as to whether or not to report the principal or local superintendent as a teacher, even though supervisors in all but the larger city systems generally taught as well as administered. Any bias introduced by omitting the supervisor would fall most heavily on small multi-teacher schools such as existed at the larger mills. The school at Newry, for instance, was credited with only one teacher in the 1900 *Report*, but the *Carolina Teachers' Journal* (October, 1900), 14, reported two teachers there for the 1900–1901 session.

Table 5. ENROLLMENT, NUMBER OF TEACHERS, AND PUPIL-TEACHER RATIOS, LARGE MILL DISTRICTS, 1900

County	*Village*	*Enrollment*	*No. Teachers*	*Pupils/ Teacher*
Aiken:	Graniteville	343	6	57.2
	Langley	299	4	74.8
Anderson:	Pelzer	673	8	84.1
Greenville:	Piedmont[a]	609	7	87.0
	Mills Mill	101	1	101.0
	Sampson-Poe	126	2	63.0
Oconee:	Newry	164	2[b]	82.0
Spartanburg:	Clifton	716	6	119.3
	Glendale	125	1	125.0
	Pacolet	369	3	123.0
	Whitney	99	1	99.0
	Victor	65	1	65.0
	Tucapau	75	1	75.0
		Statewide		38.0
		Town and city schools		45.5[c]

SOURCE: South Carolina State Superintendent of Education *Report, 1900*: Table 1, pp. 172–213, unless otherwise noted.
[a]Represents districts in Anderson and Greenville counties.
[b]From *Carolina Teachers' Journal* (October 1900), 14.
[c]S.C. State Supt. of Educ. *Report, 1900*: Table 8, pp. 262–63.

pupils. Spartanburg and Gaffney were extreme cases among larger mill centers, however, even though some others were growing at faster rates. In general the pupil-teacher ratios maintained by town school districts serving mill populations ranged above the statewide average for town schools, but rarely did their average teaching loads range above fifty pupils per teacher.[39] Although the towns of South Carolina were suffering from growing pains at the turn of the century, they were handling their school problems far more efficiently than were the benevolent despots of the mills.

39. See Table 6.

Table 6. POPULATION GROWTH AND TEACHING LOADS IN TOWN SCHOOLS AND SELECTED MILL SCHOOLS

Name of Town	*Population Growth[a] 1890–1900*	*Pupils/ Teacher 1900*
Anderson	82.2	42.4
Columbia	37.5	49.7
Gaffney	141.4	56.6
Greenville	37.8	48.0
Greenwood	263.8	48.0
Newberry	52.5	39.3
Spartanburg	105.5	60.0
Union	235.6	49.3
	Average	49.5
Name of Mill		
Glendale	36.3	125.0
Pelzer	139.0	84.1
Piedmont	18.7	87.0
Whitney	123.2	99.0

SOURCE: *U.S. Census, 1890: Population, Pt. I*, 306–310; *U.S. Census, 1900: Population*, I, 350–55; S.C. Supt. of Educ. *Report*, 1900, Table 1, pp. 172–213.

[a] The populations of unincorporated mill villages were not reported in 1900; however, in some cases individual enumerators treated mill villages as minor civil divisions, thus allowing population figures to be tallied from the manuscript census returns, available on microfilm at the South Carolina Department of Archives and History, Columbia.

The mill schools sometimes handled their overcrowding problems by instituting shifts. The above-mentioned Miss Greenleaf taught her pupils at Pacolet in two shifts of three hours each, which, however, still required her to handle from forty to fifty students of varying educational levels in each class. A newspaper writer describing her school claimed that the use of the shift system demonstrated that "children well-taught three hours in the day will learn faster than if they are kept in school eight hours and poorly taught." One need not impugn Miss Greenleaf's competence, however, to suggest that such work loads were not likely to attract teachers with the requisite superhuman skill and dedication to make the mill school a success. Furthermore, the large numbers of pupils presented perhaps the least of the mill teacher's burdens, compared to such problems as indifference or hostility in the community, absenteeism, insubordination, and interference from mill officials.[40]

While teachers were hard pressed by the inadequacies of the mill schools, the consequences bore most heavily upon the children of the community. Certainly the notoriously low enrollments at mill schools resulted at least in part from poor facilities. In 1882 a local observer estimated that there were 340 to 350 children aged six to sixteen in Clifton, and that an adequate school would require seven or eight good teachers, yet as late as 1890 only four teachers served an industrial complex which had grown large enough to require two separate buildings. Cliftonians were better equipped with school facilities than were the mill people of Columbia's Ward Five, however. None of the three mills with villages within the city limits provided schools for their operatives; that task they left to the city school system, whose response was wretched. Only in 1904 was the "experiment" of a mill school attempted, using a mill-owned building but financed and operated by the Columbia school district. Much to the astonishment of local officials, the mill children "flocked to it with an unexpected enthusiasm which almost submerged the new enterprise."[41]

Overcrowding of the schools was "mitigated" not only by low enrollments but also by irregular attendance. Data prior to the turn of the century is scanty but suggestive. In 1899 the Blossom Street School in Columbia, which drew many of its pupils from the

40. *Woman and Child Wage Earners*, I, 579. A variation on the shift system appeared at Pelzer, where some children, "whose families need their help," worked part-time in a special room at one of the mills, which shut down early so that they could receive half a day's schooling. Ellis, "Model Factory Town," 63; "Bill Arp" in Columbia *State*, November 17, 1899.

41. Spartanburg *Carolina Spartan*, June 28, 1882, September 10, 1890; Columbia *State*, December 11, 1897, November 28, 1898, November 22, 1900; *Woman and Child Wage Earners*, VII, 248. See also *Our Monthly* (Thornwell Orphanage, Clinton, S.C.), XXXVI (1899), 242; XLVI (1909), 360.

mill district, reported an enrollment of 120 but an average attendance of only 50; the local school superintendent complained that "the attendance of most of those who belonged to school was so irregular as to make real progress next to impossible." A mill pastor making an otherwise vociferous defense of the Pacolet Valley mills in 1893 had to admit that mill school attendance was proportionately low.[42] The principal source of the problem was indicated by H. H. Hickman in 1883. After the abolition of compulsory attendance at Graniteville the practice developed among operative families there of alternating children between the mill and the school according to the vicissitudes of the family finances. Children would be put to work to help out when the family was in economic difficulty, but would return to school when and if good times returned. Replying in 1890 to the already common charge that mill children were removed from school and put to work at the earliest possible opportunity, A. B. Stallworth, the principal at Pacolet, reported that 39 percent of his enrolled pupils were over twelve years of age, and that 22 percent were over sixteen. If, as seems likely, most of the older pupils were in the elementary grades, their numerical strength suggests that a pattern of sporadic attendance similar to that in Graniteville was in operation, especially in view of Stallworth's remark that the operative "could [not] send his children to school so long or so continuously as that man who is not dependent on his own labor or that of his children for support."[43]

Financial pressures on mill families may have been reinforced on occasion by direct pressures from mill management. It was the general rule among mills to require one worker per room per house; a child might thus be forced to take a mill job in order to save the family from dismissal and eviction. No cases of actual coercion have come to light prior to the twentieth century, but several cases appear in the record after 1900. Investigators in Co-

42. E. S. Dreher in Columbia *State*, November 23, 1899; Clay, "D. A. Tompkins," 117–19; J. D. Huggins in Spartanburg *Carolina Spartan*, April 5, 1893.

43. *Labor and Capital*, IV, 744; Stallworth in Spartanburg *Carolina Spartan*, December 31, 1890; *Woman and Child Wage Earners*, VII, 15. Pacolet was reportedly encouraging the practice in 1900; see Columbia *State*, December 30, 1900.

lumbia found fifteen cases of children pressed into service by the company; Grace Tompkins had to fight a running battle against her brother's mill to keep her pupils in school.[44]

There were, then, severe limits to the quality and efficiency of mill education in the late nineteenth century and afterward, limits set largely by the very mill sponsorship which was so highly valued by contemporaries. The low prevailing wages paid for mill work encouraged child labor and thus irregular attendance or nonattendance at school. More importantly, mill corporations were not educational institutions, and were rarely capable of administering a school. Publicity-conscious mill "philanthropists" tended to concentrate on supplying the more visible needs of the schools, such as buildings, furnishings, supplies, and staff, assets with which the occasional visitor could be impressed. However, they were lax in expanding school facilities to keep pace with swelling enrollments, and in hiring and evaluating teachers. Aside from Pelzer there was little concern with compulsory attendance; such social police work was irrelevant to the functioning of the mill, and might hurt the morale of a labor force whose chief concern was all too often simple survival. Above all, schooling was subordinate to the will of the stockholders, who demanded justification for all expenditures and were deeply suspicious of "frills"; the general low level of spending attested to their power. In the later words of a friendly critic, "they only make a show and noise, and appear to do what they do not do."[45]

Similar remarks can be made about the support of churches by the mills. It was rare for a village to begin its existence with a house of worship, even if the mill was in a remote area. Religious facilities were almost invariably of lower priority than the mill and the operatives' housing. Generally, church buildings were only

44. Wallace, "Hundred Years," 202; *Woman and Child Wage Earners*, VII, 55; Clay, "Tompkins," 120. Cf. *Woman and Child Wage Earners*, I, 574, describing a small mill school which the mill foremen treated routinely as a labor pool.

45. Thomas Fleming Parker, "Some Educational and Legislative Needs of South Carolina Mill Villages," *Bulletin of the University of South Carolina*, no. 24, Pt. 3 (January, 1911), 10; Parker, "The True Greatness of South Carolina," address to South Carolina Federation of Women's Clubs, May 1908 (n.p., n.d.), 9; the quote is from Parker, "The South Carolina Cotton Mill Village," 4.

erected after congregations had been established by local ministers, missionaries, or evangelists. In the self-contained mill towns the corporations were obliged at least to grant the use of some of their property for religious purposes, lest they should be thought "heathen." They also commonly contributed to the building fund and to the support of the church. Much of the "philanthropy," however, seems to have been designed less for the encouragement of religion than for its control. The larger, isolated mills preferred to build union churches, "in which all denominations might worship together, rather than for each to build a house for itself." The aim was to inhibit denominational bickering, and to a degree it worked; a Pelzer minister, for instance, praised "the harmony and love existing between the different denominations" there. By the same token, however, "unionism" placed strong obstacles in the path of any minister attempting to develop a strong, devout congregation. One Methodist minister complained that under the system "nothing definite is achieved, nothing definite undertaken"; W. P. Jacobs believed that it promoted "a lack of zeal and of true churchly spirit, and carelessness on the part of the operatives." The mills also used their power to determine which religious organizations were to be allowed in the village, discouraging activity on the part of sects they deemed disruptive.[46]

Mill support of the churches had its public relations aspects as well. While the stability imparted to the work force by the more orthodox varieties of Protestant Christianity was appreciated by some mill officials, they were hardly neglectful of the good will they could reap from their good works. The dedicatory services of the union churches at Pelzer and Clifton were gala affairs at which the benevolent donors basked in the praise of a grateful clergy. At Clifton, for example, the president of Wofford College compared the proceedings to the dedication of the Temple at Jerusalem, and the Presbyterian representative, in receiving the building for the denominations, "said a corporation was not required to erect any buildings except such as were necessary for their legitimate busi-

46. Spartanburg *Carolina Spartan*, November 5, 1884; *Southern Christian Advocate*, June 7, 1888; J. B. Hilson, *History of the South Carolina Conference of the Wesleyan Methodist Church of America* (Winona Lake, Ind.: Light and Life Press, 1950), 32, 82, 103.

ness, but this house was proof of the regard and kind consideration which the company had for its employees. It is generally believed that corporations have no souls, but that is certainly false as to the Clifton Company."[47] Manufacturers used their "munificence" to attach certain of the mill clergy to their service, using them as apologists for the industrial regime. For example, J. D. Huggins, the Baptist pastor at Clifton and Trough Shoals (Pacolet), became a vehement defender of his mill presidents, displaying on occasion almost shocking deference: "If there are such things as wrongs existing under the present labor system, I know of no men more capable or more sure of righting their wrongs than the noble mill presidents. I, for one, am willing to confide it to their wisdom and goodness. Let us leave it to them."[48]

Here, as with the schools, the praise of the mills' beneficence went beyond their actual performance. The Pelzer Manufacturing Company's annual contribution to the cause of Christ totaled two hundred dollars, divided among three or four denominations. The quality of church facilities at most mill villages provided targets for recurrent complaints in the religious press. Often in such cases a local minister would turn the ideology of mill paternalism against its progenitors, using bad publicity to shame management into making improvements. A few months after the state Methodist newspaper publicized the need for a new church building at Warrenville, in the Horse Creek Valley, the pastor announced the completion of a nine-hundred-dollar structure, toward which the mill had contributed the lot and four hundred dollars. Previously "the only place in town for religious services [had] been an old, rickety out-building, and with the exception of a very few, the people took no interest in it."[49] More rarely, there were cases of simple misrepresentation on the part of mills. A Methodist minister experienced in mill work reported that "in one of the villages where I preached is a Methodist church, and it has been publicized far and wide that it was built by the company, entirely free of charge to

47. Spartanburg *Carolina Spartan*, November 5, 1884, for Clifton; *Baptist Courier*, January 15, 1885, for Pelzer.

48. J. D. Huggins in Spartanburg *Carolina Spartan*, April 5, 1893.

49. Pelzer Manufacturing Company Receipt Book; *Southern Christian Advocate*, April 3, August 7, 1902.

everybody else, when the money to build the house came from the operatives and their interested friends, and from our Church Extension Board, which was the largest contributor to the building fund. In the last six years our mission, Sunday School and Church Extension Boards have put at least $1300 into that one church, and the mill company has given *nothing*."[50]

The paternal mill president was not as much in evidence about the mills as one might expect from the frequent expositions on his role as "educator" of the operatives. The popular image of the South Carolina cotton mill village as an "industrial plantation" is misleading if it is taken to imply that each community had its resident patriarch. In fact, the general trend, especially among the larger mills, was toward absentee presidents, as industrial leadership passed from old-time manufacturers such as Converse to the newer town classes, and as the more important industrialists built or took over new mills. Unlike his predecessor Gregg, H. H. Hickman of Graniteville chose to live in Augusta, as did W. C. Sibley of Langley. Both Hammett and Orr lived in Greenville, in order to stay close to friends and keep track of their various interests. In the middle 1880s they were joined there by Smyth, who lived at Pelzer just long enough to put his enterprise on a firm footing. Montgomery, Fleming, Sloan, and John B. Cleveland continued to reside in Spartanburg after they became mill presidents. Although Converse and his brother-in-law A. H. Twitchell lived in Glendale throughout the 1880s, in 1890 both built houses and settled in Spartanburg. By 1914 over one fourth of the state's spindleage was controlled by sixteen mill presidents living in a single middle-class ward of the City of Greenville. Undoubtedly the principal attraction of the towns for mill presidents was business convenience, but class ties and a predilection for "urban" amenities were also important. In 1896 a Yorkville man considered purchasing a small, isolated mill in Chester County, but changed his mind after an inspection of the premises. "I was so impressed with the uninviting surroundings, lack of educational facilities and civilized society,

50. Foster Speer, *Southern Christian Advocate*, March 9, 1905. Speer, though, insisted that "it is the exception, not the rule, of which we speak."

etc., that I decided that I would not move my family down there for the whole outfit as a gift."[51]

When the president of a mill lived elsewhere, day-to-day authority over the mill and its village fell to the superintendent. Some superintendents, such as Thomas Rennie of Graniteville, became as well-known within the state as any of the leading mill presidents. They generally shared the class outlook of their superiors, even though they themselves typically rose from the operative ranks, either in New England or, increasingly as time went on, the South.[52] They usually had a personal interest in the welfare and moral tone of the communities they administered, for, unlike many mill presidents, they resided in the villages and raised their families there. However, they also had jobs to do, the most important of which was to keep the stockholders happy by turning a profit. Welfare work was inevitably subordinate to the balance sheet and was thus of comparatively low priority to a hired hand such as a superintendent. Replying to a later charge that the social problems of mill villages resulted from the moral indifference of superintendents, a sympathetic mill pastor argued that most were in fact respectable and church-going, but had little control over their situation. "The superintendent then [in the middle 1890s] only demanded of the operatives what the president demanded of him; the president demanded what the directors demanded of him; the directors demanded what the stockholders demanded of them. The stockholders demanded large dividends and there is where the driving began and there is where the responsibility rests."[53]

51. Jacobs, *The Pioneer*, 97; Spartanburg *Carolina Spartan*, March 26, 1890; addresses of mill presidents are from *Directory of Greenville County, South Carolina Voters* (Greenville: W. S. Neville and Co., 1914); spindleage figures are from South Carolina Department of Agriculture, Commerce and Industries, Labor Division, *Report, 1914* (This series hereafter referred to as *Labor Division Report*). By 1914 only two presidents of mills in Greenville County still resided in their villages; both mills were small and rural.

52. W. E. Woodward, *The Gift of Life* (New York: E. P. Dutton, 1947), 38. As of 1903, thirty-eight mill superintendents had served their apprenticeships at Piedmont. Abbeville *Press and Banner*, August 1, 1883; S. S. Crittenden, *The Greenville Century Book* (Greenville: Press of Greenville News, 1903), 67.

53. W. J. Snyder, "'A Solution of the Cotton Mill Problem,'" *Southern Christian Advocate*, March 11, 1909, replying to D. E. Camak, "A Practical Solution to the Cotton Mill Problem," *Methodist Review*, XVIII (1909), 67–69.

Some superintendents did manage both duties with some success. W. F. Walker gained quite a reputation both for his ability to restore financial health to sluggish enterprises and for his strict moral discipline. Rennie "did what he could" to continue "the Gregg tradition of keeping Graniteville pious, virtuous and highly respectable" despite "a lot of sympathy deep down in his make-up for sinners and ne'er-do-wells," but even Graniteville declined in rigor from the days of Gregg's "moral despotism."[54] The lax enforcement of the education clause of Smyth's contracts by his superintendents suggests the possible gap between even the most sincere policy of "uplift" enunciated by the president of a mill and its actual execution by men whose jobs hung mainly on the profit margin.

Certainly the moral control exercised by the mills was not as tight as one might expect from the propaganda. Prohibitionists could bubble over "bright, smiling, happy, prosperous, sober Piedmont . . . in which there is not a solitary drunkard," but the saloons and bootleggers of Greenville were a mere ten miles away, and it was not for naught that the Friday evening train from the Mountain City was known locally as the "jug train." Liquor selling remained forbidden at Graniteville during the Hickman-Rennie regime, but mill jurisdiction did not reach the three saloons of nearby Madison, where "a man could get pleasantly drunk for fifty cents and dead drunk for a dollar." There was also a thriving bottle trade for women and "respectable" citizens. There was evidently little effort on the part of the mill to enforce sobriety.[55] Among the many labor problems faced by D. A. Tompkins at Edgefield were the "blind tigers" of a nearby shanty town, which allegedly sold their wares even to eight-year-old children. In the late 1880s and early 1890s Trough Shoals was surrounded by "drug stores" which were thinly disguised saloons: "All that was necessary to start one was a little calomel, castor oil, paregoric,

54. D. E. Camak, "The Power of One Man for Good," *Methodist Review*, XVI (1907), 482–86; W. E. Woodward, *Gift of Life*, 38; Wallace, "Hundred Years," 202–207.

55. *Southern Christian Advocate*, May 6, 1885; Spartanburg *Carolina Spartan*, July 12, 1882, February 5, 1890; A. S. Rowell Scrapbook (on microfilm, in SCL); W. E. Woodward, *Way Our People Lived*, 324, 334. Cf. Mitchell, *William Gregg*, 82–85, especially *re* "Wooleytown," the probable ancestor of Madison.

and a few barrels of whiskey. Back behind the whiskey a doctor sat, pen in hand, ready to sign a prescription for any one who stated that he did not feel well, and that he thought a little whiskey would do him good."[56]

Nor were other forms of good behavior besides sobriety universal in mill villages. Observers expressed enthusiasm over the deportment in the self-contained mill towns, which the rowdier operatives had to leave in order to have their fun. Mill villages adjoining towns, however, were apt to be different. As early as 1881 the operatives at Camperdown in Greenville were requesting that a city policeman be appointed to reside in the village and protect their homes and sensibilities from "young men and half-grown boys who roam about the streets tearing down fences, unhinging gates, and using the most horribly profane and indecent language." "Operative," writing in the Newberry *Herald and News*, grumbled that "while the children of God are worshipping in the chapel, we find the devil over on the hill 'going about as a roaring lion seeking whom he may devour,' carrying on a frolic." Even Graniteville had by the middle 1870s developed a reputation for violence. In general, Smyth's attempt at thoroughgoing personal control found few imitators. His most quixotic ordinance, the dog prohibition, could be found nowhere else, although it would have been endorsed by sleepless operatives all over the Piedmont.[57]

Why was there such a gap between rhetoric and achievement in the 1880s and 1890s? Furthermore, why was so little attention paid to it? An important reason for the apathy of South Carolina's middle class toward mill conditions was its overwhelming desire for economic growth, which, it was aware, depended upon cultivating an image of the state as a safe haven for capital, both "foreign" and local. "At this period of turmoil and doubt in the business world," said the Columbia *Register* in 1886, "South Carolina

56. Clay, "Tompkins," 120; Spartanburg *Carolina Spartan*, December 7, 14, 1892.

57. Newberry *Herald and News*, July 7, September 15, 1887; Wallace, "Hundred Years," 210; Greenville *Daily News*, February 1, October 18, November 23, 1881: "It is stated that there is one canine to every three human beings, and that each of the said canines average[s] at least one visitor a night. They hold caucusses [*sic*] and organize debating societies and have tea parties, all of which habitually break up in disturbances."

holds out special inducements to capital to locate in its quiet and peaceful borders." These inducements came at a price; the *News and Courier* warned its readers that "capital will not come to the South, unless they who have money to invest are sure that it will be exposed to no other hazards than those inseparable from commercial adventure. Any disregard of law, any revolutionary legislation, any threats against capitalists, discourage investments in the South and thrust from her the capital, which is anxious to come here for development in a way that will be profitable to the lender." *The State*, whose editor was more sensitive to the broadly social needs of the state than was his counterpart at the *News and Courier*, nonetheless found it necessary to place social advance behind economic growth in priority: "The State suffers no evils from the presence of capital which are at all comparable to the great evil of the hostility and abstention of capital. South Carolina is not even in a position to enact such laws as can safely be enacted in richer States. The borrower cannot make terms like the lender."[58]

Since the most cherished desire of the state's leading citizens was for economic development and prosperity, the inclination was to revere the men who brought them. Dean Swift's dictum about the economic innovator as philanthropist was frequently echoed in the local press, as in this example from *The State*: "If according to the teachings of sound political economy, the man that causes two blades of grass to grow where but one grew before should be rated as a public benefactor, then certainly he who gives constant and remunerative employment to many persons in the community that would otherwise be idle and in want perhaps of the commonest necessities of life ought to be looked upon as a much greater public benefactor." "Citizen," writing in the same newspaper, used the doctrine of Christian stewardship to urge Columbia's capitalists to place their money in productive enterprise rather than in speculation or usury; it was the part of virtue, he argued, to provide for the city's prosperity rather than to fatten on its adversity. A Clifton resident was awed by D. E. Converse, "the busiest man in the

58. Columbia *Register*, quoted in Newberry *Herald and News*, June 2, 1886; Charleston *News and Courier*, February 21, 1879; Columbia *State*, November 29, 1892.

county, [who] is doing more for the county than any other man in it. Every plan of his fertile brain, every purpose is for the advancement of the material resources and advantages of the county in which he lives."[59] If the above sentiments remind the reader of Broadus Mitchell's "philanthropic" interpretation of "the rise of the mills," it should be noted that the prevailing definition of "philanthropy" covered a broad range of behavior. A pious Greenville industrialist, touring J. B. Duke's nineteen-hundred-acre estate in New Jersey, was impressed by the goodness of the tobacco baron in giving jobs to the 150 estate workers and using them to create "beauty for people to look at"![60]

The factors cited above were important in inhibiting expressions of concern over the fate of industrial South Carolina. However, neither desire for economic growth nor the enormous prestige of the industrialists had diminished appreciably by the turn of the century, when the "cotton mill problem" became a topic of current concern. As we will see later, the mill presidents remained untouched in their social position even as debate raged over the condition of their workers. The principal difference between the period prior to 1900 and the early twentieth century was not so much the greater social concern of the latter period as the social naïveté of the former. South Carolinians of the Progressive era confronted the social changes brought by the cotton mill in a recognizably "modern" manner, dealing with them as "social problems" to be solved by concerted, rational effort. Their predecessors, however, found it difficult to think in such environmentalist terms. For them, all social questions were reduced to matters of individual virtue, virtue which, they believed, resided peculiarly in "Anglo-Saxon" racial stock. Occasional dissenters who suggested that factory life might alter for the worse those swept up by it could be silenced by the charge that they were insulting the virtue of the white race; mill apologists could thereby enlist in their be-

59. Columbia *State*, April 15, 1892; "Citizen" and editorial, *ibid.*, January 20, 1895; Spartanburg *Carolina Spartan*, September 27, 1882.

60. John T. Woodside Autobiography (MS in Southern Historical Collection, University of North Carolina at Chapel Hill), 61.

half the boundless capacity of South Carolinians to make fools of themselves for the sake of their "honor."

The contention that South Carolina's mill hands posed no threat to the social order because of their racial heritage rested, of course, on the virtually exclusive use by the mills of native white labor. Their reliance on native whites was by no means automatic; indeed, the use of immigrants and blacks as alternative sources of labor was intermittently discussed throughout the period. Interest in the possibilities of "foreign" help was particularly strong in the period immediately following the Civil War, when an influx of whites was desired to dilute the potential political and economic power of blacks, and when a body of skilled workers was deemed necessary for the state's industrial upbuilding. However, it proved difficult to obtain the "right kind of immigration." Southerners wanted northern Europeans, especially Germans, at a time when the ethnic makeup of the immigrant flow was increasingly Mediterranean and Slavic. Immigrants were repelled by southern xenophobia and southern poverty alike, preferring the ethnic enclaves and broader opportunities of the North.[61] South Carolinians, for their part, had looked askance at immigrants since antebellum times. They were feared as potential carriers of alien ideas, and their ethnic distinctiveness posed a threat to the continuing legitimacy of the vaunted southern culture. One scholar has even suggested that fear of the alien contributed materially to the inhibition of industry in the South before the Civil War.[62] Similar attitudes appeared after Appomattox, reinforced by the increasing identification of the North in general, and the New England textile industry in particular, with the immigrant. Protestant churchmen worried openly about the prospect of a Romanist deluge, and feared in addition that "the coming of foreigners into our midst"

61. Broadus Mitchell, *The Rise of Cotton Mills in the South* (Baltimore: Johns Hopkins University Press, 1921), 200–207, is a good, albeit idiosyncratic, account. Other statements of interest in immigration include Greenville *Daily News*, June 2, 21, 1881; Charleston *News and Courier*, April 13, 1881. On deterrents to immigration, see Winnsboro *News and Herald*, cited *ibid.*, May 16, 1881. On the "right kind" of immigration see *Southern Christian Advocate*, June 7, 1888; cf. Paul M. Gaston, *The New South Creed: A Study in Southern Mythmaking* (New York: Alfred A. Knopf, 1970), 76–78.

62. Genovese, *Political Economy*, 231–32.

might compromise "the boasted purity of the morals and chivalric spirit and character of the Southern people." Church editors warned that the South, like the North, might soon become "the receptacle of . . . isms, errors, and immoralities, from almost every nationality under heaven."[63]

The low opinions held of immigrant workers in the North filtered southward and were accepted there. According to a Massachusetts man, cited in the *News and Courier*, the French Canadians then pouring into the New England mill towns were the eastern equivalents of the Chinese laborers on the west coast: immoral, migratory, indifferent to education. Another northerner, reporting glowingly on southern mill conditions to the New York *Tribune*, nonetheless warned that "if the time ever comes when many foreigners are employed in southern mills, most of the conditions which I have described will be changed."[64]

The manufacturers themselves were ambivalent about foreign labor, their desire for it in time of labor shortage conflicting with distrust of its turbulence and alien ways. In 1895 D. A. Tompkins advised the South to spurn the offers of New Englanders seeking to build southern mills; they might bring New England labor with them, he warned, and "there is a type of foreign, or half-foreign, restless, dissatisfied labor there whose influence is irritating and injurious alike to the manufacturer and to the better class of labor."[65] Within the decade, though, Tompkins and other mill presidents were pressing for immigration as the solution to their increasing labor supply problem. The movement in South Carolina was led by Thomas Fleming Parker of the Monaghan Mill, the head of the Immigration Committee of the Cotton Manufacturers' Association of South Carolina. In 1906 the committee went so far

63. *Southern Christian Advocate*, May 24, 1888; *Baptist Courier*, January 22, 29, 1885; *Our Monthly*, XLIII (1906), 310.

64. Charleston *News and Courier*, February 13, 1883, May 11, 1881.

65. Tompkins in Baltimore *Manufacturers' Record*, quoted in Columbia *State*, February 21, 1895. Tompkins' allegations make little sense, as it was well known that New England mills moved South chiefly in order to exploit southern labor. It is likely, then, that Tompkins had ulterior motives in making his argument. The bulk of his business consisted of "packaging" small cotton mills for groups of local investors; large New England manufacturers would do no business with him, and the expectation of northern development would inhibit the sort of local "self-help" from which Tompkins benefited.

as to import several hundred central Europeans through the port of Charleston, in cooperation with the South Carolina Department of Agriculture, Commerce, and Immigration. By the next year, however, Parker had cooled to immigration, complaining to Tompkins that the foreigners were "filled with socialistic ideas and irreligion." The imported workers, whose expectations about their new homes and jobs had been unduly raised, proved troublesome; the easing of the labor shortage through the extensive recruitment of mountaineers, coupled with the economic slowdown following the Panic of 1907, further dampened the manufacturers' interest. Finally, an upsurge in political opposition to the state's role in promoting immigration forced the General Assembly to terminate the program in 1909.[66] Interest in outside sources of mill labor was thus spasmodic at best; such flurries aside, mill men neither needed nor wanted significant immigration.

Immigrants had to be imported, or at least enticed to the state; blacks, however, were at the mills' doorstep. Furthermore, slaves had been used extensively in manufacturing of all sorts in the South before the Civil War, even working alongside whites. In South Carolina, slave labor predominated in mills located in the central and lower portions of the state through the late 1840s. However, industrial slavery in textiles began a decline during the sustained cotton boom of the 1850s, with its attendant upward pressure on slave prices. Rising labor costs and the attraction of capital into agriculture virtually exterminated the low-country mills, while others shifted to free white workers; by 1860 only one tiny mill still made use of slaves.[67] The temporary economic tur-

66. R. Beverley Herbert, "Immigration to South Carolina" (MS enclosed in Herbert to David R. Coker, August 24, 1923, in David R. Coker Papers, SCL), 11–13; Kohn, *Cotton Mills*, 199–206; Clay, "Tompkins," 270–73. On the history of the South Carolina Department of Agriculture, Commerce, and Immigration, see its *Reports, 1904–1908*; *South Carolina Statutes at Large*, XXIV (1904), 449–52; XXVI (1909), 14–18; on opposition to the work of the department, see Columbia *State*, February 19, 20, 1908; Union *Progress*, August 11, 18, 1908.

67. Robert S. Starobin, *Industrial Slavery in the Old South* (New York: Oxford University Press, 1970), 12–14; Allen Heath Stokes, Jr., "Black and White Labor and the Development of the Southern Textile Industry, 1800–1920" (Ph.D. dissertation, University of South Carolina, 1977), 98–132; Ernest M. Lander, *The Textile Industry in Ante-Bellum South Carolina* (Baton Rouge: Louisiana State University Press, 1969), 71–80, 88–91. My

moil brought by Emancipation further discouraged the use of blacks, who by 1870 had virtually vanished from southern cotton manufacturing.[68] Black labor could nonetheless have been obtained during the postwar period at rates lower than whites would accept; in 1880 Superintendent Howland of Graniteville asserted that an all-black mill with white overseers might operate 40 percent more cheaply than an all-white mill. However, the *de facto* elimination of blacks from the mills was accompanied by a social definition of textile labor as "white" work, as manufacturers sought to attract the "better class" of native whites to tend their machinery. Under these circumstances an integrated work force would wreak havoc with white operatives; the absence of a core of experienced blacks, on the other hand, dictated that an all-black mill would have to be run entirely with "green" hands, with predictably lower productivity. Of six manufacturers questioned by J. K. Blackman in 1880, four cited the unwillingness of whites to work with blacks, and three the unfamiliarity of blacks with manufacturing, as factors deterring their use. Although the Saluda Factory near Columbia mixed twenty-five blacks and seventy-five whites with complete satisfaction, other mill men concurred with Howland in viewing black labor as "experimental" and fraught with unnecessary risk. Only as the growth of the cotton textile industry began to put pressure on the supply of native whites would interest in such "experimentation" pass beyond the merely speculative.[69]

South Carolina's textile industry, then, stood poised on the

---

discussion of the question is especially indebted to Gavin Wright, "Cheap Labor and Southern Textiles Before 1880," *Journal of Economic History*, XXXIX (1979), 669–70.

68. While South Carolina's textile industry was virtually all white prior to Emancipation, some mills in other southern states evidently shifted to whites immediately afterward; Stokes, "Black and White Labor," 134; Frank J. Huffman, Jr., "Old South, New South: Continuity and Change in a Georgia County, 1850–1880" (Ph.D. dissertation, Yale University, 1974), 75; Leonard A. Carlson, "Labor Supply, the Acquisition of Skills, and the Location of Southern Textiles, 1880–1900," *Journal of Economic History*, XLI (1981), 71, on Alabama's Bell Factory. The son of the Bell Factory's owner later blamed the abandonment of black labor on Emancipation, which made blacks less easily controlled. *Labor and Capital*, IV, 48.

69. On these points see Wright, "Cheap Labor," 670, 679–80; Carlson, "Labor Supply," 70–71; Stokes, "Black and White Labor," 134; Blackman, *Cotton Mills, passim.* On later interest in black labor, see pages 158–60, 244–45 herein.

threshold of its most spectacular development dependent almost entirely on local whites as its work force. Of such, said the publicists, was the industrial Kingdom of Heaven. Hammett argued that "our material for operatives compares most favorably" with the French Canadians and the Irish of New England. He was echoed by the *News and Courier*, which spoke of "a native population, peculiarly suited by nature, character, morals, and intelligence to make efficient and industrious operatives."[70] If foreigners were associated with strange, dissolute ways and diabolical ideas, the "Anglo-Saxons" of the southern mills were described as incarnations of orderliness and virtue. Indeed, it was an affront to describe them otherwise, for any critical comment about mill workers was considered a slander against the racial and cultural heritage of white South Carolina.

The notion that "virtue" was somehow a racial characteristic of native southern whites had its roots in the principle which had undergirded southern society for two centuries, the identity of race and class. From the end of the seventeenth century to the Civil War the class of "dependent poor" had consisted almost entirely of black slaves. Above the "mud-sill," the dominant whites shared a roughly equal social and political status, reinforced by a wide diffusion of property holding. Great disparities of wealth were indisputably present, and inevitably produced pretension on the one hand and resentment on the other; nonetheless, few whites had to surrender control over their actions to a master or an employer, and the radical (white) egalitarianism of Jacksonian political culture restrained the arrogance of the rich.[71] "Virtue," of course, had

70. Greenville *Daily News*, July 29, 1881; Charleston *News and Courier*, August 1, November 5, 1881.

71. On the origins of the racial basis of class distinctions in the slave South, see Edmund S. Morgan, *American Slavery, American Freedom: The Ordeal of Colonial Virginia* (New York: Norton, 1975); its implications for the antebellum South are stated succinctly in George M. Fredrickson, *The Black Image in the White Mind* (New York: Harper and Row, 1971), Chap. 2; and extensively in J. Mills Thornton III, *Politics and Power in a Slave Society: Alabama, 1800–1860* (Baton Rouge: Louisiana State University Press, 1978). On the diffusion of landholding in the antebellum South, see Frank Owsley, *Plain Folk of the Old South* (Baton Rouge: Louisiana State University Press, 1949); on the distribution of wealth see Fabian Linden, "Economic Democracy in the Slave South: An Appraisal of Some Recent Views," *Journal of Negro History*, XXXI (1946), 140–89; and Gavin Wright, "'Economic Democracy' and the Concentration of Agricultural Wealth in the Cotton South, 1850–

been identified in traditional republican thought with the "independence" conferred by the ownership of property, in the South essentially a white prerogative.[72] In the course of the nineteenth century, though, the spread of explicitly racist social ideas produced a curious shift in the perceived relationship of "Anglo-Saxon" blood and republican virtue. Rather than being incidental to the economic "independence" of most whites and the enslavement of blacks, virtue came to be seen as an *innate* characteristic of the white man. Thus freed from its social basis, belief in the moral superiority of *all* southern whites could persist in the face of social changes, such as Emancipation, industrialization, and the rise of white tenancy, which increasingly blurred the distinction between "independent" whites and "enslaved" blacks.

Native white workers, descended as they were from the embattled farmers of the Revolutionary age, thus had, according to industrial promoters, republican virtue for their racial heritage. A New England manufacturer touring the state spoke of "the lack of foreign or socialistic ideas" in South Carolina, where "the sacred protection to property had descended from the forefathers." A Columbia newspaper extolled the absence of "aggregations of Communistic foreigners" in the mill villages, noting that the operatives were "mostly natives of the State, identified with her people and having close family ties with every other class." The *News and Courier* answered those who feared the development of a mill class by arguing that upward mobility was "the very first principle instilled into her offspring by this great and glorious Republic"; immigrants might remain at the bottom of the ladder, but native Americans could not be held down.[73] Not only were the operatives efficient, obedient, and ambitious, but the women, at least, were

---

1860," *Agricultural History*, XLIV (1970), 63–93. The antebellum social structure, and postbellum transformation, of a region similar to the upper reaches of the South Carolina Piedmont is eloquently recounted in Steven H. Hahn, "The Roots of Southern Populism: Yeomen Farmers and the Transformation of Georgia's Upper Piedmont, 1850–1890" (Ph.D. dissertation, Yale University, 1979).

72. Morgan, *American Slavery*, 376–81.

73. Charleston *News and Courier*, October 7, 1883, November 3, 1897; Columbia *Register*, quoted in Newberry *Herald and News*, June 2, 1886. See also Columbia *State*, July 12, 1894.

beautiful. According to Hammett, "the first thing which strikes the attention of visiting business friends from the north is the superior appearance of my operatives" compared to that of the alien hordes of Lowell. Southern mill girls were "tall, shapely, with well-poised heads and faces that would do for molds of beauty."[74]

To be sure, virtue, political or moral, was not universal even among these flowers of southern womanhood, and it was here that mill paternalism played its principal role. Like the New Englanders who built Lowell, the southern manufacturers laid major stress on the rigid moral controls placed on their operatives. No quality of mill life was as harped upon by its defenders as the moral climate of the mill village. Indeed, they felt this point to be so important that they often went out of their way to make it, as in the following example.

In 1887 one Thomas Barry, a member of the executive board of the Knights of Labor, made a tour of southern mill centers, which he sharply criticized in an interview given to a Philadelphia newspaper. As a friend of the working man, he made no invidious remarks on the characters of the operatives; the targets of his criticism were the mill owners and officials, and his accusations concerned material conditions, poor educational facilities, and child labor. Naturally his remarks caused an uproar, especially around Spartanburg, where D. E Converse and John H. Montgomery each penned lengthy replies. Montgomery, however, did not content himself with replying to Barry, but added some comments in vindication of female virtue at the mills. "Disreputable women," he averred, "are not permitted about our mills," citing as evidence the dismissal from employment at Pacolet of an unwed mother "with no especial sign of reform about her." "The young people are taught by the president and superintendent to lead virtuous and upright lives, and it is a rare thing for a girl to go astray." These expatiations on "the sober and virtuous habits of our factory population" had nothing to do with Barry; rather, they were directed at the concerns of the larger society.[75]

74. Spartanburg *Carolina Spartan*, April 23, 1884.
75. *Ibid.*, January 18, 1888.

While remarks on the "schooling" influence of the factory were usually included in such apologia, the essence of mill "paternalism" lay not in "uplift" but in exclusion from the community of the idle, vicious, or discontented hand. A correspondent of the *Carolina Spartan* asserted that "the cotton mill, when well managed, is a fine adjunct of the church," but he also stated that "when [operatives] move to these mills they take step with the best people, or get away." The officers at Clifton, it was said, were "scrupulously careful to exclude bad characters, whether male or female"; "no disreputable characters [were] tolerated or allowed to dwell" in Pelzer.[76]

Obviously the exclusionary powers of the mills provided them with enormous advantages in labor control, for they could eject from their premises not only women of easy virtue but anyone else they deemed injurious to their interests. These powers were used on several occasions in the 1880s to curb labor unrest, and during the Tillman regime to control political activity.[77] The social benefits of the policy, however, are debatable. One critic admitted the superior moral atmosphere of Piedmont, but ascribed it not to innate virtue among the workers but to the despotic power of Hammett. While the industrialist was "as good a man as there is in the State," the critic wondered "if this is not a fearful power with which to invest any man," and worried about the effects of paternalism on individualism and democracy.[78] More importantly, the emphasis on exclusion did not deal with the problems of industrialization at all, but merely papered them over and postponed their solution. The mill owners were able to select a congenial work force, and the larger society could rest assured that the new industry was not nourishing an incubus of vice and disorder. Despite the rhetoric, however, exclusion was not uplift.[79] It worked, if

76. *Ibid.*, May 17, 1893; Spartanburg *Herald*, November 3, 1886 (Industrial Edition); Charleston *News and Courier*, July 9, 1885.

77. Spartanburg *Carolina Spartan*, September 14, 1887, August 31, 1892; Charleston *News and Courier*, November 17, 21, 1886; W. E. Woodward, *Gift of Life*, 71–73.

78. Abbeville *Press and Banner*, August 1, 1883.

79. The "rotten apple" school was persistent. One day, well after the turn of the century, a social worker at a Greenville mill entered the president's office and announced,

at all, only as long as the mills were few and scattered, and the workers many and importunate. Insofar as it did work it benefited chiefly the mills, which removed the most adaptable workers from the rural population while leaving the masses untouched by the blessings of mill "civilization."

The emphasis on "Anglo-Saxon" superiority and individual virtue also inhibited the use of "paternalism" as an agency for molding the personalities of mill workers. Mill churches were mere transplantations of rural denominations, with subtle management influences designed chiefly to protect the interest of the firm. Similarly, mill schools were not primarily designed to transform operative children into citizens of a new industrial society; indeed, the very notion that the safety of the state rested at the least on universal literacy, contradicting as it did the belief in innate "Anglo-Saxon" virtue, was slow to develop. Schooling was offered primarily as a frill, an inducement to rural parents who, while poor, wished to provide advantages to their children. According to one mill principal, any parent "who really wishes to educate his children, and is willing to make personal sacrifices to do it," could see them through school at one of the larger mills. The facilities were far better than any country district could provide, and "in view of the better wages which he gets here" the operative "can keep his children in school longer than his neighbor in like circumstances on the farm." Other encouragement of education by manufacturers was chiefly rhetorical and clearly subordinate to the necessities of labor; thus the president of the Greenwood Mill "encourage[d] parents to send their children to school as regularly as circumstances will admit," and at Pacolet they were urged to alternate their children between mill and school "when help is plentiful." Education was not needed to create "new men" for industrial life; the old would do nicely.[80]

"Mr. Woodside, we have some bad people in the village who must be run out." An irritated Woodside replied (as he recalled), "If all the people were good we wouldn't need you." Woodside Autobiography. Marjorie Potwin operated in much the same fashion in the 1920s, even though she admitted that expulsion was "not subjectively constructive social work." *Cotton Mill People*, 105.

80. Spartanburg *Carolina Spartan*, December 31, 1890; Abbeville *Press and Banner*, September 27, 1889; Columbia *State*, December 30, 1900.

Both the policy of exclusion and the emphasis on the racial and social superiority of southern white workers were aspects of the more general notion that the problems faced by other industrializing societies were due not to factors characteristic of industrial life or periods of social change but to the characters of the people involved in the process. Wicked industrialists ground down their workers and sloughed off responsibility for the souls of their employees. The laboring class, on the other hand, was an immoral mongrel horde, prey to strange enthusiasms. So thinking, South Carolinians felt it sufficient assurance of social stability that the characters of the operatives be screened, and that both managers and operatives be of that noblest of races, the southern "Anglo-Saxon."

Such a placid view of a society in transition ignored reality, of course. In the first place, however "superior" its racial heritage, the new proletariat was being recruited from a society far different from that being created by the townspeople. The mill hands came from a rural world in which even tenant farmers and sharecroppers lived and worked to themselves, and in which education, social discipline, and citizenship held meanings different from those accepted in town.[81] Second, the impact of the factory system itself, both in molding the operatives and in retarding their assimilation to the world of the middle class, was only dimly perceived at the time. The effects of child labor, the formation of a working class, and the impact of the mill on family life were considerations that only slowly penetrated the consciousness of South Carolina's bourgeoisie. Like the operatives, the townspeople were still in large part products of the old rural South, flavored as it was with individualism and the evangelical emphasis on personal salvation. As a result, they assumed that all social problems could be reduced to questions of personal morality and racial propensity.

How the emphases on the person and on social and racial solidarity characteristic of the South Carolinian temperament in the

81. See Jacobs, *The Pioneer*, 91, for Ellison Smyth's description of his early labor force. For the rural social structure see Hahn, "Roots"; its cultural analogue is explored in Bertram Wyatt-Brown, "The Ideal Typology and Ante-Bellum Southern History: A Testing of a New Approach," *Societas*, V (1975), 1–29.

late nineteenth century could be used to silence criticism was illustrated by the response to the most thoroughgoing attack on the cotton mills to appear in South Carolina in the 1880s. What moved Hugh Wilson to take up the cudgels against the state's industrial salvation is not clear. As proprietor and editor of one of the more important "country" newspapers, the Abbeville *Press and Banner*, he had a widespread, and deserved, reputation for crankiness. He regularly took outrageous positions on a variety of issues, ranging from the cult of the Lost Cause (which he felt revered officers' horses more than it honored the Confederate foot soldier) to violence against blacks (he modestly proposed a "close season" on the killing of Negroes, to coincide with the growing season). He was grossly inconsistent; after flailing the "princely capitalists" in the 1880s he joined them in the 1890s, becoming a director of the local mill.[82] In fact, there is reason to believe that he was less than serious in his criticisms. Wilson loved a good fight and would embrace almost any pretext for causing a journalistic fracas. He was also a persistent crusader for high standards of quality and cogency in the conduct of press controversies, and on occasion he may have deliberately intended to provoke fellow editors to make fools of themselves in order to deliver pious homilies on their unseemly behavior.[83]

Whatever his motives, Wilson's assault was frontal. His complaints were directed against neither owners nor operatives; he had nothing but praise for H. P. Hammett and insisted that "there are thousands of good and pure people in factories." He had little use for the factory system itself, however. Taking the stance of a Jeffersonian agrarian, he contended that "he who owns land, erects a home for his family, and cultivates the soil, is in partner-

82. In Abbeville *Press and Banner*, January 16, 1889, Wilson agreed to support a local mill project, and never again voiced criticism. On his election as a director see *ibid.*, May 8, 1895. By 1900 he was attacking child labor legislation and being accused of taking "the side of the strong and powerful as against the weak and defenseless." Spartanburg *Herald*, quoted in Columbia *State*, February 6, 1900.

83. Wilson thanked the Newberry *Herald* for granting him a fair hearing and praised H. P. Hammett and the Anderson *Intelligencer* for stating "solid facts, with perfect fairness and courtesy"; on the other hand, he complained of the "jibes" he received from those "who did not presume to answer our article." Abbeville *Press and Banner*, August 5, 15, September 12, 1883.

ship with God Himself"; in the manner of Jefferson he set himself firmly against the wickedness of cities and the loss of independence characteristic of factory life.[84]

He termed "the employment of little children in factories" for twelve hours a day "an outrage, which would blacken the history of any State." More to the point, mill work tended "to unfit . . . little children, physically and practically, for the ordinary duties of life," and deprived them of "any opportunity for education, or for maintaining any previously acquired education." He attacked "the hard work, poor pay, and unhealthfulness" of mill work and declared it demoralizing. On the question of wages, he showed that the estimated payroll at Piedmont yielded an average monthly wage of less than fourteen dollars for each operative. To those who praised the mills' "philanthropy" in employing women and children he commended the railroads, which "employ our men, and pay such wages as to enable them to support their families."[85] He was particularly distressed over the effect of mill life on the family. A confirmed antifeminist and social conservative, he was convinced that "it is better for a woman to be somebody's daughter or somebody's wife, than it is to be a poor dependent factory girl or woman." A mill girl learned nothing of "the duties and work of a womanly life—the life which nature and the laws of our civilization intended that she should live." Children could not be properly raised near a factory.[86]

Wilson pointed out inconsistencies in the attitudes of his colleagues. Was it not strange, he asked, that editors attacked the wicked towns and urged farm boys to stay at home, while encouraging their sisters to flock to the mill towns? If factories were such a boon, he inquired, "why is it that we in the South have so often twitted the North with the charge of cruelty and barbarism in

84. *Ibid.*, June 20, August 1, September 26, 1883.

85. *Ibid.*, August 1, 22, September 26, 1883. Hammett reported six hundred operatives together making ten thousand dollars a year, or $13.89 per operative per month. On the other hand, Hammett's estimate of monthly wages ranged between fifteen and thirty dollars a month. *Ibid.*, August 22, December 9, 1883. In April 1886, 573 operatives averaged $13.08 in total earnings; over half made less than $12.00. Piedmont Time Book (on microfilm, in SCL).

86. Abbeville *Press and Banner*, August 1, 22, 29, November 26, 1883. Wilson, of course, was a bachelor.

their treatment of factory operatives?" Above all, he warned that industrialization might bring the establishment of "caste between our own race." He recognized that "the unceasing toil, and partial exclusion from the outside world" characteristic of operatives reinforced the natural stigma placed on wage earners, deeming it improbable "that any operative would be recognized by [the stockholders of a mill] as a fit associate for their families."[87]

Wilson's attack succeeded in stirring up controversy. There were several replies, notably by Hammett and the Anderson *Intelligencer*, which addressed the issues in an intelligent, forthright manner. Several other newspapers were disapproving but respectful.[88] The generality of reaction, though, was hysterical. Ignoring for the most part the substance of Wilson's remarks, his detractors accused him of slandering "the virtuous women who prefer to earn their bread by honest toil in the cotton mills." The defenders of the mills gladly assumed the task of "manfully vindicating" the good name of the operatives and fell over each other in quest of the proper epithet to cast at their traducer. Wilson's remarks were "grossly unjust," a "foul calumny," eliciting "extreme disgust" from one mill superintendent. That Wilson touched a raw nerve is suggested not only by the heat of the replies, but by the fears occasionally suggested by them. Remarking on Wilson's warnings about "caste," one man declared that "It is evil teaching . . . even to hint at class distinction amongst us where there is no room for it, unless the evangelist of the baneful doctrine desires to see realized the horrors of another Coketown in South Carolina."[89]

While Wilson's views provoked a flurry of discussion, it was generally agreed that they had few adherents.[90] Indeed, for the most part indigenous criticism of the mills in the 1880s was so rare as to be startling when it did appear, and bewildering to the

87. *Ibid.*, June 20, August 1, September 5, 26, 1883.

88. Hammett, *ibid.*, August 1, 1883; Anderson *Intelligencer*, quoted *ibid.*, September 12, 1883; Spartanburg *Carolina Spartan*, June 27, 1883; Newberry *Herald*, August 9, 1883, which thought Wilson's views "not very unlike the views once held on the subject by Jno. C. Calhoun."

89. For a selection of indignant comment, see "The Women in the Mills: a Vigorous Defense of the Virtue of Factory Girls," in Aiken *Recorder*, quoted in Charleston *News and Courier*, September 6, 1883.

90. Charleston *News and Courier*, October 31, 1887.

spokesmen of the middle classes. When a bill to establish a ten-hour day in the cotton mills was introduced in the General Assembly the correspondent of the *News and Courier* thought it "a joke," and was surprised to find it taken seriously. When the editor of the Newberry *Herald and News*, E. H. Aull, offered some mild criticism of the 12½-hour day in the mills, Charles Petty of the *Carolina Spartan* sniffed that "energetic, pushing farmers from the first of April to the first of October are hustling around about thirteen hours a day."[91] Not only did criticism of mill conditions meet a blank wall of incomprehension, but the critics themselves, excepting the rambunctious Wilson, were inhibited by the nervousness of society toward opening questions it wished to consider settled. Aull took pains to establish his conservative credentials even while making his plea for shorter hours: "We are opposed to strikes," he said, "and opposed to arraying capital against labor, or labor against capital, and do not intend anything of that kind now."[92]

Unlike Aull, most critics could simply be dismissed as scoundrels. Before the turn of the century, for example, the most important indigenous criticism of the mills was made by followers of Governor Benjamin R. Tillman.[93] "Pitchfork Ben" and his Farmers' Movement were anathema to the townspeople, and the overwhelmingly Conservative press was only too happy to link criticism of factory conditions with the "ravings" of the "dolts or demagogues" of the "Reform" faction.[94] Yankees, of course, made even better targets, as they could be accused of playing partisan politics or of disseminating New England textile propaganda. D. E. Converse accused Thomas Barry of attempting to reincarnate the "bloody shirt" in industrial form for the 1888 political campaign,

91. The bill was defeated handily, 74–35; *ibid.*, December 7, 11, 1887. Also Newberry *Herald and News*, February 16, 1887, March 1, 1888, August 8, 1889; Spartanburg *Carolina Spartan*, March 14, 1888.

92. Newberry *Herald and News*, August 8, 1889; see also Union *Times*, May 26, 1905.

93. On Tillmanism and cotton mills, see Williamson, "South Carolina Cotton Mills"; see also pages 161–63 herein.

94. The quote is from the Columbia *State*, January 26, 1892. Editor Aull of the *Herald and News* reversed his stance on hours legislation when it became a Tillmanite issue, muttering that "the agitation of these things will do no good." Newberry *Herald and News*, November 30, December 21, 1892.

and suggested that he was backed by northerners envious of southern prosperity.[95]

Such irrelevance occasionally became ludicrous, as for example in the response to Clare de Graffenried's 1891 article in the *Century* on "The Georgia Cracker in the Cotton Mills."[96] The state press shook with abusive tirades against her "vile slanders," all of them assuming that she was a northerner with ulterior motives. A former mill teacher, for example, believed the piece to be composed of "very distant observations" by a Massachusetts woman "interested in New England cotton mills" who "by this skilful weft of fact and fiction" sought "to discourage cotton manufacturing in the South."[97] With some embarrassment the *News and Courier* had to inform the vindicators of southern decency and honor that Miss de Graffenried was a native Georgian, a protégé of the eminent statistician Carroll Wright, and an investigator whose work was considered "conscientious and thorough." Although the article appeared in a popular magazine and was doubtless highly colored, the portraits drawn seemed "true to nature—we have all seen such looking people over and over again," and it was "not unreasonable to presume that the story is generally a fair representation of facts." The Palmetto State did not lose face, however; the state press agreed that Miss de Graffenried's article was a devastating exposé of conditions in the *Georgia* mills, and urged that she "visit the factory towns in South Carolina so that she might give the Century the bright side of life in the Southern cotton mills."[98]

The awkwardness with which South Carolinians handled Miss

95. Spartanburg *Carolina Spartan*, January 18, 1888.

96. Clare de Graffenried, "The Georgia Cracker in the Cotton Mills," *Century*, XIX (1891), 483–98. Interestingly enough, she avoided attacking mill owners or the factory system, except insofar as industrial conditions encouraged the persistence of the backward "cracker" heritage. Child labor was blamed on the parents, who tricked or forced helpless managers to accept their children as employees. Both in its conservatism and in its concern with bringing a semi-primitive people into the "civilized" world, her article anticipated attitudes of South Carolina's middle class toward the "cotton mill problem" appearing during the Progressive era. See Chapters IV and V herein.

97. W. J. Thackston in Charleston *News and Courier*, February 28, 1891; W. G. Smith, *ibid.*, March 12, 1891. Smith, the foster son of a Wofford College professor, was at that time paymaster at Clifton. He subsequently became president of mills at Bamberg and Orangeburg.

98. *Ibid.*, February 28, 1891; Hugh Fox and editorial, *ibid.*, March 2, 1891; Spartanburg *Carolina Spartan*, March 4, 1891; Greenville *News*, quoted *ibid.*, March 18, 1891.

de Graffenried troubled them little, for they had long been accustomed to making awkward statements in behalf of industry. They felt little necessity to be rigorous in their discussion of the social consequences of industrialization, because in the end they failed to see any great problem. They were convinced that the state could avoid the trials faced by England and the North, even though that conviction was based on little more than sectional and racial vanity. Far from attempting to control the future of their society with social planning, middle-class South Carolinians allowed themselves to be lulled into complacency by assurances that the superiority of the southern racial stock and southern mores made concern for the future of the state unnecessary.[99]

Their naïveté was permitted by the low social profile of the early mills. Despite explosive growth in the 1880s, only 8,071 people were employed in the mills by 1890; they and their dependents probably made up less than 5 percent of the white population of South Carolina, and less than 2 percent of the total population.[100] Also, the use of water power as the principal motive force for factories in the 1880s encouraged mills to build in isolated areas, out of sight and out of mind. Even if the cotton mill operatives were not sturdy native yeomen, said the Columbia *Register* in 1886, "it would be almost impossible, from the comparatively [*sic*] smallness of their numbers, for any obstructive action they might take to have any serious permanent effect upon the business of the factories themselves or of the State at large."[101] Under such circumstances worry over the development of a working class in South Carolina seemed academic if not vaguely subversive, and any one expressing concern could logically be suspected of having ulterior motives.

The forces of doubt, however, though submerged, had never been truly vanquished. Unpressed by any necessity to deal with

99. Cf. Mitchell, *Rise of Cotton Mills*, 79.

100. *U.S. Census, 1890*, I, 2, 400–401; *ibid.*, VI, 584; Kohn, *Cotton Mills*, 86. Kohn's figures indicate that in 1907 there were 1.33 dependents for every mill operative. If the same ratio is applied to 1890 it yields a total of 18,805 people living in the state's mill villages; the figure represents 4.1 percent of the white population of South Carolina and 1.5 percent of the total population.

101. Columbia *Register*, quoted in Newberry *Herald and News*, June 2, 1886.

large numbers of foreigners, South Carolinians had been often able to advocate immigration and oppose immigrants at the same time. A similar lack of urgency had permitted them to indulge in extravagant praise of the "thrifty and industrious operatives" while privately worrying about the effect of the factory on their world. As the cotton mill worker ceased to be a novelty and became a force to be reckoned with, the middle classes began to take more serious notice of his qualities and his place in the social order. By the turn of the century even such stalwarts of the New South as *The State* began to admit that something was amiss with the old arguments, that southern heritage and Anglo-Saxon blood offered less assurance for the safety of the social order than had previously been believed. The twentieth century was to bring with it a new phrase: "the cotton mill problem."

Chapter IV

The Discovery of the "Mill Problem," 1895–1905

In January, 1898, the editor of *The State* of Columbia, one of the principal daily newspapers of South Carolina, received what was for the time a most unusual letter. Its author was a young Methodist minister named John C. Roper. Raised on a farm in the Pee Dee district of northeastern South Carolina, Roper, a recent graduate of Wofford College, had just completed his first year in the ministry, serving the congregation at the Union Cotton Mills.[1] The conditions he had found in the new, raw mill village had made a striking impact on the inexperienced and idealistic youth, and he now felt compelled to raise an alarm. While he admitted that it was "true that the cotton mill [was] a new thing in the south" and "had scarcely been in existence long enough to tell what [would] be the final result of so many country people flocking to these manufacturing towns," the evidence before him portended a frightful future. The regimen of the mills, requiring operatives to stand eleven hours a day, "breathing heated, impure, and dusty air," was already creating "a pallor known as the factory cheek." Roper feared that the physical effects of mill work would be passed on by inbreeding, ultimately producing "a monstrosity."

1. Watson B. Duncan, *Twentieth Century Sketches of the South Carolina Conference, Methodist Episcopal Church, South* (Columbia: The State Company, 1901), 270–71. It had become customary to send young, inexperienced ministers to serve mill pastorates; of the six other ministers admitted to the conference in 1896, two were assigned to mill churches at the outset of their ministries, and two others received mill charges as their second assignment.

Already he thought he discerned signs of alterations in the shapes of operatives' skulls.

Fearsome as were the putative genetic and phrenological effects of mill life, its social and moral effects on the operatives were even more hazardous. The nature of the work was "so mechanical that there [was] no opportunity for developing reasoning or logical facilities at all." The crowded life of the tenements and the promiscuous intermingling of the sexes in the mill compounded the danger. "Living an animal, sensual and mechanical life," Roper asked rhetorically, "where is any intellectual or moral development?" He called for the prohibition of child labor in the mills under age twelve and for a reduction of the limit on hours of labor to ten a day, warning that without safeguards "it is yet to be proven that the cotton mill business is not the greatest curse that has ever happened to South Carolina."[2]

Roper's fears for the future were taken less than seriously by the editor of *The State*, Narciso G. Gonzales, who, as an adherent of the "optimistic school" and a booster of industrial development, thought the minister's pessimism both ill-founded and impolitic. While the journalist, himself not quite forty, sympathized with the young minister, he failed to see any grave social problem arising about the mills. To be sure, he thought it preferable that children not have to work; fresh country air was far healthier than the lint-choked atmosphere of the spinning room, and the lack of education among child workers boded ill for the future. On balance, though, such considerations were of little importance to Gonzales. The work of the spinner was hardly onerous; indeed, it was almost play. As to its moral effects, Gonzales failed to understand "how moving from spindle to spindle and giving a little finger twist to unite two strands of yarn can bear fruit in 'infirmaries, hospitals, asylums, deformities and diseases innumerable,'" as Roper had feared. He was more understanding of Roper's position than was the offended Union man who accused the minister of making "imaginary and theoretical" charges against the town's leading enterprises; even so, Gonzales saw little need to be upset by mill con-

2. Columbia *State*, January 12, 1898.

ditions, and less need to pass corrective legislation. The great need of the state was for industrial development, and child labor reform could easily wait until the South had vanquished New England in cotton manufacturing. "When we win the race we will get the reward," he declared; "it would be folly to stop in mid-career to adjust a belt or tie a shoestring."[3]

The race had a long distance yet to run in 1900, but by then Gonzales had reversed his earlier benign estimation of the mill environment. In a ringing editorial which, curiously for a southerner, he entitled "Child Slavery in Our Mills," he threw his formidable influence into the forefront of the movement for child labor reform. His perception of the mill as a work place had changed but little: "Our cotton mills, almost without exception, are well-built and provided; they are as comfortable places to work in as cotton mills can be; they are well-heated in winter and well-ventilated in summer; the work the children do, tending the spinning frames, is light work and easily done." Whatever the conditions, however, the work was monotonous and stupefying, while the twelve hour days deprived the children of both freedom and sunshine. "The joyousness of childhood is not theirs; its freedom they do not know; they are dwarfed in mind, stunted in soul. What will their future be? What light, joy and power can come from lives like these?"

Such sentimental pleading for the child is touching, but in view of Gonzales' earlier pronouncements on the subject it strikes a false note. The conditions under which children worked in the mills had hardly worsened between 1898 and 1900, and it is unlikely that Gonzales, who had toured many mills in his journalistic career, suddenly "discovered" child labor in the interim. What *had* changed, however, was Gonzales' perception of the social consequences of child labor. "These little fellows of six and eight and ten," Gonzales warned his readers, "are one day to become our voters. . . . They are to say in the years to come who shall be our governors, who shall make our laws, who shall administer the statutes, who shall pay the taxes, who shall spend them. Can the fruit

3. *Ibid.*, January 12, 15, 24, 1898.

be any better than the tree that bears it? Can we hope for light from those who are bred in darkness?"[4]

At the time of Gonzales' enlistment in the child labor reform movement, its adherents in South Carolina were few, and the economic and political powers of the state were ranged overwhelmingly against them.[5] The ranks of the reformers were augmenting rapidly, however, and within three years they succeeded in writing at least the principle of child labor restriction into law, thanks in large part to Gonzales' strenuous advocacy of their cause. However, the influential editor's change of heart had a significance beyond the child labor reform movement. That movement was but one aspect of a spreading concern among thoughtful South Carolinians over the implications of industrialization, a concern which began to develop in the middle 1890s and by the early twentieth century became a major topic of discussion among the educated middle class. It was expressed in a wide variety of movements, for labor legislation, for "welfare work" by mill corporations, and for educational and religious missionary work. Sometimes, as in the case of child labor reform, it came into conflict with the state's industrialists. More often, however, it sought their cooperation and even their leadership. Concern over what came to be known as the "cotton mill problem" united ministers, journalists, teachers, club women, and businessmen in both a common desire for a more stable and better organized society and a common perception that one of the major barriers to its realization was a "shiftless," undisciplined operative class.

To be sure, their fears of the expanding class of mill workers could generally be expressed only obliquely, partly out of obeisance to the powerful myths of "Anglo-Saxon" superiority and equality, partly out of the traditional (and related) disinclination to admit that everyone (or at least every white person) was not a member of the "middle class."[6] As the dawn of the twentieth cen-

4. *Ibid.*, January 29, 1900. For a summary of Gonzales' attitudes on labor legislation see Lewis P. Jones, *Stormy Petrel: N. G. Gonzales and His State*, Tricentennial Studies, IX (Columbia: University of South Carolina Press, 1975), 253–56.

5. A major attempt to pass legislation in 1900 failed in the Senate by a vote of twenty-nine to eight. Columbia *State*, January 27, 1900.

6. An example of this can be found in D. E. Camak, *Human Gold from Southern Hills*

tury approached, however, the intelligent town-dwelling South Carolinian became increasingly aware of the deep cultural split existing between the people of the towns and those of the mill settlements. While he might continue to denigrate the immigrant population of the North and proclaim extravagantly that South Carolina's operatives were "to the manner (or manor) born," he increasingly perceived the mill hands as themselves aliens, immigrants from the backwoods who introduced unruly, dangerous elements into the orderly, well-regulated life of town society. Having only recently withstood the blast of rural resentment released by "Pitchfork Ben" Tillman and his followers, the townsmen feared the new "cracker proletariat" all the more. While the fundamental division in South Carolina society continued to be between whites and blacks, the cotton mill created a new and unprecedented fissure in the social landscape. In recognizing the distinction between "mill people" and "town people," South Carolinians were forced to acknowledge the fulfillment of Hugh Wilson's prophecy; the coming of the factory had indeed created "caste between our own race."

The crucial event altering middle-class perceptions of the social dimension of industrialization was the cotton mill boom of the late 1890s and the early twentieth century. The expansion came in two bursts. Twenty-three mills were organized between 1895 and 1897; after a two-year lull, an explosion of enthusiasm added twenty-four mills to the roll in 1900 and seventeen more over the next three years. Of the one hundred and forty mills extant in 1907, half came into existence during the period from 1895 to 1903.[7] At the same time, older mills expanded their operations. As a result, between 1890 and 1900 the total number of spindles in

(Greer, S.C.: private, 1960), 143, speaking of the family of a former operative who had left the mill as "living up to the best traditions of that sturdy so-called 'middle class,' of which in truth they were members all along." Another of Camak's students, an operative turned minister, spoke of "our pure stock of good, honest, middle-class common people." T. J. Carter, "The Cotton Mill Problem from An Operative's Standpoint," *Methodist Review,* LXIV (1915), 724.

7. Compiled from South Carolina Secretary of State *Reports*, using the 1907 list in August Kohn, *The Cotton Mills of South Carolina* (Columbia: South Carolina Department of

South Carolina cotton mills increased by 330 percent, vaulting the Palmetto State into second place, behind Massachusetts, among the cotton-textile-producing states of the Union; by 1905 the number of spindles had doubled again. The number of employees followed suit, rising 278 percent to 30,201 in 1900, and to 37,271 in 1905. If one estimates the 1900 mill population at 70,368, it comprised only 5.2 percent of the total population. However, its proportion of the white population in this black majority state was 12.6 percent, and within a few years it would become a commonplace of conversation that one out of every five white South Carolinians lived in a mill village.[8]

The raw statistics, however, understate the impact of the mills on the image of South Carolina as held by the townspeople, for with the increasing numbers of mill workers came a radically different distribution of the operative population. As we have seen, the profitability and varied economic benefits of the early mills attracted the attention of the towns, which began to use cotton manufacturing as an aid to local economic development. Rather than grouping the operatives in isolated communities under strict corporate control, the construction of "town" mills developed extensive mill districts within or adjacent to the towns. Cheap electricity, generated at a dam on the Seneca River and carried to Anderson over one of the world's first high-tension transmission lines, helped power a complex of eight mills in and around the "Electric City" in 1903, only one of which had been in existence before 1899. Between 1895 and 1903 six large mills were built in an arc-shaped district about the southern and western limits of the city of Greenville; by 1903 the mill population of the district was estimated at nearly eleven thousand. The formerly somnolent upcountry town of Union built its first factory in 1893. By the turn of the century it could boast four cotton mills and a knitting mill,

---

Agriculture, Commerce, and Immigration, 1907), 214–17, as a base. Whenever possible the organizational date of the *original* corporation was used. It proved impossible to determine the date of organization for four mills, all of them non-Piedmont.

8. Actually, the proportion was closer to one-sixth. U.S. Department of Commerce and Labor, Bureau of the Census, Bulletin No. 74, *Census of Manufactures, 1905: Textiles*, Tables 16 and 18. The method used in computing the mill population is that used above; see page 127n herein.

supporting a population of some four thousand people straddling the city line. The mill people were a minority of the town's total population, but they were the dominant element in one of the wards. Geographically the Union mill district was separated from the town only by the width of a street, but according to one observer "one was identified in the social mind of the community with the one group or the other according to which side of the street he lived on."[9]

Visually, the most striking instance of the new development was that of the mill district of Columbia. Taking advantage of the hydroelectric power generated by the recently completed plant on the Columbia Canal, a group of local lawyers, merchants, and bankers, headed by the mill engineer W. B. Smith Whaley, constructed a group of four cotton mills on a sandy plain in the undeveloped southwestern portion of the city between 1895 and 1900, culminating with the huge Olympia mill—with over 100,000 spindles the largest cotton mill under one roof in the world. By 1903 an estimated 8,700 people lived in the Columbia mill district; the 4,200 who lived within the city made up around 20 percent of Columbia's total population, and around one third of its white population.[10] The bulk of the new industrial Columbia, sprawling over the flatland beneath the bluff on which the older city had been built, could be viewed at a glance from the south portico of the State House, usually with pride but occasionally with anxiety.

The enormous influx of ill-paid workers into these congested districts naturally brought a considerable amount of poverty to the very doorsteps of the townspeople. In Columbia in 1896 *The State* organized a "Christmas tree" for the benefit of the poor. The party was originally to have been held on Christmas Eve; however, it was discovered at the last minute that a large percentage of the poor

9. Douglas Summers Brown, *A City Without Cobwebs: A History of Rock Hill, South Carolina* (Columbia: University of South Carolina Press, 1953), 237–40; C. W. Norryce (ed.), *A General Sketch of the City of Anderson* (Anderson, S.C.: Roper Printing Company, 1909); S. S. Crittenden, *The Greenville Century Book* (Greenville, S.C.: Press of Greenville News, 1903), 68–69; Kohn, *Cotton Mills*, 86–89; Camak, *Human Gold*, 51. See also the list of voters in Union *Progress*, April 22, 1910. Comparison with a contemporary city directory suggests that most of the city's operatives lived in Ward Four.

10. Columbia *State*, January 1, 1903. The 1900 population of Columbia was 21,108; its white population was 11,244.

children of Columbia were in fact operatives, and were expected to be at their places in the mills on the night before Christmas. Accordingly, the affair was postponed until the afternoon of the twenty-sixth, a Saturday, when the operatives got their half day off. Afterward *The State* commented on the importance of the charity effort in revealing to many Columbians for the first time the large amount of "extreme and cruel poverty" which existed in the city, much of it coming "in the wake of the factories, among a nomadic population until now strange to Columbia." Six years later another "Christmas tree," sponsored by the local Elks Club, was attended by five hundred children, two hundred of whom came from the mill district. Recognition of the poverty in the mill villages was not confined to the state capital; in 1897 virtually every relief case in Rock Hill lived in one of the five local mill communities. The rudimentary charitable societies of the period began to find themselves overloaded. In late 1897, for example, the Columbia Ladies' Benevolent Society found it necessary to issue a special appeal for funds: "Since the establishment of more factories, there is a greater number of cases calling for relief, and the illness of the past summer among this class, as well as among others, having depleted our treasury, we ask contributions from the generous-hearted whose sympathies abound for the poor."[11]

However, much of the poverty among the mill people remained invisible. Unincorporated mill districts did not benefit from organized charities, which generally limited their jurisdiction to municipalities. Mill officials generally had more pressing concerns than administering systematic relief. The principal charitable institutions of the mill villages were the churches, but their aid was rendered informally; as the bulk of destitute operatives were transients without ties to the churches and unacquainted with church members, their needs were often unknown even within the mill community itself. Thus it remained easy to dismiss the poverty among mill folk, and to continue to believe the mills to be great economic benefactors. A Columbia society woman, leafing through the 1899 city directory, was pleased to discover that "a consider-

11. *Ibid.*, December 24, 27, 1896; October 23, 1897; December 27, 1902; Charleston *News and Courier*, June 13, 1897.

able number of those who had formerly called upon me to take charge of my spare change, supernumerary garments, and superfluous food" were listed as cotton mill operatives. "Spinning and weaving will obviate the necessity of ringing me up to bestow all my goods [on] the poor, and thus help both sides," she cheerfully remarked, oblivious to the possibility that many of that "considerable number" of beggars were already operatives.[12]

While it was still possible to be complacent about the material well-being of the operatives at the turn of the century, it was less easy to ignore the possibility of labor organization at the mills. Although a flurry of union activity occurred in the state's textile industry during the 1880s, the first important period of labor unrest appeared in the years between 1898 and 1902.[13] The major contributing factor to the unionist upsurge was the economic instability produced by the mill boom, especially the increasing pressure it placed on the labor supply. As good workers became more difficult to procure, wage rates began to respond; according to fragmentary statistics collected by the United States Commissioner of Labor, between 1898 and 1902 the hourly wage of male weavers in South Carolina rose by 18.6 percent, that of female weavers rose by 14.7 percent, and that of spinning room girls rose by 23.8 percent. However, most of that improvement was canceled out by a 12.5 percent increase in the cost of living. Thus, while mill hands found their labor in demand and their wages rising, they found their pecuniary position remaining stagnant, or, in some localities, even declining, while company profits soared. The result was an upsurge in dissatisfaction among the operatives, some of it reaching public print. In Union the common complaint of the workers in the West End was that "they never in their life before seen [*sic*] the price of cotton and provisions go up but that wages went up soon," yet their pay checks were lagging behind their grocery bills. The operatives' disgruntlement was reflected in a spate of com-

12. See letter, Charles E. Weltner, in Columbia *State*, May 1, 1909; *ibid.*, September 10, 1899.

13. George S. Mitchell, *Textile Unionism and the South* (Chapel Hill: University of North Carolina Press, 1931), 22; Melton A. McLaurin, *Paternalism and Protest: Southern Cotton Mill Workers and Organized Labor, 1875–1905* (Westport, Conn.: Greenwood Press, 1971).

ment in the state press urging a "voluntary" wage increase in the industry, which, it was hoped, would "scotch the harmful agitation sure to be attempted" among the mill hands.[14]

The "agitation" was already present, for the years around the turn of the century saw an unprecedented wave of interest in organization among the operatives, whose position was enhanced by the growing labor shortage. Beginning in 1898, the National Union of Textile Workers began an organizational drive among the South Carolina mills, and received a surprisingly strong response. Efforts in the Piedmont were generally stymied by fierce opposition from management, but the union became quite powerful in certain localities. Strong locals developed in the Horse Creek Valley of Aiken County, adjacent to the union stronghold of Augusta, and in Columbia, where it received some support from a sizable contingent of skilled workers.[15]

Naturally the thought of sharing power with an organization of their own employees made mill owners apoplectic. James L. Orr, Jr., warned his fellow manufacturers that "unionism is but one step from Socialism, and Socialists but one step from Anarchists"; in the wake of a strike in 1901 a mill official was heard to mutter that "it has come to a pretty pass where a man cannot run his own affairs. We cannot afford to have the same conditions here that prevail in the North." Others besides manufacturers were perturbed by the prospect of labor troubles. Among the stronger arguments used by manufacturers against labor legislation during this period was its frequent sponsorship by unions, an argument apparently aimed chiefly at farmers fearful of unrest among their laborers. Townspeople were also nervous about unions, "which ofttimes prove[d] harmful to a community" by disrupting the local economy; they looked with foreboding upon the prospective "en-

14. U.S. Department of Commerce and Labor, Commissioner of Labor, *Report, 1904*, Table 5C, 480, on wages. U.S. Bureau of Labor, *Bulletin No. 77* (July, 1908), 197, contains a set of cost-of-living figures, compiled by census regions, for the years 1890 through 1907; I have used the figures for the South Atlantic region. Local comments on the economic situation include those of "B. F. G." and "A Weaver in Union Mills" in Union *Progress*, April 11, 1900, replying to editorial which appeared there April 4, 1900; Columbia *State*, December 2, 8, 13, 19, 1899, January 22, 1900.

15. Melton A. McLaurin, "Early Labor Union Organizational Efforts in South Carolina Cotton Mills, 1880–1905," *South Carolina Historical Magazine*, LXXII (1971), 51–52.

actment of strikes and turmoils, to which other States and other countries are subject."[16]

While the middle classes were hardly reassured by the prospect of a struggle of labor against capital in South Carolina, one nonetheless finds a surprising equanimity toward unionism among its major spokesmen, even a measure of good will. While disapproving of disorder or coercive measures connected with strikes, they generally believed that operatives had the right to organize. "Farmers, lawyers, bankers, merchants, dentists, drummers, manufacturers, editors, all have their organized societies, then why not the operatives of our factories?" asked one Labor Day orator, a former state attorney general, who proceeded to condemn attempts to destroy unions as "blow[s] to our free institutions." Even conservative newspapers were known to deprecate blatant attempts at union busting. Commenting on one such drive, the Union *Times* declared that "this is a free country and a man has a right to belong to any society or organization he sees fit, and an effort on the part of any corporation to interfere with this personal privilege will, we believe, result in disaster."[17] Management coercion was considered by many townsmen to be as wicked as union coercion, partly for ideological reasons, but also because management attempts to destroy labor organizations were sometimes as deleterious to local economies as were strikes. When W. B. Smith Whaley inaugurated an antiunion drive in his mills which culminated in a strike in September, 1901, N. G. Gonzales of *The State* was openly hostile to the management cause despite close personal ties to Whaley. "A lockout," he asserted, "is as bad for the community as a strike, and the business interests of the city demand some consideration from employers as well as employed." When it was reported at the time of the strike that South Carolina cotton manufacturers were planning to meet to discuss organizing to combat unionism, the manufacturers promptly issued an indignant denial,

16. James L. Orr, in "Addresses Delivered by Mr. G. Gunby Jordan . . . and Col. James L. Orr . . . , Warm Springs, Georgia, May 30–31, 1901" (n.p., n.d.); Columbia *State*, June 18, 1900, January 22, 23, 24, February 8, September 5, 1901, January 29, 1902; Union *Progress*, April 4, 1900; Ellison A. Smyth, "The Child Labor Question from the Standpoint of the Mill Authorities," *The Educational*, I (1902), 42.

17. Columbia *State*, September 3, 1901; Union *Times*, September 16, 1901.

reflecting a realization that concerted effort to stamp out union activity was highly unpopular. Later, when in the spring of 1902 the Horse Creek Valley manufacturers locked out their operatives in order to prevent them from supplying economic support to strikers in Augusta, they were roundly condemned by newspapers and by the state Democratic party convention. Attempts to prohibit lockouts were perennial in the General Assembly for the next several years; while none ever passed, they generally drew strong support.[18]

Not only did many people feel that organization was within the rights of the operatives, but a number felt that it was a positive good. While South Carolinians had had little experience with industrial unionism, the skilled trades were already well organized. Particularly was this the case in Columbia; the city was a railroad and printing center as well as a mill center, and could thus boast a sizable "labor aristocracy." Beginning in 1890 Labor Day was celebrated as a major holiday in Columbia, complete with a Sunday sermon by the "Labor Day chaplain," a parade of workers through the city, and a gathering of union men at the fairgrounds, where they feasted, played games, and heard speeches from politicians and others.

Like the American Federation of Labor of which they were a part, South Carolina unionists were virtually middle class in their acceptance of the existing social order and in their commitment to "enlightened self-interest." The Columbia Labor Day celebration, for example, had the "educational" purpose of encouraging fraternal feelings among workers and directing their attention to "lofty ideas." The general cast of the speeches was conservative, extolling

18. Columbia *State*, August 27, September 2, 5, 6, 1901; Rock Hill *Herald*, September 7, 1901. Whaley was married to Gonzales' cousin. McLaurin, "Early Labor Union Organizational Efforts," 56, discounts the manufacturers' denials about the purpose of the Greenville meeting, insisting that it was held in part to unify the mills behind Whaley's hard-nosed approach; however, he presents no evidence beyond the grumblings of a single mill official. The only items on the public agenda were child labor, freight rates, and a proposed exhibit at the Charleston Exposition. No organization was established. Columbia *State*, September 11, 1901; May 1, 22, 1902. Cf. the ambiguous role of Augusta, Ga., townsmen in the 1886 textile strike there, as recounted in McLaurin, *Paternalism and Protest*, 92–110; also, Herbert G. Gutman, "The Workers' Search for Power," in H. Wayne Morgan (ed.), *The Gilded Age* (Syracuse, N.Y.: Syracuse University Press, 1970), 31–53, which treats the same phenomenon but differs in emphasis from my argument.

self-improvement and self-respect, and urging that "labor and capital . . . stand shoulder to shoulder together and labor together for the upbuilding of the State."[19] The editor of the Spartanburg *Journal* extolled members of the Typographical Union as "a splendid class of citizenship; men who receive good wages and show much quiet pride in providing well for their families; big-hearted fellows who are always ready to help unfortunates in their own ranks or elsewhere." Reform-minded members of the middle classes found an ally in the South Carolina Federation of Labor, organized on Labor Day, 1900; its support of child labor and compulsory education legislation was cited by *The State* as "evidence that the forces of labor are beginning to think, and to think sanely and sensibly, of their future." Even Ellison Smyth once expressed himself privately, and fleetingly, as seeing nothing wrong with unions among "intelligent" people, although he thought them dangerous among the "ignorant."[20]

Some hoped that the spread of unionism to the operatives would be beneficial to them, that it would bring them under the leadership of the labor aristocracy, and thus serve as a means of incorporating the operatives into the society of the towns. State Senator William N. Graydon of Abbeville County, for example, condemned the destruction of a fledgeling union at the Abbeville Cotton Mill, which he argued had been primarily a mutual benefit association. "Labor unions," he declared, "can be made the means of great good if met in the proper spirit and properly managed." Senator J. Q. Marshall of Richland County (Columbia), the leading advocate of child labor reform in the General Assembly, predicted that "it will be but a short time before every mill operative in this State belongs to that union. There are associations in every calling and profession in life: doctors, lawyers, merchants, farmers—yes, and mill presidents associate themselves together to better their condition. Is there any reason why factory hands cannot do the same?

19. On the distinction between skilled workers and factory operatives, see editorial, "What Do Columbians Say?" Columbia *State*, January 22, 1900. On Labor Day, see *ibid.*, September 4, 1900, August 25, September 3, 1901.

20. Spartanburg *Journal*, June 10, 1903; Columbia *State*, December 3, 1900; January 19, 23, 1901; Smyth to D. A. Tompkins, December 7, 1905, in D. A. Tompkins Papers, Southern Historical Collection, University of North Carolina at Chapel Hill.

Organization gives dignity to every calling and profession in life."[21]

Both the darkest fears of the enemies of organized labor and the brightest hopes of its friends failed to materialize, however. The turn-of-the-century wave of union activity began to recede after 1902, and by 1905 was only a memory. Its collapse was due in large part to strong management opposition, especially the willingness of such men as Whaley to take major risks to destroy unions. A more important factor, though, was the ability of the operatives, for the next few years at least, to improve their position without recourse to organization. Ironically, the subsidence of the labor movement in the mills was due in large part to the same labor shortage which had nourished it, for in order to retain their work force the mills were forced to make a series of wage increases. Between 1902 and 1907 the wages of male weavers went up by 58.4 percent, those of female weavers by 65.2 percent, and those of spinners by 138.3 percent. In the meantime the cost of living rose by only 9 percent.[22] While incomes rose, the insatiable demand of the mills for experienced workers made it a comparatively simple matter to express grievances, not by organized effort, but by moving.

The best illustration of the limited usefulness of unions to the operatives was the strike at the Whaley mills of Columbia. It began in late August, 1901, when several hundred operatives refused to obey a mill edict requiring overtime work on a Saturday as a make-up for the approaching Labor Day holiday. The protesters, mainly members of the local textile workers' union, found themselves locked out the following Monday, and Whaley declared that no one would be rehired who did not renounce the union. The organized textile workers responded by calling a strike. However, their strategy was peculiar. From the very beginning most of the strikers assumed that they would never again work in Whaley's mills; therefore, they simply left. Some got work in the Columbia Mills across town, but many went out of the city; Union Station was reportedly "crowded with migrating help," whose household

21. Columbia *State*, February 8, 9, 1901.

22. U.S. Commissioner of Labor, *Report, 1904*, 480; *Bulletin No. 65* (July, 1906), 163; *Bulletin No. 77* (July, 1908), 169, 197.

goods clogged the platform. Far from there being any management solidarity behind the anti-union drive, numerous mills, especially in the Horse Creek Valley, were apparently anxious to hire the "troublemakers." The president of the local, a weaver named S. J. Thompson, found work in at least two other mills over the next several years, even though he attempted to organize unions wherever he went.[23]

While Whaley did succeed in destroying the union at his mills, his victory was both ambiguous and pyrrhic. The foremen, who were in charge of hiring, reportedly ignored the directives of their superiors and rehired union men without asking any questions. Even that surreptitious compromise failed to prevent Whaley's labor problems, already abnormally bad, from worsening. Dissatisfaction apparently continued among the operatives, despite a management present of a turkey to each mill household at Christmas, and the presentation by "the humble operatives" of a watch and chain to Whaley.[24] The mills had difficulty in obtaining competent help. An English visitor to Columbia in the spring of 1902 reported seeing idle machinery, excessive work loads, and a preponderance of children among the work force, despite a wage rate for spinners 25 percent above the regional average. The labor difficulties of the mills undoubtedly contributed materially to a financial crisis which resulted in Whaley's removal from their management in November, 1903, and his subsequent bankruptcy.[25] In a situation in which operatives could thus "punish" mill managers simply by seeking work elsewhere, the need for labor organization

23. McLaurin, "Early Labor Union Organizational Efforts," 53–55; Columbia *State*, August 30, September 4, 6, 1901. On Thompson, see McLaurin, "Early Labor Union Organizational Efforts," 57–58; Columbia *State*, August 14, 1912. My account of the strike differs from that of McLaurin.

24. Columbia *State*, January 5, 29, 1902.

25. *Ibid.*, September 6, 1901; Thomas M. Young, *The American Cotton Industry: A Study of Work and Workers* (New York: Charles Scribners' Sons, 1903), 68–69. A reporter for *The State* remarked that the 175 strikebreakers at the Richland Cotton Mill included over 20 "very small children" kept at work by their parents. Columbia *State*, August 30, 31, 1901. The impact of strikebreakers on productivity is suggested by the statement of a union operative at Augusta to Young, alleging that strikebreakers used by the mills there during an 1898 strike made goods so poor as to be unsalable. Young, *American Cotton Industry*, 85. On the financial crisis see Fenelon DeVere Smith, "The Economic Development of the Textile Industry in the Columbia, South Carolina Area From 1790 Through 1916" (Ph.D. dissertation, University of Kentucky, 1952), 193–209.

was unclear; it certainly was not a cause for which operatives in Columbia were willing to go to lengths to defend.

Even where conditions were most propitious for unionization the habits of the operatives tended to break up organizations and isolate the mill hands from any potential leadership. Twelve-hour days left them with little time and less inclination to fraternize with the skilled workers in town, and the widespread illiteracy, both absolute and functional, among them rendered many of them inaccessible to the printed word. The predilection of many operatives for "moving about" worked against organization. Most importantly, their backwoods individualism made them ignorant of, if not hostile to, the notion of "subordinating the rights of the individual to secure a greater benefit to the class to which he belongs." John Golden of the United Textile Workers of America declared "ignorance of the mill people in regard to textile unionism" to be the principal obstacle to organization; a survey of South Carolina operatives made by federal investigators indicated that 80 percent of them were unaware that there were any such things as unions.[26] And the extent to which they accepted the leadership of skilled workers is suggested by the Columbia mayoral campaign of 1902, conducted only a few months after the Whaley strike. One of the candidates was M. C. Wallace, a printer with *The State* and secretary of the South Carolina Federation of Labor, who hoped to win the election by uniting the labor vote under his banner. Despite his prominence as a labor leader, though, he received less than a quarter of the vote in the "mill ward," and went down to defeat.[27] The unions were hardly gone forever; indeed, as economic conditions changed in the 1910s they enjoyed another burst of popularity among the mill workers. For the time being, however, the "threat" was evanescent.

26. McLaurin, *Paternalism and Protest*, 193, 204–206; U.S. Bureau of Labor, *Report on Woman and Child Wage Earners in the United States*, Senate Document No. 645, 61st Congress, 2nd Session (19 vols.; Washington: Government Printing Office, 1910), I, 607–11. By comparison, 56.5 percent of New England operatives professed to know nothing of unions.

27. Columbia *State*, March 12, 1902. In 1906 the "mill ward" (Ward Five) rejected a typographer and a railroad man for the General Assembly, while supporting an alleged "mill slate" composed of three lawyers and a farmer from lower Richland County. *Ibid.*, August 23, 29, September 5, 1906.

A deeper and more lasting, if more amorphous, worry among the townspeople was the danger to social stability they saw in the mill population, a fear not so much of social revolution as of an individualistic form of "anarchy." The background of this worry was reflected in the disquiet over "lawlessness." Throughout the later nineteenth century there were repeated expressions of concern over the prevalence of homicide and, more importantly, the lightness with which it was often treated by public opinion; the complaint of a rural Presbyterian minister about "the spirit of lawlessness which prevails among the masses of the people" was echoed in countless other sermons and editorials in the late nineteenth and early twentieth centuries. While the propensity to murder generally knew no class boundaries, much of the blame was nonetheless attached to a "lawless class" which, it was argued, set the tone of public opinion. "The plain fact," wrote the historian David Duncan Wallace, "is that a considerable portion of our population is murder-minded. Homicide is to them merely a form of self-assertion which an exaggerated ego arrogates as its privilege."[28]

This "lawlessness" had a deeper significance, especially for the townsmen. Individual violence was seen as an aspect of an older social organization, one based not on the increasingly rigid rules and rational organization of "modern" life, but upon personal, especially family, loyalties, a strong sense of individual honor, and an insistence on the maintenance of individual prerogatives. Alongside the orderly, well-regulated society the middle classes were trying to create in the towns lay another world, governed, according to one editor, by "the law of the lawless frontiersman, . . . of the handy pistol and blood vengeance."[29] While South Caro-

28. Sermon of Rev. W. H. Reid, in Spartanburg *Carolina Spartan*, January 13, 1886; Carlos Tracy, "On Law and Order in South Carolina" (Charleston: D. L. Alexander, 1880); David Duncan Wallace, *The History of South Carolina* (4 vols.; New York: American Historical Society, 1934), III, 407–10, 413–14.

29. Spartanburg *Herald*, cited in Columbia *State*, November 5, 1903. That "older social organization" is outlined in Bertram Wyatt-Brown, "The Ideal Typology and Ante-Bellum Southern History: A Testing of a New Approach," *Societas*, V (1975), 1–29. For a fascinating discussion of crime and authority in antebellum South Carolina and their relationship to the state's social structure and social attitudes, see Michael S. Hindus, *Prison and Plantation: Crime, Justice and Authority in Massachusetts and South Carolina, 1767–1878* (Chapel Hill: University of North Carolina Press, 1980).

lina's murder rate attracted the bulk of the rhetoric, the social outlook feared by the middle classes had other implications for the well-ordered society they hoped to build. A man to whom the law on murder was irrelevant could not be expected to obey any order or accept any restrictions on his freedom of action. He would be a poorly disciplined worker, and would be hostile to the social machinery required by town life. In politics he would follow men, not principles, and, given a choice between an active, well-organized government and one which left him untrammeled in his rights, would naturally choose the latter.

In this context the enormous expansion of the mill population, especially around the towns, was seen as the injection of a new and dangerous element into community life. As we have seen, the influx into the mills came almost entirely from the countryside, which, despite the rural roots of many of the townspeople, was rapidly becoming an alien place, viewed variously as the arcadia of a fondly remembered childhood and the home of the comical "hayseed," or more darkly as the region of the agrarian agitator and the "lawless" man. More importantly, the various classes entering the mills were seen as social misfits, recruited, *faute de mieux*, to man the industrial machine but untrustworthy as members of the community. The "type" of the mill worker was developed out of a combination of older stereotypes and current conceptions, all of which tended to reinforce the suspicion that the mills were becoming a reservoir for intractable "problem cases."

Three major groups of the rural population were discerned as contributing to the mill population. The first of these was the yeomanry. Composed of small farmers and white croppers, this class was characterized as honest and hard-working, but rendered hopelessly narrow by its hard and isolated life. The yeomen were attracted to the mills as a way out of poverty and as an avenue of advancement. However, the old "philanthropic" notion of the mill as a refuge for the poor led easily to the notion that it was a catch basin for failures. A landholding mill hand in Anderson County told August Kohn in 1907 that he would never rent to any one who had ever worked in a cotton mill; not only was it an admission of ineptitude for farming, but the nature of mill work "spoiled" the operatives. "More judgment," after all, "is necessary on the farm than it is in the running of a machine that is intended to need as little executive capacity as possible."[30]

The notion that moving to a mill was an implicit admission of personal defeat is illustrated in the humorous tale of "Josh," which appeared in an up-country newspaper in 1904. Josh was an independent farmer, "seemingly a good fellow, who worked hard upon his farm, and made a good support for himself and his family"—until he made the mistake of running for political office. Despite lavish expenditure on whiskey and barbecue, financed by a chattel mortgage on his mule, he was soundly defeated. Discouraged, he took to drink and lost, in succession, his crop, his mule, and his credit. "The chilly winds of November found Josh and his family on a mill wagon moving to a cotton mill, where he put his family to work. Himself he took to the old chums who had preceded him. Josh grew from bad to worse and was soon seen with his family moving to one of the Spartan mills. Nothing more was heard of Josh, until last summer during the freshet. He was seen floating on the high tide of the Pacolet with his right arm through the handle of a big two-gallon jug."[31]

The second major source of mill labor was composed of people considered worse than failures, namely the "sandhillers" or stereotypical "poor white trash." Their "type" was noted chiefly for utter apathy and laziness. "A curious creature with no ambition, without aspiration or energy, possessing little intelligence and absolutely lacking in education," they were supposedly so degraded that commentators were at a loss to explain how they summoned the energy to move to the mills; Gonzales could do no more than suggest that they were "unconsciously drawn" there.[32] Whereas the refugee yeomen were afflicted with broken ambitions, the sandhillers had allegedly never had any to be broken. As the so-

30. Columbia *State*, December 16, 1900; Kohn, *Cotton Mills*, 29, 31.

31. "Voter" in Union *Times*, March 25, 1904. The "freshet" referred to was the Pacolet River flood of June 1903, which devastated the Clifton and Pacolet mill settlements of Spartanburg County and took the lives of many mill operatives.

32. Columbia *State*, December 16, 1900. See also the description of "sandhill tackeys" in C. Vann Woodward (ed.), *Mary Chesnut's Civil War* (New Haven: Yale University Press, 1981), 830–32.

ciety of the towns, and the efficiency of industry, depended in part on individual desires to better themselves by mastering the techniques of communal existence, the thought that a large percentage of the population might simply be indifferent to its own "betterment" was, if less than accurate, still deeply disturbing.

Most disquieting of all, however, was the third major source of the mill work force, the mountaineers, for they incarnated for the townsmen the strain of "lawlessness" and anarchic individualism. From an early day the abrupt rise of the Blue Ridge Mountains just a few miles to the northwest of what was destined to be South Carolina's cotton mill belt marked a major cultural divide. Beyond that line lay vaguely understood and seldom visited regions known as "dark corners," the most famous of which lay behind Glassy Mountain in northeastern Greenville County. John William De Forest, who had served as an officer of the Freedmen's Bureau in Greenville between 1866 and 1868, described the inhabitants of the Dark Corner as "poor, uncultured, and, in some cases, half wild," and recounted the Civil War reputation of the place as a haven for Confederate deserters and a center of hostility to the lowland government. The inclination to picture the mountain folk as an exotic breed of barbarian persisted through the nineteenth century and well into the twentieth, despite the efforts of John C. Campbell and others to dispel its more fanciful features. The Dark Corner of Greenville, to lowlanders the symbolic home of the mountaineer, was largely inaccessible; it was said, indeed, that a stranger could never find his way there. Virtually the only strangers who tried were law officers, especially revenue agents, whose forays from their Greenville base provided lively copy for the press of the period. Thus the principal conceptions held by the outside world about the Dark Corner were that it was the abode of moonshiners and a haven for lawbreakers, that its people were distrustful of the outside world, and that they regulated themselves by means of strong family loyalties, a firm code of honor, and, above all, a ferocious commitment to untrammeled individualism. Narciso Gonzales wrote of the mountaineer that "law held no terrors for him, religion presented no attractions and education was unheard of altogether."[33] To be sure, the mountaineers did observe rules; it was known that they could "be trusted to keep their word and not to violate confidence."[34] Personal honor, though, was insufficient to maintain a complex social order; in fact it could be a strong antisocial force if a man's personal loyalties conflicted with the rules and regulations of either industrial or community life. The mountain folk could be regarded simply as picturesque so long as they remained in their hollows; such condescension was no longer possible when they began to move to town.[35]

While such traditional attitudes toward the poorer whites made important contributions to the middle-class image of the cotton mill worker, they were reinforced by increasing problems of social control. Although in 1900 Ellison Smyth could still boast that there had never been a murder in Pelzer, and August Kohn could claim in 1907 that the mill villages needed no police, concern about order in the villages mounted toward the end of the nineteenth century.[36] In 1897 and 1898 a rash of bills were introduced into the General Assembly to provide for law enforcement in dif-

33. John William De Forest, *A Union Officer in the Reconstruction* (New Haven: Yale University Press, 1948), 159–62; Columbia *State*, December 16, 1900; Wallace, *History*, III, 407. See also the description of the Dark Corner of Oconee County in James Benjamin Hilson, *History of the South Carolina Conference of the Wesleyan Methodist Church of America* (Winona Lake, Ind.: Light and Life Press, 1950), 219–27, stressing the persecution of Wesleyan missionaries by the "wicked" because they sought to lift the mountaineers out of their "shame and debauchery." On the legendary remoteness of "dark corners," see E. L. Hughes in Columbia *State*, February 18, 1912. A traveler's description of Greenville's "Dark Corner" appears in Thomas R. Dawley, *The Child That Toileth Not: The Story of a Government Investigation* (New York: Gracia Publishing Company, 1912), 377–403. On violence as a component of the mountaineer image, see Henry D. Shapiro, *Appalachia on Our Mind: The Southern Mountains and Mountaineers in the American Consciousness, 1870–1920* (Chapel Hill: University of North Carolina Press, 1978), 102–12.

34. Union *Progress*, October 22, November 1, 1907. Significantly, the mountaineers referred to here were "trusties" at the state penitentiary. Two of them escaped, reportedly the first time a prisoner from the mountains had ever betrayed a trust. One subsequently returned voluntarily, having gone to visit his wife, who had lost her health working in a Greenville mill.

35. See Columbia *State*, December 1, 1912, for later observations. According to D. E. Camak, a survey of Spartan Mills taken at about the turn of the century indicated that 75 percent of the operatives there came from semi-mountainous Polk County, North Carolina. Camak, *Human Gold*, 37, 91, 136. Spartan Mills was probably atypical in this respect, as most mills drew from their localities; even so, the mountaineer element in the mills loomed large in the townsmen's imagination.

36. Columbia *State*, March 4, 1900; Kohn, *Cotton Mills*, 177. An allegation by an En-

ferent mill towns, and in 1898 a special class of mill constables was created. The law provided that, on petition of the board of directors of any industrial corporation controlling a village population of over one hundred, the sheriff was to appoint a "discreet and suitable person" as a constable to be paid by the mill. His jurisdiction was to include the mill property and all other territory within one mile of the mill.[37]

It is difficult to say how much crime and disorderliness there was in mill communities, for the crime statistics of the period did not classify convicted criminals by neighborhood or occupation. Also, there was evidently great variation from mill to mill. Remarks in the press, however, indicate that problems of order did exist at least in some locales. Commenting on a homicide in 1897, *The State* remarked that "the Richland mill village is attaining an unenviable position in criminal records," and in 1899 it remarked in passing on "the pauperism and crime which even under the best conditions are brought by a mill population." Accounts of Fourth of July celebrations among the operatives went out of their way to emphasize the "orderliness" of the crowds, and a 1900 account of the Darlington Mill noted that "the orderly behavior of the operatives has been commented upon several times by those who are accustomed to seeing the operatives in other places." Occasionally the problem of order was so serious as to inspire more direct comment. In 1900 it was reported that a wave of violence, directed chiefly against blacks, was sweeping the mill villages of Rock Hill. A full-blown "race riot" erupted in Greenville between the villagers at Poe Mill and the residents of a neighboring settlement of black fertilizer factory workers in 1899; "there was considerable firing of guns and pistols," and six men were wounded. From the operative side, a Union correspondent sadly allowed that "we are in some way becoming uncivilized. West End was once one of the

---

glish visitor in 1896 that pistol-toting was ubiquitous among the operatives at the Columbia Mills was indignantly denied by the general manager. Columbia *State*, August 5, 1896.

37. *South Carolina Statutes at Large*, XXII (1898), 793–94. Prior to passage of the general bill, special bills were introduced to provide for constables at Enoree, Pacolet, Piedmont, and Langley in 1897, and for Lancaster, Poe, American Spinning, Pendleton, and Victor in 1898. South Carolina General Assembly, *Senate and House Journals, 1897–98, passim.*

quietest places in town, to-day it is the worst. It is getting so it is dangerous for a decent person to walk at night in some quarters on this side."[38]

The apparent increase in disorder had much to do with the labor shortage. Mills could no longer pick and choose their labor force; in fact they were compelled to begin recruiting and advertising for labor. Many mills employed agents to drum up "help" in the mountains or elsewhere, even at other mills. Letters from "satisfied operatives" began to appear in the newspapers, urging "all poor people who can get here to come" to the mill. Olympia went so far as to prepare a full-page supplement, inserted in "country" newspapers, designed specifically to attract prospective workers.[39] Many mills, particularly the newer ones, were unable to maintain the controls on hiring of which the older mills boasted, especially if they had characteristics undesirable to operatives. Federal investigators reported in 1909 that certain mills, especially around the towns, developed reputations for accepting the cast-off workers of other mills; although the investigators generally found that the mill hands did not deserve their reputation for turbulence and immorality, more of the "less desirable element" were remaining at work in the mills than would have remained when the mills were few and the potential workers many.[40]

Social stability was further eroded by the propensity of many operatives for "moving about." Nomadic tendencies among the operatives appeared early in the history of South Carolina's textile industry. Between 30 and 40 percent of the operatives at Piedmont in April, 1884, had dropped off the payroll within a year; half were gone within two years. However, the small number of mills

38. Columbia *State*, March 1, 1897, July 5, 7, 8, September 30, December 15, 19, 1900; Anderson *Intelligencer*, August 9, 1899; Union *Progress*, October 2, 1901. Cf. the account in Marie Van Vorst and Bessie Van Vorst, *The Woman Who Toils* (New York: Doubleday, Page and Company, 1903), 273, describing the "Calcutta" mill village in Columbia as a place where "the knife comes flashing out at a word" and where "the women shoot as well as men and perhaps more quickly." The credibility of this account, however, is shaky.

39. On labor agents see Kohn, *Cotton Mills*, 23, and Columbia *State*, July 26, 1903. Samples of "satisfied operative" letters appear in *The State*, January 27, 1901, from Piedmont, and January 5, 1902, from Olympia; also Union *Progress*, May 15, 1901, from Lockhart. The Olympia circular appears in Edgefield *Advertiser*, September 25, 1901.

40. Camak, *Human Gold*, 57–61; *Woman and Child Wage Earners*, I, 589–90.

and the relative advantage of management over labor apparently served to inhibit the restless spirit; thus some of the older establishments, notably Graniteville, developed a fairly stable corps of employees.[41] The waning of the century, though, brought increased comment on the rootlessness of much of the mill population. The proliferation of mills and the resulting labor shortage made it easier for an operative to get a job at another mill should he become dissatisfied with his present employer. A large "floating element" thus developed, shifting from mill to mill, and to a lesser extent between the mills and the country; its size was estimated at between 20 and 25 percent of the total mill population. Thomas M. Young, an English visitor, was particularly struck by "the nomadic quality of American labour": "It is by no means unusual for a man, with his wife and family and household goods, to drive up in a wagon to the door of a Southern country mill at four or five o'clock in the afternoon and offer their services. The manager is nearly always glad to see them, and sees that they are housed before nightfall."[42]

This "restless human sea" of mill folk in incessant search of "something better farther on" was not amenable to any of the traditional institutional constraints of South Carolina society. Families disintegrated under the strain; one observer reported that it was not unusual to see small boys, or even girls, moving about through the mill sections of Spartanburg, carrying all their possessions on their backs. The shifting population was immune to the social controls of the villages. The floaters were anonymous peo-

41. Kohn, *Cotton Mills*, 24; Columbia *State*, June 14, 1897. The Piedmont estimates are compiled from Piedmont Manufacturing Company, Time Book, 1884–86 (microfilm copy in South Caroliniana Library, University of South Carolina, Columbia; hereafter cited as SCL). The imprecision of the turnover rates given is due to missing data. Between 30.2 and 41.7 percent of the names on the April 1884 payroll were missing in April 1885; 47.4 percent were missing in April 1886. The cloth room and repair shop employees were omitted from the April 1884 payroll.

42. Young, *American Cotton Industry*, 75–76. In 1922 a federal study determined that turnover in southern cotton mills was twice that of northern mills, and nearly twice that of American industry generally. Fewer than 20 percent of the southern operatives studied stayed on the job for the entire year. U.S. Department of Labor, Women's Bureau, *Bulletin No. 52* (1926), "Lost Time and Labor Turnover in Cotton Mills," 17, 106. Daniel Rodgers estimates that from 20 to 40 percent of southern operatives were "floaters" by 1910. Daniel T. Rodgers, "Tradition, Modernity, and the American Industrial Worker: Reflections and Critique," *Journal of Interdisciplinary History*, VII (1977), 670–72.

ple, employed because the mills needed their labor but otherwise unknown to the management. Most mills segregated them into special transient neighborhoods on the fringes of the village, so that class distinctions developed among the operatives themselves.[43] Although they were essential to the continued functioning of the industry, the chronic movers could not be bossed easily, for any attempt at social control by the mill or the local community might be met by another move.

The best illustration of the problems created for South Carolina, particularly the towns, by the development of the operative class can be found in its impact upon public health. Although the environmental conditions in many mill villages constituted a threat to the health of operatives, those conditions were not necessarily of concern to the towns. Typhoid, for example, was a danger in a mill village without sewerage, drawing its water from surface wells, but was of less concern to the townsman who screened out flies and drank city water. Nor was there a great deal of concern over the epidemics that swept the mill villages in the 1880s and early 1890s, for they were generally mild plagues resulting from the concentration of people hitherto isolated from exposure to the germs. "It is well known that every new town, after the manner of children, has to have the measles," asserted a Pacolet man in 1885, who boasted that of two hundred cases there not one death resulted. The development of mills near towns, however, made townspeople more vulnerable to infections spread from the villages. As early as 1886 a measles epidemic among the operatives at Greenville, then one of the few commercial towns with a contiguous mill district, spread to the townspeople.[44]

Measles, though, was a minor problem compared with what was to come, for in 1897 smallpox entered the state. The strain

43. Camak, *Human Gold*, 25, 30–33, 37; John Kenneth Morland, *Millways of Kent* (Chapel Hill: University of North Carolina Press, 1958), 210–13.

44. Charleston *News and Courier*, June 6, 1884, May 16, 1885; Newberry *Herald and News*, January 26, 1887; Baptist *Courier*, March 25, 1886. On the other hand, a measles epidemic at Piedmont in January 1886 cut the work force by one-half and production by one-third; eighteen deaths resulted, and Hammett reported the people to be "alarmed, discouraged, and demoralized." H. P. Hammett to Woodward, Baldwin and Company, January 29, 1886; Hammett to F. J. Pelzer, February 1, 1886; both in H. P. Hammett Letterbook, SCL.

was mild, and few deaths resulted; however, the disease persisted as a serious health problem until around 1905. The mill villages quickly became major foci of the epidemic, and, worse, became centers of contagion for the rest of the state. The disease could easily be controlled by means of thorough vaccination and careful quarantine of the infected communities, but the difficulties of applying either measure to the mills soon became apparent. While officials at some mills insisted that everyone in their communities be vaccinated, others were loath to take preventive measures, fearing that the resulting sore arms would hurt production or that their work forces might be demoralized. In the early stages of the epidemic some mill superintendents insisted that the disease was chicken pox, and on occasion they were seconded by townspeople who feared a loss of trade resulting from adverse publicity. Usually measures were taken only after the presence of smallpox had been confirmed. Even then, mill officials were often accused of laxity in the enforcement of either vaccination or quarantine.[45]

The major problem, however, was presented by the operatives themselves. There was widespread fear of vaccination among the mill people, just as there was among blacks and many rural whites. The old practice of using human virus instead of the recently introduced bovine virus, plus a frequent lack of sanitary precaution, had caused vaccination to be associated in the popular mind with a high risk of infection to the affected arm; if amputation proved necessary, an operative would lose his employment. At the very least a sore arm would result in lost work time, a grave consideration to working people whose economic circumstances were sufficient for their needs but left them with little in the way of a financial cushion. At the same time, the comparative mildness of the smallpox strain caused many operatives to view the risk of contracting the disease to be the lesser of the two evils; opposition to

45. South Carolina State Board of Health, *Report, 1898*, 562–63; *1903*, 516; *1904*, 941–42; Columbia *State*, February 19, 1898, May 16, 1900; Union *Progress*, April 25, 1900, in which a mill correspondent warned that compulsory vaccination there would "cause hands to leave that would not" otherwise, and thus cause "a great deal of injury to the mill company." On the other hand, for an example of prompt action by a mill abnormally solicitous of the health of its operatives, see the account of the Courtenay Manufacturing Company, in Columbia *State*, February 6, 1898.

vaccination in the mills at Yorkville died out quickly when the strain turned out to be unusually deadly, killing nine of the fifteen reported cases in the town. Finally, if anyone proposed to compel vaccination many operatives opposed it on grounds of "personal liberty." If mill officials or local health authorities insisted, the objecting operative would often move, sometimes with the blessing of the local community, which rid itself of a source of infection by sending it elsewhere.[46]

In this fashion the disease was carried from town to town by operatives moving about either to avoid the disease or to avoid vaccination, and finding a labor-hungry industry eager to hire any experienced hand anywhere.[47] By 1900 the secretary of the State Board of Health was complaining bitterly that, while he had little difficulty in controlling smallpox among Sea Island blacks or city shanty dwellers, "when it comes to the big mill towns with all their boasted good management, it is impossible to do anything." The mill villages, he charged, had become "pest holes for the corruption of the whole State."[48]

Resistance to vaccination by mill workers was not always passive. An obstreperous Rock Hill operative, for example, "swore that he would kill any physician or other person who would attempt to vaccinate himself or any member of his family."[49] A more serious disturbance occurred at Union, where in the spring of 1900 the town Board of Health launched a thoroughgoing campaign to bring the local smallpox epidemic under control, isolating cases, requiring universal vaccination, and sealing off the town to prevent flight. The mill's own doctors were in charge of vaccinating the operatives on the West End, where the Union Mills were located, but they were lax in their duties, permitting some families to refuse. As they failed to keep records of those refusing, the town

46. S.C. State Board of Health *Report, 1904*, 941; *1909*, 1387; Columbia *State*, March 19, 1898; Union *Times*, May 4, 1900; Rock Hill *Herald*, January 22, 1902.

47. Anderson *Intelligencer*, February 14, 1900. When the General Assembly provided for statewide compulsory vaccination in 1905, a provision requiring mills to vaccinate their villagers and prohibiting them from hiring unvaccinated employees was struck out without debate. Columbia *State*, February 17, 1905.

48. James Evans in Florence *Times*, quoted in Columbia *State*, May 23, 1900.

49. Rock Hill *Herald*, January 22, 1902.

physician found it necessary to make a house-to-house canvass of the mill district. What happened next is not altogether clear. The physician entered the district accompanied by constables. When an unvaccinated young man refused to submit, the physician ordered him arrested. In the meantime a crowd had gathered; later the Board of Health termed it a mob, alleging that it had assaulted the constables and freed the boy, while the operatives insisted that he had escaped and that the crowd had simply blocked pursuit by the lawmen. For the next several days relations between mill and town were tense. The Board sent excited messages to the governor alleging mass meetings of protest on "the hill" and expressing fear for their lives, while a constable reported that a woman had urged mob violence to free an arrested resister. On the other side, the president of the Union Mills, T. C. Duncan, took the part of the operatives, condemning the town physician and his assistants as "ruffians." The governor sent Secretary Evans of the State Board of Health to Union to investigate the matter, obtain a compromise between Duncan and the Board, and prevent violence. The Board, however, resigned in a body in late May, charging that Duncan, to whom responsibility for vaccination at the mill had been returned under the compromise, had neglected his duty. The old Board was replaced by a panel chaired by Duncan, which evidently softened the rigors of the campaign; smallpox was still raging in the town that December, when a local doctor stated weakly that "we hope to stamp it out if the people will allow us to vaccinate them."[50]

The difficulty in Union illustrated more than the difficulty of imposing regulations upon people not used to town life. It was one of the proliferating indications that a breach was developing between mill people and town people, that despite all the rhetorical self-assurances about white solidarity the operatives were in fact becoming a separate social class, living in sullen isolation on the outskirts of "civilized" town society. To a large degree the increasing mutual hostility was the fault of the town classes themselves.

50. My account is derived from articles in Columbia *State*, May 8, 10, 13, 26, 28, 29, June 3, December 6, 8, 1900; Union *Times*, April 20, 27, May 4, 11, 1900; Union *Progress*, May 9, 1900. Most of the documentation is in the form of correspondence between the governor and the principal parties involved, reprinted in *The State*. Coverage in the local press was sparse.

While the theme of racial solidarity continued to be exploited by different people for different ends, the notion that operatives were "necessarily vicious in their tendencies and, hence, undesirable citizens" had developed enough respectability by the turn of the century to be accepted in the public print as an admissible viewpoint rather than as an irrational prejudice to be dismissed out of hand. The fact that the town physician entered the Union mill district accompanied by constables, a precaution not deemed necessary when he toured the town, was indicative of a presumption that, as a representative of town authority, he could expect trouble from the mill people; his attitude did not escape the operatives. Nor did it escape them that their definition as a class by the outside world, especially by the townsmen, had disquieting implications for their social status. A Newberry doctor's announcement during a local epidemic that he would vaccinate white people at one hour, blacks at another, and "factory people" at a third, could hardly have been reassuring to operatives who took pride in their membership in the white race. Nor could Columbia operatives have been particularly happy about the passage in a *State* editorial in 1905 concerning them which deprecated the innate superiority of a white skin: "The white man's supremacy over the negro is in civilization: in morals and education. It is not inherent in each individual. There are many whites as uncivilized, brutish and depraved as the lower stratum of blacks; such whites deserve nothing from their connection with a superior race; they contribute nothing to its supremacy."[51] The color line remained a crucial division in turn-of-the-century South Carolina, but the old identification of race and class was beginning to break down. The townspeople increasingly viewed, not race, but "civilization" as the decisive measure of man. Furthermore, there was little doubt among most of them that the generality of operatives, whatever their "stock," did not measure up on that scale.

For their part, the mill workers responded to town condescension with deep resentment. "We are law-abiding citizens not heathen," proclaimed a Union operative at the time of the vaccination

51. Columbia *State*, May 10, December 16, 1900; January 21, 1905; Wallace, *History*, III, 425.

difficulty. "We claim civil rights; we are not under marshall [*sic*] law, and we don't intend to be forced on to measures that we don't wish by no authorities."[52] Operatives became notable for their sensitivity to slights, above all to any indication that their status was not that of "white men."

Significantly, many of the overt displays of operative hostility toward the middle classes concerned real or fancied breaches of the color line. Some involved an economic fear that black labor would be used by mill owners to reverse the economic advantage conferred on white workers by the labor shortage. The operatives had some cause for concern, for as pressure increased on the labor supply in the late 1890s the possibility of using blacks as operatives, heretofore dismissed out of hand, attracted increasing interest from manufacturers. A proposal in 1896 to employ Negroes in a projected knitting mill at Bamberg, a low-country town, stirred controversy in the state press, with the Greenville *News*, a reliable manufacturers' spokesman, leading the advocates. Although the Bamberg project failed to materialize, in 1897 an effort was made to operate the Charleston Cotton Mill with an all-black work force. The company failed in 1899, but was succeeded by a far more elaborate experiment with black labor. Named the Vesta Cotton Mill, it received heavy capital backing from Seth Milliken, and was managed by Milliken's Spartanburg ally John H. Montgomery. Montgomery was deeply committed to the success of the enterprise; were blacks to prove serviceable as operatives, he told Ellison Smyth, there would be "no more trouble about labor—no strikes, labor unions, etc. among the whites." Montgomery's enthusiasm notwithstanding, however, Milliken, the "backbone" of the enterprise, withdrew his support in 1901, and the mill closed. Although Montgomery and other manufacturers insisted that the results of the Vesta "experiment" were inconclusive, the mill's failure effectively stifled interest in black labor for some years to come. The willingness of industrialists to challenge the traditional reservation of mill work to whites in order to enhance their own power, however, was yet another indication that in the new indus-

52. "B. F. G." in Union *Progress*, May 9, 1900.

trial South a white skin was no longer a badge of automatic membership in the ruling class. Operatives saw in the Vesta experiment, said a Georgia newspaper, "either social degradation or starvation wages," and "were not slow to express themselves" on the matter. The old sense of solidarity between workers and mill presidents was shaken. The superintendent at Lockhart, commenting to a former employer on the announcement that Montgomery was trying "colored help," expressed bewilderment that a man who had "the good will of the mill operatives . . . not only of his mills but all the mills in the country" would thus betray their trust; "I would not if I could let my ambition carry me so far as that," he declared. Unable to square his admiration for Montgomery with the industrialist's treason to his race, the superintendent could only hope that he would "fail on purpose"; "if he will do that he will do the greatest piece of work he has ever done in his life."[53]

Most operatives, lacking the superintendent's identification with management, were far less trusting of the industrial leadership; furthermore, they were not averse to demonstrating their suspicions publicly. As early as 1890 an attempt by the management of the Charleston Cotton Mill to add blacks to its work force resulted in a minor race riot in which the blacks were forcibly driven from the factory. When the mill first tried an all-black work force in 1897, the three hundred displaced white operatives made threats against both the black workers and the white officials. At one point police were called in to protect the factory and its employees from milling crowds. In defense of their position the operatives issued a broadside so incendiary that the local press refused to print it. Described by *The State* as "caustic, to say the least of

53. A general discussion of turn-of-the-century interest in the use of black labor in cotton mills appears in Allen Heath Stokes, Jr., "Black and White Labor and the Development of the Southern Textile Industry, 1800–1920" (Ph.D. dissertation, University of South Carolina, 1977), 196–212, 231–61. See also Broadus Mitchell, *The Rise of Cotton Mills in the South* (Baltimore: Johns Hopkins University Press, 1921), 213–21. The quotations are from John H. Montgomery to Ellison Smyth, December 26, 1899, cited in Stokes, "Black and White Labor," 251; Athens (Georgia) *Banner*, cited in Allen H. Stokes, Jr., "John H. Montgomery: A Pioneer Southern Industrialist" (M.A. thesis, University of South Carolina, 1967), 118; and J. H. Williams to W. C. Coker, March 19, 1899, in W. C. Coker Papers, Darlington County Historical Society, Darlington, S.C. (courtesy of Mr. Horace F. Rudisill).

it," the broadside attacked President C. O. Witte as "a negro-loving mill president" who would "quake upon his luxurious couch of ease" if he ever felt the full force of the white operatives' indignation. While the Charleston disturbance was the result of an economic grievance, conflict was stirred even by hints of black encroachment upon the prerogatives of white mill hands. In 1900 operatives in Yorkville chased off a black sweeper who they felt was unduly familiar with the white woman operatives. The presence of a handful of blacks in the Columbia "Duck Mill," working at tasks, such as oiling and cleaning machinery, which were avoided by the whites, caused a disturbance in the card room in February of 1901. The blacks were ejected from the room by several of the operatives, who alleged that the blacks "got so big that they walked on the white ladies' dresses, and pushed them back from their work."[54] The less than amicable relations of mill and town in Union received a jolt at the public school commencement in June of the same year, when the pupils from the Union Mill school were placed in the balcony of the local Opera House, normally reserved for blacks; a sizable disturbance apparently resulted.[55] The extent of mill sensitivity was illustrated in 1905, when *The State*, endorsing proposed legislation for statewide compulsory vaccination, incautiously declared it to be a measure for the protection of "the negro population and the inhabitants of factory villages." A local mill minister promptly objected to the linkage of the two groups, on the ground that it was degrading to the operatives: "Common respect for the white race should have given us, at least, a separate paragraph in the statement of existing conditions. . . . We respectfully ask that in your future editorials you treat us as white men and not like we were some lower order of human beings."[56]

54. Charleston *News and Courier*, May 29, June 22, 1897; Columbia *State*, June 17, 1897, February 19, 1901. For similar disturbances elsewhere in the South see Stokes, "Black and White Labor," 205–209.

55. Union *Progress*, June 5, 1901. The Union disturbance was not reported in the local press; however, *Progress* published an explanation from the school superintendent, insisting that there had been no desire to segregate mill children involved in the seating arrangements.

56. Columbia *State*, January 17, 1905; W. J. Snyder, *ibid.*, January 19, 1905. Snyder himself did not have a mill background; he grew up in the coastal town of Beaufort and was a graduate of Wofford College. He became peculiarly interested in the mill people, however,

Aside from such race-related protests, however, the grievances of the mill people toward the towns rarely found a focus. Lacking either a tradition of class identity or the leadership with which to create one, the operatives settled into a sullen, obstinate opposition to the townspeople, based less on class consciousness than on an automatic suspicion of anything identified with the town. Such amorphous hostility provided perfect raw material for politicians. The first efforts at political mobilization of the operatives were made in the early 1890s by lieutenants of Benjamin R. Tillman. While Tillman was chiefly a spokesman for landholding farmers, and looked down upon the "damned factory class,"[57] the hostility of both rural Tillmanites and operatives toward the towns created the potential for an alliance, which was exploited in several places by local leaders. In 1890 the Factory Democratic Club was organized at Newberry; its moving spirits were two "reform" leaders, Sampson Pope and a smooth young lawyer named Cole L. Blease. In Spartanburg another young attorney, Stanyarne Wilson, who had used his legal practice to form alliances among the mill workers, used their votes in successive climbs to the state house of representatives, the state senate, and the United States Congress. Wilson was materially aided in his work by the Tillmanite editor T. Larry Gantt, who supported hours legislation in his newspaper, the *Piedmont Headlight*, and was known as a particular friend of the operatives. The appeal of these local politicians for operative support was based on more than simple anti-town prejudice, however. They were all enthusiastic advocates of legislation to limit the hours of work in cotton mills, passage of which they engineered in 1892.[58]

---

and frequently undertook to defend the operatives from "insults," especially those of fellow Methodist clergy. See *Southern Christian Advocate*, July 14, 1904, March 11, 1909.

57. Tillman insisted that the celebrated phrase was garbled and used out of context by his enemies, but his explanation was weak. Columbia *State*, August 16, 18, 19, 1892; Columbia *Register*, quoted in Newberry *Herald and News*, September 14, 1892.

58. Newberry *Herald and News*, May 15, 22, 1890; Gustavus G. Williamson, Jr., "South Carolina Cotton Mills and the Tillman Movement," *Proceedings of the South Carolina Historical Association, 1949*, 37–39. On Gantt see Jones, *Stormy Petrel*, 190–93, 211; Greenville *Daily News*, January 29, 1903. In 1887 Wilson served as attorney for a group of striking Clifton operatives contesting mill eviction notices. Spartanburg *Carolina Spartan*, September 28, 1887.

Despite their appeal, the success of the Tillmanites in attaching the operatives to their cause was partial at best. On the one hand Tillman won by a handsome margin in the traditionally class-conscious Horse Creek Valley, and in Spartanburg County Wilson was able to deliver impressive majorities for Tillman at mill villages adjacent to the city of Spartanburg. On the other hand, Tillman lost three of the four major outlying mill precincts of Spartanburg County, losing Enoree and Pacolet by landslides. Pelzer narrowly supported the Conservative ticket, while Piedmont, whose President was the Conservative (anti-Tillman) candidate for lieutenant governor, voted Conservative by better than two to one.[59] The more isolated mill communities were still dominated by the personalities of the mill officials, and their workers, living remote from other communities, still looked upon the employers as natural leaders. However, the Tillmanite majorities at the mills around Spartanburg suggested the shape of things to come. The operatives of town or suburban mills had the sort of direct experience of town disdain lacked by residents of "country" mills such as Enoree, Pacolet, or Piedmont. Their location also made them accessible to organization by young professionals based in the towns but willing to strike poses inimical to their own class for the sake of votes; men such as Blease or Wilson could organize nearby operatives with much greater ease than they could those in more remote villages where the management had greater control. The future was on their side, for the coming mill boom of the late 1890s would create large mill voting blocs adjacent to the towns, simmering with resentment toward the townspeople and ripe for exploitation.

Partial and localized as it was, the Tillmanite attempt to mobilize mill voters disturbed some townspeople, especially those convinced that the Tillman movement was somehow "radical." In the wake of the election of 1892 a Spartanburg editor complained of the unrest the campaign had stirred in the mills, and accused

59. Spartanburg *Carolina Spartan*, September 7, 1892; Columbia *State*, August 31, 1892; Charleston *News and Courier*, September 1, 1892; Aiken *Journal and Review*, August 31, 1892. No separate returns were reported for the Newberry Mill; the town voted Conservative, but the mill population was probably largely Tillmanite.

"the socialistic element in the county" of "pandering to this sentiment."[60] By the turn of the century anxiety over the "mill vote" was far more widespread; however, the concern was less over operative allegiance to any particular faction (the Tillman movement having disintegrated) than over the seeming impermeability of mill voters to town influence and control. Beginning in 1900, every election year brought increasing complaints that the mill vote was easily corruptible. By 1904 the Horse Creek Valley had acquired an unsavory reputation for the widespread practice of bribery, according to a local editor, "political corruption having been allowed to grow and flourish there" for years. One Aiken County man claimed that "he could take fifteen hundred dollars and open four or five blind tigers in the factory district . . . and get elected to any office regardless of his fitness." At about the same time a Chester man complained that "the ignorance of a large class of our citizens and the size of the purchaseable vote in South Carolina has already become a menace to good government. . . . Any candidate who fails to carry the cotton mill vote of York and Chester Counties is very apt to fail of election. And this is true of many other counties in this State. I don't mean to say that all the purchaseable vote of the State is at the cotton mills, but there is enough of it there to be politically unhealthy."[61]

The fearful attitudes of town folk toward political participation by the propertiless rabble of the mill villages inevitably led to conflict. In Union, where many operatives were disfranchised by the use of the constitutional suffrage requirements in municipal elections, complaints were voiced that the registration supervisors were deliberately discriminating against mill voters; one official was alleged to have remarked that "the majority of the factory operatives had been on the chain gang and those that hadn't there was no telling how long before they would be."[62] Stronger political expressions of mill-town enmity appeared in Columbia. The con-

60. Spartanburg *Carolina Spartan*, September 7, 1892.

61. Aiken *Journal and Review*, October 14, 1904; L. S. Trotti in Columbia *State*, December 24, 1904; W. H. Edwards, *ibid.*, January 30, 1905. See also the editorial of January 31, 1905.

62. W. E. G. Humphries to Gov. Miles B. McSweeney, April 8, 1902, in Governor Miles B. McSweeney Papers, South Carolina Department of Archives and History, Columbia.

struction of the mills there resulted in an enormous increase in the voting population of Ward Five, the southernmost ward of the city, and the new voters immediately came under suspicion from such prominent local townspeople as N. G. Gonzales. At first Gonzales feared that the various Whaley mills might attempt to control the city through the votes of their operatives; all the officers of the Democratic party ward organization were Whaley employees, the president being the superintendent of the Granby Cotton Mill. In order to forestall such control, Gonzales and his newspaper spearheaded a drive in January, 1900, to tighten the lax procedures then followed in municipal voting registration, and to require a minimum of four months' residence for city voters. The proposal was hotly contested by officials in Ward Five, the ward president accusing Gonzales of seeking "to place the poor working white man with the negro and deprive him of his right to express his preference in the choice of city officers." Gonzales, in reply, indicated that he did not consider most mill operatives to be bona fide citizens. Unlike other workmen of the city, he argued, they paid no taxes, and many were transients; more importantly, unlike railroad men and printers, they were not "independent," but could be easily herded by the mill organization. Despite heavy support from the business community, Gonzales' plan was gutted by the executive committee of the city Democratic party. Gonzales proclaimed the loss to be a defeat for "the men who have the greatest stake in the community" by agents of "the unrepresentative, shifting and irresponsible factory operatives of Ward Five and the one man power looming behind them."[63]

Gonzales' fears that operative voters would be manipulated by the mill corporations eased after 1900, but the association of the mill vote with rampant corruption continued. It was noted in 1902, for example, that the mill ward supported the same mayoral candidate as the "West End," the most disreputable section of the city, the implication being that the mill vote had been influenced

63. *Ibid.*, December 15, 1899, January 11, 20, 22, 30, February 1, 3, 1900. It was probably more than coincidental that Gonzales' first editorial against child labor in the mills appeared in the midst of this controversy.

by underworld elements.[64] Despite this and other allegations, there is little evidence that mill operatives sold their votes to any unusual degree. Their opposition to town voters was due not so much to "poor moral fiber" or even illiteracy as to a not unjustified fear that the townspeople wished to reduce them in status and control their lives. In Columbia, for example, Gonzales' attempts to restrict the franchise and his open suspicion of the mill population gave the operatives ample ground to suspect that the intentions toward them of *The State* and the "respectable," "tax-paying" element it represented were less than benign. Thus, throughout the first years of the twentieth century the vote in Ward Five consistently diverged from that polled in the four "town" wards, the mill hands often throwing their overwhelming support to the candidate least liked by the town, and especially by *The State*.[65] If a candidate's crudity offended town voters, if his cavalier approach to law enforcement scandalized the upright, or if his blatant racism and insistence upon the supremacy of all white men clashed with middle-class paternalism toward blacks and poor whites alike, his very liabilities in the town precincts became assets around the mills. To be sure, Columbia was probably afflicted with sharper class divisions than yet existed elsewhere in the state,[66] but the pattern developing there was, like the earlier Tillmanite showings, a harbinger of the future in the rest of South Carolina.

The first statewide candidate to attempt a special appeal to mill workers was James H. Tillman, nephew of "Pitchfork Ben," who was elected lieutenant governor in 1900 in part by making "special appeals and promises" to the mill voters. Described by his uncle's biographer as "reckless but affable," he was notorious as a rogue, "a free spender of his own and other people's money, a gambler, a drinker, a rascal who sometimes tried to wear the cloak of righ-

64. *Ibid.*, March 20, 1902, remarking sardonically that a victory celebration of the winning mayoral candidate, opposed by the newspaper, was "composed of the elite of the West End with a liberal sprinkling of substantial burghers from the mill villages of Ward Five."

65. *Ibid.*, March 7, 1900, March 12, 19, 1902, March 16, 1904, March 14, 1906.

66. See remarks of "The Idler" in Spartanburg *Free Lance*, August 29, 1902, noting "a little more feeling between the classes in Columbia than elsewhere in this state," although he may have been referring chiefly to the organized skilled workers.

teousness." He was also a blatant racial demagogue, an early, less successful suggestion of what his protégé Cole L. Blease was to become. He was, of course, anathema to respectable townspeople; when he ran for governor in 1902 all the newspapers of the state opposed him vehemently, none with more venom than Gonzales' *State*. Tillman's attempt to build a cotton mill bloc failed, chiefly because a "favorite son" candidate, Martin F. Ansel of Greenville, swept the mill precincts in most of the western counties. However, Tillman received strong support in Spartanburg, and his success in Columbia was spectacular; while the town wards there gave him but 22.2 percent of their votes, he swept Ward Five with 71.4 percent. In the state as a whole Tillman went crashing down to defeat, due in large part to Gonzales' relentless campaign against him. While the editor was elated with the statewide victory for "decency," he was less than happy when he viewed the local returns. The heavy Tillman vote in the mills he termed a "blind vote," cast by people impermeable to such "civilizing" influences as newspapers and indeed "predisposed to vote counter to the majority in the city proper. . . . Surely the existence of such a vote is a menace to the welfare of the community in which it is found."[67]

The part played by operatives in the traumatic sequel to Tillman's defeat brought to a focus middle-class anxieties over "lawlessness," politics, and class enmity. On the afternoon of January 15, 1903, James Tillman shot down the unarmed N. G. Gonzales on Main Street in Columbia; the editor died four days later. Tillman's trial, probably the most sensational in the history of South Carolina, took place the succeeding fall, after a change of venue had removed it from an outraged Columbia to "neutral" Lexington, twelve miles away. Despite a widespread belief that Tillman would not be punished, some viewed the trial as a major test of the willingness of South Carolinians to enforce the law and maintain order. "The jury which passes upon [Tillman's] guilt or innocence," declared the Greenville *Daily News*, "will at the same time pass

67. Francis Butler Simkins, *Pitchfork Ben Tillman: South Carolinian* (Baton Rouge: Louisiana State University Press, 1944), 380–82; Columbia *State*, August 26, 28, September 16, 19, 1902.

upon the standard of civilization of the State of South Carolina."[68]

That jury, as it turned out, included four cotton mill operatives, a fact not lost on the defense, whose strategy, it became apparent, was not so much their announced intention to plead self-defense as to convince the jury that Gonzales somehow deserved his fate. Ostensibly to demonstrate that the editor's attacks on Tillman continued after his defeat and were thus motivated not by public spirit but by personal malice, the defense placed into evidence a post-election editorial attributing Tillman's strong showing in Richland County to an unholy alliance of sandhillers and cotton mill operatives with "the law-defying element interested in illegal liquor-selling and gambling." The implied slur was repeatedly alluded to in the defense summations. Attorney George Rembert suggested that Gonzales considered mill workers "riff-raff." P. H. Nelson contended that the editor had feared the mill voters, as well as those of the sandhills, because they were "antagonistic to what he considered the best element in the county of Richland," namely "bank presidents, mill presidents, . . . the Virginia-Carolina Chemical Company and men similarly engaged." The leader of the defense forces, George Johnstone, was more charitable, arguing that Gonzales had been driven to verbal excess by his "immoderate spirit," and was not guilty of class prejudice. However, he coupled his disclaimer with a crafty appeal to the operatives' racial pride; addressing Gonzales' friends, he asked rhetorically, "Do you claim the right to class the honest factory element, the hard-working factory element of the State, bone of our bone, flesh of our flesh, marrying our people and we marrying theirs—do you class them as among the gamblers and blind tigers?" In vain did William Elliott, Jr., of the prosecution point to the editor's fight for child labor legislation and insist that he was "the best friend the cotton mill people of South Carolina ever had." The mill workers on the jury joined the other members in a unanimous vote for acquittal.[69]

68. Greenville *Daily News*, January 27, 1903.

69. From the transcripts, printed in Columbia *State*, October 8, 13, 14, 16, 1903. The "incriminating" editorial was "The Voters of Richland," *ibid.*, September 16, 1902. A brief summary of the trial appears in Jones, *Stormy Petrel*, 303–307. Rembert later became Cole L. Blease's floor leader in the General Assembly.

In the ensuing flood of indignation over the "farcical" verdict the presence of operatives on the jury was not ignored. Several newspapers printed the names and occupations of the jurors, blaming their "narrow, stupid ignorance and blinding, bitter political prejudice" for the state's "disgrace."[70] William Watts Ball's scathing final dispatch from Lexington called special attention to the exploitation of operative resentments by the defense: "Oh, what irony of fate that smooth-tongued lawyers should have convinced a mill-hand jury that the man on trial had slain their enemy—that same Gonzales whose last great political struggle sprang from his sympathy for their little children, a struggle whose motive those who opposed him honored!"[71] To be sure, two-thirds of the "mill-hand jury" were in fact farmers, and the outrage of press and pulpit was directed as much against the "ignorant" class of the countryside as that of the mills. Even so, the fact that operatives had collaborated in setting free the murderer of an unarmed journalist whose chief crime had been a zealous concern for "decency" in government, and that they had done so after appeals had been made to their hostility toward the class he represented, could not have failed to feed the fears of the townspeople that the mill villages had become seed-beds for a home-grown variety of anarchy.

If the operatives posed a major threat to South Carolina's "civilization," nonetheless their very situation presented a golden opportunity to the "civilizing" agencies of the towns. The institutions of cotton mill paternalism, perfunctory and inadequate as they were, were yet capable of development. In addition, the gathering of poor whites into communities made them accessible to a wide range of "uplift" agencies, sponsored not only by mill officials but also by religious denominations, private individuals and groups, and the state.[72]

70. Spartanburg *Journal*, October 16, 1903, quoted in Columbia *State*, October 19, 1903, and in Union *Progress*, October 28, 1903; Spartanburg *Herald*, in Columbia *State*, November 5, 1903; Greenville *Daily News*, October 16, 1903. The only direct statement from a juror on the verdict was a letter to the editor of the Spartanburg *Journal* from W. I. Risinger, a farmer, who argued that Gonzales' death was due not to murder but to "suicide by the abuse of liberty [of the press] with the wrong man." Spartanburg *Journal*, October 22, 1903.

71. Columbia *State*, October 16, 1903. Ball, then proprietor of the Laurens *Advertiser*, had opposed child labor reform.

72. *Ibid.*, December 16, 1900.

Above all, they were accessible to that organizing "town spirit" which had built so many of the mills to begin with. The businessmen of the towns had organized to increase the material welfare of their communities; toward the end of the century townspeople were beginning to develop organizations devoted to civic welfare. Particularly important were women's groups. Composed largely of career women, such as school teachers, and the wives of business and professional men, they had begun as social, cultural, or religious societies. However, they increasingly concerned themselves with applying the techniques of organized effort to such "women's concerns" as charity and child welfare. Well before the advent of Rotary, "town" women had begun to organize service clubs. In South Carolina the most notable of these was a nondenominational Christian society called the King's Daughters. Established in 1889, its members had long dabbled in "uplift" work in various localities. The cotton mill boom of the late 1890s saw an intensification of their efforts, especially in Columbia, where the local "circle" established a library and sewing room for mill girls and collaborated in the opening of a kindergarten.[73]

Such rudimentary early efforts at "uplift," however, were superficial, and were hardly more effective than the early mill "paternalism" had been. The ladies soon discovered that the "mill problem" was far larger and more intractable than they had suspected. In a letter to *The State* in the fall of 1899, a shocked clubwoman reported on her canvassing efforts on behalf of the kindergarten. She had toured the Richland Cotton Mill village seeking children under ten years of age and inviting them to kindergarten, but had been told at house after house that the children could not come—they had to work.[74] She and the other King's Daughters quickly came to the same conclusion that John C. Roper had reached several years earlier, and that N. G. Gonzales was about to reach: that the assimilation of the operatives into "modern" society required major intervention by the state into the social order. In order to extend the blessings of "civilized" life to the mill workers

73. Charleston *News and Courier*, November 16, December 4, 1890, June 13, 1897; Columbia *State*, February 8, April 13, 1896, March 29, 1899; *Carolina Teachers' Journal* (June, 1899), 6–8.

74. "A King's Daughter," in Columbia *State*, October 8, 1899.

it was necessary to extend new and unprecedented controls over the state's major industry and especially the operative class it had brought into being. Particularly was it important to control the children of the mills. Not only were they the future citizens of the state, but the plasticity of their young minds afforded an opportunity for the middle classes to breach the wall of hostility and lack of education separating them from the operatives, and to imbue the upcoming generation of mill workers with the "proper" values. "It is to the interest of South Carolina," said Gonzales, "that she shall rear up a race of white people . . . whose minds shall be illuminated by education and who shall be capable of maintaining the sturdy values of the past."[75]

In order to begin this great missionary enterprise, however, one thing was needful—the elimination of child labor. Recognizing this, the King's Daughters of Columbia persuaded their state senator to introduce child labor legislation in the next General Assembly. The introduction of this bill, along with its subsequent endorsement by Gonzales, marked a watershed in South Carolina social history; the Progressive era in social legislation had begun.[76] With that era arose a complex of issues involving the role of the state in society, the limits of individual and property rights, and above all the relationship between a paternal middle class seeking to extend its control over the remainder of South Carolina society and a fiercely individualistic operative class defending its status and perceived interests from reformers whose humanitarian motives it had reason to suspect. The battles over the major social and labor legislation of the period from 1900 to World War I, particularly over child labor reform and compulsory school attendance, provide the best illustrations not only of the basic structure of the middle-class program of "uplift" but the nature of the hostility of those to be "uplifted" toward their putative saviors.

75. *Ibid.*, November 5, 1902.

76. Elizabeth Huey Davidson, *Child Labor Legislation in the Southern Textile States* (Chapel Hill: University of North Carolina Press, 1939), 91.

Chapter V

Solving the "Mill Problem" The Reformers and the Operatives

The story of the reform movements of the Progressive era was long treated by historians as an exemplary tale, a struggle of good against evil resulting in a solid if not yet final victory by the forces of virtue. The traditional account of the movement to restrict child labor was no exception. By and large, those who dealt directly with the movement began with the understandable assumption that the prohibition of child employment is a positive good; certainly, few today are likely to advocate a return to the days when "young girls toiled in damp, dust-laden cotton mills for long hours, six days a week." Unfortunately, the general acceptance of the fruits of child labor reform tended to mute criticism of the tree that bore it. Thus, for instance, Walter I. Trattner's study of the National Child Labor Committee described its membership as "motivated by pity, compassion, and a sense of patriotism"; Elizabeth Huey Davidson's standard work on child labor legislation in the South characterized reform arguments there as "chiefly humanitarian."[1]

1. Walter I. Trattner, *Crusade for the Children: A History of the National Child Labor Committee and Child Labor Reform in America* (Chicago: Quadrangle, 1970), 11; Elizabeth Huey Davidson, *Child Labor Legislation in the Southern Textile States* (Chapel Hill: University of North Carolina Press, 1939), 62. Other studies of child labor reform in the United States along these lines include Forest Chester Ensign, *Compulsory School Attendance and Child Labor* (Iowa City, Iowa: Athens Press, 1921), and Jeremy P. Felt, *Hostages of Fortune: Child Labor Reform in New York State* (Syracuse, N.Y.: Syracuse University Press, 1965). Joseph M. Speakman, "Unwillingly to School: Child Labor and Its Reform in Pennsylvania in the Progressive Era" (Ph.D. dissertation, Temple University, 1976), takes later historical views into account, but argues that child labor reform in Pennsylvania, in its early stages at least, was basically humanitarian in intent.

A full understanding of child labor reform was further obscured by historians' preoccupation with "the greed of the capitalists" as "the chief cause of the child labor evil."[2] Manufacturers possessed not only wealth and influence but considerable argumentative skills as well; these powers, along with their obvious self-interest, made them the natural leaders of the opposition to reform. Historians thus tended to frame the debate over child labor legislation in terms of articulate reformers versus articulate manufacturers, a practice which tended to oversimplify both the nature of the reform impulse and the character of its opposition. The most serious ramification of this approach was its relegation of the workers themselves to the sidelines of the struggle, save insofar as they were spoken for by representatives of organized labor; since union officials spoke for few industrial workers at this time, especially in the burgeoning mass production industries, those most interested in the outcome of the debate seemed to have no voice in it.

Over the past quarter century, however, a different and darker picture of Progressivism has emerged. Inspired by the successive fascination and disenchantment of post–World War II intellectuals with the domination of American life by large organizations, Progressive reform has been reinterpreted in recent years as part of a "search for order." According to the revisionists, the driving force of the age was the effort of a rising business and professional elite to reconstruct American society along hierarchical, bureaucratic lines under its own firm control. Thus, for instance, Michael B. Katz and David B. Tyack argue that the expansion and elaboration of public schooling in this period was designed chiefly to domesticate and organize a turbulent and diverse society through the training of its children. By bringing the child under the supervision of a professionalized bureaucracy in tune with the dominant powers of the country, they contend, reformers hoped to replace the chaos and contention of early modern America with efficiency and order. Christopher Lasch has extended the analysis to the entire social welfare movement, arguing that the rise of the "helping professions" has been accompanied by an invasion of the auton-

2. Davidson, *Child Labor Legislation*, 63.

omy of the family by agencies of social control, a process which he terms "the proletarianization of parenthood."[3]

The revisionist interpretation of progressivism has frequently overstated its case; nonetheless, it provides, more than the traditional account, a useful framework for understanding the relationship of social reform and industrialization in South Carolina. The legislative changes enacted during the Progressive era were limited in their benefits to the operatives, and efforts to "uplift" the lower orders were often accompanied by an almost callous complacency about their economic conditions. The limits of the reformers' concerns, furthermore, bore a direct relationship to their avowed intentions. While their attitudes could certainly be described as "idealistic" or "humanitarian," their principal object was the organization of society under their leadership, a concern evinced both by their rhetoric and by their emphases. Disturbed by the growing antagonism between the mill population and the "town people," the reformers, generally middle-class themselves, proposed to use the powers of the state to attack what they perceived to be the root cause of the difficulty, the cultural segregation of the mill villager from the town, its people, and its acculturating agencies. While they certainly recognized the industrial system as a factor producing that segregation, they viewed it chiefly as reinforcing an anachronistic culture brought from the countryside by the mill hands themselves.

Far from viewing "greedy capitalists" as the principal cause of the "mill problem," the middle-class townsmen courted them, applauded their beneficences, and overlooked as much as possible their persistent obstruction of the Progressive program. The bulk of the reformers' opprobrium was directed, instead, at the opera-

3. Robert H. Wiebe, *The Search for Order, 1877–1920* (New York: Hill and Wang, 1967); James Weinstein, *The Corporate Ideal in the Liberal State, 1900–1918* (Boston: Beacon Press, 1968); Michael B. Katz, *Class, Bureaucracy, and Schools: The Illusion of Educational Change in America* (New York: Praeger, 1971); David B. Tyack, *The One Best System: A History of American Urban Education* (Cambridge: Harvard University Press, 1974); Christopher Lasch, *Haven in a Heartless World: The Family Besieged* (New York: Basic Books, 1977), 12–21. An extended analysis of child labor reform in New York City along lines similar to those suggested by Lasch is Martin E. Dann, "'Little Citizens': Working Class and Immigrant Childhood in New York City, 1890–1915" (Ph.D. dissertation, City University of New York, 1978).

tives, above all at the mill family; the attitudes and habits of mill parents, perpetuated through their children, were threats to the social order, to be combated by using state power to obtain at least partial control over the upbringing of the mill child. Since the major reforms were directed against the operatives, it was widely assumed that the "mill people," apart from an "enlightened" minority, opposed them, an assumption probably well based in fact. Most operatives were opposed to both child labor reform and such related measures as compulsory school attendance; to a lesser extent they even distrusted legislative efforts to limit hours of work. While there were various reasons for the mill workers' hostility to social reform, underlying them was a belief that the reformers were running roughshod over their interests, cared little for their welfare, and chiefly desired their subjugation under the rule of town "civilization." The campaigns for labor and social legislation in pre–World War I South Carolina thus reflected, and were shaped by, the conflict between mill and town.

As the middle classes of the towns became increasingly aware of the chasm opening between them and the inhabitants of the mill villages, and of the potential danger it posed to South Carolina under their leadership, they began to attempt a diagnosis of the problem. Some contemporaries cited the indifference or hostility of town people toward mill people as a major factor in the split. The historian David Duncan Wallace, for example, scored the aloofness of the middle class toward the mill population and urged a greater respect for the operatives. A Methodist mill minister, W. J. Snyder, complained that most discussions of the decline in church membership in the mill villages assumed that "the mill people are the only ones to blame" while ignoring the penurious treatment of mill charges by the established denominations. As Snyder's complaint pointed out, however, for the most part the causes of the "mill problem" were sought in the peculiarities of the village population.[4]

4. U.S. Bureau of Labor, *Report on Woman and Child Wage Earners in the United States*, Senate Document No. 645, 61st Congress, 2nd Session (19 vols.; Washington: Government Printing Office, 1910), I, 585–87; D. D. Wallace in *Southern Christian Advocate*,

The most important single influence in the mill village was, of course, the mill, which had brought the village into being and which monopolized the time of much of its population, men, women, and children. Until 1906 the standard work day in the mills was twelve hours, Monday through Friday, with a six-hour day on Saturday. In addition, the law permitted up to seventy hours of "make-up" time a year, and the lack of any means of enforcement of the law made it possible for the mills to run even longer. The long hours made the operatives little more than adjuncts to the machinery. A typical working day would begin at 4:30 A.M. and end at 9:00 P.M.; twelve hours would belong to the mill, the remaining four and a half being devoted largely to meals.[5] The sixty hour law of 1907 reduced the standard number of working hours to eleven, but otherwise made little difference.

The mill monopoly on the time of its workers raised a social barrier in itself. In 1911, four years after the reduction of the legal work week to sixty hours, W. P. Jacobs noted that even in the small town of Clinton the operatives were "not acquainted in the city proper, because they work all day and need to sleep all night, and [are] more or less strangers and sojourners in the city." The work day had more subtle effects as well. An operative complained that if a woman worker needed to shop on a week day she would have to "go up street" straight from the mill, without time to clean up; her "careless preparation" reinforced town stereotypes of the "linthead." The "long, dreary and deadening" work days affected the ways the operatives used their scanty leisure time. D. E. Camak reported that the older folk "would 'jist set' and smoke and gossip and dip snuff—just that and nothing more!" W. W. Ball held the long hours responsible for his utter failure to obtain subscribers at

---

August 11, 1904; W. J. Snyder, *The Cotton Mill Problem* (n.p., n.d. [probably 1909]). For a blatant example of the attitude about which Snyder was complaining see the sermon of the Rev. E. M. Lightfoot of the First Baptist Church of Orangeburg, reprinted in Columbia *State*, January 24, 1905.

5. *South Carolina Statutes at Large*, XXI (1892), 90–91; XXV (1907), 487–88; Gustavus G. Williamson, Jr., "South Carolina Cotton Mills and the Tillman Movement," *Proceedings of the South Carolina Historical Association*, 1949, 48; "Speech of Rev. W. H. Mills in Behalf of Ten Hour Bill," reprinted in Columbia *State*, January 23, 1906. Mills was a Presbyterian missionary to the Horse Creek Valley mill settlements.

the Laurens Mill for his weekly newspaper, as a result of which it "had no more influence among these people than it had in a colony in New Zealand."[6]

If the demands of factory work isolated the operatives from outside influences, the problem was compounded by the mills' use of children. While much was made of the impact of the long hours, as well as of the heat, the stale, lint-clogged air, and the poor sanitation, on the health of the mill child, the principal objection of South Carolina's reformers to child labor was that it prematurely immured the child within the ingrown world of the mill before the forces of "enlightenment" had had a chance to operate, causing it "to grow up ignorant, narrow and clannish." Narciso Gonzales warned his readers that "these little children—these infants, almost—who are set to labor in the cotton mills nearly as soon as they can toddle—are growing up profoundly ignorant. Working from dawn to dusk all the week they cannot go to school, nor can they be taught at home." Another reformer worried that "the mind in such situations . . . will be almost a blank—absolutely no opportunity will be found for its cultivation." Such a mind would not remain blank very long; if neglected by the "better classes," it would become "the tool of the politician, the butt of the demagogue . . . the plaything of Satan, victim of every foolish and hurtful lust." The lack of schooling deprived the child of the literacy required to open him to the influence of the press and deprived him of the example and leadership of the school teacher.[7]

Interestingly enough, given the frequent paeans of child labor apologists to the "habits of industry" learned at the spinning frame, reformers accused the mills of fostering indiscipline. The mill officials laid themselves open to this attack with their insistence that the work done by children in the mill was light and in-

6. *Our Monthly* (Thornwell Orphanage, Clinton, S.C.), XLVIII (1911), 82; T. S. Gettys in Columbia *State*, January 17, 1910; D. E. Camak, *Human Gold from Southern Hills* (Greer, S.C.: private, 1960), 45; W. W. Ball, "The Freedom of the Press," in Anthony Harrigan (ed.), *The Editor and the Republic: Papers and Addresses of William Watts Ball* (Chapel Hill: University of North Carolina Press, 1954), 19, 26. The possibility that the Laurens operatives might have been offended by Ball's supercilious and reactionary attitudes seems not to have occurred to Ball.

7. Columbia *State*, January 29, 1900; January 26, 1901; July 14, 1905; January 23, 1906; March 20, 1909.

termittent. Reformers were perfectly willing to admit the justice of Piedmont President James L. Orr's contention that "the work a child does (spinning and weaving) is not laborious or constant, and they [*sic*] have many spare minutes throughout the day to play with their fellows." Federal investigators reported that in South Carolina mills a typical "doffer," whose job was to change the bobbins on the spinning frames when they were filled, and who was usually a young boy, had from four and a half to five hours a day of "free" time. While reformers did not object to the free time if it was spent in play ("a thoroughly legitimate and desirable occupation for a child"), they felt nonetheless that it involved "a shocking amount of utterly wasted time. . . . In the many cases . . . where the children sit waiting to be called on, or hang around, or 'just loaf and talk,' the abundant leisure has evident and serious drawbacks."[8]

Reformers were also disturbed by the attraction of this life to many mill children over the discipline of the schoolroom. Orr reported that of two to three hundred children who had left school to enter his mill, he had never found one who did not prefer the latter: "We have money now—we don't have to sit up all day and behave, we have more fun, and we can run about all over the mill when not at work." A saltier rendition of the same point was given to D. E. Camak by a twelve-year-old operative in Spartanburg. While he himself had never been to school, "Jim—he's my pal—he tried it an' he said twan't nothin' but jist to be bossed by 'er stuck-up woman and he cussed her out an' quit—so he did." Work in the mill only reinforced such obstreperous attitudes toward "stuck-up" middle-class schoolmarms with their rules and regulations; most teachers reportedly felt that pupils returning from the mill were "harder to teach because duller of comprehension and less amenable to discipline."[9]

8. "Col. Orr's Answer to Elbert Hubbard," Columbia *State*, May 30, 1902; *Woman and Child Wage Earners*, I, 270; VII, 237–38. By contrast, in the more systematized New England mills, doffers had only three hours of free time per ten-hour day. *Ibid.*, I, 271.

9. "Orr's Answer"; Camak, *Human Gold*, 32; *Woman and Child Wage Earners*, I, 580; compare the attitudes of northern children as reported in Tyack, *One Best System*, 177–78; and Tamara K. Hareven and Randolph Langenbach, *Amoskeag: Life and Work in an American Factory-City* (New York: Pantheon, 1978), 99. Cf. Marion H. Carter, letter to New York *Times*, quoted in Spartanburg *Herald*, February 9, 1913. Carter reported being

The reformers' criticism extended to the mill village and some of its institutions. The company store frequently came under fire, often from independent merchants jealous of its competitive advantages. Reformers found the mills generally blameless of coercing the trade of their employees, saw little evidence of debt peonage, and concluded that mill store prices were, by and large, competitive with those of other local stores. Their principal criticism was directed at the common practice of extending credit to mill employees, with payment guaranteed by the mill. Credit buying, along with pay periods of two weeks or longer, supposedly encouraged the operatives to live from hand to mouth.[10] Mill ownership of housing was commonly deplored, although rarely for the power it gave to mill management over the villagers; the major concern expressed was over its encouragement of a landless, nomadic proletariat. If, as W. W. Ball contended, "the ownership of a home is the sheet-anchor of good citizenship," the swarm of rootless operatives (and tenant farmers as well) could only sap the power of the state to withstand "the devilment of the demagogue."[11]

The important role of the mill in shaping the lives of its dependents led many to believe that "the mill worker is fast becoming a type, a peculiar people, so to speak, though of the same blood and speaking the same tongue as those around them." The more common opinion, however, was that mill life simply reinforced attitudes and behavior brought from the countryside by people imbued with an essentially preindustrial culture. Commenting on Marie van Vorst's harrowing description of the Columbia mill dis-

---

told by most mill teachers that children returning to school after several years of mill work learned faster, had better memories, and were more industrious and ambitious. Carter attributed their ability to the "training" of the factory, but a more likely explanation is that those few operatives who returned to school, if they were serious, were generally highly motivated. Camak, *Human Gold*, 261–69.

10. E. J. Lister in *Dry Goods Economist*, reprinted in Columbia *State*, January 27, 1902; *ibid.*, January 21, May 8, 1900; Caroline E. Boone, *ibid.*, December 10, 1909; *Woman and Child Wage Earners*, I, 594–606. See W. C. Hamrick, *Life Values in the New South* (Gaffney, S.C.: private, 1931), 104–106, for an account of the difficulties of competing with a company store.

11. Columbia *State*, December 16, 1900, December 6, 10, 1909; W. W. Ball, "The Industrial Revolution in South Carolina," in Harrigan (ed.), *Editor*, 3–11.

trict in 1902, Narciso Gonzales insisted that, insofar as her allegations were true, the principal fault lay not with the mill but with the operatives' "antecedents." They were a people in transition, "in great part the poorest and most thriftless of the backwoods tenant farmers newly transplanted to a city and beginning life again under wholly different conditions. . . . It is too much to expect that brief residence in or near a city will effect a sudden metamorphosis in their appearance and in their customs."[12] The high illiteracy of children in the mill villages (50.3 percent by one estimate), while encouraged by child labor, was directly related to the illiteracy of their parents, a rural product.[13] Mill work made leaving school more attractive and encouraged indiscipline, but more important was the traditional indifference of the operatives and the classes from which they sprang to an education in which they saw little direct benefit. Not only did the older generation of operatives have "little conception of the duty they owe the State and nation of training their children," but its attitudes were being passed on to its progeny, uncontested by any countervailing influence. Camak's child worker justified his disdain for schooling in part by citing his father: "Pa says tain't nothin' ter it. He says he got 'long 'thout it." Other "faults" of the operatives could be passed along in similar fashion. The operatives' nomadicism and improvidence were obvious carryovers from the tenant farming background of their forebears, and their "shiftlessness" was blamed on the laxity of mill parents in raising their children. Above all, the individualistic heritage of the parents was blamed for the hostility of the younger generation to being "bossed," especially by "stuck-up" townspeople. The task of bringing the operatives under control, lest they "undermine social safeguards and make an entire wreck of organized society," involved more than restraining the excesses of the factory system; it required a determined effort to break up the operative culture itself, by challenging the exclusive influence of the mill family over the child.[14]

12. Columbia *State*, November 20, 1902; April 23, 1903.

13. *Woman and Child Wage Earners*, I, 244, 250; Lewis W. Parker to John J. McMahan, October 27, 1900, in South Carolina State Superintendent of Education, *Report, 1900*, 141; Columbia *State*, January 28, 1909.

14. Columbia *State*, January 27, 1907, July 24, 1910; Charles E. Weltner, *ibid.*, January

Remarking on the central place of the child in the efforts of Progressive era reformers, Robert H. Wiebe has suggested that "something more than sympathy for the helpless . . . explained that intense preoccupation. The child was the carrier of tomorrow's hope whose innocence and freedom made him singularly receptive to education in rational, humane endeavor. Protect him, nurture him, and in his manhood he would create that bright new world of the progressives' vision. . . . Instead of molding youth in a slightly improved pattern of their fathers, like cyclically producing like, the new reformers thought in terms of fluid progress, a process of growth that demanded constant vigilance."[15] Educated, middle-class South Carolinians, thoroughly in touch with national intellectual, political, and social trends, were deeply influenced by such Progressive attitudes. However, their social position, the nature of their society, and their strong conservatism set them apart from the Deweyan liberals and humanitarian socialists of whom Wiebe speaks in the above passage. While occasionally welcoming support from such "outsiders" as the American Federation of Labor's Irene Ashby McFayden, South Carolina's reformers insisted that their own stance was unique. Their principal mouthpiece, *The State*, complained of "officious intermeddling" by northern writers on southern mill conditions, drew careful distinctions between the "self-interest" of organized labor's support of reform and the "higher and broader" interests of "our people," and warned fellow reformers that alliances with "outside" leaders such as Alexander McKelway might fracture the broad local reform coalition.[16] Although Ebbie J. Watson, the state's chief factory inspector, occasionally collaborated with McKelway and Owen Lovejoy of the

---

2, 1909; Caroline E. Boone, *ibid.*, February 4, 1910; Camak, *Human Gold*, 32. Camak's mill boy is perhaps an extreme case in his hostility to "bosses." He left home to keep from being "bossed" by his stepmother, had just quit his doffing job at Clifton because the "boss" there had "cussed" him, and was obviously suspicious of Camak, then a college student. Compare his attitude toward discipline, and his contempt for women (his stepmother, the schoolteacher) with the attitudes of mountain boys as described in John C. Campbell, *The Southern Highlander and His Homeland* (reprint ed.; Lexington: University of Kentucky Press, 1969), 124–25.

15. Wiebe, *Search for Order*, 169.

16. On Mrs. McFayden, see Davidson, *Child Labor Legislation*, 25, 96, 99. On local attitudes toward "outsiders," see Columbia *State*, October 10, November 2, 1902, December 10, 1904.

National Child Labor Committee, he was as energetic in attacking "from-the-Pullman-car-window sociological tourists of the South" as he was in organizing the enforcement of labor laws.[17] The frequent aloofness of local Progressives from their national counterparts was due in part to their fear that opponents would cite outside alliances as proof that reform measures were of "foreign" inspiration. More important, however, was a difference in goals. While South Carolina reformers were thoroughly in harmony with the Progressive impulse to rationalize society, their goal was less "fluid progress" than stabilization. They desired to break the pattern of "like cyclically reproducing like," at least as far as mill operatives and other "problem" groups were concerned.[18] Unlike Wiebe's Progressives, however, they were not out to institutionalize social change; rather, they proposed to use reform legislation and education to tear the mill children away from the anachronistic culture of their fathers and teach them to accept the legitimacy of the new, town-dominated society being built by the middle classes. Like tuning forks, these South Carolinians vibrated sympathetically to the harmonies of humanitarianism, but, true to their natures, the notes they sounded were conservative.

Accordingly, the key social reforms pressed by South Carolina Progressives were child labor restrictions and compulsory school attendance, or at the very least an educational requirement for employment. The connection of the two measures has been frequently observed by writers on either subject, but for the most part it has been described as little more than a tactic of the manufacturers, who hoped to scuttle all labor legislation by insisting on tying it to the controversial question of compulsory education. One historian has argued that mill owners used compulsory education proposals as "amulets" to ward off the demons of reform, and in fact urged them as an alternative to other forms of labor regulation.[19] The

17. Ebbie J. Watson, "South Carolina and the Child Labor Problem," address to National Child Labor Conference, Boston, January 14, 1910 (n.p., n.d.), and his address to the Association of Labor Commissioners, Rochester, N.Y., reprinted in Columbia *State*, July 4, 1909. On Watson and the National Child Labor Committee, see *ibid.*, April 9, July 4, 1909.

18. Caroline E. Boone in Columbia *State*, February 4, 1910.

19. Davidson, *Child Labor Legislation*, 60, 92; Louis M. Harlan, *Separate and Unequal: Public School Campaigns and Racism in the Southern Seaboard States, 1900–1915*

public willingness of manufacturers to accept both child labor legislation and compulsory school attendance as a package belies the latter claim, but it is probably true that they did so in the hope of thus obstructing any legislation whatever.[20] The motives of the manufacturers, however, were less significant than was the appeal of their argument to members of the middle class, including reformers. When James L. Orr or Ellison Smyth warned against allowing mill children "to run at large on the streets and acquire habits of idleness and vice," they were addressing such men as the mill town school superintendent who worried about the large proportion of mill children already "allowed to loaf on the streets, smoke cigarettes, and engage in many other vices." In fact, behind the entire debate over labor reform lay a fundamental agreement on the part of both sides that the problem to be solved was one of control.[21]

Reformers, however, saw mill work as inculcating the same vices of indiscipline and insubordination as street life. Worse, while there were few respectable people with a vested interest in seeing a child go to ruin in the streets, there were many who benefited from imperiling his soul in the mill. Children did not go to work voluntarily, said N. G. Gonzales, but were forced to by their parents: "The children must obey. They are set to work in the mills precisely as if they were slaves, and they have no more option in the matter than slaves." Even without a compulsory education law, said Superintendent of Education John J. McMahan in 1900, it might be possible to get mill children into school, "provided there be not a stronger argument—a money consideration"—for keep-

(Chapel Hill: University of North Carolina Press, 1958), 190. Cf. Ensign, *Compulsory School Attendance.*

20. Columbia *State*, January 29, 1902, June 6, 1906, January 10, February 20, 1909, January 19, July 11, 1910.

21. "Addresses Delivered by Mr. E. Gunby Jordan . . . and Col. James L. Orr at Annual Convention of Georgia Industrial Association, Warm Springs, Georgia, May 30–31, 1901" (n.p., n.d.), 17; Orr, in South Carolina General Assembly, *Journal of the House of Representatives, 1901*, 179; Ellison A. Smyth, "The Child Labor Question from the Standpoint of the Mill Authorities," *The Educational* (March, 1902), 42; Davis Jeffries, "The Factory School Problem," *Carolina Teachers' Journal* (April, 1901), 18; Rock Hill *Herald*, quoted in Columbia *State*, February 5, 1906; W. H. Hand, "Our Schools," *Bulletin of the University of South Carolina*, No. 16, Pt. 1 (January, 1909), 38–39.

ing them out. The removal of the pecuniary motive of the parent was thus a precondition to bringing the child under the tutelage of the school. For that reason, "child labor must go, even before the schools come to the mill villages."[22]

While child labor legislation was needed both to break the hold of the factory over the child and weaken that of the parent, compulsory attendance was also necessary. "If these idle children are not sent to school," warned W. P. Jacobs, "they will certainly have the devil for their teacher." "Thousands of white children," according to *The State*, were "growing up in wild, untutored state, regardless of law or morals," and needed to be subjected to "school discipline." However, the congregation of a large proportion of these children in the state's mill villages provided "the greatest opportunity of educating the people that the State ever saw or is likely to see again."[23] The villages had been created as economic institutions; now certain of the townspeople proposed to use them as acculturating institutions, with schools as missions designed to teach "habits of regularity, neatness, kindness, obedience, and self-control" to the factory children. The school teacher was to be an emissary of the middle classes, ideally of an "exalted and noble" character, who would combat "prejudice and superstition" and "carry light into moral darkness." For the child the teacher was to be a surrogate parent, "neat and attractive in appearance, tender and sympathetic in manner, to set up as an ideal over against his mother," who was suspected of being a poor influence. By bringing the mill child under school control, reformers hoped to wean him from the attitudes of the mill village and integrate him into the "modern" world of town society. At the very least, schools could open mill children to outside voices by teaching them to read and write. Commenting, with reference to the election of 1902, on "the impossibility of any newspaper influence, good or bad, in constituencies which do not read," N. G. Gonzales urged "such an extension of education that all classes of our voting population

22. Columbia *State*, January 30, December 16, 1900; S.C. State Supt. of Education *Report, 1900*, 137.

23. *Our Monthly*, XLVIII (1911), 72; Columbia *State*, February 18, 1904; W. H. Mills, *ibid.*, July 14, 1905; Aiken *Journal and Review*, December 13, 1904.

will have at least the opportunity and the desire to read in the press both sides of every question."[24]

The drive for compulsory education was from its outset closely tied to concern with the "mill problem." In fact, some legislative proposals combined compulsory education with child labor reform, and were obviously aimed specifically at mill people. In 1901 Governor Miles B. McSweeney argued that a compulsory law limited to the children of operatives would be a better approach to the solution of the "mill problem" than a "rigid [child labor] law." While not abjuring his support for a "rigid law," N. G. Gonzales endorsed the idea. A general compulsory law, he recognized, was unpassable and unenforceable, at least in the countryside, but compulsory education was a necessary inclusion in any child labor package likely to obtain the approval of manufacturers. Then, too, the mill villages were unique in the state as to their educational situation. They contained large concentrations of unschooled people whose indifference to the schools was notorious, but whose very concentration made enforcement of a compulsory law feasible. That concentration, along with the financial power of the mills, permitted the development of school systems well beyond the means of many rural districts.[25]

No compulsory attendance law aimed specifically at mill children had any chance of enactment, thanks largely to adamant opposition from mill officials who condemned such ideas as "class legislation."[26] After the death of N. G. Gonzales and the accession of his brother William to the editorial helm of *The State*, the Columbia daily shifted its stance in favor of a general law, out of increasing concern for the educational state of the countryside, a belief that a general law could be passed, and above all a desire to

24. E. S. Dreher, "Annual Report of the [Columbia] City Schools," reprinted in Columbia *State*, December 9, 1905; Jeffries, "Factory School Problem," 18; Columbia *State*, February 23, September 19, 1902; Minnie MacFeat, "Free Kindergarten, Columbia, S.C.," *Carolina Teachers' Journal* (June, 1899), 6–7.

25. Governor Miles B. McSweeney, *Message, 1901*, 12; Columbia *State*, January 10, 15, 17, 1901.

26. Ellison A. Smyth in Columbia *State*, January 19, 1906. Obviously, insistence on a general law helped the manufacturers to maintain their argument against further child labor legislation. Also, a law applying to cotton mills alone would place them at a disadvantage in bidding for labor against the farms.

compromise with the manufacturers and thus avoid a division of the reform forces.[27] Even so, proposals applying specifically to the mills were broached sporadically prior to the passage of the first compulsory school attendance law in 1915. A bill setting an educational requirement for mill employment of children under fourteen was introduced into the General Assembly in 1906 at the behest of the Reverend William H. Mills of the South Carolina Child Labor Committee; a similar measure passed the House of Representatives in 1907, although the Senate quietly buried it at the next session. Such measures drew considerable support from those who considered general compulsory education to be an infringement of their "personal liberty," but who considered such encroachment on the prerogatives of mill parents justifiable to protect the state from the mill-hand threat.[28]

Further evidence that child labor and compulsory attendance laws were viewed as coordinate parts of a program can be found in the legislative history of the years 1910 to 1920. Under the influence of the incumbent superintendent of education, John E. Swearingen, sentiment in the state coalesced behind a local-option approach to compulsory school attendance.[29] A law embodying the local-option feature was enacted in 1915 during the burst of progressive legislation following the Blease administration. However, the law was of little benefit to mill schools, for its upper age limit of fourteen years conflicted with the child labor limit of twelve. Of the 167 mills in the state, only 21 were covered by the law by the middle of 1916; of these, 12 were located in the "town" districts of Columbia, Greenwood, and Spartanburg, in which operatives were an electoral minority, while only 5 true "mill districts" had adopted the law. In 1916 Governor Richard I. Manning urged the General Assembly to raise the child labor limit to fourteen, in or-

27. Columbia *State*, December 3, 10, 1904. However, *The State* was willing to see a general law coupled with a literacy test for mill employment. *Ibid*., January 24, 1907.

28. *House Journal, 1906*, 59; *1907*, 43; Columbia *State*, February 6, 1906; South Carolina Department of Agriculture, Commerce and Industries, Labor Division, *Report, 1909* (hereafter cited as *Labor Division Report*), 12. On the alleged "uniqueness" of the mill operatives, see B. F. Sample in Columbia *State*, May 6, 1909, and the indignant response of James L. Quinby, a Graniteville storekeeper, *ibid*., May 12, 1909.

29. Columbia *State*, March 20, 1909, January 4, 1911.

der to remove the "deterrent influence" of child employment on education. Robbed of their best weapon by the local-option law, the manufacturers could put up no resistance to the bill, thus assuring its passage despite some residual opposition.[30]

Most other social legislation desired by middle-class reformers was related to this central core of child labor reform and compulsory school attendance, or was aimed at other evils which they felt threatened to undermine society. Registration of births, which was not inaugurated in South Carolina until 1915, was advocated chiefly as a means of enforcing the child labor and (prospectively) compulsory education laws.[31] Marriage licensing, begun in 1911 after years of advocacy by both reformers and mill officials, was intended in part to prevent premature marriages by working children anxious to gain financial independence from their parents. It was also aimed at a more sinister problem arising from the footloose nature of much of the mill population, that of the "buck weavers," "unpunished bigamists who go about shamelessly from one cotton mill town to another marrying unsuspecting women only to desert them after a few weeks."[32] Even proposals to require shorter pay periods in the mills were endorsed by some reformers as a means of encouraging operatives to live on cash instead of credit, which by encouraging "extravagance" added to the pressure to employ children.[33]

Labor legislation less obviously related to middle-class concerns met with a cooler response from reformers. While sympathizing with the plight of the Horse Creek Valley operatives during the 1902 lockout, imposed by the mills to prevent their employees from giving material support to strikers in Augusta, reform leaders

30. Davidson, *Child Labor Legislation*, 191; S.C. State Supt. of Education, *Report, 1916*, 116; Governor Richard I. Manning, "Annual Message . . . 1916" (Columbia: Gonzales and Bryan, 1916), 6.

31. Columbia *State*, February 8, 1909, September 6, 1910.

32. Dan Ware, "Unmolested Bigamy," *South Carolina State Magazine*, I (1911), 18; Camak, *Human Gold*, 28–29; E. Alston Wilkes in *Southern Christian Advocate*, June 30, 1904; Ellison Smyth in Columbia *State*, January 18, 1906; A. S. Winslow, *ibid.*, June 6, 1910; *ibid.*, January 16, 19, February 1, 1911; J. P. Hollis, "The Consequences of Child Labor," address to South Carolina Conference of Charities, reported in Columbia *State*, December 20, 1910.

33. Caroline E. Boone, in Columbia *State*, December 10, 1909.

showed little interest in efforts to outlaw such behavior by employers.[34] Reform ranks were divided on the issue of hours regulation. Some reformers, notably William H. Mills, helped lead the fight for the sixty-hour week, on the grounds that longer hours of work deadened the minds and imperiled the health of the operatives, especially women and children, and also put a strain upon their family relations. Others supported the shorter work day in the hope that child workers could then get their educations part-time, in night school. On the other hand, *The State*, generally the bellwether of Progressive sentiment in South Carolina, maintained a studied "neutrality" on the subject. While believing that "the commonwealth has the right to look to its future citizens" through child labor regulation and compulsory education, it viewed hours legislation as a gratuitous interference with the right of contract. After all, "the adult operatives can make their own conditions or at least leave the mills for other fields of labor if hours and wages prove unsatisfactory." Government intervention in economic life, it believed, was only justifiable if a compelling state interest existed. Not only was the sixty-six-hour week less a threat to society than operative ignorance and apathy, but reform energy that should have been devoted to "a scheme of education which will result in a general elevation of the laboring classes" was being wasted on a proposal that contributed little to the ultimate assimilation of the operatives into "town" society.[35]

Some insights into the aims and attitudes of the reformers may be gained by looking at the provisions for enforcement of the labor laws and the man in charge of that enforcement. The framers of the child labor law of 1903 failed to make any provision for its enforcement. The law contained exemption clauses for "children dependent upon their own labor for their support" which were

34. When the 1902 state Democratic party convention passed a resolution condemning the mills of the valley for their actions, N. G. Gonzales lauded their intent but attacked the resolution as "unnecessarily harsh." The author of the resolution was Cole L. Blease. Columbia *State*, May 22, 1902. The major legislative proposal banned sympathetic strikes as well; *ibid.*, February 11, 1903.

35. "Speech of Rev. Mills," Columbia *State*, January 23, 1906; J. M. Epting, speech to South Carolina House, reported *ibid.*, February 10, 1905; *ibid.*, December 15, 1902, February 16, 1905, January 25, 1906.

easily abused. It was also open to evasion through the "helper" system, under which a child could carry a full work load without being on the payroll, his wages being placed in the envelope of a relative whom he technically "helped." In 1909, just prior to the commencement of factory inspection, federal investigators found 447 children at work in thirty-six South Carolina cotton mills; of those, over 90 percent were working illegally, 21 percent as "helpers." Of the law W. P. Jacobs said: "There are holes enough in it for anybody to drive a four-horse wagonload of children thru."[36]

In response to criticism both inside and outside the state, the General Assembly in 1909 provided for a system of factory inspection. There was little opposition to the measure, even from the manufacturers, who apparently hoped that the existence of enforcement machinery would blunt criticism of their industry. Significantly, instead of creating a separate labor bureau, the General Assembly added a labor division to the Department of Agriculture, Commerce, and Immigration, in the process renaming it the Department of Agriculture, Commerce, and Industries. The department had been created in 1904 to encourage immigration, and had evolved into a general economic development and publicity agency. While the inclusion of labor law enforcement among the department's duties was motivated partly by a desire to accommodate those legislators hostile to the creation of new government offices, it reflected a common view that factory inspection was to serve the cause of industrial development and defend the good name of the state from outside criticism.[37]

That, at any rate, was the view of the commissioner of the Department of Agriculture, Commerce, and Industries, who had long sought the addition of factory inspection to his multifarious duties. Ebbie J. Watson, the commissioner, was in many respects the quintessential Progressive. An awesomely energetic man, he had become a near legend in his youth as the enthusiastic city editor of

36. *S.C. Stats. at Large*, XXIV (1903), 113–16; *Woman and Child Wage Earners*, I, 183–91; *Labor Division Report, 1909*, 31; "A King's Daughter of Columbia," in Columbia *State*, March 26, 1904; Newberry *Observer*, quoted *ibid.*, May 21, 1905; *Our Monthly*, XLVI (1909), 82.

37. *S.C. Stats. at Large*, XXVI (1909), 14–18.

The State, and was personally and spiritually close to the Progressive Gonzales brothers. As manager of the Columbia Chamber of Commerce, and later as commissioner, he became intensely involved in every aspect of the state's economic and social development, especially as a promoter and publicist.[38] Indeed, many of his early pronouncements as "labor commissioner" suggest that he viewed that job, as well, in public relations terms, as a means of protecting South Carolina's textile industry from outside criticism. His speeches were replete with jibes at muckrakers and at "short-haired women and long-haired men, so-called sociologists." His ultimate goal, he declared, was to "bring about a condition in our industrial affairs that will give no excuse to writers on sociology, for further reflections on the people, the institutions, and the laws of South Carolina."[39]

Watson conceived his duty in far more than cosmetic terms, however. A bold administrator, he developed a system of work permits based on European models and attacked the "helper" system by ruling the presence of an under-age child inside a mill to be *prima facie* evidence of employment, whether or not he was on the payroll. These policies had no specific legislative authorization, and in fact constituted an expansion of bureaucratic power unprecedented in South Carolina. Despite some grumbling among mill officials, though, the permit system was never challenged in the courts, and was written into law in 1911.[40] Watson used his position to urge the abolition of the under-twelve exemptions in order to mollify outside critics and facilitate enforcement of the child labor law, reasoning that any profit from the 361 under-age children legally exempted in 1910 could only be "a mere drop in

38. South Carolina Commissioner of Agriculture, Commerce, and Immigration, *Report, 1906*, 12; *1907*, 11; *1908*, 12, 15; Lewis P. Jones, *Stormy Petrel: N. G. Gonzales and His State* (Columbia: University of South Carolina Press, 1973), 159–60, 270; J. C. Hemphill (ed.), *Men of Mark in South Carolina* (4 vols.; Washington, D.C.: Men of Mark Publishing Company, 1908), II, 416–23.

39. E. J. Watson, "The Textile Industry of South Carolina in the Mid-Year of 1910," address to Cotton Manufacturers' Association of South Carolina, July 11, 1910 (Columbia: The State Company, n.d.), 9; Watson, "South Carolina and the Child Labor Problem"; Columbia *State*, April 7, 1909; *Labor Division Report, 1910*, 6.

40. *Labor Division Report, 1909*, 6; Columbia *State*, April 7, 1909; Watson, address to commissioners, in Columbia *State*, July 4, 1909. Cf. Wiebe, *Search for Order*, 169–70.

the bucket, a mere bagatelle" as compared to the damage done by the exemptions to the state's image. He urged major revision of the law on hours regulation to make them simpler and more enforceable, and constantly sought extension of his authority to sanitary and safety arrangements in the mills.[41]

Watson was, in the best Progressive fashion, a man obsessed with organization, a true believer in the gospel of efficiency, whose ambition was to oversee and coordinate the orderly social and economic development of his state. He was deeply concerned that the textile industry be kept on a "safe and sane basis," and his advocacy of reforms was prompted by a desire "to relieve much of the tension and restore more cordial relations between operator and operative, for if one suffers surely their interests are so intertwined that the other must suffer, and in the end the Commonwealth itself must suffer." Of even greater importance than the maintenance of labor peace, though, was the integration of the work force into the organized and rationalized future South Carolina of Watson's dreams, a concern he expressed in strikingly mechanistic terms: "It is of supreme importance," he proclaimed, "that the efficiency, health and the brain of the human machine that is engaged in the industry should be afforded the opportunity to exercise the maximum of efficiency in productive power and in citizenship."[42]

Although Watson dreamed the dreams of a social engineer, he owed much of his success to his emphasis on "'cooperation with all individuals' to improve the conditions of life in this State." In large part the emphasis on cooperation was diplomatic in motive, as when he balanced his original inspection force between a former mill superintendent and a "conservative" member of a railroad brotherhood. His early enforcement policy, admittedly one of "extreme conservatism," was designed to assuage the fears of those who envisioned "an attempt to revolutionize existing conditions."[43] However, one senses something deeper at work in his

41. *Labor Division Report, 1910*, 13–14; *Reports, 1911–1916, passim.*

42. *Labor Division Report, 1915*, 3; *1916*, 13. The phrase "human machine" appears with disconcerting frequency throughout Watson's reports, e.g. *1912*, 6; *1916*, 8.

43. *Labor Division Report, 1909*, 5; Watson, "Textile Industry," 5, 7.

startling assertion before the National Child Labor Conference in 1910 "that the sixty-hour law, that the child labor law, and that the factory inspection law, have all found their way upon our statute books without any opposition on the part of the employers of labor."[44]

Such willingness to overlook the persistent and active hostility of mill officials to labor legislation was not confined to Watson. In 1909 a Columbia school official gave major credit for the passage of the 1903 child labor law to the mill officials; at the same time the local mill superintendents were reportedly forcing children into the mills by threatening to evict their families from company-owned housing for failing to meet their labor quotas under the "one-worker-per-room" rule. The South Carolina Child Labor Committee made a fetish of cooperation with the manufacturers, who were frequently complimented by prominent reformers. Charles E. Weltner, the pastor of Saint Luke's Lutheran Church in the Columbia mill district and a leading welfare worker, had naught but praise for Lewis Parker and other leading mill men. Joseph A. McCullough, a prominent Greenville attorney, legislator, and Methodist layman, who sponsored the 1916 act raising the child labor limit to fourteen, insisted that the child labor reform movement in South Carolina was not directed against mill owners, who "as a rule . . . are men of broad sympathies and kind hearts." Legislative proponents of child labor regulation praised beneficent mill owners, insisting that their proposals were made "in behalf of humanity rather than against corporations."[45]

On the other hand, criticism of manufacturers was strangely muted among "respectable" reformers, although it was freely indulged by union leaders, spokesmen for the Horse Creek Valley operatives, and one or two "radical" eccentrics.[46] The single major

44. Watson, "South Carolina and the Child Labor Problem," 2.

45. *Woman and Child Wage Earners*, VII, 55–56, 212; Columbia *State*, January 19, 1910; C. E. Weltner, "Social Welfare and Child Labor in South Carolina Mill Communities," *Child Labor Bulletin*, II (1913), 87–88; J. A. McCullough, in *Child Labor Bulletin*, II, 137; F. H. McMaster, speech in South Carolina House, reported in Columbia *State*, February 1, 1901.

46. For criticism of manufacturers by union men, see the reports of committee hearings in Columbia *State*, January 22, 1901, January 29, 1902, January 18, 1906. See also W. C.

exception to the rule was Narciso Gonzales, whose brilliance and instinct for the jugular made him incapable of ignoring an opponent, however powerful or subtle. Yet the crackle of his diatribes against mill officials was the product less of his understanding of the forces in play against labor legislation in South Carolina than of a sense of betrayal by men he trusted. He choked with rage when officials he had applauded as industrial statesmen of "broad views and progressive spirit," who "themselves admit in conversation that certain practices thus far tolerated are evil and should be reformed," appeared before legislative committees to fight the prohibition of those practices. His most corrosive editorials were directed at men he greatly admired, such as Orr, Smyth, and Lewis Parker, who cited the "ideal" conditions at their "show mills" as proof that "in the presence of such beatitude laws would be superfluous"; "Piedmont and Pelzer—and Greers!" he sputtered, "what crimes are committed in thy name!" To Gonzales, the crime of these men lay not in their treatment of their employees but in their infidelity to what they themselves admitted were the larger interests of the middle classes.[47]

That infidelity, however, was generally too subtle for those reformers who lacked Gonzales' brilliance or inflexibility. At any rate there is little evidence in their public statements that they realized the extent to which mill officials opposed and undercut their program. Mill pressures on families to work their children, especially through the "one-worker-per-room" rule, the preference of mills for large families, even the clause in the famous Pelzer contract requiring all children in the village over twelve years of age to work in the mill unless excused, received scant attention from reformers.[48] Their disinclination to confront the manufacturers directly stemmed partly from tactical considerations; the mills had

---

Irby, speeches to South Carolina House, reported *ibid.*, February 10, 1905, February 2, 1911.

47. Columbia *State*, January 29, December 3, 1900, January 24, February 2, 1901, January 18, 1902.

48. On mill pressure, see *Woman and Child Wage Earners*, I, 582; on preferential hiring, see testimony of Charles H. German in committee hearings published in Columbia *State*, January 22, 1901. On the Pelzer contract, see the exchange between W. H. Mills and Ellison A. Smyth, *ibid.*, February 6, 9, 1906.

attached many townspeople to their cause, particularly small stockholders and those benefiting commercially from industrial prosperity, while cotton mill attorneys were powers in the General Assembly.[49] More important, though, were considerations of class affinity and solidarity. The principal reformers were people of impeccable respectability, drawn from the business and professional classes of the towns. Their ranks included such important opinion leaders as N. G. and W. E. Gonzales, Bishops Ellison Capers and W. A. Guerry of the Episcopal Church, President H. N. Snyder of Wofford College, the distinguished Newberry editor W. H. Wallace, and his son, the historian D. D. Wallace. Living in small towns and cities in a small, compact, and largely rural state, they had close personal and even familial ties to mill officials, for reformers and mill men alike were "town people."[50] It was hardly necessary, however, for a reformer to be personally acquainted with a Smyth or a Parker for him to accept their reassurances that they, too, advocated child labor restriction—if accompanied by compulsory school attendance. After all, as even a critical northerner pointed out, the manufacturers were "men of superior mold—of fine breeding and high culture. . . . They play golf, sport automobiles, and are prominent in church and politics." If even a Yankee could find them appealing and, "at heart, as humane as their quondam critics," despite their support of "incomprehensible" practices, one need not wonder that their friends and neighbors did the same.[51]

Reformers were also inhibited by an undercurrent of anxiety

49. John Porter Hollis, "A Legislative Program for South Carolina," *Child Labor Bulletin*, I (1912), 149–50; Columbia *State*, January 26, February 5, 1901.

50. Except for the Gonzales brothers and Bishop Capers, who died in 1908, all of the above were members of the South Carolina Child Labor Committee as listed in *The State*, October 16, 1910. Among the others were Weltner; McCullough; Miss Louisa Poppenheim; Miss Sophie Carroll; Mrs. Robert Gibbes (the last three prominent clubwomen); Superintendent A. T. Jamison of the Connie Maxwell (Baptist) Orphanage; Dr. George B. Cromer, former president of Newberry College, former mayor of Newberry, and later chairman of the South Carolina Board of Charities and Corrections; J. E. MacDonald of Winnsboro; and Knox Livingston of Bennettsville (the last two, prominent lawyers and public officials). The acting secretary, John Porter Hollis, was a York attorney and former legislator whose brother, L. P. Hollis, directed welfare work in Lewis Parker's chain of cotton mills.

51. Camak, *Human Gold*, 103; Lister, in Columbia *State*, July 27, 1902.

among the middle classes over the possible effect of controversy on the social fabric. Rigorous social criticism of any sort, it was feared, might infect the "lower orders" with the germ of rebellion, and so was discouraged. This informal rule of silence was acknowledged in a 1914 letter to the editor of the Spartanburg *Herald* from D. D. Wallace. Complaining of "the neglect to large elements of our population" by the "governing classes" of Spartanburg, the Wofford College historian, whose essential conservatism did not preclude some cynicism about middle-class pretensions, playfully added that "I could say some things which would alarm some of my conservative friends along this line; but I yield to their requests and refrain." Evidently aware that he had broken a taboo, he sardonically reassured his readers that "the people with whom this hint might do 'harm' probably will not read it."[52]

The fear of those "elements" points to the most important reason why reformers declined to attack the mills. The chief target of their rhetoric, as of their program, was the operatives. Indeed, they were often willing to view the manufacturers as innocent victims of a system whose chief beneficiary was the mill parent. They nodded with understanding when mill apologists insisted that the mills preferred not to hire young children but were forced to do so by their parents, whose help was desperately needed during the labor shortage of the early twentieth century.[53] In fact, reformers turned this contention to their advantage; the mills' "inability to contend against the will of parents bent on making their children labor," said N. G. Gonzales, "is the strongest argument which could be adduced to show the necessity for the intervention of the State." Again, in advocating compulsory education for mill children, Gonzales remarked that "some of the mill managers have shown a most praiseworthy and liberal spirit in providing good schools for the children of their manufacturing towns—but what does this avail if parents prefer that their children shall work in the

52. D. D. Wallace in Spartanburg *Herald*, April 10, 1914.

53. Kohn, *Cotton Mills*, 106; *Labor Division Report, 1909*, 31; Lewis W. Parker to William Elliott, Jr., June 18, 1907, in William Elliott, Jr., Papers, South Caroliniana Library, University of South Carolina, Columbia (hereafter cited as SCL); Lewis Parker, speech at Due West Woman's College, reprinted in Columbia *State*, June 12, 1910; *Our Monthly*, XLVI (1909), 82.

mills instead of going to school or, that employment denied them, loaf at large in idleness rather than attend the schools?"[54] In part such statements were polemical in intent, clever attempts to hoist the manufacturers by their own petards. They had a deeper significance, however, for they were in line with an opinion shared by many sectors of South Carolina society, that the "mill problem" was not with the mills, but rather with the mill hands.[55]

Given that attitude, it was natural that the role of villain in the child labor melodrama be assigned, not to a "greedy capitalist," but to one of the mill people. The stereotype variously referred to as the "tin-bucket toter," "mill daddy," "mill secretary," "collector," "cotton mill drone," and even "vampire," had been in development for some time. As early as 1890 a correspondent of the *Carolina Spartan* complained of "strong, hearty men . . . with several children, who move to a mill and strut around and form secret societies and talk big while their children support the family. . . . They say some of them spend one tenth of their children's earnings for whiskey." Early supporters of child labor reform and compulsory education made the "tin-bucket toter" the target of their choicest epithets. The Reverend D. B. Clayton complained in 1896 of the "cupidity of lounging, loafing, lazy men," and the Reverend J. C. Roper attacked "those brutish characters who . . . loiter around factory towns and spend the earnings of their offspring in gratifying their heathenish propensities."[56] By 1900 the image of the "tin-bucket toter" had become the major weapon in the propaganda arsenal of reform, figuring prominently in both the child labor and compulsory education crusades. A Columbia clubwoman countered the appeals of opponents of child labor legislation to "parental rights" by describing the daily noonday procession of "stout, round-faced fathers" across the Congaree River bridge

54. Columbia *State*, January 15, February 12, 1901, January 18, 1902, February 17, 1905; *Southern Christian Advocate*, April 18, 1907.

55. See Union *Times*, February 20, 1903, December 6, 1904; Greenwood *Index*, quoted in Spartanburg *Herald*, July 4, 1913; T. Larry Gantt in Greenville *Daily News*, January 29, 1903. Numerous similar expressions in northern states are reported in Ensign, *Compulsory School Attendance*.

56. Spartanburg *Carolina Spartan*, December 10, 1890, October 21, 1891; Columbia *State*, June 7, 1896, January 12, 1898.

bearing the lunch buckets of their children, "a troup of little white-faced breadwinners."[57] N. G. Gonzales, commencing his anti–child labor campaign with a call for an intensive public inquiry into "the abuses of the child labor system," seemed certain of where that inquiry would lead. The public, he predicted, "will find the 'widowed mother' so tenderly referred to in legislative debates metamorphosed into lazy and loafing fathers, living in ease on the proceeds of their little ones' labor. It will find that these children are often victims of a system as odious as the 'padrone' system and more unnatural."[58]

The importance of the "tin-bucket toter" in the demonology of reform far outweighed his actual contribution to the child labor problem. A sample of 432 South Carolina mill families collected by federal investigators included only nine with resident and able-bodied but non-contributing fathers. By comparison, thirteen families had incapacitated fathers, and eighty were headed by widows. A survey of the Granby village in Columbia, taken by a local minister, failed to turn up a single "drone." A number of fathers, to be sure, "puttered around" at odd jobs just enough to claim to be contributors to the family income, but out of a federal sample of 202 fathers with working children under fourteen, only eighteen worked less than half the year, while 132 worked more than 250 days a year. The few true "drones" were, by and large, middle-aged men lacking the agility required for most mill work, and their dependence upon their children was due more to necessity than to choice.[59]

Whatever its deficiencies as a depiction of reality, however, the

57. Mary P. Screven in Columbia *State*, January 28, 1900. The Columbia Mills were located on the Columbia, or eastern, side of the river, while the village was built on the west bank. The term "tin-bucket toter" derived from this popular image.

58. *Ibid.*, January 29, 1900; note the implied comparison of operatives with recent immigrants. References to "tin-bucket toters" were common in the press of the period, and the image has persisted in historical writing; for an example see Harlan, *Separate and Unequal*, 191.

59. *Woman and Child Wage Earners*, I, 438–39, 444, 448, 453–54, 460; Thomas R. Dawley, *The Child That Toileth Not* (New York: Gracia Publishing Company, 1912), 76; "Homo" in Union *Times*, February 8, 1901; W. J. Snyder in *Southern Christian Advocate*, July 14, 1904; James L. Quinby, Jr., in Columbia *State*, May 12, 1909; E. J. Lister, *ibid.*,

image of the "tin-bucket toter" was highly successful as a propaganda tool. By reducing a complex social problem to a simple question of individual wrongdoing, it rendered the problem understandable to an individualistic society steeped in evangelical piety. Furthermore, it offered the middle classes a villain at once odious and powerless, a symbol of the need for social reform which enabled them to avoid the disquieting implications of an assault on powerful men and institutions. It used attitudes toward the operatives widespread in South Carolina to mobilize public opinion in favor of reform. Finally, by suggesting that large numbers of mill people were moral monsters, it provided the middle classes with a justification for an unprecedented extension of state control over the lives of fellow "Anglo-Saxons."

More rationally, if not more charitably, the reformers blamed child labor and operative "indifference" to education on the mill hands' anachronistic culture. D. E. Camak recalled that in the rural South of his youth "children, among the poor people especially, were looked upon very much as chattels, bound to work for their parents till twenty-one years of age." A. T. Jamison of the South Carolina Child Labor Committee was saddened "that any child born into the world should be regarded with the idea that in a few years he will be able to help make a living for the family."[60] Such an attitude was natural among poor rural folk for whom the family was the basic social and economic unit. John C. Campbell reported it "old mountain usage" to expect a child "to do his part in meeting the needs of the family" until his majority or his marriage, and a Gaffney mill president recalled the same custom being practiced in the Piedmont of his youth.[61] Despite their ubiquity and antiquity, such attitudes toward children were regarded by re-

July 27, August 3, 1902. Cf. Spartanburg *Free Lance*, August 15, 1902, which reprinted Lister's colorful description of a "tin-bucket toter" but omitted his conclusion that the vast majority of parents worked their children from economic necessity.

60. Camak, *Human Gold*, 27; *The Connie Maxwell* (Greenwood, S.C.; October, 1910), 2.

61. Campbell, *Southern Highlander*, 124–26; Hamrick, *Life Values*, 89; cf. Gerald W. Johnson, *The Making of a Southern Industrialist: A Biographical Study of Simpson Bobo Tanner* (Chapel Hill: University of North Carolina Press, 1952), 11.

formers as at best hopelessly narrow, and at worst "greedy and selfish."[62]

Furthermore, such attitudes provided further indications that the power of the mill parent posed a major obstacle to the goal of integrating the operatives into the new order. Said N. G. Gonzales, "We do not look to people who have been accustomed to consider their children agencies for increasing their earnings, necessary fellow-laborers, for that higher and broader conception of a child's right to development of body and mind which the informed and intelligent observer entertains." Both child labor reform and compulsory education, then, involved an attack on the mill family. They also required what was for South Carolina an innovative view of the relation of the state to the individual, laying less stress on individual rights and more on the right of the state to organize and rationalize society. "The parent is the guardian of his child, not its owner. The child is the ward of its parent, not its slave," argued N. G. Gonzales, suggesting by his word choice not only his low opinion of the mill family but also the notion that parents held custody of their children not by "natural right" but as agents of the state, obliged to serve the state's interest. Reflecting an opinion, common among the middle classes, that "the curse of the day is individualism run riot," W. E. Gonzales declared it "a fundamental fact of government" that "the right of the state is higher than that of the individual." Some urged reform measures not simply as desirable in themselves but also as a means of asserting the authority of the state. Retaining the right of a parent to exclusive control of his children "practically arrays every parent against the State and teaches rebellion against all authority," warned a pseudonymous correspondent in *The State*. In 1904 the Union *Times* blamed operative hostility to schooling on a "spirit of rebellion" stirred up by the passage of the 1903 child labor law. The authoritarian tinge of such remarks undoubtedly seemed strange to the ears of South Carolinians, and it is hardly surprising that proponents of child labor and school attendance laws were accused of

62. Hand, "Our Schools," 38; Frank Evans in Spartanburg *Herald*, August 14, 1914; *Labor Division Report, 1910*, 19.

seeking to replace "government . . . of the people, by the people, and for the people" with one "of the newspapers, by the school teachers, and for the office-holders."[63]

While the denigration of the mill operatives by the reformers was due largely to the belief that operative independence of middle-class authority posed a danger to the state, the constant harping on the alleged moral unfitness of mill parents had the more specific aim of discrediting what was generally assumed to be widespread worker opposition to the middle-class "uplift" program. To legislators who opposed child labor restriction as a measure being foisted upon an unwilling population, N. G. Gonzales insisted that "this matter should be considered without reference to what the operatives themselves wish." The insistence of reformers that "labor legislation" had nothing to do with the special interests of labor, but rather involved questions of social good, had its root in the perception of most contemporary observers that the bulk of the operatives opposed the child labor laws, compulsory education, and even hours legislation.[64]

Unfortunately, it is difficult to determine with absolute confidence the true opinion of the operatives on labor legislation. As a body they were strikingly inarticulate and largely unorganized. As a result, such "operative voices" as were heard belonged to men who, seeing little future in a labor movement, set their sights on joining the middle class, usually as a mill official. Few operatives attained political office; those who did, such as Spartanburg's W. S. Rogers, fought compulsory education and child labor legislation.[65] The sole exceptions to this pattern appeared in Columbia and in the Horse Creek Valley, where comparatively powerful labor unions existed at the turn of the century. Union leaders gave

63. Columbia *State*, January 28, 1901, February 9, 1902, January 29, February 13, 1905, June 17, 1907; *Southern Christian Advocate*, February 7, 1907, November 19, 1908; Union *Times*, December 16, 1904.

64. Union *Times*, January 28, 1901; Hollis, "Legislative Program," 152–53; Camak, *Human Gold*, 103.

65. Before entering politics, Rogers was a clerk at the Saxon Mill; see Emily Bellinger Reynolds and Joan Reynolds Faunt, *Biographical Directory of the Senate of South Carolina* (Columbia: South Carolina Archives Department, 1964), 302. See also recorded votes in *House Journal*, 1914, 1104, 1329; Columbia *State*, March 1, 1914.

fervent support to child labor legislation as a means of restricting the labor supply, and their followers made Richland and Aiken Counties strongholds of reform. Aiken even elected a union organizer to the General Assembly, where he was a leading supporter of the "uplift" program.[66]

The same geographic variation affected other modes of expression and made the operative "voice" a babel of conflicting opinion. The petitions which flooded into the General Assembly whenever a major piece of child labor legislation was considered were usually overwhelmingly opposed to any such measure; in 1901, 4,771 of 5,994 petitioners opposed the Marshall bill. However, most of the 1,223 petitioners favoring the bill lived in the Horse Creek Valley.[67] More striking were the political variations among the major mill counties, especially visible in the primary election of 1902. While all statewide candidates supported the endorsement of child labor legislation by the state Democratic party convention, many legislative candidates did not, and child labor was potentially a major campaign issue. However, only two or three races pitted child labor reform advocates and opponents against each other, and the results were clouded by "friends and neighbors" and other effects. In the major up-country counties no politician dared espouse reform, least of all before an operative audience, and the six westernmost counties of the state elected delegations which voted solidly against passage of the 1903 law. On the other hand, legislative candidates in Richland and Aiken Counties were virtually unanimously favorable, or at least acquiescent. The same was true in York County, though it seems unlikely that operatives had much to do with the election of a representative who would describe them on the floor of the General Assembly as "weak in intellect, weak in spirit, people of prejudice and the tools of wily politicians."[68]

66. Columbia *State*, September 4, 1900, January 22, 24, 1901, January 29, 1902; Melton A. McLaurin, "Early Labor Union Organizational Efforts in South Carolina Cotton Mills, 1880–1905," *South Carolina Historical Magazine*, LXXII (1971), 51–53.

67. *House Journal*, 1901, 127–57, 184–201, 231–35.

68. *Ibid.*, 387–88; Anderson *Daily Mail*, August 8, 1902; Greenville *Daily News*, August 16, 1902; Spartanburg *Free Lance*, August 1, September 5, 1902; *Keowee Courier* (Walhalla, S.C.), July 30, 1902; *People's Journal* (Pickens, S.C.), August 21, 1902; Colum-

This curious division between the big Piedmont mill counties and the mill districts along the fall line, such as Columbia and the Horse Creek Valley, was noted at the time and generally attributed to union influence in the latter areas. Manufacturers called special attention to the support of child labor legislation by the "pernicious and troublesome" unionized operatives of the Augusta area, which included the Horse Creek Valley, in their efforts to discredit the reform cause. On the other hand, Aiken County union men and representatives cast aspersions upon the evidence of opposition to reform by Piedmont operatives, accusing the mill owners of fraud and intimidation. Signatures on petitions were obtained under duress, they alleged, while labor organizations which could supply the up-country workers with independent voices were ruthlessly suppressed. G. R. Webb, a union man and representative from Aiken, remarked wryly on the rapidity with which upstate operatives changed their opinions upon breathing the free air of the valley.[69]

These accusations had some merit, especially as they involved petitions. The lack of unions in the Piedmont deprived pro-reform operatives of the organization necessary to collect petition signatures, and company control of villages could effectively be used against any independent effort. The mill managers, on the other hand, could, and did, coordinate their efforts, as is evidenced by the identical wording of many of the opposition petitions. Each mill, in addition, had a built-in organization in its "bosses," who collected the signatures of their subordinates during working hours, and perhaps took the names of those who refused.[70]

While it is likely that the unrestrained power of the up-country

---

bia *State*, August 28, 1902; Aiken *Journal and Review*, August 9, 1904; Rock Hill *Herald*, August 13, 1902; P. D. Barron, *ibid.*, February 7, 1903.

69. Columbia *State*, January 22, 24, 28, February 8, 1901, February 3, 1904, January 18, 1906.

70. *Ibid.*, January 28, 1901. In 1905 the editor of *The State* noted that a petition from Pelzer opposing proposed hours legislation was signed with a mark by 154 operatives. Resenting the implied aspersion on his vaunted school system, Smyth explained that many of the signatories had been at work and had been too busy to sign their names. *Ibid.*, February 9, 17, 1905. The petition, signed by "operatives . . . citizens, and taxpayers" and introduced by Rep. Josh Ashley, bore no outward signs of mill sponsorship. *House Journal, 1905*, 411–15.

manufacturers stifled a good deal of dissent, nonetheless the contemporary assessment of operative sentiments was probably correct. For one thing, support for reform among Horse Creek Valley operatives survived the collapse of its unions after 1902, and was probably due more to their distinctive attitudes than to any immunity from mill intimidation. In 1911 the schools at Graniteville, Vaucluse, and Langley ranked among the best mill schools in the state in terms of class size and average attendance, suggesting both high quality and unusually good patronage. The operatives at Graniteville, in particular, were frequently hailed by middle-class observers for their stability, their orderliness, and above all for that cardinal virtue of the town classes, a "spirit of self-help."[71] More than most operatives in the state, the heirs of William Gregg were "middle-class" in outlook. Their enlightened self-interest and their willingness to combine for mutual benefit shaped both their commitment to reform and their attraction to a sober, American Federation of Labor style trade unionism.

On the other hand, there is ample indication that expressions of operative sentiment in the up-country, while harmonizing with the interests of the manufacturers, were nonetheless genuine. The general unwillingness of up-country politicians to endorse child labor legislation before mill audiences, and the great success in the mill precincts of politicians who opposed both child labor legislation and compulsory education, were particularly strong indications of operative attitudes, for under the free-wheeling rules of South Carolina's Democratic party primary, which was open to virtually every white man, there was little a mill owner could do to control access to the ballot box.[72] Of course, many of the mill county legislators opposed child labor bills for reasons of their own, and reformers could properly be skeptical when cotton mill attorneys

71. McLaurin, "Early Organizational Efforts," 57; S.C. Supt. of Educ. *Report, 1911*, Tables 3 and 4; Victor I. Masters in Columbia *State*, March 21, 1904; William H. Mills, *ibid.*, January 23, 1906; William P. Etchison, *ibid.*, May 11, 1910; *Woman and Child Wage Earners*, I, 572–73.

72. D. D. Wallace, "A Hundred Years of William Gregg and Graniteville" (Typescript, 1946, in David Duncan Wallace Papers, South Carolina Historical Society, Charleston; microfiche copy in SCL), 229–30; Wallace, *History*, III, 370–71. Cf. Dawley, *Child That Toileth Not*, 424–25. A fuller discussion of cotton mill voting appears below; see page 225 herein.

and stockholders rose in the General Assembly to deplore the "insult . . . to the devoted fathers of mill children" represented by child labor legislation.[73] Even so, it was obvious to contemporaries that such speeches represented constituents as well as pocketbooks, and even labor leaders had to admit that operatives "cannot always see and say what is for their own best interests."[74]

The most obvious reason for operative hostility to child labor and compulsory education legislation was economic. While predictions that massive starvation in the mill villages would result from child labor reform were obviously hysterical, the "uplift" program had economic implications too easily shrugged off by reformers.[75] An example is the case of that stock figure of anti–child labor reform propaganda, the "poor widow" who needed her children in the mill to help support the family. By the early twentieth century her numbers were few. In 1910 the Labor Division reported that less than 1 percent of all legally employed operatives were under-age children covered by affadavits issued under the "widows and disabled fathers" clause of the law; as the abuses of the affadavit system were well known, many of the exemptions were probably fraudulent.[76] Even so, the "poor widow" and the disabled father did exist, and their plight was too frequently ignored by the reformers. The charities of the day were hopelessly inadequate. Orphanages reported a "tremendous rush" of applications from mill villages following successive child labor enactments, forcing them to stop taking children of living mothers. As for the adults, there was no public provision for the poor except the "traditionally disreputable and disgraceful Poor House." Child labor was admittedly injurious, said a mill correspondent to the Rock Hill *Herald*, "but how are we going to remedy the evil without bringing on hard times and suffering on multitudes of widows'

73. Columbia *State*, February 5, 1901; for an example, see the remarks of George Prince of Anderson County, an attorney for five cotton mills, to the South Carolina House as reported *ibid.*, February 1, 1901.

74. B. P. Carey, speech to South Carolina House, reported in Columbia *State*, February 6, 1903.

75. G. C. Propst, *ibid.*, January 27, 1901.

76. *Labor Division Report, 1909*, 33–34; *1910*, 13–14; *Woman and Child Wage Earners*, II, 212–13. For abuses of the affidavit system elsewhere, see Ensign, *Compulsory School Attendance*, 238–39.

little children?"[77] To be sure, some reformers, and even an occasional reform opponent, advocated some form of mothers' pension system or scholarships for poor children. Such proposals carried considerable price tags, however. Furthermore, they aroused fears that the "undeserving" might impose upon the taxpayer, and raised the specter of "socialism."[78] It was in the interest of the middle classes to consider child labor as a moral failing rather than as an economic problem; therefore, pension proposals never went beyond the stage of idle talk.

While few operatives were in such actual want as the "poor widows," most were not far removed from privation. Their lack of financial cushions made minor illnesses or accidents into major catastrophes, and sharpened their hunger for security and comfort. In their circumstances, any income brought in by a child was welcome, especially since the advantage of nimble young fingers in mill work meant that older children often brought home fatter paychecks than their parents.[79] Child labor was viewed by many as a means not only of keeping the wolf from the door, but of achieving family goals, building up a nest egg, or attaining a higher social status. Federal investigators reported that child workers both in New England and the South frequently entered the mill in order to help the family buy property or even to finance the education of a favored older member. The earnings of its children, saved over six years, helped a Monarch Mill family to purchase a small farm. A resident in the Greenville mill district reported that many of the operatives there brought their families to the mills "to get out of debt and to begin to save something for a rainy day," and opposed

77. *Our Monthly*, LII (1915), 197; LIII (1916), 615; *The Connie Maxwell* (January, 1910), 2–4; Camak, *Human Gold*, 104, 108; "Observer" in Rock Hill *Herald*, February 5, 1902.

78. *Our Monthly*, XLIV (1907), 82; LII (1915), 206; *The Connie Maxwell* (May, 1913), 5; *ibid.* (May, 1914), 9; *Southern Christian Advocate*, February 25, 1909; Caroline E. Boone in Columbia *State*, February 4, 1910; E. J. Watson to Mary E. Frayser, January 4, 1917, enclosed in Watson to Richard I. Manning, January 5, 1917, in Governor Richard I. Manning Papers, Department of Agriculture, Commerce, and Industries File, South Carolina Department of Archives and History, Columbia; hereafter referred to as SCDAH.

79. E. J. Lister in Columbia *State*, July 27, 1902; *ibid.*, December 12, 1904; *Woman and Child Wage Earners*, I, 487; VII, 45–50.

child labor legislation because it would throw a fresh obstacle in their path to respectability.[80]

Such sentiments could be described as short-sighted, but, coming from people all too aware that they were despised in part for their poverty, they were hardly ignoble. Reformers, of course, saw it differently. In their eyes, the working of children to pad family bank accounts was inexcusable, and the plea of poverty was nothing more than a mask for irresponsibility. "Most cases of child labor," declared Caroline Boone of the State Child Labor Committee, "are purely needless sacrifice, the result of mismanagement at home. The untaught extravagance of many a mill housewife depreciates the earnings of the family. It is a sieve through which the family resources flow, and *more wages or less do not affect the process* [emphasis mine]. Balanced against the plush album, the cheap parlor organ, or enlarged perpetrations of the family likenesses, the divine right of the child to body and brain development is nil."[81] Miss Boone's concern for child welfare was real and deeply felt, but her priggish homilies on frugality could not have endeared her cause to the mill people.

There is no evidence that operatives were impressed with the argument, put forth especially by union leaders, that the abolition of child labor would encourage the hiring of adults and thus raise the wage level. That argument was too sophisticated for people whose lives had been spent in lonely confrontation with market forces seemingly beyond their control. Their attitude was illustrated in 1915, when the depression following the outbreak of World War I produced widespread unemployment in the mill districts. At that time the McCullough bill raising the child labor limit to fourteen was pending in the General Assembly, calling forth the usual rash of operative petitions. This time, though, the operative signatories opposed the bill because "the mills are now overcrowded with

80. *Woman and Child Wage Earners*, VII, 45, 51; Union *Progress*, January 14, 1908; Abraham Jones in Greenville *Daily News*, August 16, 1902. Compare the working-class families in nineteenth-century Newburyport, Mass., as described in Stephan Thernstrom, *Poverty and Progress: Social Mobility in a Nineteenth Century City* (Cambridge: Harvard University Press, 1964), 155–57.

81. Columbia *State*, February 4, 1910; *Woman and Child Wage Earners*, VII, 51.

help and we find it hard to find sufficient work, and we fear that additional legislation will make things worse." The mill people expected no relief from something as abstract as a reduced labor pool; all they knew was that "in such stringent times, as especially the present, we need the help of our children to enable us to tide the crisis which is now upon us."[82]

Not only were the suggestions that child labor restrictions would raise wages theoretical, but they were also of dubious validity, and many reformers found them unconvincing. Some even viewed the higher-wage argument as dangerous, for it lent credence to opponents' assertions that child labor legislation would eliminate the wage differential between South Carolina and New England and thus cripple the most dynamic sector of the state's economy. N. G. Gonzales seized upon manufacturers' contentions that few young children worked in their mills to argue that any losses to the mills, or gains to the workers, from child labor restriction were "immaterial"; "surely the gain or loss of a few cents a day on the labor of a few thousand hands need not disturb the prosperity of an industry making such profits as cotton manufacturing does in the south." The low wages paid for textile work reflected factors besides child labor, involving the nature of the industry, the value of the labor, and ultimately the market economy itself, all of which were affected only slightly by the reformers' approach. Any benefit from higher wages would not compensate individual families for their losses, for the child leaving the mill would probably be replaced by a fresh recruit from the countryside, whose large reserves of rural white labor exerted a far greater downward pressure on wages than did the employment of children. Furthermore, such benefits as would accrue could only come about after an initial period of dislocation.[83]

The economic fears of the operatives were historically based. Their principal previous experience with labor legislation had been the Hours Act of 1892, which many mill workers had ar-

82. W. N. Graydon, speech to South Carolina House, reported in Columbia *State*, February 9, 1901; *ibid.*, November 5, 1902; B. P. Carey, speech to South Carolina House, reported *ibid.*, February 6, 1903; *House Journal, 1915*, 330, 363–65.

83. Columbia *State*, November 5, 1902; Camak, *Human Gold*, 104.

dently supported. When the law went into effect in April, 1893, the mills retaliated by requiring rental payments for the use of company housing, while the use of piece-work rates brought a de facto wage cut for many workers. Outraged operatives, particularly around Spartanburg, threatened a general strike, but, realizing the enormous odds against them, submitted to management. While smug newspaper correspondents hailed the lowered living standards as incentives to economy and sobriety, the mill managers tightened discipline and increased penalties for absenteeism.[84] The operatives, for their part, settled into a sullen cynicism about labor legislation. For years afterward they opposed hours regulation, fearing that it would result in another wage cut or be used as an excuse for increased work loads. More generally, they came to believe that anything done in Columbia could only redound to the benefit of the powerful and the increased oppression of the powerless. The occasionally voiced suspicion that labor legislation was designed to drive operatives back to the farms and depress agricultural wages was probably another legacy of their earlier experience.[85]

Their disillusionment was echoed, or catered to, by politicians, some of whom had supported reform in earlier days. By 1901 the author of the 1892 hours law, "Citizen Josh" Ashley of Anderson County, was attacking proposed legislation to expand cotton mill employers' liability for industrial accidents, and claiming the support of two thousand operative petitioners. Abrogation of the "fellow servant" rule, he declared, would only cause the mills to

84. Spartanburg *Carolina Spartan*, March 22, 29, September 6, 1893; Spartanburg *Piedmont Headlight*, quoted in *The Cotton Plant*, April 8, 1893; Yorkville *Enquirer*, quoted in Columbia *State*, October 18, 1895.

85. Williamson, "South Carolina Cotton Mills," 48; *Woman and Child Wage Earners*, VII, 157; Columbia *State*, February 16, 1905; "Cotton Mill Operative," *ibid.*, January 24, 1906; T. S. Gettys, *ibid.*, January 17, 1910; John H. Montgomery to Ellison Smyth, April 9, 1900, in John H. Montgomery Letterbook, SCL; "Homo" in Union *Times*, February 8, 1901. The links between hours regulation, wages, and industrial discipline are illustrated by an experiment with a ten-hour-day undertaken in the spring of 1905 by a group of Union mills, after consultation with the operatives. Despite promising early results the experiment was discontinued after a month and a half; the superintendent later blamed its failure on worker discontent. The lost time had reduced their wages, while the expected compensatory increases in productivity had failed to materialize, the workers resisting all attempts to speed up the machinery or increase workloads. Union *Times*, March 17, 24, 31, May 5, 1905, January 18, 1906.

take out insurance and deduct the premiums from the workers' wages.[86] Speaking in 1902 to an audience composed partly of mill hands, an Anderson County legislative candidate opposed to child labor restriction reminded his listeners that "the mills did not charge house rent until the legislature passed some cotton mill legislation." In 1911 a Pickens County representative, opposing the Osborne bill to abolish the under-twelve exemptions, cynically remarked that "every time any law is passed to protect the operatives the mills put on some new regulation to get it back out of the operatives."[87]

The mill workers' belief that the proponents of labor and social legislation were indifferent or hostile to their interests was reinforced by middle-class rhetoric. They were insulted by the constant allegations that they "are objects of care and pity; that they are incapable of realizing their needs; that they require special guardianship of the State." Taking offense at an article which he felt characterized the typical mill father as a "lazy, good-for-nothing wife beater, child beater, and drunkard," a mill minister declared that "it is no wonder that the self-respecting mill people have said to the outside world, 'You go your way, and I'll go mine.'" Mill people were fervent believers in the equality of all white men, and saw the middle-class program of social control as an attack on their status. Why make "laws for the special government of cotton mill employees?" asked "Homo," a teacher at the mill village of Lockhart. After all, "their hair is straight and their skins are white," and those, after all, had traditionally been considered the only necessary qualifications for the privilege of self-government.[88]

86. Williamson, "Cotton Manufacturing," 203–204; Joshua Ashley, speech to South Carolina House, reported in Columbia *State*, January 25, 1901. Ashley's contention was not altogether groundless, if somewhat fatuous. Lewis W. Parker, whose Columbia operations were plagued by employees' damage suits, became an early proponent of workman's compensation, provided that the operatives be required to pay a portion of the premium. See William Elliott, Jr., to J. Sumter Moore, May 25, 1907; Lewis W. Parker to J. Sumter Moore, June 18, 1907, in William Elliott, Jr., Papers, SCL. See also Lewis W. Parker, address to University of South Carolina, reprinted in Columbia *State*, December 15, 1909.

87. Anderson *Daily Mail*, August 8, 1902; E. P. McCravey, speech to South Carolina House, reported in Columbia *State*, February 2, 1911.

88. "Cotton Mill Operative," in Columbia *State*, January 24, 1906; W. J. Snyder in *Southern Christian Advocate*, July 14, 1904; Union *Times*, February 27, 1903.

Above all, mill workers resented the intrusion of the state into their family relations. The family was a far more important social unit to the operatives than to the townspeople with their schools and clubs, especially since the operatives' material aspirations were dependent not on a single breadwinner but on a joint effort of the entire household. To them child labor was not "parental exploitation" but an essential aspect of the role of the child in family life, and there was no contradiction in their eyes between child labor and parental love. The effect of the major reform proposals, however, was to take control of family goals out of the hands of its traditional authorities. To this the operatives objected violently. Even private charities ran afoul of their sensitivity. A mill day nursery organized by the town women of Spartanburg failed because mill mothers saw the project as a reflection on their competence. Reaction to child labor reform followed the same pattern. John Porter Hollis of the State Child Labor Committee believed that operative hostility toward "any sort of interference with or regulation of their domestic affairs" produced an opposition to the aims of the committee "more to be dreaded" than that of the manufacturers. That hostility helped explain the willingness of operatives to sign the anti-reform petitions circulated among them by the mills, according to N. G. Gonzales: "It is easy to imagine a boss going among his subordinates, men and women, and saying to them: 'They have a scheme down in Columbia to take away the control of your children from you; if you don't want that done you had better sign this paper.'"[89]

The text of those petitions was undoubtedly written by a mill official, but the plea "that we be permitted, as others are, to make our own contracts, control our own families, and pursue our chosen calling as we consider best for our interest" reflected operative sentiment. To the mill people, the purpose of reform was to rob them of autonomy, to replace their own goals for themselves and their children with those of the hated "town people." It was there-

89. Union *Times*, February 27, 1903; Hollis, "Legislative Program," 152–53; Columbia *State*, January 28, 1901. In 1914 a newspaper correspondent in the town of Piedmont noted that many operatives were concerned about the movement to raise the child labor limit to fourteen, particularly as to "how far it will interfere with home government." Greenville *Daily News*, August 23, 1914.

fore no wonder that the characteristic slogan of the operative opposition to labor legislation was "Let us alone."[90]

The opposition of mill workers to labor legislation spilled over into opposition to compulsory education, which, while not specifically aimed at mill people, was obviously designed for their control. While operative "indifference" to education was overstated, their economic status, and the lack of opportunity for educated workers in South Carolina, caused them to place a comparatively low priority on education in favor of satisfying pressing economic needs.[91] Compulsory attendance not only enforced a different set of priorities, but it also forced the mill family to bear its costs.

The opposition of mill people to compulsory education also had much to do with the schools themselves. As "town" institutions, they were perceived as alien agencies controlled by a hostile middle class. The relationship of the schools of that era to the mill villages was much like that found by John Kenneth Morland in York in the late 1940s: "The schooling experience for the Kent [York] mill child . . . is also an encounter with a somewhat different way of life. Teachers in the mill school, as well as in the downtown school, come primarily from middle- and upper-class families, some from the town section of Kent itself. These teachers hold up before the children what are essentially town standards, and the mill children discover that much of what they have learned in their homes is inadequate or even incorrect." The basic premises of public education thus seemed to be an affront to the operatives. More specifically, many operatives objected to compulsory vaccination of school children, and felt that dress and cleanliness requirements were discriminatory.[92]

Furthermore, they felt that the schools were stacked against the mill child. A mill mother at Fort Mill refused to send her child to

90. Hollis, "Legislative Program," 153; *House Journal, 1901*, 129, 233; *1915*, 363; "O. M. M." in Union *Progress*, January 30, 1901; Abraham Jones in Greenville *Daily News*, August 16, 1902; Mrs. Ethel Thomas in Columbia *State*, January 29, 1910.

91. *Woman and Child Wage Earners*, VII, 168.

92. John Kenneth Morland, *Millways of Kent* (Chapel Hill: University of North Carolina Press, 1958), 103–104; *Woman and Child Wage Earners*, I, 581; Frank Evans in Spartanburg *Herald*, October 10, 1913. Cf. Tyack, *One Best System*, 177–79, 229–55, for parallel attitudes in northern cities.

the local school "to have it 'run over' and 'imposed upon' by the 'town children,'" and her views were evidently widespread. Other objections were raised by "A Mother" in Spartanburg, who in a 1913 letter to the Spartanburg *Herald* objected to "turning the child over to the state and paying taxes on schools merely to give the college graduate a job." She complained of the large amounts of homework, which she felt gave an unfair advantage to pupils whose parents "have steamheated houses and are able to give all the time to their children," over those with uneducated, working parents, who in winter had to study in the single heated room shared by the rest of the household. More interesting was her complaint about the use of school records. In the interest of "a closer connection between the city schools and the employers of labor," Spartanburg's school superintendent, Frank Evans, permitted the inspection of individual records on scholarship, attendance, and deportment by prospective employers. "A Mother" found this embryonic dossier system tyrannical: "A boy at that age is not always what he is as a man, and it is branding him too early in life." Moreover, given the difficult situation of mill children thrown in with hostile town children (as was the policy in Spartanburg), there is little doubt that the children with the worst records were probably mill children. Middle-class spokesmen ridiculed such objections as those cited above, but they reflected a common and understandable belief among many operatives that the schools were instruments of town oppression.[93]

The depth of operative suspicion of the state is illustrated by a rumor which swept through the villages in 1910. In January of that year a report that legislation was pending to amend the sixty-hour law of 1907 to require ten-hour days brought several violent protests from operatives who believed that the proposal would eliminate the traditional Saturday half-holiday. "Why deny us every God-given right and privilege?" protested a Newberry woman. "Who has a right to deprive us of our Saturday afternoons, that are so eagerly looked forward to by all? Take Saturday afternoons

93. Fort Mill *Times*, quoted in Columbia *State*, February 6, 1906; *Woman and Child Wage Earners*, I, 582; "A Mother" in Spartanburg *Herald*, February 16, 1913; Spartanburg City Schools, *Report, 1908–09* (Spartanburg: Band and White, n.d.), 13–14.

from us, and I think you will have taken the very last work-day right and privilege left us, and I suppose it will be only a question of time when our Sundays will be ordered 'cut-and-dried' for us! . . . The thumbscrew has been applied to our interests enough. One more twist will be beyond the limits of endurance." In fact, no such bill had been introduced; but the belief that it had says much about operative attitudes toward labor legislation in general.[94]

Despite the widespread operative opposition to the middle-class reform program, the mill workers put up little overt resistance to compulsory education or child labor laws as they were enacted. This was due in large part to the poor enforcement machinery of the early laws. Statewide compulsory education with attendance officers did not come until 1919, near the end of the period covered in this study, and its enforcement was not effective until the late 1930s. The child labor law was evaded with impunity until the establishment of the Labor Division in 1909, and the general lack of birth records made later enforcement by even the most dedicated inspectors difficult. Proof of a child's age was generally provided by notarized affidavits, but many notaries processed them as a matter of routine, receiving them from the mills and failing to require that the parents swear to their accuracy; according to Watson, the practice "had reduced respect for a solemn oath to practically nil in many sections of the State."[95] Such enforcement of labor laws as there was was extremely cautious and conservative. Recognizing that they had to deal with "a large population of working people unaccustomed to legal restraint," Watson and his factory inspectors were firm but circumspect in fulfilling their duties. They saw their initial function as one of education, "thus bringing about a true regard and respect for the law, gradually." Their first prosecution was not made until 1910, and there were few others before the middle 1910s. Enforcement was inhibited

94. T. S. Gettys in Columbia *State*, January 17, 1910; Mrs. Ethel Thomas, *ibid.*, January 29, 1910.

95. *S.C. Stats. at Large*, XXXI (1919), 205–208; Camak, *Human Gold*, 273–74; Report of George D. Brown, Supervisor of Mill Schools, in S.C. St. Supt. of Educ. *Report, 1916*, 112; E. J. Watson to Richard I. Manning, March 30, 1912, in Manning Papers, Department of Agriculture, Commerce and Industries file, SCDAH. See also pages 187–90 herein.

not only by operative hostility but also by public opinion; in 1917, for example, seven defendants in child labor cases demanded jury trials, and all were acquitted, probably as a result of *ad hominem* appeals to the jury on grounds of "hardship." On the other hand there was little violence, the strongest action being the tearing down, by persons unknown, of regulatory signs posted in a York mill.[96]

Economic changes helped reconcile operatives to child labor and similar legislation. Wage increases leveled off after the Panic of 1907, which marked the end of the southern cotton mill boom, but the gains of previous years left operatives somewhat better off than they had been in 1900. In 1907 August Kohn declared that "the operatives [*sic*] classes are earning enough money now for them to be privileged to have their wives and children remain at home." In 1910 Watson predicted that the movement of South Carolina mills into the production of finer goods would raise wages to adults and eliminate the advantage of child labor to the manufacturer; already, as a result of this movement, he saw "a strong and better sentiment among the parents themselves" with regard to both child labor and education.[97]

Much of the potential for resistance by the operatives was tempered by their respect for the law. Federal child labor investigators reported that many parents who misrepresented the ages of their children to mill officials were easily induced to tell the truth by an appeal to their "desire to abide by the law."[98] While they were deeply suspicious of the government, the mill people were not anarchists; indeed, they were basically conservative. Not only did they defer to legally constituted authority, but they considered that deference to be a mark of the very respectability that they were

96. *Labor Division Report, 1909*, 4; *1910*, 7; *1917*, 24–32; Watson, "Child Labor Problem," 3, 6; Columbia *State*, May 22, 1909, January 27, 1910. In 1915 a Newry man admitted to working an underage child in the Courtenay Mill, pleading in his defense that he needed her earnings to help pay for medical treatment for his paralyzed wife. Following supporting testimony by the mill superintendent the jury brought a verdict of "not guilty." *Labor Division Report, 1915*, 48–49. Ensign's study of the development of child labor legislation in several northern states emphasizes the obstacles to enforcement raised by public opinion, especially at the local level. Ensign, *Compulsory School Attendance, passim.*

97. Kohn, *Cotton Mills*, 46; Watson, in Columbia *State*, April 17, 1910.

98. *Woman and Child Wage Earners*, I, 208.

denied by the middle classes. Their hostility toward "town people" was due not so much to a "class struggle" as to their frustrated desire to be treated as equals, as responsible fellow "Anglo-Saxons." Any massive challenge to the legitimacy of the state, on the other hand, would only confirm town suspicions that they were "lawless."

Above all, though, the failure of the operatives to resist the encroachment of the state on their "rights" was due to the same prickly individual autonomy they sought to protect. Deeply suspicious of all forms of organization, the operatives were never much more than a group of individuals facing a well-organized opposition. Not only were their social attitudes inappropriate to the complex society they had entered by moving to the mills, but those very attitudes provided them with few means of protesting their loss of status. However, they did have one major avenue of resistance open to them: the ballot box. While their votes generally only slowed the process of reform, for a time in the early 1910s they brought progressivism in South Carolina to a grinding halt. By delivering a virtual bloc vote to the "demagogue" Cole L. Blease, the mill workers of South Carolina briefly enjoyed more political power than at any time before or since. To be sure, the sound and fury of the Blease era ultimately signified nothing. Bleaseism as a creed was pure negation, and its only long-term effect was to frighten the "better element" into pressing its plans for "uplift" and control all the harder. In the short run, however, the operatives' massive support for Bleaseite politicians was the most striking manifestation of their resentment of "modern" society to appear prior to World War I. Before Blease, mill folk and town folk had merely jostled each other; with his advent on the political stage, they collided.

Chapter VI

The Bleaseite Challenge

The political heyday of Coleman Livingston Blease, stretching from his election as governor of South Carolina in 1910 until the American entry into World War I, was a period of upheaval impressive even by the tumultuous standards set by the state's postbellum history. The rhetorical bitterness surpassed even that of the Tillman era; rallies and stump meetings were punctuated with physical assaults and at times degenerated into near riots. Voting participation skyrocketed. The percentage of adult white males participating in the Democratic party primary had drifted downward from 70.8 percent in 1900 to 63.5 percent in 1910, the year Blease was elected to his first term. His stormy reelection campaign in 1912, however, saw an astronomical 80.2 percent of the voting population flock to the polls. Despite some tightening of the party rules in 1914, engineered by frightened anti-Bleaseites, 72.0 percent of the voting population cast ballots that year, as did 72.1 percent in 1916.[1]

1. W. K. Tate, "After Blease—A New Program for South Carolina," *Survey*, XXXIII (1915), 577. The voting figures used in the estimates are the total votes for governor as compiled in Frank E. Jordan, Jr., *The Primary State: A History of the Democratic Party in South Carolina, 1896–1962* (n.p.: private, n.d.). The voting population figures are from *U.S. Census, 1910: Supplement for South Carolina*, 585. For election years within the decade the population was estimated by using logarithms, assuming a constant rate of increase over the decade. My estimates vary slightly from those of J. Morgan Kousser, *The Shaping of Southern Politics: Suffrage Restriction and the Establishment of the One-Party South, 1880–1910* (New Haven: Yale University Press, 1974), 227. On political participation in South Carolina before 1910 as compared with other southern states, see *ibid.*, 233–34. On the extent of the suffrage in South Carolina at this time, see pages 202 and 225 herein.

Major changes also appeared in the basic political patterns of the state. The trend toward voter apathy prior to 1910 reflected in part the amorphous politics of a one-party state, characterized by a bewildering array of candidates, loose, evanescent coalitions built around "friends and neighbors" or an occasional issue such as prohibition, and a resulting confusion of political debate.[2] Between 1910 and 1912, however, the pattern changed abruptly, and soon the state was divided into two warring camps. Legislative and local candidates found themselves judged by their allegiance or antipathy to "Coley." Strong Bleaseite political organizations were created in several counties, notably the big manufacturing centers of Anderson and Spartanburg. In the latter county factional lines were sharply drawn; a Blease victory there in 1912 swept in an almost solidly Bleaseite legislative delegation, while an anti-Blease victory in 1914 turned all but one of the Bleaseites out of office. The bifactional pattern became so pronounced that it was even written into law; the Australian ballot law of 1918 provided for the appointment of "watchers representing different factions" by the precinct manager to assist illiterate or disabled voters. Blease made extensive use of his patronage power to create a nucleus of politically dependent campaign workers. His principal reliance, however, was not on organization but on his devoted personal following, which was both large and so persistent that its remnants were visible as late as the 1940s.[3]

The two most impressive political features of the Blease era were the enormous support given to "Coley" by mill operatives and the opposing antipathy of town voters. This mill-town split had been in evidence for some time. In 1906 Blease had run third in an eight-man race for the governorship, but had won 59.9 percent of the vote in the Horse Creek Valley, and a phenomenal 73.9 percent in Columbia's Ward Five. As the lone challenger to incumbent Governor Martin F. Ansel in 1908 Blease had taken 85.4 percent

2. Kousser, *Shaping of Southern Politics*, 231–32, gives a succinct description of South Carolina politics in the pre-1910 period.

3. Spartanburg *Herald*, September 11, 15, 1912, August 30, September 9, 1914; *South Carolina Statutes at Large*, XXX (1918), 812; V. O. Key, *Southern Politics in State and Nation* (New York: Alfred A. Knopf, 1949), 145, 400–401; Ronald D. Burnside, "The Governorship of Coleman Livingston Blease of South Carolina, 1911–1915" (Ph.D. dissertation, Indiana University, 1963), 41–44.

of the vote in Ward Five while receiving less than one-third of the vote in the four "town" wards.[4] However, up to 1912 the extent of the divisions was obscured by political crosscurrents such as the liquor issue; thus when Blease, an avowed "wet," faced a prohibitionist opponent in 1910 he lost many mill votes in the "dry" upstate counties while doing unusually well in the "wet" low country. Even in 1910, though, Blease was far stronger among mill people than he was among other up-country voters, winning 56.6 percent of the vote in the mill clubs of Spartanburg County, 63.7 percent in those of Greenville, and 67 percent in those of Union.[5]

By 1912, the high-water mark of Bleaseism, the pattern had hardened. Mill club support for Blease and Blease candidates in Spartanburg County reached over 70 percent in 1912, and ranged in the sixties in succeeding races; a similar pattern appeared in neighboring Union, the fifth largest mill county. Greenville and Anderson mill boxes persistently gave Blease 70 percent of their vote, while the Horse Creek Valley regularly delivered him 65 per-

4. Aiken *Journal and Review*, August 31, 1906; Columbia *State*, August 31, 1906, August 27, 29, 1908. In 1914 60 percent of the enrolled voters of Ward Five were operatives; see the club roll list *ibid.*, August 8, 1914. Unfortunately, only scattered precinct returns are available before 1910. It is likely that most operatives in the large upstate mill counties supported Ansel, a Greenvillian, in 1906; at two Greenville County mill boxes, Piedmont and Monaghan, Ansel received 58.4 percent of the vote to Blease's 20.5 percent. By 1908, however, Blease was defying the "friends and neighbors" effect, taking 62.6 percent of the vote at the Greenville mill boxes of Mills Mill, Woodside, and Sam-Poe. Greenville *Daily News*, August 29, 1906, August 26, 1908.

5. Greenville *Daily News*, September 16, 1910; Spartanburg *Herald*, September 14, 1910; Union *Progress*, September 13, 1910. Voting in the Democratic party primary was conducted by local Democratic clubs, analogous to, but not identical with, geographical precincts. Kousser, *Shaping of Southern Politics*, 234–35, analyzes this election by calculating the average wealth per adult white male for each county from population and tax data, and using regression analysis to compare its variation with that of the Blease vote, concluding that in the second primary Blease's support had "a fairly heavy upper income coloration." However, his high-wealth counties were generally in the low country where most of the population was black and landless, and where prohibitionist sentiment was historically weak. While Kousser suggests that antiprohibitionist sentiments were associated with the "upper class," the linkage seems far from clear to this writer. Furthermore, Kousser does not demonstrate that his averages reflect the distribution of wealth in South Carolina; indeed, he admits (p. 267) that "if sub-county differences in white wealth were consistently very large, correlations between these estimates and voting behavior would not be very meaningful." As one-fifth of South Carolina's white population lived in company-owned mill housing in 1910 and 43.9 percent of its white farmers that year were tenants or sharecroppers, the validity of Kousser's method is open to question. His analysis has other flaws; the gross inaccuracy of his principal source of data on wealth (aggregate county-level figures on assessed valuation) was notorious at the time, and the regression relationship he establishes has a correlation coefficient of only .279.

Table 7. FACTIONALISM IN SPARTANBURG COUNTY, 1910–1916

	Percentage for Bleaseite Candidates, Classified Clubs[a]					
Year	*Mill*[b]	*Town*[c]	*City*[d]	*Rural*[e]	*County*	*State*
1910[f]	56.6	34.6	33.7	44.8	46.9	52.6
1912[g]	70.9	27.0	21.6	53.3	53.2	50.9
1912[h]	68.8	30.9	26.5	51.3	53.4	—
1914[i]	62.3	27.4	21.6	41.9	45.4	43.6
1914[j]	62.7	25.1	19.3	43.7	46.4	37.9
1916[k]	63.2	31.4	26.7	49.2	50.5	48.3
1916[l]	75.1	26.6	22.6	—	53.3	—

SOURCES: Spartanburg *Herald*, September 14, 1910, August 30, 1914, September 13, 15, 1916; Spartanburg *Journal*. August 29, 1912.

[a] Percentage of total vote received by top two candidates.

[b] These are clubs organized around mills with more than ten thousand spindles, as listed in South Carolina Department of Agriculture, Commerce, and Industries, Labor Division, *Reports*. Smaller "mill" clubs are excluded as likely to include large proportions of non-mill voters. All bear the names of their mills except Arlington (Apalache Mill), Trough (part of Pacolet Mills), and Spartanburg, Ward Six (part of Spartan Mills). The others are Arcadia, Arkwright, Beaumont, Clifton Nos. 1, 2, and 3, Drayton, Enoree, Fairmont, Glendale, Inman Mills, Pacolet Mills, Saxon, Spartan Mills, Tucapau, Victor, Whitney, and Woodruff Mills.

[c] Those towns (Spartanburg, Cowpens, and Woodruff) with 1910 populations of more than one thousand. Three "mill" clubs (Spartan Mills, Beaumont, and Ward Six) are not included in the Spartanburg total, but South Spartanburg (the small Crescent Knitting Mill) is included. The Gray Mill of Woodruff and the Cowpens Mill did not have clubs of their own; their employees are included in the town totals.

[d] The City of Spartanburg (see note c).

[e] The county total minus mill and town boxes. It includes several small mills and one large one (Chesnee Mill) without a club of its own.

[f] Blease vs. C. C. Featherstone, governor, second primary.

[g] Blease vs. Ira D. Jones, governor.

[h] A. E. Hill (Bleaseite) vs. J. C. Ott (anti-Blease, incumbent), for circuit solicitor (district attorney), second primary.

[i] Blease vs. E. D. Smith, U.S. senator.

[j] John G. Richards (Bleaseite) vs. Richard I. Manning (anti-Blease), governor, second primary.

[k] Blease vs. Manning, governor, second primary.

[l] W. S. Rogers, Jr. (Bleaseite, former mill operative) vs. Ben Hill Brown (anti-Blease), state senator, second primary (incomplete).

cent. From 1908 on the Columbia mill district consistently cast 85 percent of its vote for Blease. The pattern of operative voting allegiances appears to even more striking effect in Table 9. By using the technique of ecological regression analysis to compare the proportions of operatives in a number of Democratic clubs with the

Table 8. MILL, TOWN, AND BLEASEISM IN GREENVILLE COUNTY

Mill Clubs	*Operatives, 1914* *Number*	*Percent*	*% Richards 1914*[a]	*% Blease 1914*	*1916*[a]
Brandon	178	62.2	58.4	71.1	72.0
Sam-Poe	154	57.7	58.8	68.6	64.1
Woodside	170	65.4	70.4	80.0	74.1
Judson	115	71.4	65.3	76.9	72.5
Monaghan	186	60.6	57.6	72.1	72.1
Mills Mill	169	65.0	66.0	74.1	67.5[b]
Sans Souci	173	50.1	57.5	64.3	63.2[c]
Greer Mill	72	76.6	62.7	56.2	62.1
Piedmont	139	48.9	62.7	67.3	63.3
Conestee	50	37.9	38.5	80.8	55.7
Simpsonville	62	18.4	16.9	29.7	27.2
Town Clubs					
Greenville City	112	5.2	13.8	20.8	25.2
Ward 1	5	0.6	11.4	17.3	25.2
Ward 2	0	0.0	7.6	11.3	12.7
Ward 3	2	1.3	14.7	20.1	37.6
Ward 4	48	22.6	27.0	45.6	42.6
Ward 5	51	11.7	17.3	23.7	23.0
Ward 6	6	3.9	14.9	23.2	27.7
Greer City[d]	36	8.4	25.7	30.7	28.9
Fountain Inn[e]	29	9.4	24.6	33.3	37.2
County	1,681[f]	17.2	34.8	43.5	47.0

SOURCE: For voting figures, Greenville *Piedmont*, August 28, 1914; Greenville *Daily News*, September 9, 11, 1914; September 13, 1916. For figures on the number and proportion of operatives in each club, see the discussion in the Appendix. A "mill club" here is any club organized around a mill with at least ten thousand spindles which does not include an incorporated town of over one thousand inhabitants, which is the definition of a "town" club. Fountain Inn, with a 1910 population of slightly under one thousand, is included here as a "town" club.

[a] Second Primary.

[b] Includes Dunean Club.

[c] Includes Bleachery Club.

[d] Population (1910): 1,354 in Greenville County.

[e] Population (1910): 979.

[f] Includes 36 operatives employed in three small cotton mills (Fork Shoals, Batesville, and Pelham) or otherwise not voting at any of the clubs listed above.

Table 9. ECOLOGICAL REGRESSION ESTIMATES, MILL OPERATIVE SUPPORT FOR BLEASE, 1914 AND 1916[a]

	I. Senatorial Primary, 1914 Percent			
	Blease	*Anti-Blease*[b]	*Not Voting*	
Operatives	80.5	0.7	18.8	N = 22[c]
Other Voters	29.9	59.1	11.0	R = .809, −.817, .254[d]
	II. Second Gubernatorial Primary, 1914 Percent			
	Richards	*Manning*	*Not Voting*	
Operatives	65.6	7.3	27.2	N = 22
Other Voters	23.3	56.3	20.3	R = .661, −.795, .323
	III. Second Gubernatorial Primary, 1916 Percent			
	Blease	*Manning*	*Not Voting*	
Operatives	73.7	6.4	19.7	N = 20
Other Voters	34.4	55.4	10.2	R = .755, −.769, .544

SOURCE: for voting figures, Columbia *State*, August 27, September 9, 1914, September 13, 1916; Rock Hill *Herald*, August 26, September 9, 1914, September 13, 1916; and the Greenville newspapers cited in Table 8. For a discussion of the voter enrollment data, see the Appendix.

[a]The procedure used in compiling this table is discussed in the Appendix.

[b]Includes votes for E. D. Smith, L. D. Jennings, and W. P. Pollock.

[c]The unit of observation is the Democratic Club.

[d]Represents the Pearson correlation coefficients of the estimating equations for the three columns, reading from left to right.

proportionate support of those clubs for various candidates, it is possible to estimate the degree to which the mill operatives themselves supported Blease and his faction. As Table 9 indicates, mill workers voted overwhelmingly for "Coley" in 1914 and 1916, and were only mildly less enthusiastic about John G. Richards, the Bleaseite candidate for governor in 1914.[6]

6. See Table 9 and the Appendix.

On the other hand, "town" voters in the mill counties were generally even more adamantly opposed to Blease and his henchmen than mill voters were favorable to them. The "other voters" included in Table 9, a majority of whom held nonagricultural jobs and can probably be considered "town people," usually supported anti-Blease candidates by two to one in 1914, and by only a slightly smaller margin two years later.[7] Towns in Anderson, Greenville, and Spartanburg counties generally gave Blease between a fourth and a third of their vote. While Laurens County mill clubs gave 80 percent of their vote to Blease, the towns of Laurens and Clinton gave a similar proportion to his opponents. Even Columbia, with its sizable contingent of Southern Railway employees and its comparatively relaxed attitude towards drink, never gave Blease more than 40 percent of its "town" vote, except in the apathetic, liquor-beclouded election of 1910.[8] The voting blocs of mill and town were so rigidly opposed in the upstate counties that they often balanced each other out, leaving the large and relatively unattached rural vote to decide the issue. Far from demonstrating "the propensity of intraparty politics to blur class lines in elections,"[9] then, Blease brought to a focus the sharpest class confrontation between white men ever to appear in the Palmetto State. Nowhere else does the hostility between mill and town in Progressive-era South Carolina appear in such bold relief.

How does one explain Blease's extraordinary appeal to the operatives? The historians' favorite answer has been "style," and its importance is undeniable. Blease made special efforts to woo the mill voters. His political organization was based in large part on one of

7. Of the "other voters" in Table 9, 62.7 percent reported non-farm occupations; in thirteen of the twenty clubs from which observations were drawn for the 1916 estimates, and in fifteen of the twenty-two clubs used for the 1914 estimates, non-farmers made up at least half the non-mill population.

8. For Spartanburg election figures, see Table 7; for Union, see Union *Progress*, August 27, 1912, August 25, 1914, September 19, 1916; for Greenville, see Table 8 and Greenville *Daily News*, August 29, 1912; for Anderson, Anderson *Intelligencer*, August 28, 1914; for Aiken, Aiken *Journal and Review*, September 6, 1912, August 28, 1914, September 13, 1916; for Richland, Columbia *State*, August 29, 1912, August 27, 1914; for Laurens, *ibid.*, September 16, 1910; Laurensville *Herald*, September 11, 1914; and the comment in *Our Monthly* (Thornwell Orphanage, Clinton, S.C.), LIII (1916), 450.

9. Kousser, *Shaping of Southern Politics*, 235.

the operatives' most important social institutions, the fraternal order. "Coley" himself belonged to no less than five, and was a high state and national official of the Improved Order of Red Men, whose lodges were common in the mill villages.[10] He made a practice of holding special night rallies in industrial areas, which mill hands could attend after working hours. In his speeches he attacked "respectable" people that operatives dared not attack, in language they dared not use. He flouted convention with a sometimes delightful insouciance, as for example in a barb at the temperance movement in his first inaugural address: "I . . . beg leave to call your attention to the evil of the habitual drinking of coca cola, pepsi cola, and such like mixtures, as I fully believe they are injurious. It would be better for our people if they had nice, respectable places where they could go and buy a good, pure glass of cold beer than to drink such concoctions." He served, or at least posed, as the tribune of the mill people, receiving a constant stream of complaints from operatives, especially about arbitrary treatment by the mills. He gave the mill hands recognition as part of the body politic; in Francis Butler Simkins' words, "he voiced the feelings of the common people in their own language and made them think he was one of them."[11]

The historical fascination with Blease's style, however, has led to a grave misunderstanding of his place in the history of South Carolina and the South. Most damaging has been the accusation that Blease's appeal was lacking in concrete substance and that his issues were diversionary and nonrational. Simkins declares that "Blease had scarcely any program whatever," and Rupert Vance finds "Blease's original contribution" to the practice of politics "in his ability to make a class appeal without offering a class pro-

10. Blease to Elrie Robinson (St. Francisville, La.), November 30, 1914; Blease to Mamie E. Crooks, April 16, 1914, both in Governor Cole L. Blease Papers, South Carolina Department of Archives and History, Columbia (hereafter cited as SCDAH). The Blease papers are full of fraternal correspondence, much of it quasipolitical in nature.

11. Burnside, "Blease," 6–8, 11–12, 260–63; South Carolina House of Representatives, *Journal, 1911*, 94–95; South Carolina Department of Agriculture, Commerce, and Industries, Labor Division, *Report, 1912*, 15–16; *1913*, 48 (hereafter cited as *Labor Division Report*); E. J. Watson to Cole L. Blease, February 22, 1913, March 17, 1914, and *passim.*, in Blease Papers, SCDAH.; Francis Butler Simkins, *Pitchfork Ben Tillman: South Carolinian* (Baton Rouge: Louisiana State University Press, 1944), 488.

gram." W. J. Cash argues that Blease shied away from a "tangible program" for fears of raising "class conflict," "splitting the Democratic party into irreconcilable factions[!], and thus raising the possibility of a return of the Negro to politics." V. O. Key quotes all three to argue that Bleaseism was a "nonrational" movement diverting the masses with racial appeals. Finally, J. Morgan Kousser dismisses Blease as pure wind, a cheap sensationalist who "yelled so stridently" just to attract the attention of a confused electorate which responded to "the volume more than the content of [his] remarks."[12]

All these interpretations bear a striking resemblance to anti-Blease polemics, especially in their common debt to the anti-Blease historian David Duncan Wallace, who contends that "the strength of Blease's appeal was not any program of measures, but his personality and viewpoint." The educational reformer W. K. Tate declared in 1915 that "Blease represented no consistent body of principles, and Bleaseism was an incoherent protest rather than a definite program"; D. E. Camak found Blease's speeches devoid of "constructive measure[s]." Not only have historians commonly accepted the anti-Bleaseites' low opinion of Blease, but they have also endorsed his opponents' patronizing attitude toward his following. Vance's declaration that the class consciousness of South Carolina's mill workers just prior to World War I was an "ignorant class consciousness," and Key's explanation of Blease's appeal in terms of "the ignorance of farm folk turned factory operatives overnight," are little different from H. N. Snyder's contemporary complaint about "the terrifying power of ignorance . . . to lift the empty-headed jester or the unprincipled leader into positions of trust and power."[13]

12. *Ibid.*; Rupert Vance, "Rebels and Agrarians All: Studies in One-Party Politics," *Southern Review*, IV (1938–1939), 34; W. J. Cash, *The Mind of the South* (New York: Alfred A. Knopf, 1941), 245; Key, *Southern Politics*, 144; Burnside, "Blease," 6; Kousser, *Shaping of Southern Politics*, 236. A criticism of this interpretation similar to mine appears in Clarence Stone, "Bleaseism and the 1912 Election in South Carolina," *North Carolina Historical Review*, XL (1963), 71–74. See also C. Vann Woodward, *Origins of the New South, 1877–1913* (Baton Rouge: Louisiana State University Press, 1951), 392–95.

13. Tate, "After Blease," 575; D. E. Camak, *Human Gold from Southern Hills* (Greer, S.C.: private, 1960), 138; Vance, "Rebels and Agrarians All," 35; Key, *Southern Politics*, 144; Snyder in Spartanburg *Herald*, reprinted in Union *Progress*, October 1, 1912; David

Blease did not dodge issues, however. In fact, he took firm stands on a number of questions which his constituents, at least, thought were of crucial importance. Nor is there any reason to believe that operatives supported Blease out of "ignorance." The "bloc vote" cast in the mill precincts, frequently cited as evidence that mill workers were being driven to the polls like cattle, was no more solid than the anti-Blease "bloc vote" of the towns, and both were functions of a perceived class identity and class interest. The warning of a "cotton mill boy" to the editor of the Spartanburg *Herald* not to "think for one moment that cotton mill boys haven't got brains" was well given, if not well taken.[14]

Why, then, the persistent emphasis on "ignorance," "backwardness," and "irrationality"? The ubiquitous reference to Blease's lack of a "program" suggests an explanation. All of the commentators mentioned above are heirs to a middle-class, progressive tradition that extolls a strong, activist government; "the problem of democracy," argues Key, "is . . . to grant power adequate to necessities and then to control it." A corollary is the conviction that submerged classes can, and should, use the government to promote their own welfare. How, then, to explain a "labor" politician like Blease, who "won favor by railing against measures which labor where informed and organized demands"?[15] Blease had no "program" in the usual sense, no set of proposals to use governmental power to achieve specified ends. However, his lack of a "program" is irrelevent, for he drew the hard core of his support from a constituency which regarded the government as its enemy, as an engine of oppression controlled by a hostile class. Blease's supporters were spiritual, if not intellectual, heirs of an older America whose citizens viewed all concentrations of power as dangerous, and all government bureaucracies as corrupt and self-interested. Accordingly, mill voters were devoted to Blease precisely because he was not an innovator, or even a conservative, but

---

Duncan Wallace, *The History of South Carolina* (4 vols.; New York: American Historical Society, 1934), III, 425. Wallace is a source for all the writers cited above except Cash and Key; Key's interpretation is influenced by Simkins and Vance.

14. "Cotton Mill Boy" in Spartanburg *Herald*, September 15, 1912.

15. Key, *Southern Politics*, 155; Wallace, *History*, III, 425.

rather an obstructionist. As the early-nineteenth-century Luddites smashed machinery in a vain effort to halt the encroachment of industrial capitalism on their world, so the operatives sent Blease and his lieutenants to Columbia to wreck the social machinery being created by the middle classes. The disorderliness of Bleaseism reflected a devotion to personal autonomy still prevalent among the operatives, who more than any other group of poor whites felt themselves besieged by the encroaching society of the "town people." The basic issue of the Blease era was not race, or liquor, but how society was to be organized and who would control it.

The most obvious illustration of the class conflicts underlying Bleaseism involved suffrage restriction in the primary, an issue largely ignored by historians.[16] The state constitution of 1895 restricted the franchise in the general election to adult males who were literate or who owned property of value assessed at three hundred dollars or more. Voters were also required to have paid all taxes, including the poll tax, and to have been resident in the state for two years, in the county for one year, and in the precinct for six months. Obviously the restrictions fell most heavily on the uneducated, the unpropertied, and the transient, all of whom were well represented among the operatives. However, the constitution delegated responsibility for regulating the primary to the General Assembly, which in 1888 had delegated it to the state Democratic party. The party, in turn, was generally considered to be a party in name only, and its primary a subterfuge designed to preserve universal suffrage for whites while denying the vote to blacks. Its voting requirements were few and light, and in their enforcement it customarily deferred to the prerogatives of white manhood. Thus in the early twentieth century the primary in South Carolina was open to virtually every adult white male.[17]

16. The single exception is Burnside, "Blease," 20, 139–41, 278–79, 283; his references are brief and do not alter his adherence to the view that Blease avoided substantive issues. Despite Kousser's interest in suffrage restriction (*Shaping of Southern Politics*), he wholly neglects this phase of the subject in South Carolina.

17. *Constitution of the State of South Carolina*, 1895, Article 2, Sections 4 and 10; *S.C. Stats. at Large*, XX (1888), 10; Typescript dated May 4, 1914, in James A. Hoyt, Jr., Papers, South Caroliniana Library, University of South Carolina, Columbia (hereafter cited as SCL). Cf. Kousser, *Shaping of Southern Politics*, *passim.*, on suffrage restriction as a "partisan" movement. See also Wallace, *History*, III, 370–71.

However, there was a strong undercurrent of opinion in South Carolina favorable to restricting the primary suffrage, which became increasingly powerful with the advent of the twentieth century. By 1903 such leading newspapers as *The State*, the Spartanburg *Herald*, and the Florence *Times*, noting that "the character of part of the voting population has changed in recent years," began urging that the general election restrictions be observed in all elections. Widespread complaints of corruption in mill areas produced a brief upsurge of interest in restriction following the primary of 1904; a restriction bill was introduced in the 1905 General Assembly by an Anderson mill attorney, but despite committee approval never reached the floor.[18] The restriction movement then became quiescent, but it burgeoned after Blease's strong 1908 campaign. In 1909 a bill to require registration and poll tax payment for voting in municipal primaries passed the Senate, as did a similar measure of statewide application. Both failed in the House, however, after debate.[19] A more vigorous attempt at restriction was made at the 1910 state Democratic party convention by the delegation from Richland County (Columbia). The Richland resolution lost by nearly three to one, but the margin was much closer among upcountry delegates, and *The State* was gratified at "the strong undercurrent of strength for restriction." While noting the obvious link between upstate sentiment for the proposal and the "considerable moving population" of the mill villages, the Columbia newspaper nonetheless insisted that the measure was not aimed at the "industrious and reliable" operatives but at the "menacing influence" of "the unruly element among them."[20]

18. Columbia *State*, August 11, October 3, 1903, December 15, 1904, January 30, 31, 1905; *S.C. House Journal, 1905*, 301, 334; *1906*, 736.

19. Columbia *State*, August 3, 1907, January 26, February 17, 1909; Union *Progress*, December 11, 1908; *S.C. Senate Journal, 1909*, 312, 428, 494, 552–54; *S.C. House Journal, 1909*, 75, 349, 731; *1910*, 289, 302, 374.

20. Columbia *State*, May 3, 19, 20, 1910; W. H. Edwards, *ibid.*, July 4, 1910; R. B. Caldwell to John J. McMahan, May 12, 1914, in John J. McMahan Papers, SCL. An explicit link between multiple voting in the Piedmont and "its shifting population of industrial workers" was made by James A. Hoyt, Jr., later president of the state Democratic party convention of 1914 and speaker of the South Carolina House of Representatives in 1915–16, in an address to the alumni association of Furman University, June 4, 1913 (MS in James A. Hoyt, Jr., Papers, SCL).

Despite support from many influential South Carolinians, the restriction movement was frustrated by a general disinclination to disfranchise whites and a lack of urgency on the part of the advocates of disfranchisement.[21] Its principal successes came in connection with the municipal reform movement. Abridgment of the franchise was frequently concomitant with Progressive-era urban reform in the United States, since a principal motive for reform was to strengthen the hand of the business and professional community—here the "town people"—in city government. Certainly the view that a city was in essence "a corporation, not a political division" comported well with the conception of the town held by South Carolina's middle classes. "Reform"—specifically the commission form of municipal government—helped further control by the town classes through employment of the principle of at-large elections to drown the voices of the "mill" wards, and through restriction of the electorate as much as possible to those deemed to have a "stake" in the city.[22]

Significantly, the first two cities in the state to adopt a commission form of government, Columbia and Spartanburg, contained sizable mill populations in charge of one or more wards. Enabling legislation permitting Columbia to adopt the commission form was passed in 1910 after three years of agitation by *The State* and the Columbia Chamber of Commerce. It restricted the electorate not only for municipal elections under the new form but also for the referendum on its adoption. The impact on the electorate was dramatic. The referendum turnout in the four "town" wards was 38.1 percent below that of the municipal primary of 1908; in Ward Five the total vote declined by 73.1 percent. While the shrunken mill ward gave a small majority to the commission proposal, it also cast nearly half the votes against it. The voting totals rose in the ensuing municipal election, but Ward Five still cast only

21. C. E. Spencer to John J. McMahan, May 7, 1914, in John J. McMahan Papers, SCL; Columbia *State*, May 20, 1910; D. D. McColl to James A. Hoyt, May 11, 1914, in D. D. McColl Papers, SCL.

22. See Chap. I herein; Columbia *State*, August 11, 1903, March 10, 1910; James Weinstein, "Organized Business and the City Commission and Manager Movements," *Journal of Southern History*, XXVIII (1962), 166–82.

41.9 percent of its 1908 total, as compared to 72.6 percent in the town.[23]

The adoption of commission government in Spartanburg in 1913 was accompanied by acrimonious disputes between the mill villagers and the townspeople, and between Bleaseites and anti-Bleaseites, especially over the ground rules of the elections. In the referendum the managers of Ward Six (Spartan Mills) required all voters to show tax receipts until "discovering" late in the day that the requirement had been ignored in the "town" wards. Less than one-third of the white voting population cast ballots, the town boxes voting better than four to one in favor of the reform while the mill boxes went better than four to one against it. Later that year, after a surprisingly strong showing by local Bleaseite candidates in the first municipal primary, the city Democratic Executive Committee ruled that only those who had paid taxes at least six months prior to the date of the general election could vote in the second primary. The maneuver defeated the Bleaseites, but it also disfranchised nearly a thousand registered voters, many of them mill operatives who had paid their one-dollar poll tax for the first time.[24] The mill hands' loss of power had practical consequences. Long the most neglected parts of the city with regard to municipal services, the mill neighborhoods were even worse off afterwards. In the spring of 1914, when the mill villages were still largely without sewerage, the commission was considering an extravagant scheme to light the streets of the downtown business district. Objecting to such misplaced priorities, David Duncan Wallace remarked that "the commission form of government was adopted here in the spirit of the prudent householder and business man, who wanted his affairs run on a business basis. There were other features no less valuable, such as social justice, which inhere in the plan but have not been emphasized."[25]

23. Columbia *State*, March 11, 1908, April 3, 4, 27, 1910; Weinstein, "Commission and Manager Movements," 171; *S.C. Stats. at Large*, XXVI (1910), 523–38.

24. Spartanburg *Herald*, February 12, September 6–17, 1913. A newspaper sympathetic to Blease condemned the tax ruling as a blatant factional power grab; Yorkville *Enquirer*, September 16, 1913.

25. Spartanburg *Herald*, September 11, 1913; D. D. Wallace, *ibid.*, April 10, 1914; A. F. Perkins, *ibid.*, April 12, 1914. Cf. Weinstein, "Commission and Manager Movements," 175.

While such narrow self-interest provided much of the impetus for the restriction and urban reform movements, the support of both movements by Progressive spokesmen such as Wallace and the editors of *The State* suggests that broader considerations were involved. An insight into the "Progressive" aspects of restriction can be gained by examining the attitudes of the leader of the restriction movement, Columbia attorney and former state superintendent of education John J. McMahan. On the suffrage issue McMahan was an uncompromising reactionary. As a delegate to the 1895 constitutional convention he had proposed a stiff landed property requirement for voting, the literate not excepted. As principal author of the act authorizing commission government for Columbia he had opposed the referendum, preferring to "put it on the city."[26] On social issues, however, McMahan was perhaps the most radical public man in the state. In the General Assembly of 1915–16 he supported the entire Progressive agenda, including child labor reform, compulsory education, the expansion of the school system, and medical inspection of school children. The notes he constantly made to himself were filled with stronger proposals: to force mills to expand their welfare work, to reduce the work day to eight hours, to make operatives into homeowners. He was interested in state ownership of railroads and utilities, and there are hints that he even advocated a state takeover of the cotton mills. At the same time that he sought to restrict the suffrage to property holders he proposed to use the power of the state to distribute property to every white man.[27] Nor did McMahan and other Progressives of his thinking see any contradiction in their at-

26. *Journal of the Constitutional Convention of the State of South Carolina, 1895* (Columbia: Charles A. Calvo, Jr., 1895), 152–53; typed memo re conference on commission bill, 1910, in John J. McMahan Papers, SCL. Kousser, *Shaping of Southern Politics*, 151, mentions McMahan's role at the convention.

27. See the compilation of votes in John Samuel Lupold, "The Nature of South Carolina Progressives, 1914–1916" (M.A. thesis, University of South Carolina, 1968), 65–66; John J. McMahan Papers, SCL, *passim*. McMahan was widely regarded as an impractical dreamer and a crank. Nonetheless he held the affection of many of his contemporaries among the state's close-knit middle class, who regarded him as ahead of his time and, at least privately, sympathized with his unbending stands. See D. M. Douglas to David R. Coker, July 31, 1928; David R. Coker to Kirkman G. Finlay, October 16, 1931, both in David R. Coker Papers, SCL; also, the eulogy of McMahan by James A. Hoyt, Jr. (newspaper clipping, n.d., in James A. Hoyt, Jr., Scrapbook, SCL).

titudes; in fact they advocated restriction partly in the hope that it would motivate the disfranchised to seek education, acquire property, and thus become "worthy" citizens. "Why should not the primary election laws be so designed as to inspire ambition in those who would otherwise be content with ignorance; why should not the suffrage be made to build up manhood instead of dragging down?" asked *The State*. McMahan insisted that his advocacy of the "purification" of the primary was in the interest of "the elevation of the masses of the people"; "they and their children would rejoice," he declared, "if lifted out of the filth of morals in which misfortune has placed them." In its elitism, its manipulativeness, and its willingness to abridge traditional rights in the name of a higher end, the restriction movement was thus the ultimate "uplift" program.[28]

Not surprisingly, the operatives were less than appreciative of the restrictionists' humanitarian intentions. Largely deprived of their voice in municipal affairs, Columbia mill workers struck back in the state primary. McMahan was regularly howled down at mill ward campaign meetings, and mill voters rejected him almost unanimously. Except for a brief return in 1914 his legislative career was blasted; he comforted himself with the assurance that "they make a fight on any man that tries to improve the morals of the people."[29]

The restriction issue was, of course, made to order for Blease, for it struck at his most loyal followers and could thus be used for a rallying point. From the very outset of the 1910 campaign he condemned suffrage restriction; he led the opposition to the Richland resolution at the convention and boasted repeatedly on the stump of how he had frustrated the "deep-laid scheme of the politicians to disfranchise 20,000 of the poor white men of South Carolina." He promised mill audiences that as governor he would veto any legislative proposal depriving them of a vote. While no

28. Columbia *State*, August 11, 1903; John J. McMahan, *ibid.*, August 30, 1904. Kousser, *Shaping of Southern Politics*, 260–61, notes some of the "Progressive" aspects of the suffrage restriction movement.

29. Columbia *State*, August 31, 1910, August 23, 30, September 16, 1914; memo dated August 31, 1910, and letter to *The State* dated August 26, 1916, in John J. McMahan Papers, SCL.

general restriction measure ever reached his desk, he did veto several acts extending commission government to various cities. "Under no circumstances," he declared, "would I lend my assistance to the establishing of such a form of government over any free and intelligent people."[30]

In retrospect the restriction movement seems hardly to have been a serious factor in South Carolina politics. No major campaign was ever fought on the issue; furthermore, even staunchly anti-Blease politicians publicly opposed it. Many conservatives were sufficiently attached to old democratic ideals to condemn the movement, as did Beaufort's Niels Christensen, on the ground that "universal white manhood suffrage is *right*." However, it would be a mistake to conclude from this that Blease's use of the restriction issue was "irrelevent" or "diversionary." In principle, restriction had powerful support among the "better element": "This provision," declared a Chester man, "is demanded by the good citizens of this State, not for the purpose of disfranchising, but to enfranchise our people." Anti-Blease leaders shied away from outright support of restriction, in large part out of respect for Blease's ability to mobilize opposition. An angry restrictionist blamed "political cowardice" for the failure of the anti-Blease-dominated 1912 state convention even to consider the question, while more moderate anti-Bleaseites berated McMahan and his followers for "put [ting] a stick into Blease's hands, to break our heads with." If one considers democracy, even for whites only, to be preferable to an oligarchy of the sort desired by the restrictionists, Blease's defense of universal white manhood suffrage must be given credit for keeping South Carolina from going the way of her sister southern states.[31]

30. Columbia *State*, April 24, May 19, July 4, 1910, November 12, 1911; Burnside, "Blease," 139; *S.C. House Journal, 1912*, 48; *1914*, 1308; *S.C. Senate Journal, 1913*, 631.

31. Niels Christensen to William Watts Ball, May 15, 1914, in William Watts Ball Papers, Duke University Library, Durham, N.C.; W. H. Edwards in Columbia *State*, July 4, 1910; William N. Graydon to John J. McMahan, September 14, 1912; E. S. Joynes to McMahan, May 5, 1914, quoting Columbia *Record*, both in John J. McMahan Papers, SCL. Manning reportedly complained that McMahan "had done as much for Bleaseism in this State as any other man." D. M. Douglas to David R. Coker, July 31, 1928, in David R. Coker Papers, SCL. For contemporary developments elsewhere, see Kousser, *Shaping of Southern Politics*.

Suffrage restriction and civic reform, however, were only the political manifestations of the middle-class drive to consolidate South Carolina society under its leadership; it has been Blease's stances on "uplift" legislation that have most intrigued, and confused, historians. Unable to fasten conventional labels on a governor who combined "liberal" positions on prison reform and state aid to education with "conservative" ones on labor legislation, they have often been content to term his viewpoint "incoherent" and his course "erratic."[32] Viewed as the chosen spokesman of the mill operatives and other poor whites, however, Blease appears to have been far more consistent than he has been given credit for. His early support of statewide appropriations for the public schools, for example, was motivated by a desire to counter the growing financial imbalance between the comparatively wealthy "town" schools and those of the countryside. When the anti-Blease-controlled General Assembly diverted much of the appropriation to aid town schools, however, he promptly switched to opposition. Town dwellers and educators might find such behavior perplexing, but mill operatives, aware of the inferiority of their own schools, probably found the hypocrisy of a middle class which declaimed against the "danger of ignorance" while jealously protecting the financial advantages of its own schools to be far more "opportunistic" than the behavior of their champion.[33]

Blease's position on child labor legislation was more ambiguous. In his younger days he had been a passionate advocate of child labor reform, declaring in 1892 that "if we have got to buy capital by murdering women and children, for God's sake let it go, let it go." In 1911 he signed the Osborne bill eliminating the under-twelve exemptions from the child labor law, even expressing ap-

32. Ernest M. Lander, Jr., *A History of South Carolina, 1865–1960* (Chapel Hill: University of North Carolina Press, 1960), 49–51.

33. On the growing imbalance in public school finances up to 1915, see Louis M. Harlan, *Separate and Unequal: Public School Campaigns and Racism in the Southern Seaboard States, 1901–1915* (Chapel Hill: University of North Carolina Press, 1958), 264–66; on the school tax controversy see Burnside, "Blease," 199–204. For a revealing example of the relation of mill-town hostilities to the schools, see Ben M. Sawyer to Patterson Wardlaw, May 3, 1916; W. A. Shealy to Wardlaw, May 15, 1916, both in Patterson Wardlaw Papers, SCL.

proval of the measure.[34] In general, however, he soft-pedaled his child labor stance, for much of his following was evidently of another mind. The fight against the Osborne bill was led by his powerful friend "Citizen Josh" Ashley, with the backing of other Bleaseite legislators, one of whom condemned the measure as "directed at the weak and helpless." H. K. Osborne, the bill's sponsor, was a major Bleaseite target in 1912, going down to defeat along with most of a Spartanburg County delegation which had solidly supported the proposal. In the 1913 legislative session Ashley attempted to restore the summer vacation exemption, which had been repealed by the Osborne amendment, while a Spartanburg Bleaseite introduced legislation to make it unnecessary for working children to obtain new permits when they changed employers, a measure aimed at E. J. Watson's enforcement system.[35] Those Bleaseites who survived the anti-Blease sweep of 1914, such as W. W. Dixon of Fairfield and the operative representatives W. S. Rogers and E. G. Nunn, voted against the fourteen year limit in 1916. Even as seemingly inoffensive a measure as the 1914 vital statistics bill was opposed by Ashley, Rogers, and some other upcountry Bleaseites, possibly because it would strengthen child labor law enforcement. The governor apparently approved of the bill, but prudently delayed signing it until after the 1914 primary.[36]

However equivocal his course on child labor, Blease's general opinion of "uplift" legislation was explicit. "Much has been said," he declared in his 1911 inaugural address, "about the enactment of laws in regard to the labor in our cotton mills. These people are our people; they are our kindred; they are our friends, and in my opinion they should be let alone, and allowed to manage their own

34. Charleston *News and Courier*, December 18, 1890; *ibid.*, quoted in Newberry *Herald and News*, December 14, 1892; "J" in Columbia *State*, September 12, 1910; political advertisement, *ibid.*, September 3, 1914; Burnside, "Blease," 256.

35. Columbia *State*, February 1, 2, 1911; Spartanburg *Herald*, August 10, September 11, 1912, February 8, 1913; *S.C. House Journal, 1913*, 240, 328; Charleston *News and Courier*, February 3, 1913. Both measures, however, were quietly buried by the anti-Blease-dominated General Assembly.

36. *S.C. House Journal, 1916*, 580–81; *S.C. House Journal, 1914*, 1104; Spartanburg *Herald*, September 2, 1914. Only nineteen votes were cast against the bill, and the tiny contingent of Blease men in the House was divided on the issue.

children and allowed to manage their own affairs." The same sentiment was expressed more concretely when he vetoed the annual appropriation for factory inspection, declaring to a protesting union official that adult mill workers could take care of themselves. The veto was possibly politically motivated; Blease was jealously protective of his power base, and may have feared that Watson's inspectors might subvert his mill following. Whatever its motive, there is no evidence that the well-publicized veto hurt him among the operatives, many of whom were convinced that the Labor Division was intent more on controlling them than on protecting them. Watson's early attempts to encourage foreign immigration to South Carolina were remembered by workers who had viewed those efforts as designed to undercut their economic position; his advocacy of tougher child labor laws brought complaints that "he wanted more power than any one ever had, and if he can get away with it no telling what he will want next."[37]

The essence of Bleaseism was nowhere better expressed than in its opposition to compulsory education and the use of the schools as instruments of social control. Hostility to compulsory school attendance became a touchstone of Bleaseism, a fact used by anti-Bleaseites as evidence that its factional power rested on "ignorance"; the union-oriented *Horse Creek Valley News*, for example, found Blease's stand unsurprising, for "education is a deadly foe to demagoguery."[38] "Ignorance," however, is too easy an explanation for the broad appeal of Blease's attacks on compulsory schooling. So, for that matter, is the argument that "racist" Bleaseites were opposed to compulsory education because it would promote the education of blacks, for Blease's supporters were no more "racist" than his opponents.[39] Blease and his followers objected to compulsory education for the same reasons that middle-class re-

37. *S.C. House Journal, 1911*, 95; Columbia *State*, February 19, 22, 24, 26, 1911; Joe C. Chalmers (Brandon Mill, Greenville) to Cole L. Blease, January 12, 1912; W. E. Childs *et al.* (Orr Mill, Anderson) to Blease, January 19, 1914, both in Blease Papers, SCDAH. On immigration, see pages 112–14 herein.

38. Quoted in Columbia *State*, July 11, 1910. The *News* had at one time been edited by the former UTW organizer G. R. Webb.

39. Burnside, "Blease," 214–15, concludes that Blease used the "personal liberty" argument almost exclusively in his pronouncements on the issue.

formers supported it: the hope that the school would wean mill and other poor white children away from their parents' mentality and lead them to accept that of the "town people." "In my opinion," declared Blease at his inaugural,

> compulsory education in the hands of the State means disrupting the home, for it dethrones the authority of the parents and places the paid agents of the State in control of the children, and destroys family government. Those agents stand between the child and the parent. They represent the State. They are not responsible to the parents. They impress upon the minds of the children the views of the State, and virtually say, "We have taken you out of bondage and made you free; we are giving you what your unnatural parents would not give you," and no child on earth can be subject to such influences and teachings and escape imbibing the spirit of rebellion against parental authority, and consequent disrespect and ingratitude.[40]

The fears of Blease's followers were not allayed by anti-Blease ripostes that their leader "seems exceedingly jealous for the personal rights of the parents, but don't care a farthing for the rights of the children." They believed that "the state" was in the hands of men who in the name of "children's rights" and even "law and order" sought to destroy their families and remake their children in an alien image. Against the encroaching public education establishment Blease and his noisy band of adherents in the General Assembly were their protectors; what the Bleaseite legislators lacked in numbers was made up by the governor's veto, which was used to block four different compulsory attendance bills during his second term.[41]

Closely related to the compulsory education question was the spectacular controversy over the medical inspection of school children. The idea began to attract interest in South Carolina shortly after the turn of the century, and in 1909 the Seneca school district, a "town" district containing a sizable mill population, became the third school system in the South to undertake the sys-

40. *South Carolina House Journal*, 1911, 93. Cf. the remarks of Christopher Lasch on the "proletarianization of parenthood" in *Haven in a Heartless World: The Family Besieged* (New York: Basic Books, 1977), 12–21.

41. W. H. Edwards in Columbia *State*, July 4, 1910; see the legislative histories of bills H. 93, S. 430, S. 546, and S. 811 in *S.C. House and Senate Journals*, 1913–14, *passim.*

tematic examination of pupils for diseases and physical defects.[42] By the spring of 1910 the medical inspection gospel had spread over the state, and local physicians were setting up programs in Spartanburg, Greenville, Easley, Anderson, and Columbia. Local initiative, though, was deemed an inadequate means of implementing so beneficent a reform, and almost immediately it was proposed that the state require medical inspection in all public schools, "in order to force the indifferent teachers and school boards to give it some attention." A "well-planned agitation" was begun by the South Carolina Medical Association, with backing from such Progressive bulwarks as the State Federation of Women's Clubs and *The State*.[43]

The arguments used in favor of medical inspection were similar to those used for compulsory school attendance. "The school child is the greatest asset the nation has," declared the state's pioneer medical inspector, Dr. E. A. Hines of Seneca; thus "the oversight of the child's environment and the child itself through school life" was the legitimate concern of organized society and the organized medical profession. "If the State has a right to train a child's body," argued Dr. William Weston of Columbia, "it also has a right to protect its brain and body." Dr. Rosa H. Gantt of Spartanburg likened the schools to factories "where are manufactured educated, competent men and women," and medical inspection to product testing. She added that, since the public schools mixed children of all conditions in the classrooms, they were responsible for protecting the "normal child" from children "whose parents through ignorance or neglect have not corrected deformities which are easily correctible."[44]

The virtues of medical inspection seemed so obvious to the middle classes that they were stunned when in 1912 Blease vetoed a

42. On early interest in medical inspection, see Union *Progress*, April 9, 1907; on Seneca, see M. L. Brockman, "Medical Inspection of Schools," *Southern School News*, II (October, 1910), 8–9; "Medical Inspection of Schools," *South Carolina Board of Health Bulletin*, I (1910), 22–23. The first southern schools to adopt medical inspection were in New Orleans (1908) and Atlanta (1908–1909); *ibid.*, 22.

43. "Medical Inspection," 25; Brockman, "Medical Inspection," 9; Columbia *State*, April 21, 1910, May 4, 1911.

44. Columbia *State*, April 22, 1910, February 21, December 23, 1912.

bill to apply its benefits statewide. In his veto message he proclaimed medical inspection to be an outrageous invasion of privacy, alleging that it authorized "the publishing in the records of your State and from the house-tops of your schools, that a certain child has a certain disease, thus holding it up to ridicule and scandal." In a grotesque appeal to race feeling he claimed that the bill gave black janitors the right to demand that children be examined in their presence. Most shocking, though, was his imputation of sexual overtones to the proposal. He alleged that the most intimate secrets of young girls would be recorded by the state under the provisions of the bill, and that their virtue would be endangered by lecherous examiners and "third parties." He invoked these sexual fears most violently in a 1914 veto message, in which he implicitly linked medical inspection to the "unmentionable crime," and suggested a similar solution. "I shall be honest with you," he confided: "If I had a daughter I would kill any doctor in South Carolina whom I would be forced to let examine her against her will and mine, and if any man should do this, in such a case, while I am governor, so help me, God, I will pardon him, and I will write in his pardon that he is entitled to the respect of all the people for being of the highest type of a free American citizen."[45]

On their face, Blease's objections seemed absurd. Examinations were to be in public, and did not require disrobing; all personal information was to be kept confidential, and the "janitor" issue was the product of a deliberate misconstruction of the text of the 1912 bill. The value of inspection to the welfare of mill children, on the other hand, was obvious.[46] Nonetheless, Blease's stance proved wildly popular, especially among operatives, to the utter bewilderment of the "respectable" people of the state. "Elsewhere in the world, the laboring people demand medical school inspec-

45. *S.C. House Journal, 1912*, 1089–92; *S.C. Senate Journal, 1914*, 1121.

46. William Weston in Columbia *State*, February 21, 1912; Statement of Committee on Health and Public Instruction, South Carolina Medical Association, printed in Union *Progress*, August 6, 1912. See also the text of the measure vetoed in 1912, reprinted in Columbia *State*, February 28, 1912. The bill required that all pupils, teachers, and staff be examined, but provided that a witness could be requested "by said school child, student, teacher, or janitor"; in other words, that a janitor could request that a third person be present at his *own* examination. See also Wallace, *History*, III, 430*n*.

tion laws," noted *The State*; only in South Carolina did "labor" politicians oppose them. Faced with such widespread operative resentment of "the free offering of skilled medical attention to the poor little boys and girls of the cotton mill villages," middle-class observers tended to dismiss it as the result of "credulous ignorance."[47]

However satisfactory that explanation was to the anti-Bleaseites, "ignorance" is an inadequate explanation of the inclination of mill workers to believe Blease's scandalous insinuations against the medical profession. The operatives believed Blease rather than the proponents of medical inspection because they viewed the proposal as a new attack on their integrity, and, in the words of one Blease lieutenant, "another attempt of a class to get a hold on South Carolina." Blease noted that the 1912 bill denied parents the right to forbid examination of their children, even the right to be present at the examination, thus "tak[ing] from the control of the father and mother the physical child": "Have all the people, and all the classes of the people become imbeciles and children, that the Legislature, at every turn, must pass acts creating guardianships, or do you wish to establish an anarchy and force every poor man to bow down to the whims of all professions?" he demanded. Opponents of medical inspection accused the organized medical profession of using humanitarian rhetoric to disguise its own greed and lust for power. Blease characterized inspection at one time as a scheme to subsidize incompetent doctors, and letters he received supporting his stance were littered with references to "the doctor invasion of the school," "the greatest trust on earth today," and "the self-appointed guardian of the public, 'The American Medical Association,'" which was seeking "to make slaves of our children and parents as well." The Women's Clubs were dismissed as organizations of arrogant busybodies with little respect for their womanly duties. A Bleaseite state senator complained of their wanting "to give us their dresses for our pants," while the governor boasted of the support he received from "*mothers who*

47. Columbia *State*, January 20, 1912, and quoted in Union *Progress*, July 28, 1914; Wallace, *History*, III, 430.

are more devoted to their children, to their homes, and to their State, than some who neglect all three running around, 'doing society,' playing cards for prizes, etc. [emphasis his]."[48]

The fear of middle-class encroachment characterizing the opposition to school medical inspection sometimes took a more specific form. For example, it was rumored that inspection would be used to deny schooling to "diseased" poor children, a report which mill operatives with experience of town prejudices might well find more believable than the assurances (often mixed with ridicule) of inspection proponents that the measure was intended for their benefit.[49] The principal root of hostility to medical inspection, though, lay in its symbolism. Two views of society confronted each other over the issue, the one insisting on the absolute sacredness of the person and the authority of the family, the other arguing that the welfare of the individual was best served by his subordination to a social order run along rational lines by a ruling class of experts. Even the sexual fears of the Blease following, unfounded as they were, are understandable in the light of the operatives' hostility to "modern" society. If medical examiners viewed the body of a child as a thing to be measured and recorded, a "product" of a state "factory" whose quality needed to be carefully monitored, why should they be expected to respect the person of the child in other ways? If they treated parental authority with derision, what other values were they willing to flout? In the mill a man's labor had ceased to be an expression of his personality and had become a tool to be manipulated by the "bosses"; now, it seemed, the middle classes wished to treat the bodies of his children as tools in a social factory. The link between medical inspection and fears of sexual degradation reflected a deeper fear, that individual dignity as it had been traditionally understood was being violated by the new institutions being created by the "town people" in the name of human welfare.[50]

48. Columbia *State*, February 4, 1914; *S.C. House Journal, 1912*, 1089–92; *1914*, 1344–45; *S.C. Senate Journal, 1914*, 1121. For more moderate expressions of concern over the potential for "oppression" of medical inspection, see Yorkville *Enquirer*, September 19, 23, 1913.

49. Columbia *State*, March 27, 1912.

50. In the 1920s medical inspection sometimes became quite elaborate. In Greenville's

The hostility of Blease's followers was directed indiscriminately at all "town" institutions, including the mills. Bleaseite mill hands constantly showered the governor's office with allegations of vote buying and discriminatory firings by mill officials. One of Blease's favorite rhetorical targets was Lewis W. Parker, whose Parker Mills, a chain of sixteen plants brought under a single management in 1911, employed over 10 percent of the state's operatives. The "cotton mill merger" was attacked as a combination designed to depress wages and control workers, and its president, as well as those of other mills, was accused of attempting to bribe and intimidate voters.[51] Even at the height of the Blease era, however, the governor and his following failed to make any substantive move against the mills. For one thing, they lacked the power to do so; the General Assembly, then as now the dominant power in state government, was always comfortably in the hands of their enemies. There were, as well, splits among the Bleaseite politicians; C. C. Wyche of Spartanburg, for instance, maintained cordial relations with mill officials and defended the Parker "mill merger" on the floor of the House of Representatives. The governor himself, despite his rhetorical denunciations of industrialists, had a few friends among the mill presidents and "bosses." While commiserating with operatives over their "outrageous" treatment by the mills, he carefully avoided committing himself to any concrete action. Not only did the use of state power to protect operatives

---

Parker School District, a showcase of southern "welfare capitalism," each child was required to undergo daily inspection and to answer a series of questions, including whether or not he had slept on clean linen and had had a bowel movement the previous day. Walter T. McFall, "Mouth Hygiene Program, Parker School District," *South Carolina Education*, VII (January, 1926), 138–39. Compare the mill workers' attitudes with those of Jewish immigrants on the Lower East Side of Manhattan, who in 1906 or 1907 rioted over attempts by a local school to have children operated on for enlarged adenoids without their parents' consent. David B. Tyack, *The One Best System: A History of American Urban Education* (Cambridge: Harvard University Press, 1974), 179; *Southern Christian Advocate*, October 18, 1906, gives a different version of what was probably the same incident.

51. Affidavit of A. L. Dyson (Hartsville), August 17, 1914; letters to Cole L. Blease from S. M. Miller (Sampson, Greenville), April 26, 1914; E. C. Hendrick (Dunean, Greenville), March 1, 1914; Will T. Neal (Piedmont), May 11, 1914; R. C. Simpson (Monaghan), March 23, 1912; G. W. Pigler, March 24, 1911; and J. E. Thompson, March 18, 1911, all in Blease papers, SCDAH; Burnside, "Blease," 260–61; Columbia *State*, June 27, July 26, August 23, 1912.

smack of the "state guardianship" he despised, but he instinctively realized that any direct intervention on his part in industrial matters would probably alienate some portion of his support.[52] Given the costs of a direct assault on the manufacturers, Bleaseites preferred to express their sympathy with the oppressed workers by obstructing real or fancied "pro-mill" legislation. For example, a 1913 proposal to investigate the possibility of a workman's compensation system for South Carolina was opposed by nearly all the Bleaseite House members from mill counties, who, noting that many manufacturers advocated such a system in order to reduce their losses from damage suits, darkly suspected a "nigger in the woodpile." The fact that the principal "labor plank" in the platform of Ira D. Jones, Blease's 1912 opponent for the governorship, was a call for a workman's compensation system was thus probably more a liability than an asset to his campaign, for it helped make him a symbol of the shadowy "conspiracy" of the "town people" against the mill people.[53]

The essence of the "paranoid style" that underlay Bleaseism was best expressed in the response of the mill people to a bizarre rumor circulating in the villages during the 1912 campaign. According to the rumor, the election of Jones was to be followed by the formation of a gigantic cotton mill trust, presumably under Parker's control, which would dictate the passage of a law to control migration from one mill village to another. On its face the report was pre-

52. Gabriel Rocquie to C. C. Wyche, January 20, 1913; Wyche to Rocquie, February 1, 1913; A. M. Law to Wyche, January 21, 1913; Wyche to Law, January 24, 1913; L. W. Parker to Wyche, January 30, 1913, all in C. C. Wyche Papers, Duke University Library, Durham, N.C.; J. M. Davis (Newberry) to Cole L. Blease, May 20, 1914; B. B. Gossett (Anderson) to Blease, April 20, 1914; Blease to Gossett, April 21, 1914; Blease to A. I. Gragg (Spartan Mills), December 9, 1913; Blease to Sam W. Walker (Greenville), December 5, 1911; Blease to C. P. Lockey (Arcadia, Spartanburg), December 20, 1913, all in Blease Papers, SCDAH.

53. Columbia *State*, January 29, 1913. Two of the investigation bill's five cosponsors, Wyche of Spartanburg and John T. Miller, a union member and printer with *The State*, were Bleaseites; however, they were the only members of their faction to support the bill. The fears of the majority of Bleaseites may have had some validity. In 1912 W. J. Thackston of the American Cotton Manufacturers' Association urged mill officials to accept the inevitability of workman's compensation. There would be no danger of increased costs, he suggested, if the manufacturers placed themselves in a position to influence the administration of the program and assure the "fairness" of the compensation schedules (Columbia *State*, April 14, 1912). Jones' platform appears *ibid.*, June 20, 1912.

posterous, and anti-Bleaseites seized upon it as yet another indication of the "ignorance" of the governor's following. However, even the wildest fear of conspiracy is backed with some evidence, and this one was no exception. The mills were known to be concerned over high employee turnover, which not only disrupted production but encouraged "labor raiding" and contributed to upward pressure on wages. Proposals to use the power of the state to curb the "moving about" of operatives had been made in the past; furthermore, embryonic enforcement machinery was already in existence in the Labor Division of the Department of Agriculture, Commerce, and Industries, where E. J. Watson had developed a system of "transfer permits" to keep track of working mill children under fourteen years of age.[54] Unsubstantiated though it was, the allegation against Jones and the mills was given great credence by those who saw it as a manifestation of the malignant arrogance they expected in a "town" candidate, and as a logical extension of the middle-class drive for order and control.

If the operatives supported Blease and his faction for their stand against the encroachments of modern industrial society, many of the "town people" condemned him for the same reason. The Progressives among them were distressed by the Bleaseites' obstruction of their attempts to expand public institutions and organize society along more "rational" lines. One hardly needed to be a reformer, however, to view Bleaseism as a threat to the expanding power of the town classes, and thus in their eyes to the social order itself. Blease's extensive use of patronage to benefit his own faction and discomfit his opponents brought howls of rage from the "respectable" element, who alleged that the governor was turning out "able" men and replacing them with hacks.[55] They accused him of

54. Columbia *State*, December 3, 1900, August 4, 26, 1912; D. D. Wallace, "The Democratizing of an Old Commonwealth" (MS address, probably 1913, in David Duncan Wallace Papers, South Carolina Historical Society, Charleston; microfiche copy in SCL), 15; *Labor Division Report, 1909*, 6.

55. Burnside, "Blease," 52, 110, 135; Wallace, *History*, III, 429. Of course the "most able" men were men like themselves; when the anti-Bleaseites regained control of the governorship in 1914 many of them were determined that "none but good men, who are known and can be depended upon as anti-Blease" receive appointive office. L. L. Wagnon to Richard I. Manning, February 16, 1915, in Richard I. Manning Papers, SCL.

stealing votes and buying voters, even though they were perfectly capable of doing both in the name of "good government."[56]

More seriously, the middle classes condemned Blease for his racial attitudes, especially for his open advocacy of lynching; in fact, it is for his violent race baiting that Blease, along with other southern "demagogues," is chiefly remembered. The attention paid to Blease's racism has, unfortunately, been both inordinate and inadequate. On the one hand, some writers have alleged that Blease used the race question to distract his followers from more "legitimate" issues; other historians, rightly noting that both factions were well endowed with "racists," have concluded that there were no real differences between them.[57] Certainly Blease's upright opponents were no paragons of liberal enlightenment, being as willing as he was to drag the "Negro question" into politics. However, to conclude from the pervasive racism of the society that factional contentions on the race question had no substance is too facile. While the anti-Blease faction contained a broad range of racial attitudes, its tone was largely set by a sizable contingent of what one historian has termed "accommodationist racists." In essence they were the sort of whites who eagerly accepted the major propositions of the so-called "Atlanta Compromise": that, while blacks must remain subordinate, they were an integral part of southern society whose "uplift" was necessary to the region's social and economic progress. "Accommodationist" views involved a qualification of traditional attitudes, eschewing a simple white supremacist social order in favor of one in which the lower classes, white and black, were to be "developed" by their betters for the greater good of the whole.[58]

56. Burnside, "Blease," 166–68. On anti-Blease shenanigans see J. E. Jones to E. N. Austin, September 13, 1916; H. T. Mills to Richard I. Manning, September 15, 1916, both in Manning Papers, SCL; C. C. Wyche to T. B. Pearce, September 15, 1916, in C. C. Wyche Papers, Duke University Library, Durham, N.C.; J. G. Brown (American Spinning, Greenville) to Cole L. Blease, April 25, 1914; R. J. Hollady (Mills Mill, Greenville) to Blease, October 13, 1913, both in Blease Papers, SCDAH.

57. An example of the first is Key, *Southern Politics*, 144; of the second, Kousser, *Shaping of Southern Politics*, 232–36.

58. See George Fredrickson, *The Black Image in the White Mind* (New York: Harper and Row, 1971), Chap. 10.

To such paternalists Blease's racial stance was utterly irrational, for its emphasis on the color line worked against their goal of a society ruled not by a superior race but by "superior" people. Constant harping on white supremacy, they complained, encouraged insubordination among the poorer whites. According to D. D. Wallace, "Our ignorant people have been told so often that they are the grandest people on the face of God's earth that too many have concluded that raw Anglo-Saxonism is all sufficient, regardless of education and character, and the result has been a supreme self-satisfaction and egotistical contentment with themselves as they are, and a passionate rebellion against any attempt to improve that which by this logic can need no improvement." The Fortner bill to forbid whites to teach in black schools, introduced in 1914 by a Spartanburg Bleaseite with heavy-handed support from the governor, was condemned by many anti-Bleaseites as inimical to a rationally conducted school system.[59] On another occasion *The State* attacked Bleaseite antipathy to spending money on health care for black school children as ignoring the interdependence of blacks and whites in the South: "A negro cannot be ill in a community without endangering the health of whites. Disease knows no color line." The Columbia daily argued against Bleaseite racial legislation on broader economic grounds, pointing out that the wage competition of a degraded class of blacks depressed living standards for poor whites as well.[60]

Despite such arguments, Bleaseite mill workers could be rightly suspicious that racial "accommodation" might be used as a weapon against their own economic and social position. A specific example was the question of black labor in the mills, which generated some heat during the Blease and Manning administrations. The flurry of interest in the use of blacks as operatives in the late 1890s had died down after the failure of Montgomery and Milliken's Vesta Mill at Charleston in 1901. Although mill owners in suc-

59. Wallace, "Democratizing," 14; Columbia *State*, January 29, February 3, 11, 1914. A large number of anti-Bleaseites, especially from up-country counties, joined the Blease contingent in supporting the bill, but many did so reportedly out of fear of being branded "nigger lovers" if they opposed it. *Ibid.*, January 28, 1914.

60. Columbia *State*, July 7, 1912; February 12, August 13, 1914.

ceeding years acquiesced in the general social consensus forbidding an integrated work force in areas where women were employed and reserving most mill jobs to whites, and even used fears of "social equality" to discredit union organizers, they continued to view the black labor pool with hungry eyes, employing blacks in numerous menial and marginal tasks.[61] While the Segregation Act of 1915, effectively prohibiting the use of blacks in most mill occupations, received bi-factional support, mill representatives fought to weaken it, and in the years following its enactment took ample advantage of its loopholes.[62] Although Babbitry was not yet prepared to openly challenge bigotry in the South Carolina of the Progressive era, the intrinsic hostility of free-market capitalism to all human values, good or evil, not determined in the market place, could already be seen lurking behind the "accommodationist" rhetoric.

The economic implications of "enlightened" middle-class racial attitudes, however, were less disturbing to Bleaseites than their social implications, for they were aware that the accommodationists' view of blacks as objects of "uplift" paralleled a similar attitude on their part toward mill workers and other poor whites. When Blease warned his audiences that suffrage restriction advocates wished to "place you cotton-mill men and you farmers on the same basis as a free negro!" he was describing the status anxieties of his followers with the most vivid metaphor possible in a society obsessed with race. The operative audiences which howled their

61. On earlier interest in the use of blacks in mills, including the Vesta experiment and operative reaction, see pages 158–60 herein; on the use of blacks in cotton manufacturing at this time see U.S. Department of Commerce, Bureau of the Census, *Negro Population, 1790–1915* (Washington: Government Printing Office, 1918), 527, 535. For an appeal to race feeling used as an antiunion tactic by a mill official, see paid advertisement of L. W. Parker in Greenville *Daily News*, July 17, 1914.

62. While the Segregation Act was sponsored by an anti-Blease legislator, its strongest proponents were Bleaseites. When Clement F. Haynsworth, Sr., of Greenville attempted to remove the cleaning of machinery from the list of occupations forbidden to blacks by the bill on the ground that whites considered the job too menial, the Bleaseite W. C. Irby replied that whites would be willing to do the work if they were sufficiently paid. Greenville *Daily News*, February 20, 1914. On enforcement of the act, see *Labor Division Report, 1919*, 23–25; *1920*, 10, 24–25. On continued interest in black labor among manufacturers, see Broadus Mitchell, *The Rise of Cotton Mills in the South* (Baltimore: Johns Hopkins University Press, 1921), 218–21.

approval when Blease described blacks as "apes and baboons" were lashing out not only at a subject race but at a middle class inclined to treat blacks and poor whites alike as "children."[63]

"Accommodationist" sentiment was by no means universal among anti-Bleaseites, but even the more traditional racists were often shocked by Blease's endorsement of lynching. Antilynching sentiment, however, generally had less to do with a concern for social justice than with fears for social stability. While some members of the middle classes maintained their theoretical sympathy for lynching if its victim was guilty of the "unmentionable crime," beginning in the 1890s they were increasingly fearful that its logic led to "conclusions that would be destructive to all social order." The wave of economically motivated vigilantism that swept much of the South during the first decade of the twentieth century caused many townsmen to worry that a weapon whose use against a despised race they had once condoned might well be turned against themselves. The *Southern Christian Advocate* warned that the "spirit of anarchy shows forth and grows whether the mob lynches a negro for some outrageous crime, or slays a property owner for insisting on his legal rights, or burns the barns of those who seek the best available market, or posts a cotton ginnery with threats. Each such act unpunished but encourages repetition often in a less justifiable and more wanton form. . . . Today the negro, tomorrow the prominent attorney."[64] The class hostilities of the Blease era heightened their nervousness; feeling as they did that they were sitting on a powder keg, they were frightened when their governor not only applauded mob violence against Negro "brutes," but refused to enforce antilynching laws against the mobs. A 1911 lynching at Honea Path was led by Blease's most powerful ally, "Citizen Josh" Ashley; in 1913 the Bleaseite mayor of Spartanburg

63. Union *Progress*, July 14, 1914; Columbia *State*, July 6, 1911. Cf. J. Mills Thornton III, *Politics and Power in a Slave Society: Alabama, 1800–1860* (Baton Rouge: Louisiana State University Press, 1978), 443–44, on the obsession of antebellum southerners with the danger of "enslavement."

64. George Brown Tindall, *South Carolina Negroes, 1877–1900* (Columbia: University of South Carolina Press, 1952), 249–54; Columbia *State*, December 8, 1901; *Southern Christian Advocate*, November 19, December 10, 1908; Yorkville *Enquirer*, October 13, 1911. On the "Black Patch" war and similar disturbances, see Woodward, *Origins*, 386–87.

made no effort to disperse a mob of several thousand which terrorized the city in a vain attempt to storm the county jail and seize a suspected rapist. In both cases the governor ignored urgent requests from other local officials that he call out the militia.[65] In 1913 Ashley went so far as to introduce a bill in the General Assembly to legalize lynching if "the preponderance of the testimony" proved that the victim had been guilty of rape or attempted rape.[66]

The circumstances surrounding another lynching, at Laurens in August 1913, are illustrative not only of Blease's attitude toward mob justice but also of the potential of the passions aroused by it to spill over into broader social and economic conflict. During the lynching, repeated telephone calls to Columbia requesting militia protection for the victim were ignored by the governor. "I was told several times there was a long distance call for me from Laurens, but I had a very sick nephew in the hospital, and I was out there with him and didn't have time to bother with any telephone communications, and didn't bother myself about it," he wrote later to a political lieutenant in Laurens, assuring him that "I was not going to call out the Militia on a case like that." The mob had included many of the "cotton mill boys" of Laurens Cotton Mill, and the affair raised tensions between the white weavers at the mill and a handful of blacks employed to do menial work in the weaving room, who were finally driven from the mill by the whites. Contending that the blacks were performing necessary tasks spurned by the whites, the mill's general manager, W. S. Montgomery, insisted that they be allowed to work unmolested and vowed to dismiss anyone violating his order. The weavers countered with a charge that the blacks had been hired in preference to whites; rather than submit to Montgomery's demand, thirty-seven walked off the job, leaving four hundred looms idle. In a letter to the protesters, Blease applauded their stand, declaring, "I do not believe

65. Wallace, *History*, III, 400–406; Columbia *State*, November 12, 1911; Frank Evans in Spartanburg *Herald*, June 29, 1913; *ibid.*, August 19, 1913. The near victim of the Spartanburg mob was subsequently acquitted, the jury having been convinced that the supposed rape had been hallucinated by the girl. *Ibid.*, September 21, 1913.

66. *S.C. House Journal, 1913*, 565, 595; Yorkville *Enquirer*, February 14, 1913. The bill received no support.

in white people allowing themselves, if they can possibly help it, to be placed in any such position."[67] As the Laurens incident suggests, lynching, and the governor's benign attitude toward it, was more than simply disorderly; such uncontrolled collective action could be disruptive of an economic and social order increasingly bent on lumping blacks and poor whites together in its "lower class."

Blease's defense of lynching was hardly new to South Carolina; in fact it closely resembled the argument which Senator Tillman had long been making on the Chautauqua circuit. However, "Pitchfork Ben's" rhetoric was balanced by his strong advocacy of effective antilynching laws.[68] Not only was Blease a far more thoroughgoing adherent to the credo of the mob than his erstwhile leader, but he and his followers seemed disposed to elaborate it into a general social philosophy. He was notorious for his pardons, setting free more than seventeen hundred convicts in his four years in office, at that time a national record. The "wholesale loosing of felons and firebrands" so unnerved the insurance industry that its trade paper warned that South Carolinians might become uninsurable risks should Blease persist in office. He was inclined to be lenient with crimes of passion, considering unpremeditated murder to be frequently an understandable mistake. While there was no great increase in crime during Blease's administration, the spectacle of a governor who winked at murder in a state where personal violence had long been endemic was deeply disquieting to the state's "respectables."[69]

Still worse were Blease's routine appeals to violence and disruptive behavior, especially when they were directed against the "professional and trading classes" of the towns. He was promiscuous

67. On the lynching, see John M. Cannon to Cole L. Blease, August 12, 1913; W. R. Richey to Blease, August 12, 1913; Blease to Cannon, August 13, 1913; and Blease to Richey, August 14, 1913, all in Blease Papers, SCDAH. On the incident at the mill see Albert E. Sloan *et al.* to Blease, August 21, 1913, in Blease Papers, SCDAH; Anderson *Daily Mail*, August 22, 1913; Spartanburg *Herald*, August 22, 1913.

68. Simkins, *Pitchfork Ben Tillman*, 173–74, 224–25, 304–305, 396–98.

69. James Taylor Brice, "The Use of Executive Clemency under Coleman Livingston Blease, Governor of South Carolina, 1911–1915" (M.A. thesis, University of South Carolina, 1965), 72; Burnside, "Blease," Chap. 6; O. L. Warr, "Mr. Blease of South Carolina," *American Mercury*, XVI (1929), 28; Columbia *State*, July 6, 7, 1911.

with promises to pardon assailants of his political enemies, be they election officials suspected of irregularities or mill officials influencing votes; Lewis Parker interpreted one Blease utterance as an implied threat of personal violence against himself. Blease sometimes went further; in a speech to a night rally of Spartanburg mill hands he came close to advocating a general strike, promising, according to a local editor, that "the silk dresses of the wives of the mill presidents would cease to dazzle the operatives should they stop work." Shortly afterward, the editor, in "a little talk" to the mill people, grimly informed them that what they had heard was "anarchy . . . the same dangerous doctrine for which men and women are arrested in the great cities of the country as enemies of organized society."[70]

"Anarchistic" in any strict sense Blease certainly was not, but the word indicates the fear of social upheaval which to the "town people" was embodied in "Coley" and his faction; "Bleaseism leads to anarchy" was the principal theme of Ira Jones in the campaign of 1912. The more common epithet was "lawless," however, for while anarchy was perceived as a foreign importation, Bleaseism was strictly home grown, a gushing forth of the hostilities generated by the advance of "modern" society and the expanding power of the town classes. The townsmen of South Carolina saw their civilization threatened not by foreigners plotting in unintelligible languages but by grinning "good ol' boys" like the caricature "I. W. Justice," who in his spurious letters to *The State* swore eternal loyalty to "Coley," "so long as he lets us shute peoples and du all other kinds of things and go free."[71]

Town fears of "lawlessness" were intensified by increasing labor tensions in the mill villages. Between the Panic of 1907 and the prosperous World War I period cotton manufacturers were caught in a squeeze between high cotton prices and a labor shortage, on the one hand, and stagnant demand, on the other. The mills alleviated the pressure in part by curtailing production; the traditional

70. Columbia *State*, August 26, 1912; Spartanburg *Herald*, August 10, 11, 1912, July 19, 1914.

71. Burnside, "Blease," 143; "I. W. Justice" in Columbia *State*, July 8, 1911. The pseudonym may well have been a play on "I.W.W."

summer shutdown, still practiced in the southern textile industry, originated at this time.[72] The principal remedy, however, was to squeeze more production out of the operatives. In some cases it took the form of what later came to be known as the "stretchout." In 1914, for instance, the mill at Converse reduced its force of loom fixers; despite a compensatory 10 percent wage increase, the remaining loom fixers promptly struck in protest against the heavier work loads. More commonly the mills took advantage of the loopholes and inadequacies of state hours laws to extend production time. They made liberal use of the "make-up time" provisions in the law; they ran their machinery overtime, obliging operatives to tend it "voluntarily" or risk having their work taken from them. Thus a work day legally eleven hours long could be stretched to thirteen, even fifteen hours in length.[73]

For their part, the operatives, many of whom had previously opposed hours legislation, began to shower both the Labor Division and the governor with complaints. Unfortunately, though, the inadequacies of the law tied Watson's hands, with consequent grave damage to the legitimacy of the government. "The employees believe," snorted a sarcastic Watson in 1914, "from the name of the Act itself, that there is actually a sixty-hour per week law on the statute books of the State"; being so misled, they "naturally think that, under the law, they have been deprived of their rights, and that the State authorities have failed to give them the relief they naturally think the law provides." An anonymous complaint sent to anti-Blease Governor Richard I. Manning in 1915 put it more bitterly: "You claim to be such a law enforcer. . . . The Greenwood Cotton Mills Greenwood South Carolina Do as they please under Manning."[74]

72. Mill apologists characteristically credited the "philanthropy" of the mills for the inauguration of the custom; it was also hoped that the "vacation" would help curb absenteeism. A. S. Rowell in Greenville *Daily News*, August 12, 1914.

73. Spartanburg *Journal*, July 18, 1914; *Labor Division Report, 1915*, 7–10. The substitution of piece work for day work among weavers made the existing law on hours virtually irrelevant; an operative paid by the piece could work for extra hours while not being technically "employed" to work them. The use of piece work rates also brought pressure from some operatives to keep the machinery running during lunch hours, especially after the widespread introduction of the automatic loom, which could be left unattended for as long as half an hour. *Ibid., 1910*, 21.

74. *Labor Division Report, 1912*, 15–16, 23; *1913*, 4, 34, 36–41; *1914*, 6, 37,

By 1914 operatives began to take matters into their own hands. While some disturbances occurred in the comparatively militant Horse Creek Valley, there was even trouble in the traditionally conservative Piedmont, where mill workers engaged in a brief, startling flirtation with the Industrial Workers of the World. The "Wobblies" moved into Greenville in early 1914, and by May were claiming two thousand members. Although they figured in a minor incident at one of the mills at the end of May, they attracted little attention until early July, when a wildcat strike at Lewis Parker's Monaghan Mill escalated into a major confrontation. There were rallies and parades, one of which featured the "very novel sight" of a red flag being carried down Greenville's Main Street. Joseph Ettor, who had led the famous Lawrence strike the previous year, rushed to South Carolina and spent the late summer preaching the anarcho-syndicalist gospel about the up-country mill villages. IWW support in the Piedmont proved shallow, however. The strike at Monaghan had been the result of an accumulation of petty grievances, and was rapidly defused by the willingness of Parker to consult with a workers' committee. Far from accepting the ideology of the "one big union," the strike leaders denied to Parker that "there is a man at Monaghan who would damage you at all," and generally showed far less knowledge of IWW principles than did Parker himself. As a result they were easily maneuvered by the mill magnate into a settlement which acknowledged his absolute authority on the factory floor. Several more strikes occurred in up-country mills that summer, but the strikers were immediately fired and moved away. By the fall IWW support in South Carolina mills was nowhere to be found.[75]

43–45; *1915*, 9–13, 31, 37–38, 40–44, 52–56. See also letters to Cole L. Blease from Sam W. Walker (Greenville), December 4, 1911; J. H. Parker (Monaghan), February 24, 1912; James Metcalf (Dunean), April 27, 1913; Neal Bass (Pelzer), February 9, 1914; T. V. Blair (Pelzer), November 30, 1914; and C. M. Cooper (Whitmire), December 1, 1914, in Blease Papers, SCDAH.

75. *Labor Division Report, 1914*, 28–29; Greenville *Daily News*, July 11–18, 26, August 4, 16, 18, September 2, 6, 1914; Spartanburg *Journal*, August 21, 1914; Pickens *Sentinel*, September 3, 17, 1914; S. W. Miller to Cole L. Blease, April 26, 1914; J. T. Blassingame to Blease, June 9, 1914; B. E. Brookshire to Blease, n.d.; Deed (?) Cobb and R. F. Langford to Blease, May 4, 1914; all four in Blease papers, SCDAH. Not only did Parker confer with a strike committee, but he had the bulk of the conference proceedings transcribed and published in the Greenville *Daily News*, July 17, 1914.

Interest in the "Wobblies" may have been evanescent, but the tensions which generated it remained, and even worsened. The depression marking the onset of World War I, which added wage cuts to the hours difficulties, brought an unprecedented wave of strikes. The most important of these, at Anderson in 1915 and 1916, involved the United Textile Workers of America, an American Federation of Labor affiliate, and represented the first serious interest in unionism among operatives since the collapse of the turn-of-the-century unions. Major reform legislation on hours was finally passed in 1916 by the "Progressive" Manning assembly, but only after Watson convinced them that immediate action was necessary to avert a major explosion in the mill villages.[76]

The Bleaseites, of course, did little to calm the waters. Although W. C. Irby of Laurens, a leading Bleaseite with close ties to the operatives, worked closely with Watson on the problem of hours abuses, Blease himself provided little leadership, probably recognizing that the blame for the situation was falling on Watson rather than on him. On labor disputes Blease maintained a studied ambiguity. He and his lieutenants were deeply suspicious of unions, which they regarded as potential competitors. When a Columbia union official remonstrated with the governor over his veto of the appropriation for factory inspectors, he replied that "he knew more about the conditions of the factory people and their needs than any representative of a labor organization," and could handle their problems himself. A Blease factional leader in Greenville warned the governor to nip the IWW in the bud as potentially divisive of Bleaseite support.[77]

On the other hand, Bleaseites were fervent advocates of the right to strike. In 1912 the governor urged the mill workers of Columbia and Spartanburg to walk out of the mill and "be white men" if the company attempted to dictate their votes. In 1914 Bleaseite sheriffs Hendrix Rector of Greenville and Joe M. H. Ashley of An-

76. *Labor Division Report, 1915*, 3, 25–26; *1916*, 3, 22–23. See also George Sinclair Mitchell, *Textile Unionism and the South* (Chapel Hill: University of North Carolina Press, 1931), 35–38.

77. Burnside, "Blease," 257–58; E. J. Watson to Cole L. Blease, February 22, 1913; J. T. Blassingame to Blease, June 9, 1914; both in Blease Papers, SCDAH; Columbia *State*, February 24, 1911.

derson (son of "Citizen Josh" Ashley) gave public support to the Monaghan strikers; Blease himself carefully avoided making either an endorsement or a condemnation of the IWW, but urged the workers to "stick together and stand back of their homes and wives and children" against company eviction threats. At a later meeting in Anderson the governor promised operatives that "so long as I'm Governor I won't allow any scabs to come in here to take your place in the mills," and in 1915 he decried the turning of "women and children out of their homes into the snow and into the night, at the behest of a corporation."[78] Significantly, the major disturbances of the 1915–16 strike wave occurred in Anderson County, the bailiwick of Sheriff Ashley, who was openly hostile to management attempts to use the law to break strikes. By the fall of 1916 his "encouragement of lawlessness" had become so flagrant as to provoke Governor Manning to abandon his earlier policy of nonintervention in labor disputes and use National Guardsmen to evict strikers from company houses.[79] Aside from such overt incitements, many townspeople felt that the Bleaseites' "way of doing things" had encouraged the "lawless element" among the operatives. "The friends and lieutenants of Blease," warned a Spartanburg newspaper in 1912, in striving "to array the mill employees against their employers . . . are working up a class feeling that will bear evil fruit long after Blease and Jones have passed away."[80] The "lawlessness" of Bleaseism, then, was perceived by the "town people" as far more than a surface phenomenon; it was an attitude which threatened the core of their society. The hysteria of the anti-

78. Charleston *News and Courier*, quoted in Union *Progress*, July 23, 1912; Greenville *Daily News*, July 11, 18, 1914; Columbia *State*, July 11, August 23, 1914; Spartanburg *Herald*, August 10, 1912; Yorkville *Enquirer*, December 31, 1915; Cole L. Blease to George R. Koester, April 24, 29, 1914; Blease to S. W. Miller, April 29, 1914; Blease to J. T. Blassingame, June 10, 1914; all three in Blease Papers, SCDAH.

79. *S.C. House Journal, 1917*, 514–25, contains Manning's report on the affair. See also James L. Gossett to Manning, November 22, 1915; Robert E. Ligon to Manning, October 19, 1916; M. L. Bonham to Manning, September 16, 25, 1915; William J. Muldrow to Manning, September 21, 1915; all in Manning Papers, SCL; R. E. Ligon to David R. Coker, October 5, 1916, in David R. Coker Papers, SCL.

80. James H. Merritt in Greenville *Piedmont*, quoted in Anderson *Daily Mail*, August 6, 1914; Tom W. Tatham in Anderson *Daily Mail*, August 11, 1914. See also the comments of Tillman in Spartanburg *Herald*, August 15, 1914; Spartanburg *Journal*, quoted in Union *Progress*, August 6, 1912.

Blease press, which with one or two exceptions was the state press, and the enormous margins for anti-Blease candidates in the up-country "town" wards, reflected a widespread fear among the middle classes that their leadership, and with it their values, were in jeopardy.

That fear, by and large, was shared by mill officials. Contrary to the traditional contention that Blease "drew effective and quiet support from mill owners," the evidence indicates that, at least during his governorship, Blease was adamantly opposed by most cotton manufacturers. During the campaign of 1912 Lewis and Thomas Parker, Ellison Smyth, Leroy Springs, J. I. Westervelt of Greenville, James D. Hammett of Anderson, Arch Calvert and Aug W. Smith of Spartanburg, and A. Foster McKissick of Greenwood were all publicly anti-Blease; the governor's papers give no indication that their private opinions were any different. Even in 1916, when Richard I. Manning's efforts at conciliating the workers during the strikes of 1915 and 1916 left many manufacturers openly unhappy, there was little movement on their part to Blease. Of six prominent mill presidents polled by J. W. Norwood, a Greenville banker and grudging Manning supporter, before the second primary in 1916, three refused to vote at all while two opted for Manning as the lesser evil; only Ellison Smyth went with Blease, holding his nose as he voted. Manning's close friend David R. Coker assured him that, to his knowledge, most manufacturers had supported his reelection, adding that the managers of the Darlington County mills "not only voted but worked" for the incumbent. To be sure, Blease was not completely bereft of friends among the mill presidents; furthermore, there was much in his record of which they could approve, particularly his opposition to labor legislation and his suspicion of "outside" unions. The benefits they gained from Blease's distrust of concentrated power, however, were far overshadowed by the dangers posed when that distrust was directed at them. Manufacturers were offended by the governor's attacks on the "mill merger" and the allegations of bribery and voter intimidation he leveled against some of them; they were disconcerted by his endorsement of worker resistance and his denunciations of their strike-breaking tactics. Above all, "mill men" shared the values and outlook of the "town classes" of which they were a part, and joined their fellow townsmen in abhorrence of Bleaseite "disorder." As residents of South Carolina, they shared with their compatriots what D. D. Wallace called the "humiliation" of having Cole L. Blease for a governor.[81]

How was the "respectable element" to meet the Bleaseite challenge? "Purify the primary," was one answer, especially after the fraud-tainted 1912 primary; Blease's ascendancy gave the quiescent restriction movement a new lease on life. Almost immediately after the primary John J. McMahan, William Watts Ball, and others began a campaign to have the general election restrictions imposed on the primary by the 1914 Democratic convention, which unlike the General Assembly was usually dominated not by politicians with their "counsels of caution and compromise" but by private citizens. By the spring of 1914 restrictionist activity was furious, and reform resolutions were pushed through a number of county conventions; the "reform" element organized its own caucus, which met just prior to the state convention on May 19 to formulate a common strategy.[82]

Despite everything, however, the "counsels of caution and compromise" prevailed, even in the caucus. The convention agreed to require a complete new registration, raise the residence requirement, and place elaborate safeguards on the registration process,

81. The traditional view appears in Key, *Southern Politics*, 144; Wallace, *History*, III, 425; Burnside, "Blease," 263. See Columbia *State*, June 30, August 4, 25, 26, 1912; J. B. A. Mullaly to Cole L. Blease, January 5, 1912, in Blease Papers, SCDAH; letters to J. W. Norwood from W. M. Hagood, James C. Self, John A. Law, A. F. McKissick, and J. P. Gossett, enclosed in Norwood to David R. Coker, September 15, 1916; Ellison A. Smyth to Norwood, September 8, 1916; Coker to Richard I. Manning, September 14, 1916; all in David R. Coker Papers, SCL; D. D. Wallace, Memorandum of conversation with A. S. Salley, in "Blease and Bleasism" file, notes for *The History of South Carolina* (Typescript in David Duncan Wallace Papers, South Carolina Historical Society, Charleston; also on microfiche at SCL). Most direct evidence of collusion between Blease and mill officials dates from the 1930s; see page 270 herein.

82. John J. McMahan to Thomas F. McDow, September 30, 1912, in John J. McMahan Papers, SCL; McMahan to D. D. McColl, September 17, 1912, in D. D. McColl Papers, SCL; W. H. Edwards in Columbia *State*, September 19, 1912; Union *Progress*, October 8, 1912; Spartanburg *Herald*, September 21, 1913; April 28, May 1, 1914. See the McMahan and McColl Papers, April–May 1914, *passim.*, for correspondence concerning the reform movement.

but refused to impose literacy or property tests on primary voters. Even these mild restrictions were bitterly attacked by Blease, who argued that the higher residence requirement fell heavily on nomadic operatives and that the personal registration rule was humiliating to illiterates. Objections were also raised to the brevity of the registration period (six weeks) and the early closing date (one month prior to the primary). In response, anti-Blease election managers frequently bent over backwards to register mill voters, even to carrying the books into the homes of invalids in the mill villages; when the books were closed in late July the total registration was larger than the record vote of 1912.[83]

Nonetheless, evidence from club rolls indicates that operatives were underrepresented in the 1914 electorate. In Greenville County, where a third of the white population lived in mill villages, only 17 percent of the enrolled electors were identifiable as mill workers. In York County, where one-quarter of the whites were "mill people," only 15 percent of the occupations listed on the rolls were mill-related. The 1914 vote totals were lower than those of 1912, and both sides agreed that the new rules had been instrumental in bringing about the anti-Blease victory that year.[84]

Most of the reasons for the failure of the restriction movement

83. *Rules of the Democratic Party of South Carolina, Adopted . . . May 20th, 21st, 1914* (n.p., n.d.), Sections 3–19, 50; Union *Progress*, May 26, July 14, 21, 1914; Columbia *State*, August 16, 1914; Yorkville *Enquirer*, May 29, 1914; D. D. McColl to S. E. Liles, July 6, 1916; McColl to W. C. McGowan, June 1, 1914; both in D. D. McColl Papers, SCL. On the other hand, there were occasional attempts to deny registration to mill voters by various means; see Spartanburg *Herald*, July 8, 1914; Spartanburg *Journal*, July 3, 1914.

84. Spartanburg *Herald*, September 8, 1914; Sam McNinch to Cole L. Blease, September 1, 1914; J. H. Hill to Blease, September 13, 1914; J. W. S. Pigler to Blease, August 20, 1914; all three in Blease Papers, SCDAH. For enrollment figures, see above, Table 8, and Yorkville *Enquirer*, July 28–August 21, 1914. The mill population estimates are from *Labor Division Report, 1910*, 33. A number of factors contribute to the disparity between population and enrollment. The large size of operative families and the age-sex composition of the work force probably lowered the relative size of the voting population in mill areas. The mill population estimates were compiled by the Labor Division from reports made by individual mills, and thus may be defective. Finally, the method of counting used in analyzing the club rolls leaves out clerical and managerial workers, as well as occupations, such as teamsters, machinists, etc., not explicitly related to mill employment. However, it is doubtful that the evidence for low voting participation by mill people in 1914 can be completely explained by the above factors. Unfortunately, comparative data for earlier years is lacking.

have been discussed earlier.[85] Also important, however, was the realization among some members of the middle classes that the deep divisions within South Carolina society could not be dealt with simply by denying poor whites a voice in the government. "Cole Blease as Governor is comparatively a trivial incident," remarked *The State* in 1911, "but if the soul of South Carolina is a Blease soul . . . the minority in the commonwealth have something to ponder." The sickness of the state's soul was strikingly revealed to the townsmen by the Blease victory of 1912. "Has the light been shed in South Carolina?" asked *The State*. "It has to the best of the ability of a large majority of civilization's torch-bearers. It has been shed from pulpit and press. In the name of patriotism and righteousness much has been printed and spoken." And all, apparently, to no avail. Especially disturbing was Blease's hold on the mill vote, which the "town people" saw as rejection of their leadership. The hostility of the operatives, warned a Spartanburg "Observer," would remain even should Blease and his cronies be overthrown; they would view an anti-Blease regime as "class rule" and refuse to respect its legitimacy.[86]

It was necessary, then, for the middle classes to convince the mill voters who made up the hard core of Blease's constituency that the government was an instrument that could be used to further their welfare, and that the law protected them as well as the powerful. McMahan blamed "the deep-seated hatred that certain classes cherish" not only on "ignorant prejudice" but also in part on "the government's neglect for their welfare." *The State* found one of the principal lessons of the 1912 elections to be the "danger" stemming from "the existence of a large group of workers who do not believe themselves prosperous, who dumbly feel that they are laboring too much and getting too little." By 1914 the Bleaseite challenge and associated fears of social disruption were producing widespread support among the middle classes for Progressive social proposals: "Let the classes feel that the ignorance and misery

85. See page 231 herein.

86. Columbia *State*, April 14, 1911, August 29, 1912; *Our Monthly*, LII (1915), 146; Spartanburg *Herald*, September 11, 15, 1912; "Observer," *ibid.*, August 16, 1914.

of the masses threatens their own well-being or even safety," observed D. D. Wallace, "and then right quickly will they discover that they are their brother's keeper."[87]

The anti-Bleaseite victory of 1914 was viewed as a mandate for "affirmative and constructive legislation," and the governor and General Assembly elected that year were accordingly the most activist the state had ever seen. A number of pro-labor measures were enacted during the sessions of 1915 and 1916 which exhibited both a desire to conciliate the operatives and the general Progressive impulse to "rationalize" labor relations. Mills were prohibited from paying operatives in store goods, discounting of mill checks was forbidden, and racial segregation customs in the industry were written into law. Despite strong opposition from mill officials the Assembly revamped the troublesome hours regulations, prohibited the docking of wages for lost time, and required weekly pay checks.[88] At the same time Governor Richard I. Manning, the scion of an old planter family but himself a banker and businessman from the low-country city of Sumter, made an earnest effort to prove to the operatives that the law applied to all classes. When the president of the Brogon Mill in Anderson requested that Manning call out the National Guard to suppress a 1915 strike, Manning replied that the function of government was not to take sides in industrial disputes, but to see them resolved peacefully and in the best interest of the state; the Guard was not to be used except in time of insurrection against the public order.[89] Manning did not approve of strikes, however, preferring arbitration as a more "orderly" means of handling labor disputes. At his

87. John J. McMahan to Thomas F. McDow, September 30, 1912, in John J. McMahan Papers, SCL; Columbia *State*, August 29, 1912; D. D. Wallace in Spartanburg *Herald*, April 10, 1914; Wallace, "Democratizing," 16–17; Tate, "After Blease," 576.

88. Columbia *State*, September 8, 1914. On the first Manning administration, see Robert M. Burts, *Richard Irvine Manning and the Progressive Movement in South Carolina* (Columbia: University of South Carolina Press, 1974), Chaps. 7 and 8; Lupold, "South Carolina Progressives."

89. Richard I. Manning to James P. Gossett, November 19, 1915; Manning to R. E. Ligon, October 13, 1916; both in Manning Papers, SCL. Manning's labor policies were supported by several major dailies; see Columbia *State*, August 28, 1916; Greenville *Piedmont*, quoted in "The Voice of the People," a Manning campaign pamphlet, in Manning Papers, SCL.

urging the General Assembly in 1916 created a Board of Arbitration and Conciliation made up of an industrialist, a labor representative, and a "public" representative.[90] Manning's stiff-necked adherence to the middle-class values of government by law and a more rational social order caused great unhappiness among mill officials who preferred a more flexible approach when the law went against their own interest, and their coolness nearly cost Manning his reelection in 1916. However, Manning's policy of ostentatious even-handedness was applauded by many leading anti-Blease spokesmen.[91]

The labor policies developed during the first Manning administration represented an unprecedented intrusion of the state government into economic life. However, they produced no major changes in the economic order; the free market mechanism remained the ultimate arbiter of labor relations, although it was hedged with regulations designed to make it less chaotic and to remove sources of friction between managers and operatives. Nor did such legislation remove the differences in fundamental values which lay at the root of the hostility of the mill villagers toward the towns. Thoughtful anti-Bleaseites were well aware of this, in their own self-serving fashion. The root of Bleaseism, declared "Observer" in 1914, was "a lack of understanding of the privileges of the ballot, the duties of citizenship, the social, moral, and economic conditions of the commonwealth, and what the state is for." Bleaseism was, in short, the product of "ignorance," specifically ignorance of the benefits to be gained from submission to the conventions of "modern" society. Accordingly, education was the keystone of the program developed by the more thoughtful anti-Bleaseites; it was no coincidence that the raising of the child labor

90. Richard I. Manning to D. D. Wallace, December 21, 1915; Wallace to Manning, December 16, 1915; both in Manning Papers, SCL; *S.C. Stats. at Large*, XXIX (1916), 935–36. Cf. James Weinstein, *The Corporate Ideal in the Liberal State, 1900–1918* (Boston: Beacon Press, 1968), 7.

91. M. L. Bonham to Richard I. Manning, August 24, 1916; John G. Clinkscales to Manning, August 24, 1916; both in Manning Papers, SCL; Thomas M. Lyles, Sr., to John J. McMahan, June 29, 1916, in John J. McMahan Papers, SCL; David R. Coker to Manning, September 14, 1916, in David R. Coker Papers, SCL; Columbia *State*, August 28, 1916. See also Union *Progress*, September 5, 1916.

limit to fourteen and the enactment of the state's first compulsory education law came in the wake of the anti-Blease victory of 1914.[92]

Associated with the reaction to Blease was an upsurge of concern over the quality of the mill schools. Most of the ills attendant on the company schools of the late nineteenth century were still evident in the middle teens. State Superintendent of Education John E. Swearingen complained in 1914 that control of the mill schools by the mill corporations resulted in wildly varying standards, and he called for state supervision of "one of the weakest links in our educational chain."[93] A mill school supervisor for Spartanburg County was appointed in 1915, and in 1916 the General Assembly created the office of state mill school supervisor under the control of the state superintendent of education. Over the next decade the supervisors gathered and published detailed information about the quality of mill schools, their buildings, equipment, sanitation and staff. While diplomatically praising mill officials for their educational efforts, they used the threat of publicity to encourage adherence of mill schools to state-determined standards. Most significantly, the professional educators who filled the office encouraged the gradual elimination of the mill school in favor of tax-supported public schools, which, incidentally, were more easily controlled by "expert" public educators; in 1919 Supervisor W. A. Shealy declared that the only proper management for a school was "the regularly constituted authorities," adding that "very few mill experts are school experts." Mill schools were further regulated by a 1918 act requiring that all mill schools receiving public funds make at least eight grades available to their pupils.[94]

92. "Observer" in Spartanburg *Herald*, August 16, 1914; Wallace, *History*, III, 435–36, 440–41.

93. On early mill schools, see pages 94–103 herein; for Swearingen's comments, see *S.C. State Supt. of Educ. Report, 1914*, 42–43.

94. *S.C. Stats. at Large*, XXIX (1915–1916), 332, 1037; XXXI (1918), 1–2. Beginning in 1916 a mill school supervisor was also employed in Greenville County; *ibid.*, XXIX, 1001. For the reports of the mill school supervisors, see *S.C. State Supt. of Educ. Reports, 1916–17, 1919–23, 1925–26*, especially *Report, 1919*, 167–80. The position had a rocky and brief history; in its ten years of existence it had five occupants, and the post was vacant in 1918 and 1924. Due to the continuing ambivalence of South Carolinians toward recognizing class distinctions among whites, there was always some discomfort about the

Although mill schools were hardly up to town standards by 1920, some progress was made. World War I profits financed new buildings and enlargements of old ones. Enrollments rose and teacher work loads shrank; a comparison of forty-eight mill schools in 1913 with the same schools in 1920 indicates that, while the number of enrolled pupils rose by 56.4 percent, the pupil-teacher ratio dropped from 66.7 to 50.3, or a decline of nearly a quarter. Obviously, much remained to be done; fifty pupils per teacher was far too great a work load even by contemporary local standards, and average attendance remained low. Even so, education for mill children in 1920 was far closer to "modern" standards than it had been at any time prior to the Blease era.[95]

Paralleling the new concern for the schooling of mill children was the growth of interest in adult education, for rural whites as well as those in the mills. Prior to the 1910s there had been sporadic attempts to set up night schools in various mill centers, notably Charles E. Weltner's school in the Columbia mill district.[96] The first really sizable effort in adult education, however, was inaugurated in 1913 in the mill villages of Spartanburg County. Its guiding spirit was Miss E. Julia Selden, a well-educated and independently wealthy young woman with experience teaching mill

---

office, and it was finally abolished in 1926 on the pretext that the mill schools were now "among the very best schools in the state." *South Carolina Education*, VII (1926), 288. Nevertheless, the position, especially during the tenure of W. A. Shealy, was a major force in effecting the integration of the mill schools into the state public school system.

95. The data on enrollment and pupil-teacher ratios are from *S.C. State Supt. of Educ. Report, 1913*, 141–480; *1920*, 162–88. A "mill school" is defined as a school located in a mill village whose building was owned by the mill corporation. Comparative figures are available for fifty of these in 1912 and 1920; however, two have been removed from the list because by 1920 they had become primary schools, the older grades attending nearby "town" schools. A large proportion of the increased enrollment was due to the statewide compulsory school attendance law of 1919; in thirteen large mill school districts enrollment rose by 26.2 percent between 1918–19 and 1919–20. *Ibid., 1920*, 162–63. Of twenty-six mill schools for which figures on average attendance are available for 1920, the average school had only 62.8 percent of its pupils in attendance on any one day; in 1913 the figure was 59 percent. *Ibid., 1913*, 141–480; *1920*, 241–69.

96. Wil Lou Gray, "Evolution of Adult Education in South Carolina," *Interstate Bulletin on Adult Education*, II (1927), 3–4; Mrs. Charles E. Weltner to Estella Smoak Herndon, March 25, 1928; Mrs. Weltner to Wil Lou Gray, March 25, 1931; J. W. Thomson to Miss Gray, January 6, 1927; Frances Beaty to Miss Gray, December 5, 1926; Lottie C. Estes to Miss Gray, January 10, 1930; Davis Jeffries to Miss Gray, December 4, 1926; all six in Wil Lou Gray Papers, SCL.

children, who by the summer of 1913 had become convinced that "political conditions in South Carolina were in such a deplorable condition" that something needed to be done to educate the "masses." She obtained backing from such pillars of the local establishment as President Snyder of Wofford College, Superintendent Frank Evans of the Spartanburg City Schools, and Secretary John Wood of the Chamber of Commerce, and "with a little persuasion" arranged financing from the mills and the county government. In October 1913 fifteen night schools opened with an enrollment of over eleven hundred pupils. The program received a setback in 1914, when the mills "cried hard times" and cut back their support; however, the 1915 General Assembly made up the difference and integrated the night schools into the county public school system. In 1913 a similar network of night schools was established in Rock Hill under mill sponsorship.[97]

The adult education movement was given added stimulus by the re-registration required by the primary reform of 1914, which permitted illiterates to sign the roll with a mark. Incomplete statewide figures gathered by Superintendent Swearingen indicated that around 20 percent of enrolled primary voters were illiterate. Furthermore, most of the illiteracy was in rural areas and in the mill villages. In Spartanburg County, for instance, 29.5 percent of rural voters, and 29.2 percent of mill voters, signed with a mark, as opposed to 5.9 percent in "town" clubs, and 2.7 percent in the nonmill wards of the City of Spartanburg. The disparity in literacy between mill and town was striking in its similarity to the disparity in politics between mill people and town people, and reinforced the townsmen's identification of Bleaseism with "ignorance."[98]

97. Alice Love (ed.) *Pioneer Women Teachers of South Carolina* (Rock Hill, S.C.: White Printing Company, 1958), 47; E. Julia Selden, MS dated "just before Miss Selden's death" in 1927, in Wil Lou Gray Papers, SCL; *Southern School News*, V (December, 1913), 15; VI (November, 1914), 14; VII (March, 1916), 16; Spartanburg *Herald*, September 27, 28, 30, October 5, 1913, April 16, 1914; *S.C. Stats. at Large*, XXIX (1915), 332; R. C. Burts, "Night Schools in Rock Hill," *South Carolina Education*, III (October 15, 1921), 10.

98. *S.C. State Supt. of Educ. Report*, 1914, 23–26; Spartanburg *Herald*, August 21, 1914. The use of aggregate figures for mill clubs understates the illiteracy of mill voters. The writer has located one registration book for a mill club, that at the Bennettsville mill village in Marlboro County. Here 45.3 percent of the enrolled voters were unable to sign the roll, but 58.7 percent of those identified as operatives used their marks. The sample, to be sure,

The large number of illiterate voters, declared Wil Lou Gray, a Laurens County school official, "denied the privilege of forming their own opinion through the printed page, is too large for the safety of our democratic institutions, for the highest good of society, and for the greatest degree of material progress." Miss Gray responded by developing a system of night schools in both rural and mill areas of Laurens County, patterned after the work of Miss Selden in Spartanburg and Cora Wilson Stewart in Kentucky.[99]

The next several years saw a marked expansion in adult education, especially of mill people, due in large part to the zeal of Misses Selden and Gray. In 1916 the General Assembly made its first statewide appropriation for night schools. At the same time the State Federation of Women's Clubs prevailed upon Governor Manning to appoint an Illiteracy Commission. For two years the commission existed only on paper; after the entry of the United States into World War I, however, it was able to obtain support from the State Council of Defense and make considerable progress by taking advantage of wartime mobilization. In particular the commission linked the eradication of illiteracy to the war effort, making much of the high illiteracy rate among South Carolina inductees into the armed forces, higher, it noted, than that of New York "with its large foreign element." Moreover, attacks on the war effort by Blease and some of his associates provided the anti-illiteracy crusaders an opportunity to exploit factional and patriotic loyalties simultaneously. "Russia's fall was caused by German propaganda among the ignorant classes," asserted Miss Selden in early 1918, adding that "there is a fertile ground for German propaganda in our State, and . . . it is going on all around us."[100]

---

is small (eighty-six were enrolled, forty-seven of them operatives) and atypical (the Bennettsville Mill was small, and its Pee Dee location placed it well away from the major industrial regions of the state); nonetheless it is probably adequate as an indication. See Marlboro County Democratic Club Rolls, in SCDAH. At any rate, the relation of Bleaseism to illiteracy is probably not very strong if rural voters, as well as those of mill and town, are considered.

99. Wil Lou Gray, *A Night School Experiment in Laurens County* (Columbia: State Department of Education, 1915); the quote appears on 7–8.

100. *Southern School News*, VIII (December, 1916), 11–12, and numerous other articles; E. Julia Selden to Patterson Wardlaw, May 10, 1918, in Wil Lou Gray Papers, SCL; Miss Selden, circular letter dated March 1918, in David R. Coker Papers, SCL. On Blease

By 1919 the commission had prodded the General Assembly into establishing the nation's first statewide, state-supported adult education program, headed by the commission's field director, Wil Lou Gray. An awesomely energetic woman, "Miss Wil Lou" was also an adept politician and a public relations genius who in a few years created a constituency for adult education that carried it through the depressed decade of the 1920s.[101]

While adult education work was by no means limited to mills, well over one-third of all night schools operating in South Carolina in 1920 were in mill villages, where illiteracy was concentrated and where facilities and financial support were available from the corporations. The same factors made mill night schools generally more elaborate than rural schools. Continuation schools, designed to give continuing training to adult operatives, were established in several mill centers, notably Gaffney, Rock Hill, Pelzer, and Monaghan. While most night school teachers were "moonlighting" day school teachers, a group of "special teachers," paid jointly by the state and participating companies, served full time in some mill villages as combination teachers and social workers. In 1920 special teachers were at work in a dozen villages, to the general satisfaction of mill officials. "Coming in contact with such characters as the teachers is elevating and will help to make the people less suspicious, as these people usually are," said one mill president, adding that "this work will make the people appreciate their work, and make them more efficient to their employers."[102]

The educational "awakening" of the World War I period was

---

and World War I, see Daniel Walker Hollis, "Cole Blease: The Years Between the Governorship and the Senate, 1915–1924," *South Carolina Historical Magazine*, LXXX (1979), 14–16; Terry Lynn Helsley, "'Voices of Dissent': The Anti-War Movement and the State Council of Defense in South Carolina, 1916–1918" (M.A. thesis, University of South Carolina, 1974).

101. *S.C. State Supt. of Educ. Report, 1919*, 186–88; Mabel Montgomery, *South Carolina's Wil Lou Gray: Pioneer in Adult Education* (Columbia: Vogue Press, 1963). The state of New York created a similar program at about the same time. For a general account of adult education in South Carolina, differing somewhat from mine, see Norfleet Hardy, *Farm, Mill, and Classroom: A History of Tax-Supported Adult Education in South Carolina to 1960* (Columbia: College of General Studies, University of South Carolina, 1967), 35–44.

102. Of the 178 night schools for whites taught in 1919–20, 68 were "mill" schools. *S.C. State Supt. of Educ. Report, 1919*, 195–97, 211; *1920*, 192–205, 210.

closely linked to a conception of the schools as agencies of social indoctrination. Playing to the fears of the "respectable" element, public educators stressed their role as acculturating agents of "modern" society, especially in the realm of "citizenship." The teaching of the three Rs was designed to break down the barriers between classes and make mill operatives and other poor whites more accessible to middle-class leadership. Said one grateful night school pupil in the early 1920s, "I find that the educated people are my friends. I used to have a feeling of distrust towards every man I bought things from. I find now that my grocery man makes as many mistakes in my favor as he does in his." Second in importance only to the three Rs was the teaching of "civil government." The setting of the compulsory attendance age limit at fourteen and the requirement that mill children have eight grades of study made available to them were both probably based in part on the desire to hold students in school until they were old enough for serious civics instruction, which generally began in the seventh grade. Arguing that "no subject . . . is more needed at this crisis than civil government," one educator urged in 1913 that civics teachers "exert moral inspiration and civic uplift" and "give their classes . . . true and just interpretations of existing affairs." "Civil government" courses were also a key feature of private ventures in mill education such as the Textile Industrial Institute of Spartanburg, whose founder, D. E. Camak, felt that a recognition by the operatives of "how important it is to have the right men in office" was essential if in the future the state was to be spared such scenes as he had witnessed that August day in 1912.[103]

The adult education program was permeated with propaganda. Classroom materials and assignments preached not only thrift and good health habits but also more political causes such as good roads and, especially, public education.[104] A larger purpose of the mill schools was to inculcate the middle-class Progressive view of

103. *Ibid.*, 1922, 249; E. H. Hanna in Columbia *State*, February 13, 1913; Camak, *Human Gold*, Chaps. 11, 12.

104. See "Our Paper," a four-page list of simple sentences for copying, used in Newberry County sometime between 1914 and 1917; also the *Lay-By School Messenger*, August 7, 1920. (Both items in Wil Lou Gray Papers, SCL.)

society with its curious blend of democracy and paternalism. The most comprehensive statement of the educators' approach to society was D. D. Wallace's "Lessons in Democracy," a series commissioned by Wil Lou Gray for use in teaching adult illiterates "some of the lessons of good citizenship."[105] In the first lesson, "What Is Democracy?," Wallace praised democratic government for making the power of the governors dependent on their contributions to the welfare of the people; however, he made it clear that he did not consider Bleaseism to be true "democracy." He decried "lawlessness" and "anarchy," and declared that "stirring up class against class, either in politics or in industry, is the very opposite of democracy; for it is the attempt to set up the despotic rule of one part of the people over the rest of the people, and to put a part of the people under a disadvantage." On the other hand, true "democracy" consisted in those of lesser ability deferring to the leadership of their betters; democracy no more meant "that an ignoramus was to be elected to the legislature" than it meant "that children were to have the same authority in running the home that the older people have."[106]

The second part of the series, "Why Taxation?," was a plea for a stronger and more active government. Attacking popular beliefs that taxes were too high, Wallace argued that in South Carolina they were actually too low, for the lack of adequate funds inhibited the necessary extension of government services. Addressing the sentiment that the government was a brigand exacting tribute from the people for the profit of those who controlled it, he asserted that a combination of democracy and "public officials of the highest character for intelligence and honesty" would prevent a more powerful government from becoming a more oppressive one. The third lesson, "Labor and Capital," was a defense of the capitalist system in the same terms of "mutual interest" used in his defense of the "best men." While admitting that the system suffered from abuses, and advocating action, including labor orga-

105. The series was reprinted serially in the state's major teachers' journal and was commended by the editor for its "soundness of doctrine and simplicity of statement." *South Carolina Education*, I (October 15, 1919), 4.

106. *Ibid.*, I (October 15, 1919), 4–5.

nization and social legislation, to correct them, he warned his readers not to tamper with a regime which had brought such an "immense improvement in the condition of the laboring class." The recurrent theme of all the "lessons" was that the welfare of the people was best served by a society dominated by powerful organizations, both public and private, run for the public interest by qualified "experts" whose leadership was to be accepted as proper by those who were to be governed.[107]

The policies developed by the "town classes" in response to the "social threat" of the operatives and other poor whites, particularly as expressed in Bleaseism, then, involved inducing the operatives to accept the legitimacy of middle-class rule, both by demonstrating that rule by the "best men" was beneficial to working people and by educating them to accept the fundamentally conservative values of Progressive "democracy." The anti-Bleaseites got the opportunity to implement their policies in 1914, when the effect of the new primary rules and a general reaction to the tumult of the previous four years enabled them to place Manning in the governor's chair and elect a General Assembly both heavily Progressive and heavily anti-Bleaseite. However, despite Manning's scrupulously even-handed approach to labor disputes, and the numerous pieces of labor legislation passed during his first two-year term, the mill workers remained steadfast in their loyalties to Blease and Bleaseism. For example, John J. McMahan, who had returned to the Assembly in 1915, could boast a solid record of support for labor reforms and welfare legislation, yet the operatives of Columbia, among whom his paternal concern counted less than his elitist political views, continued to howl him down on the stump and rejected him *en bloc* at the polls. In his 1916 reelection campaign against Blease, Manning and his allies used the record of his first term to court mill voters, emphasizing his refusal to invoke

107. *Ibid.*, I (November 15, 1919), 9, 11–12; (December 15, 1919), 7–8, 13–14. A fourth lesson, "Town and Country," *Ibid.*, I (March 15, 1920), 10–11, preached a similar theme of "mutual interest" to farmers suspicious of "town people." Cf. the characterization of school materials designed for immigrants, in Tyack, *One Best System*, 235–36. Many of the ideas of adult educators in South Carolina were borrowed from the "Americanization" movement; see, for instance, the reading list in *Adult and Night Schools* (Columbia: South Carolina Superintendent of Education, 1920).

"bayonet law" to settle strikes and the opposition to his reelection by mill owners, who were supporting a third candidate.[108] However, Manning's efforts to win over the operatives were to little avail. "Not all the mill workers are union sympathizers," a skeptical friend pointed out to Manning; on the other hand the old antagonisms persisted, and were even exacerbated by such measures as the fourteen-year child labor limit and compulsory school attendance, both enacted by the General Assembly under Manning's leadership. To be sure, there may have been some marginal movement among operatives away from Blease toward Manning in 1916, as Tables 7, 8, and 9 suggest; *The State* estimated that Blease support in the villages dropped by about five percentage points. The evidence of a shift, however, is far less conclusive than is that of a continuing firm allegiance to Blease on the part of the mill hands. The fundamentally conflicting views of society held by Blease's mill following and the predominantly anti-Blease townsmen could not be reconciled by a few reforms. Noting the continuing electoral chasm between mill and town in Laurens County, the now aged W. P. Jacobs remarked that "evidently there is some root of bitterness, somewhere, that ought to be eradicated."[109]

The educational program of the "town people" had somewhat greater success in "eradicating" the "root of bitterness" than did the legislative program, but its results could only show in the long run; by 1920 the effort to incorporate the mill people into town society had only begun. Blease remained a persistent force in South Carolina politics, retaining his grip on the mill vote as late as 1932; even in 1918, when some early antiwar utterances en-

108. John J. McMahan, notes for stump speech at state fairgrounds, August 26, 1916; typescript of letter to *The State*, August 26, 1916; both in John J. McMahan Papers, SCL. See the 1916 circulars "Why Manning?" and "Who Is Your Friend Mr. Mill Voter?" and the pamphlet "The Voice of the People," all in Manning Papers, SCL; Columbia *State*, August 23, 24, 26, 28, 1916.

109. M. L. Bonham to Richard I. Manning, August 24, 1916; H. C. Tillman to Manning, September 13, 1916, in Manning Papers, SCL; *Our Monthly*, LII, 274; LIII, 450; Greenville *Daily News*, September 13, 1916; Spartanburg *Herald*, September 13, 15, 1916; Union *Progress*, September 19, 1916; Columbia *State*, September 23, 1916. Due to the small number of observations, the difference in Table 9 between the 1914 and 1916 Blease vote among mill workers can largely be dismissed as due to sampling error, although some small movement did occur.

abled his enemies to label him "disloyal," he apparently won a majority of the vote in the state's mill boxes. Certainly Wil Lou Gray's 1922 boast that since the establishment of the state adult education program "27,000 ignorant, prejudiced creatures have been transformed into enlightened, thinking men and women," and that the spread of learning in the state had banished forever the days "when political demagogues swayed men and women too ignorant to form their own opinions," was premature.[110] Not only had the "demagogues" not yet vanished, but the labor upheavals of 1929 and the 1930s were still in the future. The more general goal of gaining acceptance of "town" values among the operatives was necessarily slow and frustrating work. In 1920 a "special teacher" in Gaffney confessed to Miss Gray that she had toyed with resigning in despair, being "fully persuaded that 95 percent of the mill population is wanting in elements which go to make up character"; however, believing that "with the influence of education a better community could be developed," she decided to remain.[111]

Thus the gap between mill and town persisted well past 1920, reinforced by the continuing segregation of the operatives in mill villages; not until midcentury, with the impact of the automobile and the New Deal, would that bedrock institution of the "mill culture" begin to break up.[112] Despite the continuance of "millways," however, they never again inspired the widespread fears of "anar-

110. Hollis, "Cole Blease," 14–16; Spartanburg *Herald*, August 28, 1918, September 10, 1930, September 14, 1932; Union *Progress*, July 30, 1918; Aiken *Journal and Review*, September 4, 1918, September 10, 1930, September 14, 1932; Greenville *News*, September 10, 1930, September 14, 1932; typescript, n.d., in Wil Lou Gray Papers, SCL.

111. Era Littlejohn to Wil Lou Gray, November 10, 1920; also, W. H. Hand to Mrs. Annie I. Rembert, January 5, 1927; MS report of Altalee Davis, probably 1930; all in Wil Lou Gray Papers, SCL.

112. On the break-up of the mill village, see Harriet Laura Herring, *The Passing of the Mill Village: Revolution in a Southern Institution* (Chapel Hill: University of North Carolina Press, 1949); Liston Pope, *Millhands and Preachers: A Study of Gastonia* (New Haven: Yale University Press, 1941), 191–95. In some areas, at least, mill village culture has survived into the very recent past, if not the present. See three pieces by John Kenneth Morland: *Millways of Kent* (Chapel Hill: University of North Carolina Press, 1958); "Kent Revisited: Blue-Collar Aspirations and Achievement" in Arthur B. Shostak and William Gomberg (eds.) *Blue-Collar World: Studies of the American Worker* (Englewood Cliffs, N.J.: Prentice-Hall, 1964), 134–43; and "Educational and Occupational Aspirations of Mill and Town School Children in a Southern Community," *Social Forces*, XXXIX (1960), 169–75.

chy" found among the townspeople during the Blease era. The Blease movement faded as fast as it arose, chiefly because in essence it was little more than a sort of electoral *jacquerie*. While Bleaseites had an ideology of sorts, it was essentially backward looking, and could offer no intelligible alternative to the corporate society of the "town people." The only weapon available to the Bleaseites for use against that society was obstruction; while their obstructionism pleased their hard-core support in the mill villages, the mass of voters in the countryside who held the balance of power finally agreed with the townspeople that the Bleaseites had little to offer except continued strife and disorder. The Blease faction lasted through the 1920s, but after World War I it was a worn-out shell; its leader made his peace with the mill officials and became a conservative and drearily conventional racial demagogue. The Blease of 1930 who was relied upon by the mills to "keep the hands quiet" by distracting their attention from economic issues with "liquor and niggers" was a far cry from the "anarchist" of the teens.[113] Blease finally lost the allegiance of the "lintheads" altogether in 1934, to a former mill hand who had received his education at D. E. Camak's Textile Industrial Institute, a teetotaling Baptist with "liberal" leanings named Olin D. Johnston. While Johnston was capable of strange behavior (he once declared the State Highway Department to be in a state of insurrection, and had its headquarters occupied by the National Guard), he was generally a far more sober and respectable politician than Blease could ever be. More importantly, in his sympathy for organized labor and New Deal liberalism Johnston showed himself to be a man willing to accept "modern" society and to work within it, a position far removed from the wholesale rejection of modernity represented by Blease in his heyday. The ascendancy of Johnston over Blease was thus something of a watershed for the operatives. While their shift in allegiance did not represent a surrender to the "town people" (who, fearing that Johnston was a "red," gave their votes for the first time ever to Blease), it did signify their recogni-

113. Hollis, "Cole Blease," 16–17; Elliot Janeway, "Jimmy Byrnes," *Life*, January 4, 1943, p. 66.

tion that the society the "town people" had created was the society in which they would have to live.[114]

By 1920 the future of South Carolina society plainly lay with the town classes and their vision of a well-organized, rationally run society. The operatives themselves implicitly admitted as much by their response to the social and economic attraction of the mills the "town" people had built. Lured by the prospect of a better material life, they had accepted, in fact if not in principle, the industrial discipline imposed by the mill owners. Having made that choice, however, they had little alternative but to submit to the social discipline and subordination which was decreed for them by "industrial society" and the classes that ruled it. They sent their children to school and attended night schools and "opportunity schools" because, despite their unhappiness over their loss of autonomy in the new world of industrial South Carolina, they had chosen to live in that society and recognized that their hopes for social mobility and a modicum of human dignity depended upon their playing by its rules. In the end they gained a good deal for their submission; their material conditions were greatly improved, and the abolition of child labor and the extension of educational opportunity, both products of middle-class paternalism, were boons to the mill child. However, the benefits came at a price. The "assimilation" of the mill workers into "town" society produced the same sorts of generational tensions faced by their immigrant contemporaries in the northern cities.[115] They suffered some economic hardship along the way, and they lost much of their former control over their lives. The hostilities of the period before 1920 produced an antipathy toward the town that is still discernible in southern mill centers, and the grievances of the operatives of that age against reformers live on in the operatives' present-day distrust of unions and liberals. Occasionally their resentments are focused by a charismatic leader such as George Wallace, whose promises to throw the bureaucrats' briefcases into the Potomac resemble in their iconoclasm Blease's attacks on the bureaucrats' rationalizing

114. Camak, *Human Gold*, Chap. 12; Key, *Southern Politics*, 139, 145–46.
115. Morland, *Millways of Kent*, 104.

predecessors.[116] Lacking such a leader, however, they settle into apathy and a passive dislike of a social order over which they have little control.[117] The mill workers of South Carolina remain today as they have for most of this century, acquiescent but not quite willing participants in a world not of their making.

116. Due to the enormously more complex socioeconomic structure of the modern Piedmont, and the incorporation of blacks into the voting population, it is difficult to determine mill worker voting behavior in the election of 1968 with non-survey data. However, as Numan V. Bartley and Hugh D. Graham point out, George Wallace's support among southern whites in that year varied inversely with their income level, while that of his Republican opponent, Richard Nixon, varied directly with income level. The Democratic candidate, Hubert Humphrey, received few votes from any whites. See Numan V. Bartley and Hugh D. Graham, *Southern Politics and the Second Reconstruction* (Baltimore: Johns Hopkins University Press, 1975), 126–34.

117. In the presidential election of 1972 the voter participation rate in the Fourth Congressional District of South Carolina (Greenville and Spartanburg) was the third lowest of any congressional district in the country. Michael Barone, Grant Ujifusa, and Doug Mathews, *Almanac of American Politics, 1980* (New York: Dutton, 1980), 801.

Appendix: A Note on Table 9

The estimates of mill operative support for Cole L. Blease and John G. Richards given in Table 9 were made by means of ecological regression analysis of Democratic club-level data on voting and enrollment. The details of the statistical technique and its application to historical problems have been discussed elsewhere by historians far more expert at statistics than I am.[1] Here I wish simply to set forth the nature of my data and certain peculiarities of my procedure.

The election figures I used are taken from tallies published in local newspapers, as cited in Table 9. The precinct enrollment figures, and the occupational data from which the proportion of mill operatives in the membership of each club was derived, come from several sources. In 1914 the South Carolina State Democratic Party Convention called for a complete reenrollment of primary voters. Under the new system all voters were to enroll in person, and were to identify themselves, not simply by name, but also by address, age, and occupation.[2] In the month between the closing of the books and the primary election, some local newspapers published the county club rolls, in order to give private citizens the opportunity to verify them and call the attention of party officials to possible irregularities. Complete newspaper records of this sort,

1. See J. Morgan Kousser, "Ecological Regression and the Analysis of Past Politics," *Journal of Interdisciplinary History*, IV (1973), 237–62.

2. See pages 255–56 herein; *Rules of the Democratic Party of South Carolina, Adopted . . . May 20th, 21st, 1914* (n.p., n.d.), Section 11.

providing occupational data, survive for two important mill counties, Richland (Columbia) and York. While the Greenville *Daily News* failed to give occupational information in its listing, a local printer later published the rolls for use as a county directory. In the directory the names were grouped by post office, but a comparison with the club lists appearing in the *News* permitted me to determine the proportion of each club consisting of operatives.[3] The occupational designations were not standardized; I chose to count as an "operative" any person reporting an explicitly textile-related occupation, excepting supervisory and white collar positions. Since some skilled mill employees, such as machinists, could not be linked to the textile industry, this definition probably understates the true proportion of mill operatives in the voting population. No data comparable to the 1914 rolls exists for 1916; therefore the 1914 proportions were used in making the 1916 estimates.

It proved impossible to obtain complete enrollment totals for 1916.[4] One Greenville club, Brandon, was not reported at all to my knowledge. The reported enrollment at Mills Mill in Greenville was lower than the total number of votes cast at the box; it was excluded from the 1916 analysis along with a newly created club, Dunean, whose members had previously voted at Mills Mill. Another new club, at Union Bleachery in Greenville, was combined with its parent, Sans Souci. The net loss of two observations between 1914 and 1916 does not significantly affect their comparability; excluding Brandon and Mills Mill from the 1914 estimates would alter them by less than half of a percentage point.

Preliminary analysis of the club data revealed some distortion in the estimates, such that the proportions totaled well over 100 percent. An inspection of the data suggested that the difficulty lay in the inclusion of Greenville City wards in the data base; except for Ward Four, which was one-quarter mill operative, these boxes were generally more anti-Blease than was predicted by the regres-

3. Columbia *State*, August 8, 10–14, 1914; Yorkville *Enquirer*, July 28, 31, August 11, 18, 21, 1914; Greenville *Daily News*, August 19, 1914; *Directory of Greenville County, South Carolina Voters* (Greenville: W. S. Neville and Company, 1914).

4. Columbia *State*, August 2, 1916; Rock Hill *Herald*, August 3, 1916; Greenville *Daily News*, September 2, 1916.

sion line. Greenville City's deviance from the other observations was probably due to the overwhelmingly "town" cast of its electorate. If the proportion of voters in each club engaged in neither mill work nor agriculture is used as a surrogate for "town" voters, no club outside of Greenville City had more than 55 percent of its membership consisting of "town" people. Within the city, though, only Ward Four ranged as low as 75 percent "town"; the others ranged from the middle eighties to the upper nineties. The "urbanity" of Greenville City voters was largely a reflection of the size of the city (15,741 in 1910, fourth largest in the state) and the residential segregation of most local mill workers outside the city limits. It also reflected a peculiarity of the 1914 primary rules. Since voting was by Democratic club rather than by precinct, and since there were no boundaries drawn between clubs, voters could enroll at the club most convenient to their homes; thus many rural folk voted at such "town" boxes as Greer or Rock Hill. However, an explicit exception was made in the case of the state's four cities of over ten thousand population; voters there were not permitted to cross municipal or ward lines to enroll or cast ballots.[5] Thus the voting membership of the Greenville City clubs was restricted to city residents, few of whom considered themselves "farmers." Given the peculiarity of Greenville City voters, and the apparent effect of that peculiarity on their voting behavior, it was deemed best to exclude the Greenville wards, including the "normal" Ward Four, from the data base. The resulting estimates showed some reduction in correlation but significant gains in clarity. A more sophisticated measure of "town" orientation among voters, used to divide the "non-mill" population into its component parts, should further improve the estimates.

5. *Rules of the Democratic Party*, Section 8.

Essay on Sources

I. Primary Sources

A. Manuscripts

Since this study has been concerned chiefly with social behavior and public attitudes, it has made comparatively little use of manuscript sources. Nonetheless, a number of collections have proven useful for illuminating specific points. At the Southern Historical Collection of the University of North Carolina at Chapel Hill, the "Recollections" of W. K. Blake and the McBee Family Papers contain interesting remarks on economic life in South Carolina in the years immediately following the Civil War, while the John V. Stribling Papers describe the industrial expectations of the late 1870s through the eyes of a small entrepreneur. The typescript "Autobiography" of John T. Woodside is colored by the author's efforts to come to terms with his business failure in the Great Depression, but is otherwise a good account of the rise of a Greenville merchant and industrialist. Limited use has been made of the large Daniel Augustus Tompkins Collection, chiefly for the period between 1902 and 1905. The Perkins Library of Duke University, Durham, North Carolina, contains the papers of Cecil C. Wyche, who in the 1910s was in charge of Cole Blease's political organization in Spartanburg County. A limited sampling was made of the massive William Watts Ball Papers, which contain correspondence concerning his mill investments as well as a wealth of material on his political and journalistic activities during the Blease period.

The credit ledgers of the R. G. Dun and Company Collection at the Baker Library of the Harvard University Graduate School of Business Administration contain large quantities of systematically gathered data on mercantile firms in South Carolina and a number of other states from the late 1840s to 1880; no student of the nineteenth century American middle class can afford to ignore them.

The most useful single repository is that of the South Caroliniana Library of the University of South Carolina in Columbia. Among mill records available there are sundry accounts of the Graniteville and Pelzer Manufacturing Companies, a stockholders' minute book, 1899–1912, of the Olympia Cotton Mills, and a time book, 1884–1886, on microfilm, of the Piedmont Manufacturing Company. Letterbooks of H. P. Hammett, 1885–1886, and John H. Montgomery, 1899–1901, both on microfilm, provide useful information on the work and attitudes of two major South Carolina industrialists. Unfortunately, few other mill records are available for this period, although an extensive collection of Graniteville Manufacturing Company material is available at Graniteville, and a massive, as yet unorganized collection of twentieth-century records of the Courtenay Manufacturing Company has recently been uncovered and placed in the University of South Carolina School of Business Administration.

Other collections dealing with matters of relevance to this study are also available at the South Caroliniana Library. A scrapbook, 1876–1894, on microfilm, kept by A. S. Rowell, the foreman of the cloth room at Piedmont and a leading local citizen, contains clippings of his voluminous newspaper correspondence and a variety of vital and historical records of the village. The papers of William Elliott, Jr., Columbia attorney for the Parker interests, contain much material on the legal aspects of labor and community relations. The John J. McMahan, James A. Hoyt, Jr., and D. D. McColl Papers deal with Progressivism, the middle-class response to Blease, and the ramifications of electoral reform. The Richard I. Manning Papers contain revealing correspondence concerning the strikes of 1915 and 1916. The Patterson Wardlaw Papers, dealing with his leadership of a movement to place control of the Richland County (Columbia) schools in the hands of "professionals," contain illuminating material on class tensions in the public schools. By comparison, the papers of John E. Swearingen, state superintendent of education from 1909 to 1923, contain little of value. The Wil Lou Gray Collection deals principally with her pioneering work in adult education, but also contains material on virtually every social problem faced by South Carolina in this century. The papers of David R. Coker, merchant and planter of Hartsville and one of the most influential men in the Pee Dee region, deal only tangentially with cotton mills; Coker's friendship with Manning and his statewide connections, however, enabled him to mediate between the governor and the Piedmont industrial elite during the elections and strikes of 1916, and the collection for that period thus contains important documentation of the political attitudes of the industrialists and their allies.

By and large, the post-Reconstruction documents housed at the South Carolina Department of Archives and History in Columbia are unorganized and inaccessible. The most easily used collections are the Governors' Papers, of which the most important are those of Cole L. Blease and Richard I. Manning. The Blease Papers are eccentrically organized but rewarding in content, since political correspondence and affairs of state are promiscuously (but appropriately) intermixed. The Manning Papers are grouped by subject matter, and are of comparable importance to those of his predecessor. The charter books and loose papers kept by the secretary of state beginning in 1887 were my chief reliance in compiling the list of mill directors analyzed in Chapter II.

Several collections at other repositories are worthy of note. The David Duncan Wallace Papers, some of which were consulted at Wofford College, are now housed at the South Carolina Historical Society in Charleston, with a microfiche copy available at the South Caroliniana Library. They include his correspondence, the notes for his *History of South Carolina*, and numerous manuscripts, notably that of an address, "The Democratizing of an Old Commonwealth," probably first delivered in 1913, which contains penetrating observations on mill-town relations in the Blease era and sets forth Wallace's own position in the contemporary debate over "democracy." The W. C. Coker Papers at the Darlington County

Historical Society contain correspondence, 1898–1899, between Coker and J. H. Williams, a former superintendent of the Darlington Mill who had moved to Lockhart; while concerned primarily with the day-to-day problems of mill management, they also contain some striking sentiments on John H. Montgomery's Vesta experiment.

B. Government Documents

Publications of the federal and South Carolina State governments are second in importance only to newspapers as sources for this study. The reports of the various U.S. Censuses, particularly those from 1880 through 1920, are of obvious value. Of special importance are materials generated by several massive investigations of industrial conditions, undertaken in order to provide comprehensive information regarding what was in most areas of the country a fairly new phenomenon. U.S. Senate Committee on Education and Labor, *Labor and Capital: Report Upon the Relations Between Labor and Capital, and Testimony Taken by the Committee*, Vol. IV (Washington: Government Printing Office, 1885), contains a stenographic record of committee hearings held in the South, including testimony taken in Augusta from Horse Creek Valley industrialists. The U.S. Industrial Commission's *Report . . . on the Relations and Conditions of Capital and Labor*, Vol. VII (Washington: Government Printing Office, 1901) contains testimony largely favorable to the industrialists, thanks in part to the efforts of Commissioner Ellison Smyth. More hostile is the U.S. Bureau of Labor's *Report on the Condition of Woman and Child Wage Earners in the United States*, Senate Document No. 645, 61st Congress, 2nd Session (1910), 19 vols., which, though animated by a bias in favor of child labor reform, is much less impressionistic and more heavily statistical than the earlier reports. For this study volumes I (*Cotton Textile Industry*) and VII (*Conditions Under Which Children Leave School to Go to Work*) are particularly useful. The U.S. Commissioner of Labor, *Nineteenth Annual Report . . . 1904* and the U.S. Bureau of Labor *Bulletins* supply background information on wages and living costs during the period.

Relevant records of the State of South Carolina fall into two categories, legislative and executive. The first consists of the *Statutes at Large*, the *Journal of the House of Representatives of the General Assembly of the State of South Carolina*, and the *Journal of the Senate . . . of South Carolina*, all three of which have been examined for the period 1880–1920. While the *Journals* contain no verbatim records of debates, they do contain governors' messages and occasionally reprint petitions, memorials, and committee reports. They can also be used to construct legislative histories of both successful and unsuccessful bills, which can then be used to obtain fuller information from extraordinarily detailed newspaper accounts of Assembly proceedings. Of the various state agency reports, three series are of special importance. The South Carolina superintendent of education *Annual Reports* first pay attention to mill schools in 1900, but are generally of little value until the superintendency of John E. Swearingen, when they begin to include comprehensive data on individual school districts (in 1911) and on individual schools (1913). The later addition of reports by the supervisor of mill schools, commencing in 1915, and the superintendent of adult and night schools, beginning in 1919, enhances its value as a source of information on mill education. The South Carolina Department of Agriculture, Commerce, and Industries, Labor Division, *Annual Reports* (1909–) provide information on labor law enforcement, labor relations, and sanitary conditions in factories, and, through the dominating personality of E. J. Watson, shed light on the attitudes underlying the local brand of Progressivism. The South Carolina State Board of Health *Annual Reports* are of more limited usefulness, their chief value lying in their documentation of the epidemiological problems posed by the mill population; they have been examined for the period 1897–1910. Some publications of local governments have also been used, notably the City of Columbia *Annuals*, 1910–1914, and the Spartanburg City Schools *Annual Reports* for 1904–1905 and 1908–1909.

C. Newspapers and Periodicals

The bulk of the supporting evidence used in this study has been obtained through extensive research in the collection of postbellum newspapers in the South Caroliniana Library. Between the Civil War and the 1890s the dominant newspaper in South Carolina was the Charleston *News and Courier* (1879–1890), whose English-born editor, Francis W. Dawson, was perhaps the most powerful individual in the state. He used his enormous influence to promote industrialization and, on occasion, ward off threats to industry. Dawson's, and the *News and Courier*'s, place among New South spokesmen has been exaggerated, being in part the product of self promotion, but the newspaper remains invaluable. For the period between 1879 and 1886 I have been guided by a list of articles pertaining to industrial and commercial development compiled by Allen H. Stokes, who has graciously permitted its use.

After 1891 the *News and Courier* was partially displaced in influence by the Columbia newspaper *The State* and its first two editors, N. G. Gonzales and W. E. Gonzales. The files of *The State* constitute the most important single source for this study, in part because of the newspaper's location at the state capital, itself a sizable cotton manufacturing center, but chiefly because of its position as the leading spokesman for the "Progressive" element among the "town people." While the *News and Courier* hardened into a backward conservative stance on the social questions of the early twentieth century, *The State* led most of the Progressive era crusades and was Blease's most bitter opponent. The Columbia paper also provided paraphrased accounts of legislative debates, reprinted numerous speeches, and provided a platform for scores of local commentators of varying abilities. Its value as a source is enhanced by the existence of indexes for the years 1892–1901 and 1903–1912; their quality is poor (they were composed by widows of *State* employees as a make-work project), but they provide an indispensable tool with which to handle a massive body of material.

Despite their location, daily newspapers in the Piedmont prove less valuable. The Greenville *Daily News* (1881; 1902; 1914) was controlled by cotton manufacturers, notably D. A. Tompkins and Ellison A. Smyth, and reflected their interests in the most predictably narrow fashion. The Spartanburg *Herald* (1910–1914), on the other hand, was owned by the Gonzales family, and its editor,

Charles O. Hearon, pursued policies similar to those of *The State.* The principal value of the two major up-country dailies, as with the Spartanburg *Journal* (1902–1903; 1912) and the Anderson *Daily Mail* (1902; 1910–1914), lies in the information they provide on local class relationships.

Semiweekly and weekly newspapers have been consulted more for the period prior to 1900 than for the later period. For the 1880s and 1890s the principal "country" newspapers used are (1) the Spartanburg *Carolina Spartan* (1879–1893), edited by Charles Petty, an ardent proponent of manufacturing and an adamant opponent of early proposals for labor legislation; (2) the Newberry *Herald* and its successor, the *Herald and News* (1883–1893), whose editor, Elbert H. Aull, combined industrial advocacy with some concern over working conditions; (3) the Anderson *Intelligencer*, a more or less conventional "booster" organ; and (4) the Abbeville *Press and Banner*, whose editor, Hugh Wilson, made the unique attack on industrialization described in Chapter III. The Union *Times* (1900–1906) and the Union *Progress* (1900–1921) supply evidence on class relationships and attitudes in a small up-country manufacturing center. Of the handful of newspapers sympathetic to Blease, the Yorkville *Enquirer* (1911–1915) was the most widely respected. Other weekly and semiweekly newspapers consulted include the Rock Hill *Herald* (1883–1888; 1902–1903), the Orangeburg *Times and Democrat* (1880–1882; 1896; 1900–1902), the Laurensville *Herald* (1895–1897), the Spartanburg *Free Lance* (1902), the Edgefield *Advertiser* (1897–1902), the Edgefield *Chronicle* (1907–1908), and the Aiken *Journal and Review* (1904–1906). Extensive use was made of two church newspapers, the *Baptist Courier* (1880–1890) and the Methodists' *Southern Christian Advocate* (1880–1890; 1897–1910). An agricultural paper, the *Cotton Plant* (1887–1894), which during the early 1890s served as the organ of the South Carolina Farmers' Alliance, also proved to be of value, especially in expressing the ambivalent attitudes of farmers toward the mills.

The most important South Carolina periodicals used are the teachers' journals, whose history reflects the expansion and organization of South Carolina's public schools. Such early journals as the *Carolina Teacher* (1885–1888) and the *Palmetto School Journal* (1890–1891) were short lived, and the *Carolina Teachers' Journal* (1897–1901) and its successor the *Educational* (1902–1904) fared little better. The *Southern School News* (1909–1917), however, was more elaborate and more successful, as was *South Carolina Education* (1919–1930), which was published by the School of Education of the University of South Carolina. While the school journals rarely took sides on political issues, they were invariably favorable to expanding the scope and functions of public education. Among other periodicals, the most remarkable is *Our Monthly* (1881–1917), published by the Thornwell Orphanage at Clinton and edited until his death in 1917 by the Rev. Dr. William Plumer Jacobs. Jacobs' interests were wide-ranging, but they were filtered through an almost antique Calvinist mentality which, for example, led him to oppose child labor reform. The magazine of the state Baptist orphanage, the *Connie Maxwell* (1909–1920), is more conventionally humanitarian. Two promotional magazines, the *Home Seeker and Business Guide* (1893–1895) and the *Exposition* (1900–1902), contain some items of value.

D. Books, Articles, Addresses, etc.

Much of the evidence concerning the rise of the towns has been gathered from several contemporary promotional accounts. The *Historical and Descriptive Review of the State of South Carolina* (3 vols.; Charleston: Empire Publishing Company, 1884) is remarkably informative, especially the volume allotted to the upcountry towns (Vol. III). More comprehensive and statistically rigorous, but also more general, is Harry Hammond, *South Carolina: Resources and Population, Institutions and Industries* (Charleston: Walker, Evans, and Cogswell, 1883), a promotional handbook commissioned by the State Board of Agriculture. Among the more useful business directories are R. G. Dun and Company, *The Mercantile Agency Reference Book*, for various years between 1867 and 1900; the *Southern Business Directory and General Commercial Advertiser* (Charleston: Walker and James, 1854), and the *South Carolina State Gazetteer and Business Directory for 1880–1881* (Charleston: R. A. Smith, 1880). D. A. Tompkins,

Cotton Mill: Commercial Features (Charlotte, N.C.: By the Author, 1899), is useful both in itself and in its inclusion, as an appendix, of William Gregg's *Essays in Domestic Industry*, the most important argument for manufacturing to appear in the antebellum South. [J. K. Blackman], *The Cotton Mills of South Carolina* (Charleston: The News and Courier Job Presses, 1880), was the most important literary product of the *News and Courier*'s "cotton mill campaign."

Some important information on contemporary conditions and attitudes can be gleaned from memoirs and other autobiographical writings. Of these the most valuable is D. E. Camak, *Human Gold from Southern Hills* (Greer, S.C.: By the Author, 1960). Although his memory of historical detail is occasionally fuzzy, Camak's account is a well-rounded depiction of the industrial transition in South Carolina as seen through the eyes of a socially conscious Methodist minister and welfare worker. One of Camak's early students reminisces in Robert Carl Griffith, "God Can't Use a Quitter" (address to South Carolina Methodist Conference, n.d.). W. E. Woodward, the popular historian and inventor of the verb "to debunk," grew up in Graniteville in the 1880s; he has left two accounts of his childhood, in *The Way Our People Lived* (New York; Liveright, 1944) and *The Gift of Life* (New York: E. P. Dutton, 1947). W. C. Hamrick, *Life Values in the New South* (Gaffney, S.C.: By the Author, 1931), is the autobiography of an upcountry cotton manufacturer. Thornwell Jacobs, in *My People* (Clinton, S.C.: n.p., 1954) and *Step Down, Dr. Jacobs: The Autobiography of an Autocrat* (Atlanta: The Westminster Publishers, 1945), recounts his youth in Clinton, and in his edition of the *Diary of William Plumer Jacobs* (Oglethorpe University, Ga.: Oglethorpe University Press, 1937) provides us with a partial record of his father's thoughts.

The rise of the "cotton mill problem" to public consciousness around the turn of the century stimulated a good deal of controversial writing. A number of writers based outside the state were moved for various reasons to comment on mill conditions. Some were approving. Leonora Beck Ellis, in "A New Class of Labor in the South," *Forum*, XXXII (1901), 60–65, applauds the benevolent despotism of "show mills" such as Pelzer. Paul H. Goldsmith, *The Cotton Mill South* (Boston: Boston Transcript Company, 1908), is also positive, but Goldsmith relies heavily on other, biased sources and his own observations are impressionistic; his viewpoint is that of a native southerner turned fashionably conservative New England minister. Thomas R. Dawley, *The Child That Toileth Not: The Story of a Government Investigation* (New York: Gracia Publishing Company, 1912), makes some useful observations on mountain people, but his research is sloppy and his biases, particularly his sometimes vicious antipathy toward child labor reformers, are flagrant.

Many outside observers, however, were not approving. Clare de Graffenried, "The Georgia Cracker in the Cotton Mills," *Century*, XIX (1891), 483–98, is not directly concerned with South Carolina, but is important as an early examination of southern industrial conditions by a trained observer. Miss De Graffenried's standards, unfortunately, were not followed by some of the popular journalists of the day, representative pieces of which include Elbert Hubbard, "White Slavery in the South," *The Philistine*, XIV (1902), 161–78; Bessie and Marie Van Vorst, *The Woman Who Toils* (New York: Doubleday, Page, and Company, 1903); and Marie Van Vorst's industrial novel *Amanda of the Mill* (New York: Dodd, Mead and Company, 1905). Fortunately, the reformers associated with the National Child Labor Committee were more sober, though no less devastating. Two NCLC pieces of particular usefulness are John C. Campbell, "From Mountain Cabin to Cotton Mill," *Child Labor Bulletin*, II (1913), 74–84, a reply to Dawley; and Alexander J. McKelway, "Child Labor in the Carolinas," *Charities and the Commons*, XXI (1909), 743–57, which includes one of Lewis Hine's most famous photographic essays.

The one important "outsider" without an axe to grind is Thomas M. Young, *The American Cotton Industry: A Study of Work and Workers* (New York: Charles Scribner's Sons, 1903). Young, a business reporter for the Manchester *Guardian*, made a tour of American mills in 1901–1902 with the object of assessing the competitive position of the American industry vis à vis the British industry. As with most travelers, his impressions are frequently superficial, but his technical and economic expertise enable him frequently to make penetrating analyses.

Writing on mill conditions by South Carolinians was generally less polemical in tone, although the movement for child labor reform stimulated some controversial writing. Of these, by far the most important is August Kohn, *The Cotton Mills of South Carolina* (Columbia: South Carolina Department of Agriculture, Commerce, and Immigration, 1907). Kohn was sympathetic to the manufacturers' case, and his book is badly marred by a tendency to accept obvious public relations releases as depictions of reality, but it remains one of the most important single sources of information on mills and mill people. A speech of James L. Orr, reprinted in "Addresses Delivered by Mr. E. Gunby Jordan . . . and Col. James L. Orr at Annual Convention of Georgia Industrial Association . . . Warm Springs, Ga., May 30–31, 1901" (n.p., n.d.), gives the views of one of the more extreme manufacturers. J. P. Hollis, "Child Labor Legislation in the Carolinas" (pamphlet, National Child Labor Committee, n.d.) and "A Legislative Program for South Carolina," *Child Labor Bulletin*, I (1912), 149–53; J. A. McCullough, "South Carolina" (in symposium on "Child Employing Industries in the South") *Child Labor Bulletin*, II (1913), 133–38; and C. E. Weltner, "Social Welfare and Child Labor in South Carolina Cotton Mill Communities," *Child Labor Bulletin*, II (1913), 85–90, state the case of the reformers. The published addresses of Ebbie J. Watson, notably "The Textile Industry of South Carolina in the Mid-Year of 1910" (Columbia: The State Company, n.d.) and "South Carolina and the Child Labor Problem" (n.p., n.d.), delivered at the National Child Labor Conference in Boston in 1910, provide glimpses into Watson's social engineering outlook. A group of pieces by Thomas Fleming Parker, "The South Carolina Cotton Mill: A Manufacturer's View," *South Atlantic Quarterly*, VIII (1909), 328–37; "The South Carolina Cotton Mill Village: A Manufacturer's View," *South Atlantic Quarterly*, IX (1910), 349–57; "Some Educational and Legislative Needs of South Carolina Mill Villages," *Bulletin of the University of South Carolina*, No. 24, Part 3 (January, 1911); "How the Sunday School Can Assist in Village Welfare Work," *Bulletin of the University of South Carolina*, No. 25, Part 2 (April, 1911); and "The True Greatness of South Carolina" (address to South Carolina Federation of Women's Clubs, May 1908), discuss the "cotton mill problem" from the standpoint of a pioneer "welfare capitalist." Remarks on the social impact of industrialization from a worried conservative appear in Anthony Harrigan (ed.), *The Editor and the Republic: Papers and Addresses of William Watts Ball* (Chapel Hill: University of North Carolina Press, 1954).

Although their role was inadvertently slighted in this study, churchmen generated a large body of commentary on the "mill problem" as it affected organized religion. The leading clerical specialist in the "problem" was D. E. Camak, who promoted his proposals in "The Power of One Man for Good," *Methodist Review*, LVI (1907), 482–86; "A Practical Solution to the Cotton Mill Problem," *Methodist Review*, LVIII (1909), 67–79; and "Religion That Cares," *Methodist Review*, LXIII (1914), 137–46. He received help from his associate Thomas Jefferson Carter, in "The Cotton Mill Problem from an Operative's Standpoint," *Methodist Review*, LXIV (1915), 711–24. W. J. Snyder, "The Cotton Mill Problem" (pamphlet, n.p., n.d. [prob. 1909]), is in part a reply to Camak. Disgruntled comments on mill life and modern life in general from an old-fashioned Methodist minister appear in E. Alston Wilkes, *The Circuit Rider's Sketch Book* (Columbia: R. L. Bryan, 1907) and *Echoes and Etchings* (Columbia: R. L. Bryan, 1910). Contemporary pieces on the Blease period include W. K. Tate, "After Blease—A New Program for South Carolina," *Survey*, XXXIII (1915), 575–78; James C. Derieux, "Crawling Toward the Promised Land," *Survey*, XLVIII (1922), 175–80; and Osta L. Warr, "Mr. Blease of South Carolina," *American Mercury*, XVI (1929), 25–32. Miscellaneous pieces of value include Carlos Tracy, "On Law and Order in South Carolina" (Charleston: D. L. Alexander, 1880), an early protest against the strain of violence in South Carolina society; and W. H. Hand, "Our Schools," *Bulletin of the University of South Carolina*, No. 16, Part 1 (January, 1909), a general discussion of the state of public education in South Carolina.

II. Secondary Sources

A. U.S. History

For my general approach to the Progressive era I am obviously indebted to Robert H. Wiebe, *The Search for Order, 1877–1920* (New York: Hill and Wang, 1967). Samuel P. Hays, in *The Response to Industrialism, 1885–1914* (Chicago: University of Chicago Press, 1958) and in "The Politics of Reform in Municipal Government in the Progressive Era," *Pacific Northwest Quarterly*, LV (1964), 157–69, delineates the conflict underlying much "reform," as does James Weinstein in "Organized Business and the City Commission and Manager Movements," *Journal of Southern History*, XXVIII (1962), 166–82, and *The Corporate Ideal in the Liberal State, 1900–1918* (Boston: Beacon Press, 1968).

Treatments of child labor reform are generally still dominated by older views pitting idealistic reformers against selfish business interests. Walter I. Trattner, *Crusade for the Children: A History of the National Child Labor Committee and Child Labor Reform in America* (Chicago: Quadrangle, 1970); Jeremy P. Felt, *Hostages of Fortune: Child Labor Reform in New York State* (Syracuse, N.Y.: Syracuse University Press, 1965); and Joseph M. Speakman, "'Unwillingly to School': Child Labor and Its Reform in Pennsylvania in the Progressive Era" (Ph.D. dissertation, Temple University, 1976), are well documented, but implicitly credit the reformers with their own moral sensibilities; Speakman, while noting criticisms of the arrogance and coerciveness of reformers, argues that the beneficence of the reform justified their behavior. An older study, Forest Chester Ensign, *Compulsory School Attendance and Child Labor* (Iowa City, Iowa: Athens Press, 1921), contains a wealth of material on the legislative history of reform.

Most criticism of the child labor reform movement has been made in connection with the revisionist work on public education which has been appearing over the past fifteen years. Representative works include Michael B. Katz, *The Irony of Early School Reform: Educational Innovation in Mid-Nineteenth Century Massachusetts* (Cambridge: Harvard University Press, 1968) and *Class,*

Bureaucracy, and Schools: The Illusion of Educational Change in America (New York: Praeger, 1971); and, especially, David B. Tyack, *The One Best System: A History of American Urban Education* (Cambridge: Harvard University Press, 1974). The impact of the rising social service professions on the American family is speculated upon with gloomy grandeur by Christopher Lasch in *Haven in a Heartless World: The Family Besieged* (New York: Basic Books, 1977). In a similar vein is Martin E. Dann, "'Little Citizens': Working Class and Immigrant Childhood in New York City, 1890–1915" (Ph.D. dissertation, City University of New York, 1978), which contains some useful material but is generally poorly done.

The most useful treatments of working-class history have been those which treat unions as peripheral. Stuart Brandes, *American Welfare Capitalism, 1880–1940* (Chicago: University of Chicago Press, 1976), sets southern "paternalism" in a broader national context, while Daniel Rodgers, "Tradition, Modernity, and the American Industrial Worker: Reflections and Critique," *Journal of Interdisciplinary History*, VII (1977), 655–81, deals with American attitudes toward work. Herbert G. Gutman, "The Workers' Search for Power" in H. Wayne Morgan (ed.), *The Gilded Age* (Syracuse, N.Y.: Syracuse University Press, 1970), is suggestive about the ambivalence shown by "town people" toward labor organization; his "Work, Culture, and Society in Industrializing America, 1815–1919," *American Historical Review*, LXXVIII (1973), 531–88, since republished as the title essay in an anthology of Gutman's writings on labor history, deals with concerns parallel to my own, and is a mine of insights.

The increasing number of community studies produced in recent years have provided us with new understanding of the more intimate details of American social history. By using local and regional studies of nonsouthern locales for comparative purposes it is possible to consider afresh the ancient question of southern "uniqueness," avoiding the too frequent tendency of southern historians to compare the South to a liberal-bourgeois "America" whose historical existence is moot. The extensive literature of midwestern boosterism, including both the general observations of Stanley Elkins and Eric McKitrick, "A Meaning for Turner's Frontier, I—Democracy in the Old Northwest," *Political Science Quarterly*, LXIX (1954), 321–53; Daniel Boorstin, *The Americans: The National Experience* (New York: Random House, 1965), Pt. 2; and Leslie E. Decker, "The Great Speculation: An Interpretation of Mid-Continent Pioneering" in David M. Ellis (ed.), *The Frontier in American Development* (Ithaca, N.Y.: Cornell University Press, 1969), 357–80; and the more localized studies of Robert R. Dykstra, *The Cattle Towns* (New York: Alfred A. Knopf, 1968), and Don H. Doyle, *The Social Order of a Frontier Community* (Urbana: University of Illinois Press, 1978), suggest numerous parallels between town development on the western frontier and that on the "commercial frontier" of the late-nineteenth-century South. The nature of local elites in the North, their frequently "paternalistic" relationship to their workers, and their efforts to handle social change with traditional, especially religious, controls, are explored in rich detail by Paul E. Johnson, *A Shopkeeper's Millennium: Society and Revivals in Rochester, New York, 1815–1837* (New York: Hill and Wang, 1978), and Anthony F. C. Wallace, *Rockdale: The Growth of an American Village in the Early Industrial Revolution* (New York: Alfred A. Knopf, 1978). Stephan Thernstrom, *Poverty and Progress: Social Mobility in a Nineteenth Century City* (Cambridge: Harvard University Press, 1964), suggests the ways in which the priorities of working-class families differ from those of middle-class families, particularly in their deemphasis of occupational mobility in favor of economic security. The interrelationship of family, work, and culture are explored in Virginia Yans-McLaughlin, *Family and Community: Italian Immigrants in Buffalo, 1880–1930* (Ithaca, N.Y.: Cornell University Press, 1977), and Tamara K. Hareven and Randolph Langenbach, *Amoskeag: Life and Work in an American Factory-City* (New York: Pantheon, 1978), which reveals a remarkably traditional society, comparable in many respects to that of southern mill villages, flourishing in the very maw of an early twentieth-century industrial complex. Indeed, all in all, the studies listed above, and numerous others of less immediate relevance, suggest that "traditional" values, institutions, and practices have played far greater roles in the making of "modern," urban, industrial America than many historians have appreciated; to that extent, southern society is considerably less "un-American" than some southerners, and southern historians, have cared to admit.

B. The South

The most important general history of the period of southern history covered here remains C. Vann Woodward, *Origins of the New South, 1877–1913*, A History of the South, IX (Baton Rouge: Louisiana State University Press, 1951). Other volumes of use in the LSU series include E. Merton Coulter, *The South During Reconstruction, 1865–1877* (Baton Rouge: Louisiana State University Press, 1947) and George B. Tindall, *The Emergence of the New South, 1913–1946* (Baton Rouge: Louisiana State University Press, 1967).

Anyone seeking to trace the evolution of the post–Civil War South must have an image of the antebellum South as his starting point. At the outset of this study that base point was provided by Eugene Genovese, notably in *The Political Economy of Slavery* (New York: Pantheon, 1965); I have since concluded that his model of a planter-dominated region rejecting liberal-bourgeois values leaves much to be desired as a way of understanding what the South became after the destruction of the slave regime. The story told above, I decided, could better be understood if it began with a different view of the slave South, emphasizing the economic independence, social individualism, and political egalitarianism of the southern white population, resting as it did atop a mudsill of black slaves. Economic and political aspects of this interpretation are explored in such older works as Frank L. Owsley, *Plain Folk of the Old South* (Baton Rouge: Louisiana State University Press, 1949), and Fletcher M. Green, "Democracy in the Old South," in J. Isaac Copeland (ed.), *Democracy in the Old South and Other Essays by Fletcher M. Green* (Nashville: Vanderbilt University Press, 1969), 65–86. The racial dimension of southern "*herrenvolk* democracy" is discussed in George M. Fredrickson, *The*

Black Image in the White Mind (New York: Harper and Row, 1971), Chap. II, and its colonial roots are excavated in Edmund S. Morgan, *American Slavery, American Freedom: The Ordeal of Colonial Virginia* (New York: Norton, 1975). The southern concern with family and personal honor is explored in Bertram Wyatt-Brown, "The Ideal Typology and Ante-Bellum Southern History: A Testing of a New Approach," *Societas*, V (1975), 1–29. The "white democracy" view of the antebellum South receives its greatest elaboration from J. Mills Thornton III in *Politics and Power in a Slave Society: Alabama, 1800–1860* (Baton Rouge: Louisiana State University Press, 1978). On antebellum commerce, Lewis Atherton, *The Southern Country Store, 1800–1860* (Baton Rouge: Louisiana State University Press, 1949), and Harold D. Woodman, *King Cotton and His Retainers: Financing and Marketing the Cotton Crop of the South, 1800–1925* (Lexington: University of Kentucky Press, 1968), are crucial, although Woodman accepts a fundamentally Genovesean explanation for the lack of prewar southern commercial development. On urban history, David R. Goldfield, *Urban Growth in the Age of Sectionalism: Virginia, 1847–1861* (Baton Rouge: Louisiana State University Press, 1977), and Fred Fein Siegel, "A New South in the Old: Sotweed and Soil in the Development of Danville, Virginia" (Ph.D. dissertation, University of Pittsburgh, 1978), are suggestive, although their usefulness for the cotton South is limited by their upper-South subject matter. Gavin Wright's *The Political Economy of the Cotton South: Households, Markets, and Wealth in the Nineteenth Century* (New York: Norton, 1978) contains numerous insights into southern economic behavior. On antebellum industry, a new book, Fred Bateman and Thomas Weiss, *A Deplorable Scarcity: The Failure of Industrialization in the Slave Economy* (Chapel Hill: University of North Carolina Press, 1981), corrects numerous misconceptions but offers no strong explanation of antebellum southern industrial "failure" to take their place.

If the social historiography of the Old South has long been a "dark and bloody ground," that of the New South may well become one. Woodward's heretofore hegemonic thesis that the South of the Gilded Age was dominated by merchants and industrialists has recently been challenged by several historians who propose to extend Genovese's, and Barrington Moore's (in *Social Origins of Dictatorship and Democracy: Lord and Peasant in the Making of the Modern World* [Boston: Beacon Press, 1966], Chap. III), analysis of the antebellum South across the chasm of the Civil War. Jonathan M. Wiener, for example, in *Social Origins of the New South: Alabama, 1860–1885* (Baton Rouge: Louisiana State University Press, 1978), and, more recently, "Class Structure and Economic Development in the American South, 1865–1955," *American Historical Review*, LXXXIV (1979), 970–92, argues that a persistent planter elite used its control of the land to inhibit both political liberalization and economic development well into the twentieth century. Less defensibly, Dwight B. Billings, Jr., *Planters and the Making of a "New South": Class, Politics and Development in North Carolina, 1865–1900* (Chapel Hill: University of North Carolina Press, 1979), contends that planters in the Tarheel State actively pursued economic development in the (presumed) manner of Prussian Junkers or Japanese nobles, ultimately creating a quasi-fascist state within the American Union. I set forth some of my own objections to the "Prussian Road" school in "'Builders of a New State': The Town Classes and Early Industrialization of South Carolina, 1880–1907" in Walter J. Fraser and Winfred B. Moore (eds.), *From the Old South to the New: Essays on the Transitional South* (Westport, Conn.: Greenwood Press, 1981). See also the replies of Robert Higgs and Harold D. Woodman to Wiener, "Class Structure," and Wiener's reply to them, in *American Historical Review*, LXXXIV (1979), 993–1006, and Woodman's historiographical essay "Sequel to Slavery: The New History Views the Post-Bellum South," *Journal of Southern History*, XLIII (1977), 523–54. Roger Ransom and Richard Sutch, *One Kind of Freedom: The Economic Consequences of Emancipation* (Cambridge: Cambridge University Press, 1977), present an economically sophisticated restatement of Woodward's argument, while Steven H. Hahn's superb study "The Roots of Southern Populism: Yeomen Farmers and the Transformation of Georgia's Upper Piedmont, 1850–1900" (Ph.D. dissertation, Yale University, 1979) seeks middle ground. The later chapters of Woodman, *King*

Cotton, and Wright, *Political Economy* treat postbellum economic developments, Woodman stressing the rise of the merchant while Wright stresses the postwar decline of the cotton economy. Among the more useful southern, but non–South Carolinian, community studies are Samuel M. Kipp III, "Old Notables and Newcomers: The Economic and Political Elite of Greensboro, North Carolina, 1880–1920," *Journal of Southern History*, XLIII (1977), 373–94, and Frank J. Huffman, Jr., "Old South, New South: Continuity and Change in a Georgia County, 1850–1880" (Ph.D. dissertation, Yale University, 1974), which pioneered the use of quantitative methods in the study of a southern community across the Civil War era but is not interpretively strong. In intellectual history, Paul M. Gaston, *The New South Creed: A Study in Southern Mythmaking* (New York: Alfred A. Knopf, 1970), is a good study of one strain of postbellum southern thought, but by presenting the promotional statements of "New South" spokesmen as somehow "mythic" he loses sight of many complexities and tends to exaggerate both southern optimism and southern detachment from reality. On political matters, V. O. Key, *Southern Politics in State and Nation* (New York: Alfred A. Knopf, 1949), though dealing with a period later than my own, is still the basic work. J. Morgan Kousser, *The Shaping of Southern Politics: Suffrage Restriction and the Establishment of the One-Party South, 1880–1910* (New Haven: Yale University Press, 1974), brings a new sophistication to bear on his central question, but his handling of such secondary subjects as the "white primary," the "demagogue," and the broad social consequences of suffrage restriction is less satisfactory. Elizabeth Huey Davidson, *Child Labor Legislation in the Southern Textile States* (Chapel Hill: University of North Carolina Press, 1939), displays a mild bias in favor of the reformers, but nonetheless is probably the best study of southern child labor reform. Louis M. Harlan, *Separate and Unequal: Public School Campaigns and Racism in the Southern Seaboard States, 1901–1915* (Chapel Hill: University of North Carolina Press, 1958), despite minor flaws, is a perceptive general history of public education in the Southeast during the Progressive era as well as a study of segregation. John C. Campbell, *The Southern Highlander and His Home-*

land (New York: Russell Sage Foundation, 1921), is a classic description of one of the major sources for South Carolina's mill population; Henry D. Shapiro, *Appalachia on Our Mind: The Southern Mountains and Mountaineers in the American Consciousness, 1870–1920* (Chapel Hill: University of North Carolina Press, 1978), deals in a turgid, unsatisfying way with the response of the outside world to the mountaineer.

C. South Carolina

The student of South Carolina history in this period is fortunate to have as his guide David Duncan Wallace's *The History of South Carolina* (4 vols.; New York: American Historical Society, 1934). Wallace writes from the standpoint of a conservative Progressive and a certified member of the local establishment, but he combines careful scholarship with a deep personal concern for the welfare of his native state to produce an illuminating work that has deserved its wide influence. A posthumously published abridgment, *South Carolina: A Short History, 1520–1948* (Chapel Hill: University of North Carolina Press, 1951), leaves out much of the commentary, but adds some new material. Ernest M. Lander, Jr., *A History of South Carolina, 1865–1960* (Chapel Hill: University of North Carolina Press, 1960), is less valuable.

Studies of specific periods vary widely in quality. Francis Butler Simkins and Robert H. Woody, *South Carolina During Reconstruction* (Chapel Hill: University of North Carolina Press, 1932), an early, tentative revision of the then-standard interpretation of the "tragic era," was also a pioneer in eschewing a narrow political focus to discuss the broader social and economic developments of the period. William J. Cooper, *The Conservative Regime: South Carolina, 1877–1890* (Baltimore: Johns Hopkins University Press, 1969), attempts a similar survey for the succeeding period, but is more valuable for its assemblage of material than for its conclusions. No comparable study exists for any period after 1890, the closest equivalents being several biographical studies of important governors, which naturally focus on political events and on occurrences of direct concern to their subjects. Francis Butler Simkins' *Pitchfork Ben Tillman: South Carolinian* (Baton Rouge: Louisiana

State University Press, 1944), is deservedly a classic, but aside from its chapter on Blease is of limited usefulness here. Ronald D. Burnside, "The Governorship of Coleman Livingston Blease of South Carolina, 1911–1915" (Ph.D. dissertation, Indiana University, 1963), is conventional but well-crafted, as is Daniel Walker Hollis, "Cole Blease: The Years Between the Governorship and the Senate, 1915–1924," *South Carolina Historical Magazine*, LXXX (1979), 1–17. The same cannot be said for Robert M. Burts, *Richard Irvine Manning and the Progressive Movement in South Carolina* (Columbia: University of South Carolina Press, 1974), which is sloppily written and edited, contains serious misstatements of fact, and has virtually nothing to say. Both Manning and the Progressives deserve better.

Other, more specialized studies can be consulted with some profit. Lewis P. Jones, *Stormy Petrel: N. G. Gonzales and His State*, Tricentennial Studies, No. 8 (Columbia: University of South Carolina Press, 1973), contains much information about a pivotal figure in turn-of-the-century South Carolina. The life of another prominent journalist is chronicled in John D. Stark, *Damned Upcountryman: William Watts Ball, A Study in American Conservatism* (Durham, N.C.: Duke University Press, 1968). John Furman Thomason, *Foundation of the Public Schools of South Carolina* (Columbia: The State Company, 1926), was designed in part to counter those who attacked public education as a "Radical" importation, and as a result exaggerates the importance of its indigenous roots; however, it contains some good information, especially for the antebellum period. Michael S. Hindus, *Prison and Plantation: Crime, Justice and Authority in Massachusetts and South Carolina, 1767–1878* (Chapel Hill: University of North Carolina Press, 1980), is a fascinating and revealing, if not completely successful, effort to understand antebellum South Carolina through studying its criminal justice system. Another good antebellum study is Alfred Glaze Smith, Jr., *Economic Readjustment of an Old Cotton State: South Carolina, 1820–1860* (Columbia: University of South Carolina Press, 1958). George Brown Tindall, *South Carolina Negroes, 1877–1900* (Columbia: University of South Carolina Press, 1952), is a good background source on racial attitudes. Norfleet Hardy, *Farm, Mill, and Classroom: A History of Tax-Supported Adult Education in South Carolina to 1960* (Columbia: College of General Studies, University of South Carolina, 1967), is superficial. Of the plethora of local histories the most informative are the Federal Writers' Project, *A History of Spartanburg County* (Spartanburg: Band and White, 1940); Bobby Gilmer Moss, *The Old Iron District: A Study of the Development of Cherokee County, 1750–1897* (Clinton, S.C.: Jacobs Press, 1972); and especially Douglas Summers Brown, *A City Without Cobwebs: A History of Rock Hill, S.C.* (Columbia: University of South Carolina Press, 1953). The latter-day growth of scholarly interest in local history has not left the Palmetto State untouched, but the fulfillment of its promise lies in the future. A pioneering effort, though not strictly germane to this study, is O. Vernon Burton's grandiloquently titled "Ungrateful Servants? Edgefield's Black Reconstruction: Part I of the Total History of Edgefield County, S.C." (Ph.D. dissertation, Princeton University, 1976). The most useful extant study is Lewis J. Bellardo, "A Social and Economic History of Fairfield County, South Carolina, 1865–1871" (Ph.D. dissertation, University of Kentucky, 1979), which pays special attention to the relations of town and country in the aftermath of the Civil War. The forthcoming work of Lacy K. Ford on the South Carolina up-country should be a major contribution. Another noteworthy local study, anthropological rather than historical, is Ralph C. Patrick, Jr., "A Cultural Approach to Social Stratification" (Ph.D. dissertation, Harvard University, 1953), a study of the "town people" of York, S.C.; his analysis is utterly wrongheaded.

D. The Southern Textile Industry

Despite general acknowledgment of its flaws, the basic general work on the southern textile industry prior to World War I remains Broadus Mitchell, *The Rise of Cotton Mills in the South*, Johns Hopkins University Studies in Historical and Political Science, Series 39, No. 2 (Baltimore: Johns Hopkins University Press, 1921). A more recent study, Jack Blicksilver, *Cotton Manufacturing in the Southeast: An Historical Analysis* (Atlanta: Bureau of

Business and Economic Research, School of Business Administration, Georgia State College, 1959), is essentially a business history; it relies chiefly on secondary sources, and is sketchy by its own admission. Sister Mary Josephine Oates, *The Role of the Cotton Textile Industry in the Economic Development of the American Southeast, 1900–1940*, Dissertations in American Economic History (New York: Arno Press, 1975), is an economic study endeavoring to explain why the southern textile industry was so unsuccessful in stimulating auxiliary industries and general economic growth. For the antebellum background of the industry, Richard W. Griffin's numerous articles, notably "Ante-Bellum Industrial Foundations of the (Alleged) New South," *Textile History Review*, V (1962), 33–43, have made available a large body of material but have exaggerated prewar industrial development. On the other hand, Ernest M. Lander, Jr., *The Textile Industry in Ante-Bellum South Carolina* (Baton Rouge: Louisiana State University Press, 1969), while narrowly empirical, is careful and balanced. Gavin Wright, "Cheap Labor and Southern Textiles Before 1880," *Journal of Economic History*, XXXIX (1979), 655–80, presents an intriguing explanation both of antebellum industrial development and the textile industry's shift to an all-white work force. For South Carolina after the war, Gustavus G. Williamson, Jr., "Cotton Manufacturing in South Carolina, 1865–1892" (Ph.D. dissertation, Johns Hopkins University, 1954), is an indispensable piece of business history. The most important economic study of the industry in a specific South Carolina locale is Fenelon DeVere Smith, "The Economic Development of the Textile Industry in the Columbia, S.C. Area From 1790 Through 1916" (Ph.D. dissertation, University of Kentucky, 1952).

As the South's pioneer industry and largest manufacturing employer, the textile industry has been the subject of much social comment as well as economic study. The general literature is too large for review here, but a few of the more important items can be noted. Broadus Mitchell and George Sinclair Mitchell, *The Industrial Revolution in the South* (Baltimore: Johns Hopkins University Press, 1930), is a collection of short pieces written on southern industrial conditions in the 1920s, following the basic lines laid down in *The Rise of Cotton Mills*. A more recent study, John G. Van Osdell, "Cotton Mills, Labor, and the Southern Mind, 1880–1930" (Ph.D. dissertation, Tulane University, 1967), is, despite its title, chiefly concerned with the strike wave of 1929. Van Osdell's ideas are unoriginal when not puzzling, and his coverage is spotty; his chapter on South Carolina does not cite a single local source. On the 1929 strikes, and much else besides, a far more valuable source is Liston Pope, *Millhands and Preachers: A Study of Gastonia* (New Haven: Yale University Press, 1941), which remains the best work ever written on the social history of the southern cotton mills. Gastonia is also the focus of a new study by John Earle, Dean Knudsen, and Donald R. Shriver, *Spindles and Spires: A Re-Study of Religion and Social Change in America* (Richmond, Va.: John Knox Press, 1976). Melton A. McLaurin, *Paternalism and Protest: Southern Cotton Mill Workers and Organized Labor, 1875–1905* (Westport, Conn.: Greenwood Press, 1971), is overdrawn in its depiction of struggle between militant operatives and villainous, conspiratorial management, but is the best labor history, although George S. Mitchell, *Textile Unionism and the South* (Chapel Hill: University of North Carolina Press, 1931), remains useful for periods not covered by McLaurin. Allen H. Stokes, Jr., "Black and White Labor and the Development of the Southern Textile Industry, 1800–1920" (Ph.D. dissertation, University of South Carolina, 1977), is the most complete treatment yet of an oddly neglected topic; however, see also Leonard A. Carlson, "Labor Supply, the Acquisition of Skills, and the Location of Southern Textiles, 1880–1900," *Journal of Economic History*, XLI (1981), 65–71, who offers an interesting hypothesis regarding the failure of southern manufacturers to make greater use of blacks.

Several social studies of the mills have dealt with South Carolina. The earliest "sociological" work, Marjorie Potwin, *Cotton Mill People of the Piedmont* (New York: Columbia University Press, 1927), was written by a social worker at a Spartanburg mill; it is largely impressionistic, and displays flagrant bias in favor of the manufacturers, especially her employer, whom she subsequently married. A considerably darker picture is presented in Lois MacDonald, *Southern Mill Hills* (New York: Hillman Brothers, 1928).

By far the most useful community study is John Kenneth Morland, *Millways of Kent* (Chapel Hill: University of North Carolina Press, 1958), part of a trilogy on York, S.C., which also includes Patrick, "A Cultural Approach to Social Stratification," mentioned above. Morland's investigations were conducted in the late 1940s when the company-owned mill village was beginning to disappear; nonetheless his mill people display many of the same traits as their ancestors. Indeed, Morland found that little had changed when he returned to York for a follow-up study ten years later; see his articles "Educational and Occupational Aspirations of Mill and Town School Children in a Southern Community," *Social Forces*, XXXIX (1960), 169–75; and "Kent Revisited: Blue-Collar Aspirations and Achievements" in Arthur B. Shostak and William Gomberg (eds.), *Blue-Collar World: Studies of the American Worker* (Englewood Cliffs, N.J.: Prentice-Hall, 1964), 134–43.

A collective description of South Carolina's industrial entrepreneurs appears in Carlton, "'Builders of a New State,'" cited above. W. P. Jacobs, *The Pioneer* (Clinton, S.C.: Jacobs Press, 1934), is chiefly a biography of Ellison Smyth, but contains sketches of other early manufacturers. Its tone is uniformly uncritical and adulatory, as is James L. Young (ed.), *Textile Leaders of the South* (Columbia: R. L. Bryan, 1963). Broadus Mitchell, *William Gregg, A Factory Master of the Old South* (Chapel Hill: University of North Carolina Press, 1928), is more scholarly, but is all the same overly sympathetic. On the other hand, Howard B. Clay, "Daniel Augustus Tompkins: An American Bourbon" (Ph.D. dissertation, University of North Carolina, 1950), is a sometimes unreasonably hostile biography of the Charlotte engineer, manufacturer, and publicist. One of the most interesting studies of an early manufacturer, despite its brevity, is Allen H. Stokes, Jr., "John H. Montgomery: A Pioneer Southern Industrialist" (M.A. thesis, University of South Carolina, 1967). Mary Baldwin Baer and John Wilbur Baer, *A History of Woodward, Baldwin and Company* (Annapolis, Md.: Private, 1977), is a short but informative chronicle of one of the most important commission houses. Other northerners active in southern textiles are treated in Samuel B. Lincoln, *Lockwood Greene: The History of an Engineering Business, 1832–1958*

(Brattleboro, Vt.: Stephen Greene Press, 1960), and George Sweet Gibb, *The Saco-Lowell Shops: Textile Machinery Manufacturing in New England, 1813–1949*, Harvard Studies in Business History, Vol. XVI (Cambridge: Harvard University Press, 1950). Articles dealing with various social aspects of industrialization include Gustavus G. Williamson, Jr., "South Carolina Cotton Mills and the Tillman Movement," *Proceedings of the South Carolina Historical Association*, 1949, 36–49, and Melton A. McLaurin, "Early Labor Union Organizational Efforts in South Carolina Cotton Mills, 1880–1905," *South Carolina Historical Magazine*, LXXII (1971), 44–59; the latter piece suffers from the same melodramatic approach that afflicts McLaurin's larger monograph.

Index

Abbeville, 65, 66, 68
Abbeville Cotton Mill, 141
Abbeville County, 31, 66, 141
Abbeville *Press and Banner*, 122
Adger, James, 44
Agriculture: in postbellum South, 6–7; in postbellum S.C., 7–8, 17–20, 67; in 1860s, 16–17; and newspapers, 33; towns dependent upon, 38–39
Aiken County, 90, 138, 163, 200, 201
American Federation of Labor, 140, 180, 202, 252
"Americanization" movement, 267*n*
Anderson: early development, 14, 15*n*, 16; and agriculture, 24, 67; postbellum development, 24, 31; appearance, 26; merchant elite, 29–30; cotton manufacturing, 34, 46, 66, 69, 134; leadership, 35; school, 37; industrial elite, 50–51, 55–56; medical inspection, 236; strikes, 252–53, 258
Anderson Cotton Mill, 55, 66, 82
Anderson County: agricultural growth, 18, 19, 24; and Blease, 216, 217, 221; strikes, 252–53; mentioned, 31, 45, 90, 98, 146, 207, 208
Anderson *Intelligencer*, 67, 124
"Anglo-Saxons," 2, 10, 83, 111, 116–18, 120, 121, 128, 132, 197, 244
Ansel, Martin F., 166, 216
Anti-Blease faction: on Blease, 223; and commission government, 228; and suffrage restriction, 231; corruption, 242–43; and race issue, 243–46; and "town" voters, 274–75
Arbitration, labor, 258–59
Ashley, Joe M. H., 252, 253
Ashley, Joshua W., 207, 233, 246, 247, 253
Atlanta and Charlotte Air Line Railroad, 22, 23, 24. *See also* Southern Railway
"Atlanta Compromise," 243
Augusta, Ga., 24, 31, 75, 106, 138, 140, 186
Aull, E. H., 125

Bailey, Mercer S., 53, 80*n*
Bailey, W. J., 53
Baldwin, Summerfield, 59
Ball, William Watts, 3–4, 6, 168, 175–76, 178, 255
Bamberg, S.C., 158
Banks: antebellum, 14, 31; postbellum emergence, 17, 31–32
Barry, Thomas, 118, 125–26
Beaufort, 36
Beaufort County, 231
Beaumont Mill (Spartanburg), 54
Beecher, Henry Ward, 79
Belton, S.C., 95, 96
Bennettsville, S.C., 262*n*
Billings, Dwight, 46
Birmingham, Ala., 49
Birth registration, 186, 212, 233
Black Belt, 48
Black labor in mills, 75–76, 112, 114–15, 158–60, 244–45, 247. *See* Segregation Act of 1915
Blacklisting, 143
Blackman, J. K., 60, 115
Blacks: as "mudsill," 11, 116–17; as social concern, 37; and "mill people," 150,

247–48; and vaccination, 154, 155, 160. *See also* Black labor in mills; Race issue
Blake, W. K., 16
Blease, Cole L.: on the stump, 1–2; and class divisions, 5; as champion of "mill people," 11, 214; early career, 161, 162; and James H. Tillman, 166; political impact, 215; and mill voters, 216–20, 221–22, 224, 267–69; and "town" voters, 216, 221, 224; his "style," 221–22; racial appeals, 222–23; lack of "program," 222–25; and suffrage restriction movement, 226, 230–31; and "uplift" legislation, 232–39; and school appropriations, 232; and child labor reform, 232–33; and factory inspection, 234; and labor unions, 234, 252, 254; and compulsory school attendance, 234–35; and race issue, 234, 237, 243–44, 245–48, 270; and medical inspection, 236–39; and violence, 237, 246–49; and cotton manufacturers, 240–42, 248–49, 254–55, 270; alleged corruption, 242–43; and lynching, 246–48; and strikes, 247–48, 249, 252–53, 254; and 1914 reforms, 256; and World War I, 263, 268–69; compared to George Wallace, 271; voting estimates, 273–75
Blease faction: formation, 216; and commission government, 228; and child labor reform, 233, 234; and compulsory school attendance, 235; and medical inspection, 238; and cotton manufacturers, 240–42; patronage, 242
Bleaseites: described by Camak, 2–3; and "ignorance," 223–24
Bleckley, Sylvester, 29, 30
Blue Ridge Mountains, 14, 40, 148
Boone, Caroline, 205
Boosterism, 9, 13, 33–34, 37–38, 61–71, 74
Boston, Mass., 56, 57, 85, 86
Bounderby, Josiah, 87
Brogon Mill (Anderson), 258
Brown, E. W., 30

Calvert, Arch, 254
Camak, D. E., 1–3, 5, 11, 175, 178, 179, 197, 223, 265, 270
Camden, S.C., 25, 31
Campbell, John C., 148, 197
Camperdown Mill (Greenville), 109
Capers, Ellison, 28, 193
Capital: local, 20; Charleston, 43–45; northern, 56–57, 58, 59
Cash, W. J., 223
Centennial Exposition (1876), 69
Chambers of Commerce, 38
Charleston: commercial decline, 22, 23, 43–45, 73; role in cotton textile industry, 43–46; as cotton manufacturing center, 72–76; labor disputes, 1890s, 159–60; mentioned, 14, 16, 20, 24, 25, 27, 31, 35, 54, 70, 114, 244
Charleston Cotton Mill, 72, 158, 159–60. *See also* Vesta Cotton Mill
Charleston *News and Courier*: as industrial promoter, 64, 72, 73–74, 75, 77, 78; on social conditions, 85, 110, 113, 116, 117, 125, 126
Charlotte, N.C., 22, 43, 52
Charlotte and South Carolina Railroad, 24
Cheraw, S.C., 31
Cherokee Falls, S.C., 97
Chester, S.C., 14, 31, 52, 163, 231
Chester County, 24, 106–107, 163
Child labor: potential labor source, 76–77; England, 84–85; and schooling, 102–103, 120; criticized by Wilson, 123; de Graffenried on, 126*n*; Gonzales on, 130–32; Columbia, 1900s, 143, 169; isolating effects, 176; intensity of work, 176–77; and discipline, 176–77, 182; and illiteracy, 179; extent, 188, 206; blamed on parents, 194–99; rural background, 197–98; and mill family, 197–98, 203–205, 209; and economic changes, 213; mentioned, 118, 121
Child labor laws: Act of 1903, pp. 132, 187, 191, 198, 200; Act of 1916, pp. 186, 191, 205, 259–60, 268; enforcement, 187–90, 212–13, 233, 242; Act of 1911, pp. 189, 208, 232–33
Child labor reform: beginnings, 130–32, 169–70; and N. G. Gonzales, 131–32, 167–68; and unions, 141; historiography, 171–73; characterized, 173–74; and national organizations, 180–81; and compulsory school attendance, 181–86, 194–95; and mill parents, 198–99; stance of "mill people," 199–203; election of 1902, p. 200; economic impact on families, 203–206; and wage levels, 205–206; McMahan and, 229; and Bleaseites, 232–33

Child, mill: target of reform, 11, 170, 174, 181; education, 176, 177–78, 183–84; illiteracy, 179; and "moving about," 152
Christensen, Niels, 231
Churches: role in towns, 30–31; and cotton manufacturing, 78–81; and cotton mills, 104–106, 119; and immigrants, 112–13
Churches, mill: at Pelzer, 91–92; described, 93–94, 103–106, 120; and poverty, 136
Civil War, 8, 13, 15, 19, 44, 56, 85, 87, 88, 148
Clarkson, Thomas, 84
Clayton, D. B., 195
Clement Attachment, 66, 76, 78
Clergy: and postbellum towns, 28; and cotton mills, 104–106
Clerks, 30, 52, 53
Cleveland, John B. (elder), 53
Cleveland, John B. (younger), 106
Clifton, S.C., 54, 90, 97, 101, 104–105, 110, 119
Clifton Manufacturing Company, 54
Clinton, S.C., 27, 53, 65, 68, 70–71, 79–81, 175, 221
Clinton Cotton Mill, 80
Coerced labor, 92, 102–103, 178, 191
Coker, David R., 254
Coketown, 80, 87, 124
Columbia: background of "mill people," 76; mill schools, 101–102, 261; coerced labor, 102–103, 191; poverty, 135–37; labor unions, 138, 140, 142–43, 144; mill-town relations, 157, 163–65, 166, 230; "welfare work," 169, 170; and van Vorst, 178; child labor, 195–96; and child labor reform, 199, 201; Blease vote, 216–17, 218, 221; commission government, 227–28, 229; mentioned, 14, 23, 25, 27, 31, 73, 185, 236
Columbia and Augusta Railroad, 22
Columbia Chamber of Commerce, 189,227
Columbia Mills, 142, 160
Columbia *Register*, 109–10, 127
Columbia *State*: on social conditions, 110, 128; and "mill people," 129, 130, 135–36, 150, 157, 159–60, 165, 166, 169, 183, 198; and labor unions, 139, 141; and Progressive reform, 180, 184, 187, 188–89, 198, 229, 236, 237–38, 244, 257; and political reform, 226, 227, 229, 230; mentioned, 36, 38, 144, 241*n*, 268
Commerce: antebellum, 14–15; and Civil War, 15; postwar revival, 16–17; and Emancipation, 17; and cotton monoculture, 18–20; postbellum, focused on towns, 21; late-nineteenth-century, 67
Commission government, 227–28, 229, 230, 231
Compulsory school attendance: at Pelzer, 92, 96, 103, 108; nineteenth-century, 92, 95–96, 103, 108; and unions, 141; opposed by "mill people," 174, 199, 210; and child labor reform, 181–86, 194–95; Act of 1915, pp. 185, 260, 265, 268; role of government, 198–99; Act of 1919, pp. 212, 261*n*; enforcement, 212; opposed by Blease, 234–35; and mill family, 235; mentioned, 170, 229
Constitution of 1895, p. 36
Converse, S.C., 250
Converse, D. E., 40, 55, 90, 106, 110–11, 118, 125–26
Cotton: postbellum stagnation, 13, 17; expansion of cultivation, 18–19, 24; and white farmers, 18–20; and banks, 31; as raw material for mills, 47–48; and cotton textile industry, 64–65
Cotton manufacturers: and compulsory school attendance, 181–82, 184–85, 193; and child labor reform, 172, 173, 181–82, 184, 186, 188, 189, 191–93, 201–202; and Blease, 240–42, 248–49, 254–55, 270; and Manning, 254, 258–59, 268; and adult education, 264
Cotton Manufacturers' Association of South Carolina, 71*n*, 113–14
Cotton manufacturing: and "town people," 9, 50–51; and boosterism, 13, 74; and newspapers, 34; and town growth, 36–37, 38, 39; "religious" motives, 42, 71, 78–80; profits, 59–61; motives, 59–80; as "community enterprise," 59, 61–71; as "philanthropy," 60, 71, 72–81, 110–11, 123, 146; and land speculation, 62; and local population growth, 62–63; and diversified economic development, 63–64; and cotton trade, 64–65; and agriculture, 65–67; and town rivalries, 67–68; and social improvement, 70, 78; and churches, 70, 78–81; Charleston, 72–76; potential work force, 72–77
"Cotton mill campaign," 72, 74
"Cotton mill merger." *See* Parker Mills

Cotton mills: clustered around towns, 46–49, 134; and farmers, 65–67, 83, 93; as symbols, 68–69; and "town people," 83; and churches, 103–106; social impact, 121; criticism before 1900, pp. 118, 122–27; criticized by Wilson, 122–24; and mill family, 123; and Tillmanites, 125; sanitation, 129, 130, 131, 176, 190
Cotton prices: after Civil War, 16; late nineteenth century, 24, 25, 67; and mills, 83; c. 1900, p. 137; 1910s, 249
Cotton textile industry (New England), 11, 63–64, 112, 113
Cotton textile industry (South Carolina): postbellum expansion, 6, 7–8, 40–41; pre-1880, pp. 20, 40, 55; leadership, 42–59; role of Charleston, 43–46; role of merchants, 50–56; northern capital, 56–57, 58, 59; 1880s, 61; late nineteenth century, 82, 127; immigrant labor, 112–14; black labor, 114–15; boom, c. 1900, pp. 133–35; and Panic of 1907, p. 213; shift to finer goods, 213; difficulties in 1910s, 249–50
Cotton textile industry (southern), 41–42, 63–64
Cotton trade: Civil War, 15; in postbellum towns, 23, 24, 25, 33, 39, 49, 52, 53, 54; Charleston, 43
Countryside: as focus of southern history, 6–7; Reconstruction, 17–20; and towns, 38, 39; and cotton mills, 93; viewed by "town people," 146; and industrial wages, 206; and Blease, 221, 270
Courtenay Manufacturing Company, 45, 98
Credit: agricultural, 9, 17–18, 67; at mill stores, 178, 186
Cromer, Dr. George B., 193*n*
Crop-lien system, 17–18

"Dark Corner," 148
Darlington County, 254
Darlington Manufacturing Company, 58, 150
Davidson, Elizabeth Huey, 171
Dawson, Francis W., 72, 73, 74
Deering, Milliken and Company, 57–59
De Forest, John William, 148
"Democracy": debate over, 3–4; decline, 11; D. D. Wallace on, 266–67. *See also* Equality, white
Democratic party, 1, 140, 164, 200, 202, 215, 225, 226
Democratic party primary, reenrollment (1914), 255–56, 262, 267, 273–75. *See also* White primary; Suffrage; Suffrage restriction movement
Department of Agriculture, Commerce and Immigration, 114, 188
Department of Agriculture, Commerce and Industries, Labor Division, 188–91, 203, 212
Depression, Great, 7
Directors, mill, 25, 42–57 *passim*
Dixon, W. W., 233
Dogs, prohibited at Pelzer, 91, 109
Duke, J. B., 111
Dun, R. G., and Company, 31
Duncan, T. C., 156

Easley, S.C., 236
Edgefield, S.C., 108
Edgefield Manufacturing Company, 97, 103
Education, public: revisionists on, 172–73; expansion, as response to Blease, 259–67; adult, 261–67, 269, 271
Electric power, 46, 134, 135
Emancipation, 8, 13, 17, 115, 117
Employers' liability, 207–208
Engineering, textile, 57–58
England, 84–85, 86, 127
Enoree, S.C., 162
Enoree Manufacturing Company, 45
Equality, white: postbellum decline, 11; in nineteenth-century South, 116–17; threatened by industrialization, 124; deprecated, 157; and black labor in mills, 158–59; asserted by mill people, 160; in politics, 164, 165; threatened by reform, 208; and restriction movement, 227, 231. *See also* Race issue; "Democracy"
Ettor, Joseph, 251
Evans, Frank, 211, 262
Evans, Dr. James, 156
Evins, Alex, 30

Factories, criticism, 84–86. *See also* Cotton mills
Factors, 8, 15, 21, 22, 26, 43, 45
Factory inspection, 188–91, 212, 234, 252
Family, mill: and child labor, 102, 197–98, 203–205, 209; impact of factory, 121,

123; and "moving about," 152; target of child labor reform, 174; and "mill culture," 179; and state intrusion, 209–10; and compulsory school attendance, 210, 235; and medical inspection, 238–39
Fant, O. H. P., 16, 30
Farmers: and newspapers, 33; and "town people," 33; as mill officials, 49–50, 51; and mfg. tax exemptions, 62; and cotton mills, 65–67, 83
Farmers' Movement, 3. *See also* Tillman movement
Fertilizers, 20, 54
Fingerville, S.C., 97
Fitzhugh, George, 84
Fleming, C. E., 54, 58, 106
Florence *Times*, 226
Fork Shoals, S.C., 32
Fort Mill, S.C., 70, 210–11
Fortner bill, 244
Fraternal orders, 30, 222
French Canadians, 113, 116
Fretwell, J. J., 30

Gaffney, S.C., 23, 27, 28, 36, 38, 98–99, 197, 264, 269
Gantt, Dr. Rosa H., 236
Gantt, T. Larry, 161
Gastonia, N.C., 43
Georgetown, S.C., 31
Georgia, 14, 126, 159
Glendale, S.C., 40, 106
Gluck Mills (Anderson), 56
Golden, John, 144
Goldville Manufacturing Company, 49
Gonzales, N. G.: on child labor, 130–32, 176, 182, 194–95, 196, 198, 199, 206, 209; and cotton manufacturers, 139, 192; on "sandhillers," 147, 167; on mountaineers, 148–49; and "mill people," 164–65, 167, 169–70, 179; death, 166–68, 184; on education, 183–84; on compulsory school attendance, 184; as reformer, 189, 193
Gonzales, W. E., 184, 189, 193, 198
Government, role of: and Progressives, 10–11, 224; and "mill problem," 169–70; hours regulation, 187; factory inspection, 188–90; and "parental rights," 198–99; intrusion into family, 208–10; and "mill people," 224–25; Manning's administration, 259; Wallace on, 266–67
de Graffenried, Clare, 126–27
Granby Cotton Mill, 164, 196
Graniteville, S.C., 40, 44, 90, 102, 106, 107, 108, 202
Graniteville Manufacturing Company, 60, 94–95, 152
Gray, Wil Lou, 263, 264, 266, 269
Graydon, William N., 141
Grayson, William J., 84–85
Gregg, William, 40, 44, 90, 95, 106, 108, 202
Greene, Stephen, 57–58
Greenville: early development, 23, 24, 25, 31; early conditions, 26, 27, 28, 68, 108, 109, 153; leadership, 34; manufacturing, 46, 63, 67, 134; "mill people," 109, 150, 153, 204–205, 239–40*n*; IWW in, 251, 252; voting behavior, 274–75; mentioned, 73, 87, 106, 111, 148, 166, 191, 236, 254
Greenville and Columbia Railroad, 17
Greenville County: cotton production, 18, 19; Blease vote, 217, 219, 221; voter enrollment, 256; voting behavior, 272*n*, 274–75; mentioned, 75, 90, 96, 148, 245*n*
Greenville *Daily News*, 32, 158, 166–67, 274
Greenwood, S.C., 13, 68, 185, 250, 254
Greenwood Cotton Mill, 120, 250
Greer, S.C., 192, 275
Guerry, W. A., 193
Gutman, Herbert G., 10

Hamburg, S.C., 31
Hammett, H. P., 55, 56, 60, 90, 106, 116, 118, 119, 122, 124
Hammett, James D., 254
Hammond, Harry, 18, 21, 23
Hammond, James Henry, 84, 88
Haymarket riot, 87
Haynsworth, Clement F., Sr., 245*n*
"Helper" system, 187–88, 189
Hickman, H. H., 90*n*, 94, 95, 102, 106, 108
Hines, Dr. E. A., 236
Hollis, John Porter, 193*n*, 209
Hollis, L. P., 193*n*
Holyoke, Mass., 79
Honea Path, S.C., 246
Horse Creek Valley: antebellum manufacturing, 40; union stronghold, 138; lockout (1902), 140, 186; and Tillmanities, 162; alleged corruption, 163; and child

labor reform, 191, 199–201, 202; Blease stronghold, 216, 217–18; disturbances, 1910s, 251; mentioned, 75, 90, 105, 143
Horse Creek Valley News, 234
Hours of labor: England, 84; 1880s, 85; Roper on, 130; isolating effect, 144, 175–76; 1910s, 250
Hours of labor, regulation: 1880s, 125; Act of 1892, pp. 161, 206–207; and "mill people," 174, 199, 207, 211–12, 250; Act of 1907, p. 175; and reformers, 187, 190; McMahan and, 229; enforcement, 250; Act of 1916, pp. 252, 258
Housing, mill, 75, 91, 178, 207, 208

Illiteracy, 144, 179, 262, 263
Illiteracy Commission, 263–64
Immigrants: use in mills, 112–14; absence in S.C., 117; attitudes toward, 128, 133; feared by "mill people," 234; compared to "mill people," 263, 271
"Industrial plantations," 42, 46, 89, 106
Industrial Workers of the World, 251, 252, 253
Irby, W. C., 245*n*, 252

Jacksonian era, 4, 5, 116
Jacobs, W. P., 27, 53, 68, 70–71, 79–81, 104, 175, 183, 188, 268
Jacobs, W. P. II, 71*n*
Jamison, A. T., 193*n*, 197
Johnson, Gerald W., 64
Johnston, Olin D., 270
Johnstone, George, 167
Jones, Ira D., 2, 241, 242, 249, 253
Justice, I. W., 249

Katz, Michael B., 172
Key, V. O., 223, 224
Kindergartens, mill, 169
King's Daughters, 169, 170
Knights of Labor, 118
Kohn, August, 48, 146, 149, 213
Kousser, J. Morgan, 217*n*, 223
Kyle, John, 16

Labor Day, 139, 140–41, 142
Labor disputes: 1880s, 119; and black labor, 159–60, 247–48; Blease era, 247–53; and Manning, 267; after 1920, p. 269
Labor legislation: and "cotton mill problem," 132; under Manning, 258–59, 267
Labor recruiting, 151
Labor shortage: Charleston, 1880s, 74–75; and immigration, 113–14; and unions, 137, 138, 142–44; and social instability, 151, 152; and public health problems, 155; interest in blacks, 158; and child labor, 194; 1910s, 249
Labor unions: and "paternalism," 90; c. 1900, pp. 137–44; and black labor, 158; and child labor reform, 172, 180, 191, 199–200, 201–202, 203, 205; and Blease, 234, 241*n*, 252; and race issue, 245; 1910s, 251–53; D. D. Wallace on, 266–67; and "mill people," 268, 271; and Johnston, 270
Lancaster, S.C., 51, 52, 67
Lancaster Cotton Mill, 62
Lancaster County, 18, 24
Langley, S.C., 44–45, 90, 95, 98, 106, 202
Langley Manufacturing Company, 95
Lasch, Christopher, 172–73
Laurens, S.C., 16, 56, 68, 221, 247–48
Laurens Cotton Mill, 58, 176, 247–48
Laurens County, 49, 53, 65, 80, 221, 263, 268
Laurensville, S.C. *See* Laurens, S.C.
"Lawlessness": in S.C., 145–46; and mountaineers, 148; and Bleaseites, 1–3, 249, 253–54
Lexington, S.C., 166, 168
Ligon, W. S., 30
Liquor: in early towns, 27, 70; in mill villages, 91, 108–109. *See also* Prohibition
Lockhart, S.C., 159, 208
Lockouts, 139–40, 186
Lockwood, Amos, 57–58
Lovejoy, Owen, 180
Lowell, Mass., 79, 118
Lynching, 246–48

McCaughrin, R. L., 55
McCulley, P. K., 29
McCullough, Joseph A., 191, 193*n*
McFayden, Irene Ashby, 180
McKelway, Alexander J., 180
McKissick, A. Foster, 254
McMahan, John J., 182, 229–30, 231, 255, 257, 267
McSweeney, Miles B., 184

Manning, Richard I.: and child labor reform, 185–86; and mill voters, 220, 267–68; and labor disputes, 250, 253;

and cotton manufacturers, 254, 258–59, 267–68; administration, 258–59, 267–68; and Illiteracy Commission, 263
Manufacturing, in postbellum South, 7
Marriage licensing, 186
Marshall, J. Q., 141
Medical inspection of school children, 229, 235–39
Memminger, Christopher G., 35, 88
Merchants: antebellum, 8; postbellum, 9, 16–18, 20–21, 26; as "town people," 9; pivotal in postbellum economy, 13; during Civil War, 15; and crop-lien system, 17–18; and cotton monoculture, 20; personal relationships, 29–31; as town leaders, 34–35; and cotton manufacturing, 49, 51, 52–56; careers, 52–55
Miles, William Porcher, 78
Miller, John T., 241*n*
Milliken, Seth M., 57–59, 158, 244
"Mill people": at stump meeting, 1–3; as class, 5, 124, 133, 135, 157, 178; characterized, 8, 10–11; rural background, 10, 77, 121, 133, 146–49, 173, 178–79; as social threat, 83, 88, 131–32, 146, 147–49, 257–58, 267; de Graffenried on, 126; numbers, 127, 134; poverty, 135–37; and unions, 137–38, 142–44, 268, 271; illiteracy, 144, 179, 262–63; disorder, 149–51; and blacks, 150; and vaccination, 154–56; resentment of "town people," 156, 157–58, 160, 161, 162, 167, 168, 174, 271–72; and black labor, 159–60; and child labor reform, 172, 174, 199–203, 208–10; compulsory school attendance, 174, 210; attitudes toward education, 179, 184, 197; cynicism about legislation, 206–208; resentful of reformers, 208–10; and schools, 210–11, 232, 271; resistance to reform, 212–14; respect for law, 213–14; and factory inspection, 234; and immigrants, 234; and medical inspection, 237–39; and racial accommodation, 245–46. *See also* Child, mill; Family, mill; Parents, mill; Voters, mill
Mills, William H., 185, 187
Mill villages: general, 91; as business necessities, 93–94; rowdyism, 109; moral climate, 118–19, 130; law enforcement, 149–50; sanitation, 153, 228; epidemics, 153–56; criticized, 178; as "uplift" institutions, 183; adult education, 264*n*; persistence, 269
Mitchell, Broadus, 46, 61, 72–73, 78, 111
Monaghan Mill (Greenville), 113, 251, 253, 264
Monarch Mill (Union), 204
Montgomery, John H., 48, 54, 56, 58, 90, 97–98, 106, 118, 158–59, 244
Montgomery, W. S., 247
Morland, John Kenneth, 210
Mothers' pensions, 204
Mountaineers, 114, 148–49
"Moving about": and poverty, 136; and unions, 142–44; general, 151–53; and public health, 155; and tenancy, 179; and political corruption, 226; rumored restriction, 241–42

National Child Labor Committee, 171, 180–81
National Child Labor Conference, 191
National Union of Textile Workers, 138
Negro. *See* Blacks
Nelson, P. H., 167
Newberry, S.C., 14, 31, 38, 55, 56, 109, 157, 161, 193, 211
Newberry College, 193*n*
Newberry Cotton Mill, 62, 65, 69
Newberry *Herald and News*, 109, 125
New Deal, 269, 270
New England: capital, 56, 57; economic competition, 63–64, 131, 206; criticized, 84, 85; superintendents, 107; and immigrants, 112, 113, 116, 117; criticism of South, 125, 126; mentioned, 11, 80, 204
Newry, S.C., 98
Newspapers: role, 32–34; and agriculture, 33; and boosterism, 33–34; and "mill people," 176, 183–84; and Blease, 253–54
Norris Manufacturing Company, 49
North: commercial relations, 17, 22; as model, 36; economic competition, 38, 63–64; and S.C. textile industry, 43, 49, 56–59; cultural influence, 86–88; as home of "radicals," 87–88; "paternalism" in, 89; as home of immigrants, 112, 113, 133; critical of southern industry, 118, 125–26; industrial conditions criticized, 123–24; and strikes, 138; mentioned, 127
North Carolina, 14, 43, 78, 79

Norwood, J. W., 254
Nunn, E. G., 233

Oconee County, 18, 19, 45, 66
Olympia Cotton Mill, 135, 151
Orangeburg, S.C., 75
Orangeburg *Times and Democrat*, 36
Orr, James L., 106, 138, 177, 182, 192
Osborne, H. K., 233
Osborne bill. *See* Child labor laws: Act of 1911

Pacolet, S.C., 90, 97–98, 100, 102, 105, 118, 120, 153, 162
Pacolet Manufacturing Company, 45, 54, 55, 57, 58, 62
Pacolet River, 54, 90, 147*n*
Pacolet Valley, 102
Panic of 1907, pp. 114, 213, 249
Parents, mill: Progressive assaults, 11; targets of reform, 174, 181; influence on children, 179; responsible for child labor, 182–83, 194–99; and compulsory education, 235; and medical inspection, 238
Parker, Lewis W., 191, 192, 193, 208*n*, 240, 241, 249, 251, 254
Parker, Thomas Fleming, 113–14, 254
Parker Mills, 240, 254
Parker School District, 239–40*n*
"Paternalism," 83, 89–109, 118–20, 121, 168. *See also* "Welfare capitalism"; "Welfare work"
Pay periods, reform, 186, 258
Pelzer, S.C., 45, 90–93, 96, 97, 98, 103, 104, 106, 119, 149, 162, 192, 264
Pelzer, Francis J., 44, 45, 92
Pelzer Manufacturing Company, 45, 57, 90–93, 95, 96, 105
Peonage, 178. *See also* Coerced labor
Peoples, John E., 29
Petty, Charles, 33, 125
Phosphate mining and manufacturing, 44, 45
Pickens County, 18, 19, 49, 208
Piece work, 207, 250*n*
Piedmont (region): antebellum towns, 14; manufacturing heritage, 20; growth of towns, 21, 25; banks, 31; newspapers, and manufacturing, 34; economic development, 40–41, 64, 82; industrial leadership, 42–51; as "commercial frontier," 68; unions weak, 138; customs, and child labor, 197; and child labor reform, 199–202; strikes, 1910s, 251–53; mentioned, 6, 11, 30
Piedmont, S.C., 67, 90, 97, 98, 108, 119, 123, 162, 192
Piedmont Manufacturing Company, 45, 57, 60, 75, 151*n*, 177
Planters, and industrialization, 42, 49–50
Poe Mill (Greenville), 150
Politics: nineteenth century, 4–6; Blease era, 5, 6, 215–21
Pope, Sampson, 161
Populism, 4
Porter, A. Toomer, 16
Presidents, mill: and newspapers, 32; residence, 43, 106–107; occupations, 49, 51; duties, 55; prestige, 110–11, 193
Progressivism: characterized, 10, 111, 170, 171–74; and the child, 180–81; Ebbie J. Watson, 188–90; and suffrage restriction, 227, 229–30; as response to Blease, 257–69
Prohibition: as political issue, 216, 217, 221, 225; satirized by Blease, 222
Public health: and "mill people," 153–56; and race, 244

Race issue: and Blease, 222–23, 225, 243–44, 245–48; and compulsory school attendance, 234; and "accommodationists," 243–46
Railroads: antebellum, 14; postbellum expansion, 21–23, 24; and towns, 36, 38, 68; and Charleston, 44, 73; and cotton mills, 46–49
Reconstruction, 3, 23, 35, 38, 85, 89
Rector, Hendrix, 252
Reedy River Factory (Greenville Co.), 96
Reformers, and "mill people," 10–11. *See also* Child labor reformers
Rembert, George, 167
Rennie, Thomas, 107, 108
Report on Woman and Child Wage Earners, 93–94
Richards, John G., 219, 220, 273
Richland Cotton Mill, 150, 169
Richland County, 141, 167, 200, 226, 274
Rock Hill, S.C.: early, 24–25, 26, 27, 28, 31, 35, 52–53, 63, 65; "mill people," 136, 150, 155; adult education, 262, 264
Rock Hill *Herald*, 203
Roddey, John, 52
Roddey, W. J., 52–53

Roddey, W. L., 52–53
Rogers, W. S., 199, 233
Roper, Rev. John C., 129–30, 169, 195

Salisbury, N.C., 78
Saluda Factory, 115
Saluda River, 45, 57, 90, 91
"Sandhillers," 147–48, 167
Savannah River, 24, 69, 90
Savannah Valley Railroad, 31
Saxon Mill (Spartanburg), 96–97
Schools, mill: at Pelzer, 91, 92–93; function, 93; described, 93–103; costs, 94–95, 103; standards, 96; length of term, 96–97; compared to "town" schools, 96–100; facilities, 97, 101, 103, 118, 261; teaching loads, 97–101, 261; attendance, 101–102, 103, 261; as "frills," 120; as "missions," 183; Horse Creek Valley, 202; improvements, 1910s, 260–61
Schools, public: Progressive era, 10–11; antebellum, 35; in postbellum towns, 35–37; and cotton manufacturing, 70, 78; and "mill people," 210–11, 271; expansion, 1910s, 229, 232
Segregation Act of 1915, pp. 245, 258
Selden, E. Julia, 261–62, 263
Selling houses, 48, 57–59
Seneca, S.C., 23, 235–36
Seneca River, 134
Sharpe, W. S., 30
Shealy, W. A., 260
Sibley, William C., 90*n*, 95, 106
Simkins, Francis Butler, 222
Simpson, Bishop Matthew, 79
Skilled workers, 138, 140–41, 144
Slavery, 4, 8, 41, 84–85, 88, 89, 114, 116–17
Sloan, J. H., 54, 106
Smallpox, 153–56
Smith, Aug W., 254
Smyth, Ellison A.: establishes Pelzer, 44–45; regime at Pelzer, 90–93, 95, 96, 108, 109, 149; on unions, 141; and child labor reform, 182, 192, 193; and Blease, 254; mentioned, 57, 106, 158
Snyder, H. N., 193, 223, 262
Snyder, W. J., 160*n*, 174
South: postbellum transformation, 5–6; postbellum economy, 6–7; impact of industry, 41–42
South Carolina Child Labor Committee, 185, 191, 193*n*, 197, 205, 209
South Carolina College, 78
South Carolina Federation of Labor, 141, 144
South Carolina Federation of Women's Clubs, 236, 238–39, 263
South Carolina Medical Association, 236
South Carolina State Board of Health, 155, 156
South Carolina State Council of Defense, 263
Southern Baptist Convention, 28
Southern Christian Advocate, 79, 246
Southern Railway, 49, 221. *See also* Atlanta and Charlotte Air Line Railroad
Spartan Mills, 54, 58, 69, 82, 147, 228
Spartanburg: stump meeting, 1–3, 5; postwar development, 13, 16, 23, 25, 31, 34, 68, 70, 90; cotton manufacturing center, 46, 53–55, 58, 63, 69, 77; schools, 98, 99, 185, 211, 265; Tillmanites in, 161, 162; "mill people," 178, 207, 209, 211, 252, 253; adopts commission government, 227, 228; attempted lynching (1913), 246–47; adult education, 262, 263; mentioned, 26, 27, 79, 96, 106, 118, 158, 199, 236, 254
Spartanburg *Carolina Spartan*, 33, 62, 63, 77, 79, 119, 125, 195
Spartanburg County: cotton production, 18, 19; cotton mills, 45, 54; mill schools, 97, 98, 260; and Tillmanites, 162; and J. H. Tillman, 166; Bleaseites, 216, 217, 218, 221, 233; night schools, 261–62; voting, 272*n*
Spartanburg *Herald*, 32, 194, 211, 224, 226
Spartanburg *Journal*, 141
Spartanburg *Piedmont Headlight*, 161
Springs, Elliott White, 70
Springs, Leroy, 51–52, 62, 67, 254
Stallworth, A. B., 102
Steam power, 46
Stewart, Cora Wilson, 263
Stores, mill, 83, 91, 178
"Stretchout," 250
Stribling, John V., 78
Strikes: and "paternalism," 90; and "town people," 125, 138, 140; Columbia (1901), 142–43; Laurens (1913), 247–48; Blease and, 247–48, 249; 1910s, 250–53; Anderson (1915–16), 252, 253, 258
Suffrage: and debate on "democracy," 3–

4; antebellum, 3, 4; and "mill people," 8; restricted in Union, 163; in white primary, 202, 225
Suffrage restriction movement: in primary, 225–27, 229, 230–31; and Blease, 226, 230–31; and commission government, 227–28, 229; and Progressivism, 227, 229–30; 1914, pp. 255–57; mentioned, 11
Superintendents, mill, 107–108, 159
Swearingen, John E., 185, 260
Synthetic fiber industry, 64

Tate, W. K., 223
Tenant farmers, 5, 17, 117, 121, 146, 179, 217*n*
Textile Industrial Institute, 2, 265, 270
Textile machinery industry, 57, 63–64
Thackston, W. J., 241*n*
Thompson, E. P., 10
Thompson, S. J., 143
Tillman, Benjamin R., 3, 65–66, 125, 133, 161, 162, 165
Tillman, James H., 165–67
Tillman era, 119, 215
Tillman-Gonzales trial, 166–68
Tillmanites, 161–63, 165
Tillman movement, 33, 83, 125. *See also* Farmers' Movement
"Tin bucket toters," 195–97
Tompkins, D. A., 97, 103, 108, 113, 114
"Town people": at stump meeting, 1; characterized, 8–11, 13–14; and "cotton mill problem," 10–11; importance of community, 26, 28; pursuit of profit, 27–28; kinship, 29; and churches, 30–31; and farmers, 33; and North, 36, 56–59; and cotton manufacturing, 39, 50–51, 61–71; social fears, 80–83; and cotton mills, 83; desire for development, 109–10; and unions, 138–42; and countryside, 146, 168; disdain for "mill people," 174; fear of controversy, 193–94; and mill "extravagance," 205; and Blease, 216, 221, 224, 242–43, 270, 274–75; and municipal reform, 227–28; and lynching, 246; and Johnston, 270
Towns: postwar expansion, 9, 21–26; antebellum, 14–15; early crudity, 26–27, 28; liquor, 27; factionalism, 27, 38; banks, 31–32; newspapers, 32–34; as "enterprises," 34; leadership, 34–35; public improvements, 34–37; public schools, 35–37; and boosterism, 37–38; and countryside, 38, 39; dependent upon agriculture, 38, 39, 52, 67; dependent upon cotton trade, 39; industrialization, 39; locations of mills, 46–49; rivalries, 67–68
Transportation, 9, 13, 15, 21–23. *See also* Railroads
Trattner, Walter I., 171
Trough Shoals, S.C., 54, 108–109
Twitchell, A. H., 106
Tyack, David B., 172

Union, S.C., 31, 56, 129–30, 134–35, 137, 150–51, 155–56, 157–58, 160, 163
Union Cotton Mills, 129, 155–56, 160
Union County, 217
Union *Times*, 139, 198
United Textile Workers of America, 144, 252

Vaccination, 154–56, 157–58, 160, 210
Valley Falls, S.C., 96
Vance, Rupert, 222, 223
Vandiver, Edward, 29
Vaucluse, S.C., 202
Vesta Cotton Mill (Charleston), 158–59, 244. *See also* Charleston Cotton Mill
Violence, 2–3, 145–46, 246–49
van Vorst, Marie, 178
Voters, mill: Columbia (1902), 144; and Tillmanites, 161–63, 165; alleged corruption, 163, 164–65, 167, 226; discrimination, 163, 228, 256*n*; opposed to towns, 163–65, 166, 257–58; and J. H. Tillman, 165–66; and "demagogues," 176, 178; and child labor reform, 200, 202–203; and Blease, 214, 216–20, 221, 224, 267–69, 270; and suffrage restriction, 226, 227–28, 230; and commission government, 227–28, 230; and 1914 reforms, 256; and Manning, 267–68; and Johnston, 270; behavior, estimates, 273–75

Wages, industrial: 1880s, 75, 85; England, 84; criticized, 123; c. 1900, pp. 137–38; after 1902, p. 142; Columbia, 1900s, 143; of children, 204; and child labor reform, 205–206; and agriculture, 207; after 1907, p. 213; and labor turnover, 242; and black competition, 244, 245*n*;

cuts (1914), 252; legislation under Manning, 258
Walhalla, S.C., 32
Walker, Fleming and Company, 53–55, 58
Walker, Joseph, 34, 53
Walker, W. F., 108
Wallace, David Duncan, 3–4, 6, 145, 174, 193, 194, 223, 228, 229, 244, 255, 257–58, 266–67
Wallace, George, 271
Wallace, M. C., 144
Wallace, W. H., 193
Warrenville, S.C., 105
Water power, 20, 40, 45, 46, 54, 90, 127
Watson, Ebbie J., 180, 188–91, 212, 213, 233, 234, 242, 250, 252
Webb, G. R., 201
"Welfare capitalism," 89, 239–40*n*
"Welfare work," 75, 107–108, 132, 229. *See also* "Paternalism"
Weltner, Charles E., 191, 193*n*, 261
Westervelt, J. I., 254
Westminster Cotton Mill, 66, 77
Weston, Dr. William, 236
Whaley, W. B. Smith, 135, 139, 142–43
White primary, 3, 202, 225. *See also* Suffrage; Democratic party
Whitney Mill (Spartanburg), 54
Widows, 196, 203–204
Wiebe, Robert H., 180, 181
Williamson, Gustavus G., 74
Wilson, Hugh, 122–24, 125, 133
Wilson, Stanyarne, 161, 162
Winnsboro, S.C., 14, 31, 36
Witte, C. O., 160
Wofford College, 1, 69, 92, 104, 129, 193, 194, 262
Women: in agriculture, 76; in mills, 73–75, 76–77, 123
Women's Clubs, 169, 170, 238–39
Wood, John, 262
Woodside, John T., 119–20*n*
Woodward, Baldwin and Company, 57–59
Woodward, C. Vann, 6, 11, 41, 61*n*
Workman's compensation, 241
World War I, 205, 249, 252, 261, 263
World War II, 7
Wright, Carroll, 126
Wyche, C. C., 240, 241*n*
Wylie and Agurs, 52

Yeomanry, 146–47
York, S.C. *See* Yorkville
Yorkville, S.C., 31–32, 106, 155, 160, 210, 213
York County, 24, 163, 200, 256, 274
Young, Thomas M., 152